PRAISE FOR *OCEANS OF GRAIN*

"*Oceans of Grain* is the best work of history I have read in a very long time. Witty and wise, it reveals how conspirators and heads of state, workers and entrepreneurs, and philosophers and economists turned the human struggle for daily bread into wars and empires, revolutions and conquests, feasts and famines. It takes readers from the granaries and ancient trade pathways of Europe to the US Civil War and the overthrow of slavery, the founding of empires, the slaughterhouses of the First World War and the Russian Revolution, and, finally, to our contemporary, interconnected, and profoundly unequal world. Along the way, Scott Reynolds Nelson introduces us to the individuals who made and remade this world. Some are welcome new acquaintances and others—like Abraham Lincoln and Vladimir Lenin—are shown in such new light that it feels as if we are meeting them for the first time."

—ANDI ZIMMERMAN, GEORGE WASHINGTON UNIVERSITY

OCEANS
of GRAIN

HOW AMERICAN WHEAT

REMADE THE WORLD

Scott Reynolds Nelson

BASIC BOOKS
NEW YORK

Basic Books
Hachette Book Group
1290 Avenue of the Americas, New York, NY 10104
www.basicbooks.com

Printed in the United States of America

First Edition: February 2022

Published by Basic Books, an imprint of Perseus Books, LLC, a subsidiary of Hachette Book Group, Inc. The Basic Books name and logo is a trademark of the Hachette Book Group.

The Hachette Speakers Bureau provides a wide range of authors for speaking events. To find out more, go to www.hachettespeakersbureau.com or call (866) 376-6591.

The publisher is not responsible for websites (or their content) that are not owned by the publisher.

Print book interior design by Trish Wilkinson

Library of Congress Cataloging-in-Publication Data

Names: Nelson, Scott Reynolds, author.
Title: Oceans of grain : how American wheat remade the world / Scott Reynolds Nelson.
Description: First edition. | New York : Basic Books, 2022. | Includes bibliographical references and index.
Identifiers: LCCN 2021032198 | ISBN 9781541646469 (hardcover) | ISBN 9781541646452 (ebook)
Subjects: LCSH: Wheat trade—United States—History. | Wheat trade—History. | World history.
Classification: LCC HD9049.W5 .U66 2022 | DDC 338.7/61664722—dc23
LC record available at https://lccn.loc.gov/2021032198

ISBNs: 9781541646469 (print), 9781541646452 (ebook)

LSC-C

Printing 1, 2021

To my grandmother,
Mildred ("Mimi") Lofquist Brown (1912–2009),
whose grandparents Mormor and Morfar left Sweden in 1887
after living through what she called the "real Great Depression."
She taught me to darn a sock, hem a torn pocket,
and save a jam jar for the next depression.

CONTENTS

Oceans of Grain: The region that is sometimes called Europe on the left, its Black Sea breadbasket on the right, and the vital pinch point on the Bosporus Strait, c. 1912

Kate Blackmer

RAILROADS
1 Hamburg–Baghdad
2 Odessa–Königsburg

St. Petersburg

FOREST

Moscow

ARABLE STEPPE

Königsburg

RUSSIAN EMPIRE

2
Brest-Litovsk

Vistula

Kiev

SEE INSET

Dnieper

Don

DRY STEPPE

UNGARY

Dniester

S. Bug

Volga

Mykolaiv

Mariupol

Kagul

Rostov-on-Don

ROMANIA
Danube

Odessa

Caffa

SER

Eupatoria

BULGARIA

Sebastopol

Black Sea

Caspian Sea

Bosporus Strait

TTOMAN EMPIRE

Sinope

Constantinople/Istanbul

Bursa

OTTOMAN EMPIRE

Aegean Sea

GR

Konya

Mediterranean Sea

Suez Canal

EGYPT

CENTRAL RUSSIAN
AGRICULTURAL GUBERNIAS

Volhynia

Poltava

Kiev

Podolia

Ekaterinoslav

Kherson

Bessarabia

Taurida

CRIMEA

INTRODUCTION

I N THE SPRING of 2011, I first flew into Odessa to research an international financial crisis, but not the one you have probably heard about. Two and a half years earlier, on October 1, 2008, I had written an article in the *Chronicle of Higher Education* predicting that problems with the mortgage market suggested a deeper problem with international trade that could hinder bank lending and lead to a global depression. I knew this, I wrote, because I saw similarities between modern problems with mortgage banking and my obsession: the panic of 1873. My editor asked me to conclude with a few paragraphs about what might happen if 1873 were similar to 2008. I predicted a steep decline in trade, widespread unemployment, hoarding of cash by financial firms, shifts in the currency used for international trade, scapegoating of immigrants, and finally a surge of nationalism and tariffs. Newspapers all over the world translated and reprinted my article even as the stock market began to plunge.[1] Between October 1, 2008, and March 9, 2009, the Standard & Poor's Index dropped over 50 percent. By 2011 all the things I predicted had happened.[2]

By 2011 I had finished a book about the American origins of financial panics, which I argued had much to do with drastic changes in commodity prices.[3] Drawing me to Odessa were the often invisible connections between booms and busts in the history of a single commodity: wheat. By the spring of 2011, we were already seeing some of the longer-lasting results of the 2008 downturn. For example, a surge in the price of grain had led Arab states—which import most of their food—to stop subsidizing the price of bread in cities. Bread riots followed in an "Arab Spring" that would soon topple governments in Libya, Egypt, Tunisia, and Syria.[4] Newspaper reporters were flying to the Arab world because of protests there, but as a historian I was heading to Odessa. Egyptian protesters called for "bread, freedom, and social justice" in 2011. I was thinking about calls for bread, freedom, and justice in the French Revolution of 1789, the downfall of Sultan Selim III in 1807, the European Revolutions of 1848, the Young Turk Revolution in 1910, and the Russian Revolution in 1917. Wars and revolutions now, just as in the past, have much to do with wheat. That is the topic of this book.

Taking off from Budapest on an antique commuter plane, a dozen Hungarian tourists and I headed south over the Eurasian steppes. Through my window, I could see endless wheat fields laid out below like a massive *Tetris* game, with interlocking squares and rectangles of land straddling the main highways. The railways and roads that sliced through the black soil followed a straight path southward to the Black Sea. Neither the Russian Revolution nor the Second World War nor the Orange Revolution of the 2000s had erased those sharp grid lines laid down in the nineteenth century.

Ukraine has what may be the richest soil in the world. Called chernozem, it is a dark, beautifully aerated loam that allows worms and bacteria to thrive. In 1768, the tsarina Catherine II sent more than a hundred thousand Russian troops through this region and across the Black Sea to capture it. She had an audacious plan to build the Russian Empire by borrowing food, seizing the steppe, planting wheat here, and then feeding all of Europe. Five thousand miles away, American colonists had a similar plan, and both seemed utterly utopian. Then a revolution in Paris over the price of bread, the rise of Napoleon, and the burning of thousands of wheat fields in Europe changed all that. Odessa became a grain-exporting boomtown and made the tsars who followed Catherine and their landowning nobility rich. Wheat grown in those black rectangles traveled by oxcart to Odessa, where workers loaded the sacks onto Greek-owned ships bound for Livorno, London, and Liverpool to feed European cities at war. Wealth poured into Russia's newly built port. In a few decades, French émigré architects, refugees from the Revolution, had designed the Vorontsov Palace, along with Alexander Square, the Odessa Opera House, and the majestic summer dachas of southern Russia's moneyed estate owners and grain traders. The most beautiful dachas surrounded the imperial botanical gardens.

After Napoleon's defeat, these vast fields of Russian wheat did not delight European landlords. They faced what is called "Ricardo's paradox," in which rents drop when food gets cheap. For forty years taxes on foreign grain slowed cheap sacks of Russian Azima and Ghirka wheat. But then a water mold, unknowingly carried in from America, killed potatoes and brought food insecurity that forced European states to open the trading floodgates to wheat again in 1846. A century-long contest emerged between the wheat fields of Russia and the wheat fields of America to feed Europe's working class.

In the 1860s, as both empires were forced to end slavery and serfdom, a powerful Russia and a weak United States switched positions. Russia's boom went suddenly bust when larger boatloads of cheap American wheat burst across the ocean to European markets in the wake of the American Civil War. A group of US capitalists I call the boulevard barons helped break the power of southern enslavers and then stole a march on Russia's grain trade. The boulevard barons who sold grain internationally had partnered with the Union Army to create a new financial instrument called the futures contract, which allowed a London merchant to buy ten thousand bushels of wheat in Chicago and sell it for future delivery on the same day in Liverpool, nearly eliminating the risk of price fluctuations. Other innovations cheapened the cost of delivering American wheat. An Atlantic telegraph allowed purchase of a futures contract. Portable nitroglycerin widened American rivers and cut through the Appalachian Mountains that separated American prairies from the coast. Huge sailing ships that could never pass through the Suez Canal were forced onto the Atlantic. While Odessa at its peak could export a million tons of wheat each year, New York in 1871 was putting a million tons of grain afloat every week. As a result, European grain prices dropped nearly 50 percent between 1868 and 1872, and merchant fees fell along with them. Grain ships came back to the United States nearly empty, cheapening the price of passage from Europe to America. Within a few years millions of European immigrants were climbing into "steerage" holds just emptied of American wheat, their American journey subsidized by sales of American grain.

European workers in cities—previously plagued by low birth weights, high infant mortality, rickets, and malnutrition—benefited enormously from cheap grain, but Odessa faced what its committee on trade and manufactures had by 1873 called "ruinous competition." The committee predicted that the problem of cheap American grain, first noticed in 1868, would lead Odessa to "a period of absolute decline."[5] By the middle of 1873, Ricardo's paradox had done its work, not just in Russia but in much of Europe. The Bank of England, fearing that banks were using interbank lending credit to buy up real estate, raised interest rates in a series of shocks. A real estate bubble burst almost simultaneously in Odessa, Vienna, and Berlin. This so-called Agrarian Crisis set off a financial panic and then an economic downturn in agricultural Europe that was so severe, it was known, until the 1930s, as the Great Depression. In other words, oceans of grain had flooded Europe, and the flush times in Odessa and much of central Europe had ended, sending shock waves around the world.

States that had once been Europe's most powerful agricultural empires, including the Ottoman and Austro-Hungarian empires, then faced four decades of decline. The European states with cities that consumed the most American and Russian grain—Britain, Germany, France, and Italy—grew in importance by comparison. Political leaders in three of the grain-consuming "great powers"— Germany, France, and Italy—responded to the Agrarian Crisis by imposing lucrative taxes on imported wheat. As critics at the time put it, they picked workers' pockets to buy gunboats. These grain-powered great powers then built navies and merchant marines that scrambled to turn Asia, Africa, and the Middle East into outposts of disparate, brutal patchwork empires.

In 1884 Russia responded with state-supported railroads and cheap farm loans to emulate the grain-credit system of the United States, which allowed Russia to compete directly with its Atlantic competitor by the 1890s. The audacious plan to plant grain in Siberia and Central Asia attracted French investors and funded railway corridors all the way to a new grain port in Manchuria. In 1905 the Japanese Empire forced Russia to slink back to its old source of wealth in Odessa.

Russia's catastrophic failure in Asia, including the humiliation of its army, the loss of most of its fleet, and revolts among soldiers and sailors, brought Russia's first revolution in 1905 and forced one of the world's greatest powers to refocus on exporting grain through Odessa. By 1914 Russia's anxiety that Turkey might halt Russian grain shipments on the Black Sea helped start World War I—a war over nothing less than foreign bread. If Russia lost a hundred thousand men in the Russo-Japanese War, it would soon lose millions more in a fight over oceans of grain. The loss of those men, who would never again harvest wheat, brought Russia again to the brink of revolution.

The American part I understood well, having written about food, technology, and railroads in the United States for over thirty years. I have tried to explain here the way that Russia and the United States were yoked together on an international market and the frequently catastrophic effects. Trained as an American historian, I have been working through this tension between the United States and imperial Russia for over a decade. I spent those years researching in multiple languages and literatures, piecing together the relationship between the economic changes that came with the American Civil War (a subject I know) and the economic and political events in Europe that led to World War I and the Russian Revolution (a subject I have been studying ever since).

The further I dug, the more I was helped along by the brilliant analysis of a Russian grain trader and revolutionary writing under the pseudonym Parvus, who had grown up in Odessa during the 1873 crisis and in fact coined the term "Agrarian Crisis" in 1895.[6] In his many books and opinion pieces, he claimed that paths of grain made and destroyed empires and argued that this was true not just for his own time but going back to antiquity.[7] These trading pathways were not created by empires but rather were formed by traders—empires simply rode on top of them.[8] Parvus argued that trade was an active force of its own that "took on different forms and gained different meanings" in different societies, ancient, medieval, and modern. Trade, he thought, shaped the structure of a society in ways impossible to fully understand. Empires assembled themselves on paths of trade, he argued, but were vulnerable on the very lines that connected them to their inner and outer rings; they were thus prone to what he called *Zusammenbruch*: crash, breakdown, or collapse.[9] He devoted his life to understanding how trade routes and empires overlapped, how crashes occurred, and the radical changes in social structure that followed.

PARVUS WAS A famous revolutionary whom you have probably never heard of. Born in a shtetl in Belarus, Alexander Israel Helphand grew up large and broad-shouldered, the son of a former dockworker. Yet, all his adult life, Parvus dressed as a dandy, with a starched collar, vest, tie, and polished black leather shoes. His fancy clothes, it was said, drew one's attention away from his growing waistline. *Helphand* is a Russian pronunciation of the Yiddish word for "elephant" (*Gelfand*), and his friends called him the elephant or "fatty" behind his back. A student of the world economy and conversant in Greek, Latin, Russian, Ukrainian, Turkish, and German, he wrote newspaper editorials in a sarcastic, bombastic manner that irritated monarchs and politicians all over Europe. Kicked out of at least five German cities for his radical editorials and hounded by the Russian police for most of his life, he nevertheless became, by 1910, a confidential advisor to foreign secretaries in the Ottoman and Prussian empires who sought to understand Russia's power over grain. A philanderer and voluptuary, he alternately courted female revolutionaries and actresses. He was a radical with tens of thousands of loyal readers—German, Russian, and Turkish workers mostly—who learned about the world economy in the half dozen cheap radical newspapers that he founded in his life.

Parvus was not just a scholar and a writer but also a key player in the changes that brought about the collapse of imperial Russia. He smuggled weapons and grain to Istanbul during the Balkan Wars, helped the Ottoman Empire build up its defenses at Gallipoli, and became a multimillionaire. In the middle of World War I, he persuaded the German government to send more than fifty million deutsche marks and a sealed train of revolutionaries to Saint Petersburg to start the Russian Revolution. Married, with at least one illegitimate son, he lived through the 1920s in an opulent mansion in Berlin's Wannsee district. Radicals called it a revolutionary salon; critics called it a private bordello.[10] But in 2011 no one I met in Odessa had ever heard of the man who saw the world's fortunes pivoting around the grain that came through this port.

By 2020 Parvus had become famous all over again, at least in Russia, Turkey, and much of the Middle East. In 2017 he became the star of *Demon of the Revolution*, an opulent two-part costume drama on the history of the Russian Revolution, first broadcast on Russia's national television station, RT1. As Vladimir Putin's government moved sharply toward nostalgia for the Russian Empire that had been dead since 1917, Russian media recast Parvus as the wily Jewish speculator who during World War I tricked the German military into funding Vladimir Lenin's seizure of power in the Russian Revolution. This Parvus was not fat but a buff crime lord with chauffeurs, Rolls-Royces, and young mistresses. His secret agents were in the shadows, prepared to strangle any of the tsar's loyal subjects who crossed him. The new Russian Empire increasingly needed a beefcake villain like Parvus to justify Putin's hold on power. The story about Parvus's role in the revolution was exaggerated but partly true.

Meanwhile, in Turkey, Parvus had for a hundred years been considered a minor founder of the Turkish national state. In fact, Parvus arguably helped save Turkey from being wiped off the map during World War I. But then, after Recep Tayyip Erdoğan successfully defended himself from a military coup in 2015, Turkish national media turned sharply to an Islamist view of the world that glorified the last days of the Ottoman Empire. A Turkish National Television series, *The Last Emperor* (2017–2020), turned Parvus into the slender grand vizier of a global Jewish conspiracy. In season 2, the scheming Parvus floods the Ottoman emperor's chamber with poison gas using a newfangled radiator, killing nearly everyone but the emperor himself. Here was a different Parvus, secretly allied with Britain, the Catholic Church, and the Freemasons. He was bent on starting World War I to break up the Ottoman Empire to create a Jewish state in Palestine. If the Russian version of historical revisionism via television show got a few facts right, the Turkish version was paranoid, anti-Semitic fantasy.

WHEN THE PLANE landed outside Odessa, I reconfirmed the limits of my expertise. My spoken Russian was not good enough to bargain with the private cab drivers whose Ukrainian-accented Russian I found difficult to parse. I finally located someone who spoke a little German and a few words of English. When I showed him the address of my hotel, he looked me up and down, twice, then shrugged before motioning for me to get into the car. When we arrived, I discovered why he had seemed so surprised at my destination. "Russkaya mafiya," he said, nodding, as I stared at the men in camouflage jackets who guarded the front gates of the building with Kalashnikovs. The sightlines from two sniper towers converged on our taxi. I had, apparently, booked a hotel room in a Russian-mafia quarter. My broken Russian and printed reservation got me past the guards.

Outside the compound, I had seen crumbling roads, massive flea markets, and public transportation older than my grand-mother. Inside, I saw shocking opulence that reminded me of the wealth of old Odessa: oversize Humvees, late-model Benzes, and the multimillion-dollar summer homes of the newly rich Russians close to Vladimir Putin. My hotel in this gated community looked out onto a pool and beyond it to the Black Sea. Young women in bikinis swam in the pool while their elderly boyfriends, in dark sunglasses and sweatpants, watched from their deck chairs. This was the new Ukraine. Its wealth, as Russia's economic colony and breadbasket, was over a century in the making.

From my fancy room of tile and glass—I didn't dare go down to the pool—I planned my research itinerary. I would travel from the ports to the grain pathways, visit museums, read city records, and walk the Jewish quarter. There were warehouses to gawk at and roads to wander down. I had to see the city from the water. I hoped to see the pathways, to understand how Odessa became the place where Ukrainian grain found the sea. Istanbul, the ancient spout through which Black Sea grain entered the world, would be my next stop. How, I wondered, could cheap American grain persuade a tsar and tens of thousands of French citizens to invest in a railroad to Riga in the 1880s and then an impossibly long one to Manchuria? In 1895, Parvus declared that the debt accrued to build these pathways would lead Russia on a path to famine, world war, and revolution. In following Parvus's tracks, I learned so much more.

One

THE BLACK PATHS

10,000–800 BC

T HE NEXT MORNING, I left the mafia compound, waved good-bye to the guards, and headed out to visit Odessa. My goal was to traverse what Ukrainians call the "black paths" (*chorni shlyakhy*). These are the ancient oxen trails that cut across the Ukrainian plains to Black Sea ports.

I was looking for paths, but traces of empire jumped out at me. When I found a bus stop down the road, the bus shelter had a large sign advertising a brand of kvass: a sour, slightly alcoholic drink made from bread crusts soaked in water. A peasant beverage for ten centuries, kvass was an iconic symbol of imperial rule, the daily drink the steward of a Slavic noble household rationed out to serfs. It so symbolized the bond between lord and serf that critics of the tsar in the 1800s referred to crass expressions of expansionist Russian nationalism as kvass-patriotism. The drink, now carbonated, filtered, and sweetened, has recently reemerged in Ukraine and Russia as competition for expensive American sodas.[1]

Kvass is an emblem of empire, but its sour and fizzy flavor comes from yeast still alive in the crusts of rye bread. That tangy taste can give you a sense of some of bread's mysteries. Yeast and water are naturally plentiful on this planet, but a complicated chemistry takes place when they are mixed with ground-up grain. Recent archaeological research from the Fertile Crescent (near what is now Jordan) suggests that baked, slightly leavened bread is at least 14,400 years old.[2] That makes bread older than writing, older than cities, and older than most domesticated animals. In many societies between the British Isles and the eastern edges of China, the mystery of summoning food from this mixture of wheat, bacteria, and yeast was transmitted for thousands of years. Some of the earliest Mediterranean folktales preserve bread's secrets.

The ancient song of Demeter, reproduced in the Homeric hymns of 700 to 800 BC, suggests how to store the seeds of flowering weeds like emmer, wheat, and rye. Some ancient scholars believe that the story was taught to children as survival lore, to be remembered in case of famine, flight, or early separation. One-third of the seeds were gathered at harvest and placed in an underground vault. Thus Demeter's "slim-ankled" daughter Persephone is snatched from the fields and shoved "into the misty gloom" at a time when the narcissus flowers are blooming (late winter). Persephone, trapped in the underworld, stays preserved there, pining for her family. She waits months for rescue: "For so long hope charmed her strong mind despite her distress. The mountain peaks and the depths of the sea echoed in response to her divine voice." Wheat kernels in seed vaults can be preserved for many months in vitro without "spoiling," that is, without either growing into wheat plants or serving as a host for bacteria and yeast. If wheat kernels in their adolescent, Persephone-like form remain tightly sealed and thus untouched by yeast, they can be transported and planted the next season, in either spring or fall.[3] Saving grain for the next season is just as important, for long-term survival, as harvesting, grinding, and baking.

How does the remaining amount of raw grain become food? With the hymn of Demeter as our guide, we learn that the kernel must be dried with fire for nine days (Demeter searches for her daughter with a torch and does not bathe her skin in water). The heat allows the outer hull to be removed (Demeter doffs her dark cloak). The kernel is set by the family hearth (in the household of Metaneira). Then the kernels are mixed with water, barley, and pennywater (Demeter asks the family for this drink). This would provide enough yeast to start the process. At this point wild fungi and bacteria do the seemingly magical, invisible work of saccharification. At a microscopic level, the two microbes digest the wheat's starch and cellulose, expelling simple sugars. As the fungi breathes out carbon dioxide, the product rises. Once risen, the mush can then be heated and fed to children to make them grow strong. In the fable, Metaneira is too old to nurse her infant son, and so Demeter feeds the boy with this miraculous product. Because the yeast is still alive in bread, the leftovers, stored in a closed vessel for a few days, yield beer or kvass, an important source of calories for peasants and farmers.

Persephone's ability to stay preserved in a jar or sack made a long-distance trade in grain possible. Traders moved in caravans of a hundred carts lashed together, each laden with a ton of goods: fish and salt for the trip north, leather and grain for the journey south. One of those black paths led all the way north and west to the Black Forest in what is now the German state of Baden-Württemberg. Traders occasionally rode on navigable stretches of the Dniester River to save time and energy. Beside these paths lay ancient kurgans—burial mounds for these ancient travelers when their traveling was done.

The black paths, according to Ukrainian legend, were formed by a band of ancient warrior-merchants, predecessors of the Cossacks, called the *chumaki* (Turkish for "stick" or "spear"). Two oxen pulled each cart, and the *chumaki* walked beside them. When attacked by roving bands of horsemen—Avars, Khazars, Haidamaki, or Tatars—the *chumaki* gathered in a circle, spears out. The *chumaki* had distinctive stories, sorrow songs, signaling horns, and burial rituals. The Ukrainian name for the Milky Way—the long band of stars that moves over us at night—is Chumatski Way. The *chumak*, depicted as a man in *chumaki* songs, sang as he traveled and sang when he returned home:

By the river along the shore
Walked a chumak *with his whip,*
Hey-hey!
Home from the Don.

A sack on his back
And a patched-up caftan—
Hey-hey!
I've had enough of chumaking.
. . .
"If I fail to find destiny,
I'll go to the publican's tavern,
Hey-hey, and forget my trouble!"[4]

Ukrainian folklorists have long claimed that the *chumaki* are older than the ancient world. According to folklorist Ivan Rudchenko, who interviewed them in the 1860s, the *chumaki* came before "class society," before "civilization," even before "homelands." For untold centuries, he was told, the *chumaki* used oxen to find destiny, hauling wheat from farming towns on the Ukrainian plains to stone fortresses that dotted the northern coast of the Black Sea. Empires rose and fell—Persian, Athenian, Roman, Byzantine, Mongol, Venetian, Genoese, Ottoman—trying to get their hands on *chumaki* grain. Along with leather, lead, and slaves, the *chumaki* filled the Black Sea fortresses with grain.[5] The paths waxed and waned as human settlement was wiped off the plains multiple times.

Geographers, by comparison, loved the paths but ignored the traders. They argued that empires came first, believing them to be defined by their control of trade lines, usually rivers or oceans. Between around 2270 and 1600 BC, "potamic" (river-based) states controlled a river or rivers and drew grain as tribute from nearby. The Akkadian Empire, in what is now Iraq, Kuwait, and

14

southwestern Iran, drew grain from farmlands up and down the Tigris and Euphrates Rivers. The Egyptian Empire collected grain from farmers along the Nile. By the third century BC, new "thalassic" (ocean-based) empires had emerged. The Mauryan Empire on the Indian subcontinent collected food on the Arabian Sea and the Bay of Bengal; the Han demanded grain from farmlands in the west but also took food from farmers across the East China Sea; Athenians took farms in Italy and western Turkey and along the Black Sea coast.[6] An empire was a grain pump: grain traveled inward from an empire's "inner ring" of farmland to feed capital cities; grain also spread outward to land and water frontiers where it fed far-flung sailors and soldiers. Absorbing food from the inner ring, the city center repaid *chumaki* traders with cloth, wine, and leather goods.[7]

Historians, like geographers, have long treated grain ports, like those on the Black Sea, as the children of thalassic empires, with *chumaki* as their worker bees. The ancient Greek word for such a provisioning port is *emporion*, the source of the word "empire." Port traders in these emporia specialized in gathering, drying, and storing food for shipment. Grain came as trade, tribute, and tax to the emporia to feed the arms of an empire, its armies. In the historian's imagination the Roman Empire built trade in western Europe, for example, with Roman roads, mileposts, and armies. There was no China, the story goes, until Han canals fused the region into a single domain of trade. New archaeological evidence suggests that the folklorists have it right and that the black paths are prehistoric, nearly as old as bread itself. The proof that trade pathways were ancient is a tiny bacillus that traveled inside *chumaki* traders' bodies: *Yersinia pestis*. This is the bacillus that causes what we now call plague but which Slavs called *chuma*. The *chuma* crossed these plains many times, each time riding on trading paths, each time decimating human populations in the towns where grain was gathered and stored. *Chuma* rode with the *chumaki*.

The first appearance of *Y. pestis* was a prehistoric plague that struck in roughly 2800 BC, centuries before any river-ruling empire existed. In 2019 archaeologists traced the oldest extant *Y. pestis*, found in human molars, to Trypillia, a Copper Age city about three hundred miles north of Odessa. From Trypillia the plague must have followed black paths west, south, and east. Within five hundred years it had killed humans from China to Sweden. We only know about these Copper Age trade routes because the bacillus evolved as it traveled, and it traveled distances too great to be explained by migration or war. Using genome-wide next-generation sequencing, geneticists can now trace the movement of millions of humans over thousands of years using only a few hundred DNA samples.[8] Any large-scale movement of people over long distances will show up as genetic drift. Genetic-drift analysis for this period suggests that no human traveled even a fraction of the distance between China and Sweden between 2800 and 2300 BC. Yet trade between thousands of *chumaki*-like traders, inadvertently carrying the bacillus from town to town, must have brought the *pestis* into millions of households across the world.

In fact, trade by people like the *chumaki* may be how agriculture started. Anthropologists who study the origin of farming around 10,000 BC have suggested that grain growing originated in moist habitats—near springs or lakes—that travelers found between areas of scarce, valuable resources, such as obsidian or seashells. Prehistoric travelers would drop seeds in these "settlement cells" and return the next season, cutting the grain and grinding it for food before moving on. The first wheat "farmers" may in fact have been travelers or traders who, after decades of migration, stayed behind in these way stations. Over time, apparently, settled communities gathered at these stopping points.

It is easy to view traders as leeches who profit from the work of others. That is certainly how the Russian tsars viewed Odessa's Jews who arranged delivery of grain onto ships. But the trading and dropping of seeds may actually be the world's oldest profession, and farms, towns, states, empires, and armies are the beneficiaries of the bounty that planetary traders scattered beneath their feet.[9]

While we can only guess at mortality figures for ancient strains of *Yersinia*, the strain that left Trypillia in 2800 BC and traveled the black paths did so at roughly the same time that, DNA records suggest, human populations around the world plummeted in what is called the Neolithic decline. After this Neolithic decline, empires sprouted along the pathways. Centuries later the city-state of Uruk fell to the Akkadians, who developed one of the world's first empires in what is now mostly Iraq.

How would empires emerge along trading lines? We lack written evidence. Perhaps a local warlord found an existing crossroads between paths and demanded payment for passage. Perhaps a group of traders blocked competitors, then bound themselves by pledges into military households. Perhaps a group of armed traders took advantage of weakened city-states to assert their control. Trading networks apparently came first, then *Y. pestis*, and then, perhaps in the devastation, soldiers who claimed multiple crossroads and nearby farming towns. An empire could establish a protection racket along *chumaki* pathways and in a few generations assume the mantle of imperial rule.[10]

If we think of the paths from the perspective of the *chumaki*, the laboring people whose oxen first brought the world together, empires did not create trade but slowed, bounded, and taxed it. Empires, for their part, claimed to police and protect trade. Indeed, imperial origin stories often emphasize their capacity to drive out competing tax agents (commonly called robbers, highwaymen, or pirates). Thus Thomas Carlyle, in extolling the growing empire of Frederick the Great, argued that his greatness came from defeating the robbers that demanded tribute for trade over the Rhine River and were ruining Germany. "Such Princes, big and little, each wrenching off for himself what lay loosest and handiest to him, found [robbery] a stirring game, and not so much amiss."[11] The heroic Frederick the Great replaced local robbery with an even more stirring game: taxing robbers.

For their own benefit emperors might cheapen trade by forcing imperial subjects to improve roads, build milestones and lighthouses, and deepen ports. In improving prehistoric trade routes between towns, an empire could decrease the price of what I will call, using an obsolete medieval term, "tollage," a travel cost measured in pennies per ton per mile.[12] This was simultaneously a measure of cost, weight, and distance. Absolutist states turned rivers into canals and built roads across rivers. Decreasing tollage centralized imperial authority and quickened trade.

The efficiency of black paths—the blood vessels for traded food—is no small matter. The United Nations and World Bank measure the density of every country's traffic in ton-kilometers (tkm). In the 2020s, for example, a country's tkm multiplied by 650 will give you a close approximation of that country's gross domestic product (GDP) in US dollars. The connection between GDP and tkm works in both directions. GDP growth apparently fuels demand for improving the black paths that become roads, while improving black paths increases GDP. When it comes to a society's economic well-being, the black paths are everything. Both the World Bank and the United Nations emphasize that cheapening the *efficiency* of these paths (in cents per tkm) can accelerate a nation's production. The more efficient the black paths, the more a country, village, empire, or town can assemble products together for further processing and trade.[13]

Empires imposed a tax on black paths, as did disease. Bacilli like *Y. pestis* hijacked black paths repeatedly after 2800 BC. In bringing devastation they were, in a way, a natural tax on trade. In the Bible, John of Patmos's vision in the book of Revelation (written around AD 95) gives us a memorable metaphor for how pestilence traveled along the paths. The prophet John describes the apocalypse coming with four riders. The rider on the white horse "went forth conquering"; the man on the red horse took away "peace from the earth"; the one on the black horse took advantage, selling only "a measure of wheat" but demanding an exorbitant penny for it; and finally, the rider on the pale horse brought death. *Y. pestis*, reproducing and feeding on the bodies of riders, surely brought all four when *chumaki* brought pest-infected trade goods into settlements. After the Neolithic collapse, humans abandoned these plains for centuries, then slowly repopulated them. Humans returned, black paths connected them again, and empires rose to thrive on the bounty. The bread pathways constantly surged underneath, sustaining the empires but also carrying the forces of their own collapse. What brought humans back to these plains was the fading of memory and the promise of sharing bread.

As empires grew along trading paths, they absorbed and adapted the mysteries of grain and yeast. Women and men in the Roman Empire took the Greek myths of Demeter and Persephone and forged them into the Eleusinian mysteries—rituals for initiation into the cult of Demeter and Persephone, a cult built around knowledge of grain and fungus, life and food. Actors depicted the mysteries in rituals performed in underground theaters for those who swore not to reveal the cult's secrets. By that point Roman matrons and priests had turned the Greek goddess Demeter into the Roman goddess Ceres. Her cult seems to have been similarly practical—something like a college class in wheat storage, cultivation, fermentation, and baking preserved in imperial ritual. In Egypt the cult of Nepri likewise served as a combination of legend, planting guide, and cookbook but also as justification for control by imperial elites. In Russia and Ukraine the Slavic god of spring, Jarilo, was (like Persephone) preserved for a time in a coffin, then buried in the soil. People should copulate in the fields, in more than a few legends, to seal the deal with the gods and thus lead the wheat plants to fruit.[14]

But if the preservation, storage, and heating of a yeasty bun is impossibly ancient, it was also wickedly expensive in terms of the resources brought together. We can divide the process into three parts. Part one was planting and harvesting on an open plain. Part two was storing and shipping to bread eaters, the emporium part. Part three was cracking, separating, and winnowing into flour, mixing with yeast and water, then rising and baking. Cities often did that part. Of course, armies on the move could harvest, crack, and bake grain as bread. Roman soldiers carried scythes along with their swords for impromptu taxation.[15] For at least fifty centuries, considerable human labor was devoted to part two: carrying grain from dry, flat places where wheat grew best to spots that had stone, leather, clay, or salt where it was most easily prepared. Empires emerged to engross and centralize part two, feasting on the networks that bonded farming towns together, inserting their own justifications for sovereignty into myths older than the empires themselves.[16]

Though empires come and go, the technologies of grain planting, collection, storage, and conversion to food remain as their deepest fundaments. The grain pathways connecting humans are older than written words, so deep and hard to see that they are almost invisible. But for people accustomed to watching grain move—grain traders, in particular—they are the ancient man-made circulatory system that makes civilization possible. When the paths are diverted or blocked, the *horrea* will be quickly emptied. Laws, armies, kings, and the marble columns sustaining them will crumble. We can only mourn the passing of grain like Demeter crying for her lost Persephone.

Looking at my maps, I could see the black paths but not how these lines could build up or destroy empires. To do that, I needed to follow the paths into deep water. I understood that Odessa could not have existed without the weakening of the imperial city at the gates of the Bosporus. It was first called Byzantium, then Constantinople, then Istanbul. In 1896, Parvus said that this city had been at the center of the world's trade for thousands of years, and its weakness had made Odessa great. How, I wondered, was that possible? [17]

Two

THE GATES OF CONSTANTINOPLE
800 BC–AD 1758

IN THE EIGHTH century BC, Ionian Greek traders established stone trading posts that extended all the way to the northern side of the Black Sea. From each post they collected a thousand or more sacks of grain and loaded them onto massive ships bound for the granaries of Rhodes and Athens. The foreign grain would feed those cities along with Sparta, Pylos, Mycenae, and Thebes. Throughout the century a new elite, the *aristoi*, emerged who made their wealth from trade with the Greek cities. Their banquets were legendary, but they were not well loved. Greek odes recalling a lost golden age attacked the *aristoi* for their wealth, their outsized influence, and their corruption of Greek cities.

In response to criticism, the *aristoi* paid poets, singers, and storytellers to spin stories of their wily trading, clever deals, loneliness, and bold adventuring. The legacy of their grain expeditions were adventure tales, including *The Iliad* and *The Odyssey*. While the puffed-up fables of their spectacular conflicts with hydras and sirens on the Black Sea were memorable, the grain traders' burdens were rather more prosaic. The greatest burden on the Black Sea was a tyrannical tax. To feed Greek cities, every year the ships of the *aristoi* had to pass through the mile-wide Bosporus Strait and the nearby Dardanelles. The "tyrants on the Bosporus," as one of Aristotle's students called the rulers of Byzantium, controlled the *aristoi*'s gateway to life-giving Black Sea grain. Throughout history the tyrants used derelict ships, iron chains, and Greek fire to block grain traders who tried to rush the gates. Stand and deliver, said the highwayman at the crossroads, and so said the tyrants who ruled Byzantium.[1]

The *aristoi* long resented Byzantium's monopoly control of this low-friction corridor that separated Greece from its grain. Using pinch points in the trade for grain is, like bread and the *chumaki*, older than recorded history. According to one fable, an oracle had told Byzas, son of the water god Poseidon, to settle on the narrow strait of the Bosporus that connected the Black Sea to the Mediterranean. Byzas built Byzantium on the hill that overlooked the Bosporus so that he could dominate waterborne trade between East and West. Over the centuries Persians, Spartans, Athenians, and Romans captured the city whose markets and bazaars gathered together the goods of an ancient world economy that stretched from France to China. Byzantium was a city that taxed but also a city of trade, a meeting point for leather, spices, silk, wine, and grain. In the ancient world, the second phase of the grain-to-food pathway—the gathering and shipping—could stretch hundreds of miles and demand considerable energy.

By the fifth century BC, the "ten thousander" ships of the *aristoi* could carry about ten thousand sacks of grain (roughly four hundred tons) from the Mediterranean to the Black Sea. They used both square sails and galley slaves who stood two and three abreast on each oar, hauling grain from the stone ports on the Black Sea to hungry ancient cities on the Greek peninsula and its many islands. In the centuries that followed, the Persians, Macedonians, and Romans copied these ships, but they never matched their size. The last ten thousander owned by one of the *aristoi* must have sailed through the Bosporus before AD 300. Ships that large would not regularly travel any ocean in the world until the Spanish galleons of the sixteenth century.[2]

For the *aristoi* in the loosely organized Athenian Empire, grain represented wealth: concentrated and dried calories, the crucial raw material that fed cities and armies. Grain collection at Rhodes paid for a famous statue, the Colossus of Rhodes, one of the ancient wonders of the world. We know that wealthy grain merchants probably paid for the original statue because when it collapsed in an earthquake, the city solicited Greek grain traders to rebuild it.[3]

Two hundred years after the first ten thousander passed through the gates of Byzantium, in the third century BC, the Romans defeated the Hellenistic kingdoms, taking the Greek islands and peninsula, and by 129 BC the Romans could in turn draw tribute from the city of tyrants. But the Greeks, to paraphrase Horace, also captured her uncivilized conquerors by bringing skills to rustic Rome.[4] When the Romans captured Byzantium, they sacked the stone ports on the Black Sea and rebuilt them, while adopting the mysterious Greek techniques of grain gathering, drying, and storing.[5]

Romans called Byzantium "the eye of the Universe." Recognizing its unique power and position, they built aqueducts into the city and extended roads to it, including the Via Appia and the Via Egnatia. The roads expanded Byzantium's reach, giving it access to the Aegean, Ionian, and Adriatic Seas. At around the same time the massive grain ships of the *aristoi* disappeared from archaeological records, perhaps because Roman roads diminished the power of waterways or because smaller ships were required on the shorter route from the Black Sea to Byzantium.

In AD 324, after the Roman caesar Constantine defeated his rivals and declared himself emperor, he relocated the Roman Empire's imperial capital to Byzas's hill, the safe and defensible pinch point that could command the fruits of Europe, Asia, and Africa. In AD 330, Constantine planted a column—Cemberlitas—at the forum in Byzantium, rededicated Byzantium as New Rome, and invited wealthy and well-connected families throughout the old Roman Empire to settle there. At some point later it became Constantinople, in Constantine's honor. Traders from the Black and

Aegean Seas delivered grain to *horrea*, massive grain banks large enough to feed citizens during long sieges by rival empires.[6]

These granaries of the Greek, Roman, and Byzantine empires were the predecessors of modern banks.[7] Elite citizens made deposits and withdrawals of grain by wheelbarrow. Individual vaults in a *horreum* stored valuables, just as safety-deposit boxes do in many downtown banks today. A receipt for grain stored in the *horreum* could be bought or sold, used as collateral for contracts, or seized in cases of debt. These grain receipts collectively became what we now call money.[8] On the edge of two oceans, the voracious, grain-eating port of Constantinople stood as the crossroads for much of Eurasia's trade. As Byzantine princess Anna Komnene later described it, the empire commanded "the two pillars at the limits of east and west." The western pillars of Hercules in southern Spain are now called the Strait of Gibraltar. The pillars of Dionysus in western India may be the Strait of Hormuz.[9] Rome's empire reached across this route, but the prehistoric trade that made it possible long predated *aristoi*, Greece, Persia, Macedonia, or Rome.

When Constantinople became the Roman capital after 330, Greek merchants—familiar with the pathways—fed the city from the Black Sea as their ancestors had fed Rome and Athens before it. They referred to Constantinople as "the City" and called its granaries *Lamia*, referencing a massive, mythological shark, to describe the empire's voracious appetite for wheat.[10] To satisfy it, the Eastern Roman Empire's soldiers erected more trading fortresses on the Black Sea, including Chersonesus, Pantipacaeum, Phanagoria, and Berezan. Grain pathways on the Black Sea and the Mediterranean fed Constantinople for over a thousand years, from before 300 to 1453. The imperial city's wealth rose and fell as the black paths converging on the Bosporus expanded and contracted.

During that centuries-long reign, *Yersinia pestis* struck again. Twice it changed the course of the grain trade and thus the course of history. One strain emerged in 541 and another in 1347. Each strain reached Constantinople, then spread outward. Trading lines tangled and tore, bringing fundamental changes to planting, harvesting, and eating practices for tens of thousands of miles in every direction. Empires shrank down to baronies in Europe, and new empires came to the fore in the Middle East, though the city on the Bosporus survived them all.

In 541, the Plague of Justinian brought an end to the ancient world. The four horsemen had returned, carrying a newly evolved *Yersinia*, and ushered in the Middle Ages in Europe and the Middle East. According to the first complete literary account, written in Constantinople, *Yersinia* started south and west of the Black Sea, near Alexandria. For the Byzantine Empire, the apocalypse that ended the ancient world came not by oxcart or horse but by ship, riding in the stomachs of black rats, ship captains, and galley slaves who pulled the ships into the Golden Horn, the city's natural inlet and port.

The grain emporia that had been the nodes for the empire's food circulation became nodes for infection. Beginning at the docks, the plague quickly overwhelmed the city. Refugees carried the plague on the improved roads and water routes that stretched from the empire's seaports to farming towns in every direction. We can only guess at the mortality rate. In Constantinople, firsthand accounts suggest that five thousand people died per day in the city in 542 and that the mortality peaked at ten thousand in the final days, though many historians dispute these numbers. So few people were left to bury the dead, according to one account, that Emperor Justinian's subordinate, the *referendarius*, had the roof removed from one of the city's defensive towers, the bodies dropped inside, and then the roof replaced to prevent further contagion. Within two years *Yersinia* had leaped from the center of the ancient world economy to its edges, reaching from Ireland to Manchuria. Waterborne trade between East and West diminished again, and grain ships and agricultural settlements were abandoned. The steppe became again a flat table of feather grass at the end of the ancient period, visited by herdsmen for a season or two. Horsemen in mobile empires spilled across the plains in spectacular raids: Huns and Avars, later Khazars and Mongols.[11]

Justinian's Plague depopulated trading cities along the coast of the Mediterranean and Black Seas, briefly forced Europeans to revert to a barter economy, and contributed to the growth of insular monasteries. The plague apparently benefited new medieval dynasties that grabbed ancient land pathways. These post-Justinian grain gatherers included the Capetians in the West, the Persians and the Abbasids in the East.[12] Over the next 450 years, Islamic empires— Umayyad, Abbasid, and Almohad—stretched over much of the same East-West expanse as the Byzantines had, renaming the pillars of Hercules as Jabal-al-Tariq (Gibraltar).[13] What the Roman Empire called the pillars of Dionysus probably became the trading city of Hormuz.[14] But now much of that trade came overland on the backs of plague-resistant camels. Plague-bearing rats could ride almost invisibly over long distances inside wooden ships and oxcarts. But a desert journey in sacks and the chance of exposure in the caravanserai that awaited traders at twenty-five-mile intervals would have acted as a brake on *Yersinia*'s transmission.

At the same time a new kind of grain-bread-state structure emerged on the northern and western part of the Black Sea after 541. Peasants built closely connected, partially underground, family-sized buildings with stone hearths in the corner. Their organization is what we would call medieval: a dozen or so buildings surrounded a larger one with communal ovens and clay pans. Gathering, collecting, and cooking bread took place in metafamily groups of roughly thirty or more people, much smaller than the prehistoric city-states or the far-flung thalassic empires of Emperor Constantine's day. Knowledge about the mysteries of grain— drying and delivery—shrank considerably with the depopulation that came with plague. With less food to share, the planting and harvesting part became more critical. Innovations like the flail, the plow, and three-field rotation made these smaller, land-based grain-growing units more self-sustaining; *Yersinia*'s decades-long infestation of waterborne trade routes may have made these medieval fiefs necessary.[15]

Medieval grain growers on the Black Sea became even more important to Constantinople when plague contributed to its loss of colonies in the eastern Mediterranean and Egypt in the 600s. Constantinople thus tightened its hold on the Slavs, who, as a result, alternately admired and despised the Byzantine Empire in Constantinople, which, while it often ignored the people north of the Black Sea, could nonetheless pinch off their passage to the western ocean. The city on the Bosporus also faced a Bulgarian Empire that gobbled up Byzantine grain pathways on the western half of the Black Sea. The grain producers' threat to Constantinople waxed and waned. In 907, Prince Oleg of the Rus laid siege to Constantinople. He allegedly got close enough to nail his shield to its gates. A legend arose inside the city that the Byzantine emperor used pieces of the Virgin Mary's gown to repel the invaders. Shortly after the Rus were defeated, the Byzantines celebrated by commissioning a mosaic at the Hagia Sophia, the largest temple in the Western world, pledging church and city to Mary's protection.[16]

Its empire nearly broken in the west and narrowly saved in the north and east, the Byzantines extended their influence northward to these Slavic communities by sending missionaries like Cyril and Methodius back in the boats that brought Constantinople its life-giving grain. By spreading Christian gospels, advice manuals, and lives of the Byzantine saints along with Cyrillic writing, the Byzantines imposed patterns of religion, culture, and governance on the far-flung regions of their empire. Grain flowed along pathways of trade. Cultural ideas and practices flowed back. Slavic princes slowly converted to Orthodox Christianity, emulating and adapting Constantinople's religious rituals of possession and control. Icons, draperies, and clothing in Kiev and Moscow mirrored Byzantine styles.[17]

Medieval western Europe, often cut off from regular trade with the East after 542, changed drastically. Just as bread made prehistoric fables and fed ancient empires, it increasingly defined medieval serfdom as lordship over smaller communities by bread-making masters. Formal slavery declined in Eurasia after the Plague of Justinian, though historians hotly debate whether that was a result of the plague. Aristocratic landlords derived their control in part by monopolizing grain milling and distribution, just as the kings of ancient empires had done, but on a much smaller scale. In medieval England, for example, the word "lord" comes from *hlāford*, meaning "loaf-ward": the person who guards the loaves distributed from the medieval mill and bakery. The word "lady" derives from *hlǣfdīge*, meaning "loaf-kneader": a maker of loaves. In part because the communal bakery turned wheat or rye into bread, controlling the loaf meant controlling people.

The outer boundary of a ruling family's manor house—including bakery, mill, and fields—was called in old English the *soke*. The *soke* defined where a lord could "seek" out subjects to investigate complaints, all for the lord's "sake." Men legally bound to the space were his "sokemen." Those who escaped the lord's justice were out of his laws ("outlaws") and thus "forsaken." Control of mill and bakery, then, entailed control not just of grain and yeast but also of people, their labor, the lord's laws, and the homes that surrounded the bread-making hearth. The ritual of bread making, delivery, and consumption defined the lord, the land, and the people.

Western European and Slavic feudalism differed in many small ways, but both derived their rituals from a common Christian practice in which men, women, and children took bread—the body of the savior—at a common table from a man who called himself their lord. Christ's torture, death, placement in a tomb, and resurrection, too, became deeply bound up with the rituals of the grinding, resting, and magical rising of bread after saccharification.[18] In other words, the feudal power of bread delivery reenacted the gospels, reaffirmed a lord's power, and yet appeared as natural as eating. That said, bread's day-to-day form for feudal subjects was not a loaf or wafer but a pottage or stew composed mostly of leavened grain sprinkled with small amounts of turnips, cabbage, fish, and salt.[19] We have few documents for early medieval Slavic communities, but hundreds of years later the *domostroi*, a 1550s Russian instruction manual for nobility, described in detail how to manage a manorial bread-making community: which servants got served when and in what quantities, how to store food, and how the boyar, or lord, of the medieval Slavic household should instruct his steward to serve his bread.

In Europe, the centuries between 541 and 1100 were the age of the so-called robber barons. Constantinople used its pinch point across the Bosporus Strait to tax incoming vessels. Likewise, the barons built gates with guarded castles at the narrowest points of low-friction trading corridors in western Europe, like the Rhine, the Danube, and the Thames. From these castles they taxed grain and other goods that river traders brought between towns.

After 1100 the Hanseatic League emerged along the Baltic and North Seas. Organized as military trading companies of young, unmarried men, the league drove away robber barons along with Viking raiders and highwaymen who interfered with their trade along the rivers and between their ports. Rye and wheat traveled under their care between Poland and ports in northern Europe. The league's secretive, oath-bound agents made fortunes buying and selling rye and grain in times of famine, though the total quantity of grain shipped was modest by the standards of the *aristoi*. Hanseatic goods stayed locked in sealed-off port districts on the edges of Prussian, English, Swedish, and Dutch towns. By the sixteenth century the league fell, to be replaced by Russian-speaking English traders who kept estates in Saint Petersburg and brought rye and wheat for sale on London's Baltic Exchange.

In time, absolutist states in Europe grew by breaking the power of inland robber barons. They improved trading pathways, widening rivers, arming traders, and starving fortresses into submission. South of Constantinople, the caliphs chosen by the Prophet Muhammad expanded east and west in the area previously controlled by Constantine. By 1300 the caliphs had built a long, efficient, and relatively safe southerly route between Byzantium's eastern and western gates. Sugar cultivation and plantation slavery accompanied the expansion of these new Islamic empires.

Then, in 1347, the four horsemen appeared again, heralding the return of *Yersinia*. The bacillus probably came from the eastern steppe over the Silk Roads that stretched across the Mongol World Empire into the khanate of the Golden Horde. *Yersinia*'s first documented arrival from this route was in the Black Sea emporium of Caffa. According to legend, Mongols besieging the emporium became infected with plague. They then allegedly used catapults to launch infected corpses over the city gates.[20] While there are reasons to doubt the story, new genetic evidence suggests that the plague's expansion from Central Asia onto the steppes as early as the 1200s may have helped the Mongol Empire's expansion east and west from what is now Mongolia.[21] The plague started overland but found access to water by 1340. Genoese and Venetian traders had by this time established long-distance sea routes from the Black Sea to the Mediterranean, as chartered agents of Constantinople. Along with grain and slaves, traders again brought plague through the gates of Constantinople to western Europe.

Historians have called these Genoese and Venetian traders the first capitalists.[22] As authorized agents of the Byzantines between eastern and western ports, and as competitors with the Islamic empires in the south, they combined the technologies of both trading corridors. Early in the fourteenth century they blended ancient

Roman and more recent Islamic traditions, including Arabic numerals and legal agreements, to craft private bills of exchange. Using advances from Islamic algebra, these capitalist traders helped to develop and define double-entry bookkeeping. The first European central bank, the Camera del Frumento in Venice, purchased grain from ports along the Black Sea, then resold it to cities on the Mediterranean. Merchants borrowed from local citizens by drafting bills of exchange in banks with a promise to pay in ninety or more days when the ships came in. These bills of exchange were private credit instruments, guaranteed by the name of the trader, which any citizen could buy. A bill of exchange increased in value between the time it was issued and when the ship came in, allowing it to act as a privately issued, appreciating currency.

The bill of exchange was a physical symbol of a deal not yet consummated, charting the invisible route between ports. Wealthy landowners and traders with extra wealth bought bills of exchange because they were small, easy to store, appreciated in value, and could be quickly sold to someone else if hard currency was needed. As a representation of grain and other goods in transit, it named the port that a shipment came from and the port it was bound for, along with the traders involved and the bank that would make final payment.[23]

Y. pestis colonized these far-reaching Genoese and Venetian pathways, growing and spreading inside the bodies of black rats, snug under the decks of grain ships that ventured from port to port. Fully infected ships drifted into European ports, their captains and galley slaves sickened or dead. Grain ships had become "plague ships." Humans, rats, fleas, and the *Y. pestis* inside them traveled as far north as Ireland. Again *Y. pestis* devastated Eurasia, taking roughly twenty-five million people in Europe alone, perhaps a third of Europe's population. It stayed for two hundred years, erupting in smaller plagues, until a combination of harsh winters and new trade regulations limited its spread. Eventually ports imposed quarantine: ships were forced to wait forty days before unloading. (*Quarantena* is a corruption of the Latin word for "forty.") We now know that forty days was long enough for infected grain rats to die, along with their fleas, and for the feces to have dried enough to kill the last *Yersinia* on the ship. The solution was not well understood, but trial and error ensured that quarantine would hinder the transit of plague from ship to city. After quarantines were established to stop the plague, the Byzantine Empire held onto Constantinople, the gates of the Black Sea, for nearly a hundred years, though at times it could scarcely feed its soldiers and citizens.

Another candidate for control of the gates of Constantinople waited in the wings. The Ottoman Turks comprised an Islamic emirate that had assembled itself from farmers, traders, and horsemen in Anatolia in 1299. After establishing a capital at Bursa south and east of Constantinople, they expanded in part by serving as a mercenary army for a war between two competing regencies in the capital city in the 1340s and again in the 1350s. With each military victory the emirate acquired more territory. Over the next hundred years, the Ottoman Turks seized one Byzantine port after another on both the Black Sea and the Mediterranean, on both the Asian and the European sides of the city. Then, in 1451, Ottoman sultan Mehmed II found the pinch point that would fully destroy the Byzantine grain monopoly and the empire that straddled it. He located another spot across the Bosporus as narrow as Constantinople's, the site of an abandoned Roman fortress a few miles north of "the City." Within months his army had built a new fortress (Rumeli Hisari), which Mehmed called Boğazkesen, meaning "strait cutter." It also means, not coincidentally, "throat cutter." Using this fortress and another on the Asian side, he blocked all Black Sea vessels from delivering grain to Constantinople.

In 1453 the Byzantine Empire, increasingly starved of its grain-exporting fortresses, collapsed in a titanic battle with the

Ottoman Turks. The invaders moved ships over greased wooden rollers into the port at the Great Horn, then breached the city's walls with cannon. The Ottomans built a new empire on the fallen city, renaming Constantinople as Istanbul (probably from the Arabic for "to the City"). Just like the Greeks and Romans before them, they kept the city's immense granaries and built new fortresses on the Black Sea for collecting grain to feed a new empire's soldiers and citizens.

Thus, if we look at the world from the gates of Constantinople, the trading paths came first and successful empires simply straddled them. Athenian, Persian, and Roman empires did not build grain pathways but rather taxed them and tried to extend them. The Ottoman and Russian empires grew along those same paths by seizing or co-opting medieval sokes, fiefs, families, and noble houses.

If the route to grain was vital, the grain itself was the prize. Between 541 and 1347, control of bread became baked into the laws of medieval European, North African, and Arabian empires that surrounded the Bosporus Strait. Kings, queens, aristocrats, sultans, and tsars built their power on grain, regulating the size of loaves and carefully controlling grain and the boundaries where it was grown. As late as 1835, bakers in Britain remained public employees paid by the state for each loaf of bread they produced. The same was true in Istanbul, where the *nan-i 'aziz*, or standard loaf, weighed exactly 110 *dirhem* (just over thirteen ounces). If a baker's loaf weighed less, a market inspector might instruct local police to parade him through the streets or, after multiple offenses, nail his ear to the door of his shop.[24]

Control of grain did not just come from monarchs. Workers in towns from Cork in Ireland to port cities on the Yellow Sea enforced what they considered a "just price" for bread from the imperial bakeries. Deviations from the norm by bakers led to citywide protest, violence, and even revolutions. Empires' unstable hold on power meant controlling the harvest, controlling mills, and controlling bakers. High bread prices in cities could lead to revolution: bread riots preceded imperial collapse in Constantinople in 1453, in Paris in 1789, and again in Istanbul with the downfall of the Ottoman sultan Selim III in 1807.

And just like a combination of fungus and flour, modern empires rose, thriving on the policing of bread. As Britain's cities grew after 1600, the British Empire extended its bread regime across the sea to Ireland, subsidizing Protestant landowners (called "Undertakers") to establish "plantations" to plant, dry, and transport grain. Imperially subsidized fleets of ships gathered the grain from English emporia established in Dublin and Cork. In their rocky sheds, Irish agriculturalists grew and cooked potatoes for themselves, while sending the bounty of Irish plantations—flour, beef, and butter—to feed Bristol, Liverpool, and London and its urban classes. Britain, like its imperial predecessors, built an empire that depended on grain that came from what historians call the empire's "inner ring."[25]

Contests between empires, too, relied on bread making. After the Ottomans seized the granaries and bakeries of Constantinople in 1453—renaming it Istanbul—Russia, under Ivan the Great (1440–1505), imagined a centuries-long struggle to take the city on the Bosporus from them. Russia, according to Ivan's plan, would erect a thalassic empire to control two oceans: the Black Sea to the south and the Baltic Sea to the north and west. With grain for armies gathered at southern ports along the coast, Russia would recapture "the City," Istanbul, and build a third Rome there. In 1472, Ivan sought out Sophia, niece of deposed emperor Constantine XI, proposed marriage, and then chose the double-headed eagle (Byzantium's symbol) as Russia's imperial crest. The rulers assumed the name tsar—caesar in Russian. For four centuries the tsars meticulously planned their assault on Istanbul, giving the city a new aspirational title of Tsargrad: city of the tsar. Among the places they needed to control was the area that is now western Ukraine but was then southern Poland.

In this area, a hundred miles north and west of Odessa, the dry steppes meet the forest. Flat and wet, with deep black soil, it is one of the best spots on the planet to grow grain. The western portion, called Podolia, was, according to early nineteenth-century Ottoman court chronicler Mehmet Esad Efendi, "fertile soil, watered by an infinity of rivers."[26] In Podolia and the neighboring district of Kiev, wheat and rye grew easily in the dark soil on flat, black loam called chernozem. Proximity to trees in Podolia meant that houses, boats, and carts could be built locally. If we imagine the chernozem belt as a spread eagle, the western wing starts at Podolia, the head reaches as far north as Riazan, and the eastern wing reaches to Orenburg. The body extends all the way across the northern reaches of the Black Sea with a western foot in Crimea and an eastern foot reaching to Terek, between the Black and Caspian Seas. Beginning as early as the fifth century BC, cultivated wheat in this vast region broke up into "landraces," regional varieties adapted to particular mixtures of climate, soil, and moisture levels. Rye, originally a weed that grew up alongside wheat, also diverged into subspecies. Suited to colder climates, it grew more readily north of the eagle.

When the Ottomans took over Constantinople in 1453, they had nominal control of Podolia but shortly lost it to Polish and Russian princes who warred over the bread lands on those rivers. While the princes put their names in chronicles, farmers north of the Black Sea did the more vital work over the centuries, seeking and recombining nearby strains of wheat to suit the weather. We have little worthwhile from the princes, but the thousands of unremembered farmers left us something much more vital for humanity's long-term survival: dozens of varieties of wheat suited to dozens of microclimates and seasons. The later settlement of western Canada, the northern United States, Argentina, and Australia would have been impossible without the many landrace strains of wheat that developed over centuries in this region.[27]

From 1455 to the 1560s, often using loans from Dutch merchants, the Polish Empire briefly dominated the wheat and rye fields of Podolia. This was the western edge of the eagle's wingspan on the western, or "right bank," of the Dniester River.[28] Borrowing from the capitalist playbook of the Venetians, Dutch merchants lent Polish nobles the resources they required. Some rye and wheat harvested from these estates still went south on *chumaki* caravans to Black Sea ports and fed Istanbul. But most grain after the Ottoman takeover traveled north to the Vistula River and the port of Danzig on the Baltic Sea, where Dutch merchants sold it in markets as far away as London. Polish and Lithuanian nobles, to enforce their claims to soil and people, imposed a new kind of state-enforced serfdom on the mostly Ukrainian-speaking farmers after 1496. Serfs would plant and harvest wheat and rye through eastern Europe and Russia.

Polish control of the bread lands did not last. By the 1570s Russian princes were building *cherta*, or notched frontier lines, south and west of Moscow that brought them closer and closer to the land of infinite rivers. A series of wars between Russian and Polish princes, along with peasant uprisings around 1650, produced protracted and bloody conflict and killed perhaps a third of Poland's population. A unified Russia then forced Ukrainians—peasants, the *chumaki*, and the roving bands of Ukrainian Cossacks—to swear perpetual oaths to the Muscovite crown. Russia slowly began to assimilate these bread lands while forging rough pathways that led back to the imperial core, acquiring the lands east of the Dnieper by 1689 with designs on the land farther west and south.[29] For Russia, however, access to the Black Sea was always crucial to these plans.

There are many different definitions of "empire." Some emphasize a common law, a single emperor, and multiple ethnic groups;

another describes a core of ruling gentry surrounded by military districts; others emphasize gentlemanly families with rank who draw from holdings at the periphery.[30] But at its deepest level an empire may be a monopolizer of food along ancient grain pathways that it never fully understands. Empires survive only as long as they control the sources of food needed to feed soldiers and citizens; they fund themselves by taxing those who sell it. Before empires, ancestors of the *chumaki* traded food over long distances along with salt and leather. International trade shrank in periods when *Yersinia pestis*, in the bellies of rats, found a way to hitchhike on those same trade routes. This microscopic pestilence cleared the path for another parasite, one orders of magnitude larger than a bacillus. Ancient thalassic empires, I believe, surged along the pathways cut by *Y. pestis*, building grain ports as stepping-stones for further conquest, often to feed armies at imperial borders.

Around 542, at the beginning of what we call the Middle Ages, *Y. pestis* severed the paths connecting western Europe to China, forcing smaller states to focus on increasing agricultural yields to compensate for the loss of international trade. This contributed to the creation of medieval sokes, fiefs, and noble houses throughout Eurasia. In the wake of the 1347 plague, postmedieval empires grew by incorporating and dominating hundreds of these communities.

Then, in the 1760s, a new military-fiscal-banking structure grew up in Russia that weakened and nearly demolished the empire at the gates of the Bosporus. When Napoleon emerged to briefly dominate most of Europe's ports, Russia turned Odessa into something entirely new: an emporium that no longer fed its own empire but now fed Europe. Russia, the Mediterranean, and western Europe would never be the same.

Three

PHYSIOCRATIC EXPANSION
1760-1844

B ETWEEN 300 AND 1762, when *Yersinia pestis* colonized human trading pathways, empires had been forced to innovate to protect themselves. Like spiders after a rainstorm, they rebuilt their webs. Sometimes they shrank to garrisoned kingdoms or hived themselves off in monastic compounds, as in much of late-medieval Europe. Sometimes empires abandoned oceans and colonized trading pathways on steppes and deserts, like the Safavid, Mongol, and Abbasid empires in Central Asia and the Near East. *Y. pestis* killed travelers, causing empires to quarantine and innovate, to discover again how to rotate crops, mill grain, and live for another season.

In the 1760s the relationship between empire and grain changed again under the reign of tsarina Catherine II, who embraced an unprecedented policy of selling unprocessed grain to increase the size of the Russian Empire. Before Catherine's rule, empires seized agricultural land, expanded ports, and moved grain inward to feed cities and outward to feed armies and navies. But Catherine was influenced by the physiocrats, a group of French economists and imperial advisors. Imagining the economy as an exchange of goods between farmers, landlords, artisans, and merchants, the physiocrats believed that merchants who exported grain benefited an empire by trading excess grain for scarce foreign goods. While their predecessors regarded international trade as unsavory or dangerous, these gentlemen argued for the state support of grain growing, the elimination of internal barriers in trading grain, broad-based education, and the careful control of imports and exports. They were not free traders in a modern sense but believed that grain exports, properly managed, could be the foundation of an empire's wealth.

Catherine's reading of the physiocrats was filtered through her jealousy of the Polish counts who drew their wealth by selling grain up the Vistula River to Gdansk and then to markets on the Baltic and North Seas. She wanted to seize this trade by rebuilding an ancient grain export corridor down the Dnieper to the Black Sea. How to achieve this was her burning question. After closely reading the physiocrats François Quesnay, Anne Robert Jacques Turgot, and Pierre Samuel du Pont de Nemours, she founded the Free Economic Society, an institution to promote new methods of planting, tilling, and rotation and the use of New World food crops like the potato. She created a modest system of public education, built printing houses, and established libraries that would spread physiocratic principles to large landowners. Two years later Catherine further interpreted these physiocratic principles to fit the Russian situation in a hundred-page document that she had printed and circulated throughout Russia. She called it the *Nakaz*, or mandate. "The basis of trade," she declared, "is the export and import of goods to favor the state." "Customs," she continued, drew from this well of trade; it was "the routine collection from this export and import to favor the state."[1]

To facilitate intensive grain production, Catherine created a system of private property in Russia that would have profound effects on the empire's future. She sought to make serfdom more like New World slavery. She gave serf owners private property in the land, including rights to own farmland personally. New laws would prevent the tsar from ever claiming it in cases of treason; relatives instead would receive the property. Not only could serf owners sell their land to other serf owners, but they could sell the serfs to others or to the state as soldiers. Serfs, by comparison, she denied a shared right to the land, making them less distinguishable from slaves. Indeed she called them *raby* (slaves) rather than *krepostnyye* (serfs). Under the new dispensation, they had no rights, just an unenforceable promise that she would keep them safe from beating, torture, and execution. Serfs could be sold and forced to marry against their will; legally they could possess no assets. By giving personal property in land and people to serf owners, Catherine intentionally made Russian serfs into something more like colonial slaves. The plan, as she saw it, was to turn the landed gentry into something like colonial enslavers, all to support wheat growing.[2]

Her plan for imperial warfare also centered on grain. She borrowed grain from outside her empire to feed armies that would seize flat and arid plains. Next, she subsidized foreign settlers, lavished resources on ports, and sold grain abroad for foreign exchange. After pausing to consolidate, she would then expand again. Russia's tsars and imperial officials would continue her policy for wheat-based expansion for over a century. This physiocratic expansion turned empires inside out. In expanding, wheat field by wheat field, large families accumulated trading wealth centrifugally, at the empire's edges. As a result, much of Russia's wealth would forever after lay on its outer rim, unlike in ancient and medieval empires before it.

Catherine II's physiocratic expansion allowed her to incorporate Poland into her empire and brought her close to turning Istanbul into Tsargrad. Beginning around 1762, the tsarina introduced military reforms that radically strengthened the Russian army and navy. The Russian advantage over Ottomans and Poles came partly from iron-making capacity. Russian-made light artillery loaded with tubes of lead and sawdust (called canisters) could blast devastating holes into massed Turkish or Polish infantry.

But more importantly, Catherine gave Russian officers a new way to feed armies on the march. She dictated that Russian officers after 1762 should bring bills of exchange to Ottoman- and

Polish-controlled territories to buy grain at ports and farm gates. In 1768 Catherine relied on another note to trade for her army's wheat: the assignat. The assignat, like the British pound, became an imperial currency and represented the tsarina's *future* promise to pay for provisions. In the same period Catherine seized land previously owned by the Russian Orthodox Church inside Russia's borders. Serf owners could buy this land with assignats. This made the assignat a particularly valuable form of currency.[3] While Venetian bills of exchange represented grain in motion, Catherine's assignats represented recently seized land and future land her empire would take by force.

The assignat was a bold move, one France soon adopted when French revolutionaries seized lands from the Roman Catholic Church.[4] Catherine created a national debt in a strategy that would be embraced by an infant empire created at nearly the same moment: the United States. Indeed both Thomas Jefferson and Benjamin Franklin plunged into the same physiocratic waters that Catherine did. Physiocratic ideals shaped their vision of agricultural colonization of the West, investment in education, and plans for the export of grain. Those ideals would define their plans for independence.[5] While French reformers defined American and Russian plans for expansion by wheat, the plan to turn national debt into currency likely came directly from capitalist traders in the Dutch Empire. Hope and Company in the Netherlands advised all three empires. A Hope representative would have pointed out how in the seventeenth century the Netherlands had established a national debt, created a national bank to issue that debt, and then used debt to expand its military empire around the world. Shortly after the Dutch expansion, Great Britain appropriated a deficit-based expansion strategy when English lords persuaded the Dutch prince William and his wife Mary to take the English throne. William formed the Bank of England in 1694. British consols and bonds helped fill the Atlantic with English ships. Historians have called this the financial revolution.[6]

While the Dutch and English empires had used their banks to pay for a navy and fund a merchant marine, Catherine's physiocratic model was aimed at seizing land where wheat could grow. On the Baltic and Black Seas both, Russian armies and navies used bills of exchange drawn on Dutch and English banks. Assignats and bills of exchange together acted as loans to feed troops, rough gambles on the success of Russian arms in the drive to Istanbul.[7] What makes the case especially interesting is that the bills of exchange allowed the Russian army to provision itself in Polish- and Ottoman-controlled lands without using the ancient strategy of seizing territory and then demanding grain from it, which could lead to revolt. This strategy used the Ottoman grain monopoly against itself. Because Istanbul controlled the strait, it imposed a *miri*, or set price, for wheat. But enforcing low prices for grain, as any physiocrat will tell you, will induce farmers to sell grain to a competing empire at market rates.[8]

While Catherine purchased grain with promises, officers in the Ottoman Empire by comparison assembled bread using direct taxation, following trade and tax pathways laid out centuries before by the Byzantines. Turkish officers ordered the grinding and baking of whatever grain lay stored in its stone fortresses, while carrying silver and gold to buy additional supplies at the fixed Ottoman price. But the weight of carrying gold, silver, and grain made the sultan's armies bulky and slow-moving on the Black Sea, particularly along the Danube and Pruth Rivers, which entered the sea from the northwest.

Catherine's strategy of borrowing grain while paying market rates made her army more mobile. Russian officers could more cheaply transmit the Russian Empire's bills of exchange and assignats. As Ottoman chronicler Mehmed Esad put it, "They bore on them the value of all that they had in bills of exchange or notes payable by administrative funds. Whenever they needed funds, they changed one of these notes for cash; if, in a rout, or by any event whatsoever, these papers were taken from them by the Muslims, they could not make use of them."[9] Though Ottoman merchant guilds had been using bills of exchange for centuries, the empire itself used a medieval instrument—the *hawala*—that could only be transmitted from one *hawala* broker to another. The *hawala* did not represent future credit and could never be retraded or resold. The empire had no long-term borrowing instrument until decades later.[10]

Key to the Ottoman failure was grain owners' gamble on Russia's ability to seize bread lands. In 1768, when the third Russo-Turkish war began, the older grain-tax system that the Ottomans had used successfully for centuries collapsed catastrophically, according to Esad, producing famines inside their own lines. The Ottoman Empire, successful for three hundred years as a grain-gathering empire and the most fiscally efficient empire in the world a century earlier, could not feed its Janissaries, cavalry, or drafted militias. These had been for three centuries the most feared warriors in Europe. But in 1768 contractors could not build the ovens quickly enough to feed the troops; they tried to replace wheat with millet; some added lime to whiten inedible black bread, which killed some of the soldiers who ate it. Lacking proper bread, tens of thousands of Ottoman troops either revolted, starved, or died of food poisoning in the trenches outside Ottoman fortresses along the Danube and Pruth after 1768.[11]

The loss of grain for the Ottoman army turned the tide of war. In a climactic battle on the Pruth near Kagul (now Cahul, in present-day Moldova), Russian general Pyotr Rumyantsev's army of fewer than 40,000 men defeated the bulk of the Ottoman imperial army of 150,000. By 1774, eight centuries after Prince Oleg and three centuries after Ivan the Great, Russia's forces appeared poised to finally capture the holy city on the Bosporus and turn it into Tsargrad. *Yersinia* played its part in the battles too, for the bacilli that long lived among rodents once more entered human hosts weakened in the chaos of war.[12]

Catherine's grain-borrowing model worked, but she failed to capture the Bosporus Strait. The Austrian Habsburgs, whose armies had helped Catherine take the fortress near Kagul, became alarmed by Russia's lightning successes on the Black Sea. It was one thing for the Russians to seize grain-growing regions along the Black Sea. It was another to capture the chokepoint for all the grain, including grain that might flow out of Habsburg lands along the Danube through the Black Sea and the Bosporus to the world. To prevent Russia's seizure of Istanbul, the Austrians and Prussians together threatened to make peace with the Ottomans *against* Catherine. With the threat of a Catholic-Protestant-Muslim military alliance against Orthodox Russia, Catherine sued for peace in 1771. Though she won control of the Crimea and access to trade on the Black Sea, the German-speaking kings preserved a constricted Ottoman Empire and blocked her capture of the Bosporus and Dardanelles Straits. The European powers' crucial requirement, that grain ships of Russia and other empires could safely leave the Black Sea through the straits, ensured that European states would compete to keep the Ottoman Empire alive even if Ottoman control of grain fields shrank. None of the other European empires wanted Russia to become as powerful as Constantine or Justinian had been, with an impregnable fortress on two oceans that might enable it to build, as Constantine had done, an empire from Spain to India.

To appease voracious Catherine, the European princes tore grain-producing Poland into pieces. She accepted forty thousand acres of Poland as payment for withdrawing from the Danube and the Pruth. From the Ottomans she took all the steppe land between the Dnieper and Southern Bug Rivers, and she demanded the autonomy of the Tatar khans on the plains, as well as influence in regions farther east. From her share of the partition of Poland, she claimed that "fertile soil, watered by an infinity of rivers," which she used to pay off her many loans and to guarantee her assignats.

Catherine's utopian combination of military, fiscal, and bread-based expansion succeeded. The *chumaki* trails again rapidly expanded along the ancient black paths. A thousand *chumaki* wagons in the 1760s would, by the 1830s, become tens of thousands. The reemergence of a southern Russia along the black paths of the steppe produced its own problems, however: the rebuilt black paths carried plague to Moscow and Saint Petersburg, killing tens of thousands. But over the long term, her strategy brought grain back to the ancient steppe lands. Catherine began assigning Russian and Greek names to rivers and cities in the Crimean Peninsula.[13] Just as in the United States' expansion along the Great Lakes, thousands of native peoples were persuaded to ally with the physiocratic conqueror to dispossess others. While Catherine's annexation of Crimea forced some Tatars to cross the ocean and join the Ottoman Empire, her willingness to accept Muslim officers in Russian ranks persuaded six Tatar divisions to form up in Russian service and participate in the invasion of Poland in 1792.[14]

After conquering the steppe, Catherine set out to build a free port, exempt from import or export taxes. In 1791, Catherine's cabinet planned a new city to gather the golden grain from the *chumaki* trails that spread all the way to historic Poland. Claiming to recivilize the steppe and restore it to its condition under the ancient Greeks, the tsarina named the new port after a lost Black Sea emporium called Odessos, whose ruins, some believed, lay nearby. According to legend, Catherine gave it its feminine ending: Odessa.

A grain port required thousands of new farmers, of course. That part she had already secured. In the year after seizing power, in 1763, Catherine had issued a decree, or *ukaz*, permitting foreigners to settle in Russian lands, granting them seventy-five acres of land, exempting them from military service, and giving them freedom of religion. Before the docks at Odessa had been completed, her request for emigrants attracted multiple, non-Turkic people onto the plains: Ukrainian peasants, Greek captains, Jewish traders, Polish landowners, Bulgarian refugees, independent Cossacks, and displaced German Protestants. As Catherine concentrated control over eastern Poland, she claimed Polish towns that had become the refuge for millions of Jews. This newly Russian-controlled area was the Jewish "pale of settlement." Catherine and her successors forced many of Russia's Jews to resettle inside the pale, including in the plains just north of the Black Sea. When the empire promised to suspend taxes on Jewish communities that relocated to Odessa, millions of Polish Jews followed the *chumaki* trails south to seek new opportunities in Russia's new grain outpost.[15]

Odessa, then, was a masterpiece of physiocratic social engineering. Before Odessa, the Athenian, Byzantine, and Ottoman empires had located grain-growing communities, dominated and taxed them, and drawn tribute as grain *inward* to the imperial center, where it was stored in immense granaries, and also *outward* in wars of expansion. The Ottoman Empire had done so in 1453 when it seized the Byzantine Empire's ocean routes and bread roads on the Black Sea. The Qing Empire did the same after 1636, expanding from Beijing to tributary states in Southeast Asia. Imperial agents blazed a trail for grain traders who went north to gather grain and soy cakes; others went south to gather rice. Emporia, through tribute and trade, fed imperial centers.[16] But Odessa, the newest emporium on the Black Sea, would sell grain abroad to feed the cities of Europe. For the first time since the days of the ancient *aristoi*, massive ships of grain bound for distant ports would fill the Black Sea. By 1860, seven hundred thousand *chumaki* wagons brought grain to the Black Sea coast every year, providing the food for an industrial revolution in Europe.

Founded in 1794, the flat and dusty grain port of Odessa has none of the crooks or bends of a medieval city. It was laid out with boring mathematical precision to funnel out raw grain: two squares facing the water, one side for grain, another for the army and plague quarantine. The natural crook of the bay required that the squares intersect at forty-seven degrees.[17] The residents of Odessa came from distant parts of the world, filling up what still looks like a French coastal town. Or as Alexander Pushkin described "dusty Odessa," it was "already Europe":

> *There everything breathes, diffuses Europe,*
> *Glitters of the South and is gay*
> *With lively variety.*
> *The language of golden Italy*
> *Resounds along the merry street,*
> *Where walk the proud Slav,*
> *The Frenchman, the Spaniard, the Armenian*
> *And the Greek, and the heavy Moldavian,*
> *And that son of the Egyptian soil,*
> *The retired corsair, Morali.*[18]

EIGHT THOUSAND MILES away, the North American cities of New York, Philadelphia, Boston, and Baltimore had emerged as grain ports long before Catherine laid out her battle plans on the Black Sea, though before the American Civil War the American cities offered Odessa no practical competition in the export of grain. With the exception of tobacco, the principal exports of North American coastal colonies were semi-manufactured foods grown to supply Caribbean slave regimes or to provision the Royal Navy that defended them. As part of the apparatus of a far-flung British Empire in the Americas, American port cities were not visionary physiocratic cities but simple adjuncts to plantation slave regimes. Between 1660 and 1770, they were mostly food-growing regions lashed to the value-producing, slave-destroying tropical island colonies that stood between ten and twenty degrees north of the equator. The tropical colonies had a powerful lobby in London, the so-called West India Interest, which was nearly as powerful as the "India interest" that dominated and drew resources from South Asia. For the absentee landowners of Britain's Caribbean islands, North American port cities were food pumps, providing over a million barrels a year of flour and approximately seven hundred thousand barrels combined of beef, pork, rice, and cornmeal for the slave regimes, which in turn exported addictive, equatorial drugs—coffee, sugar, and cocoa—that made British elites rich. Though enslaved people grew food in small gardens on Caribbean plantations, the Caribbean islands remained utterly dependent on provisions that came from North America.[19]

In gathering food for tropical slave regimes, these North American port cities resembled the middle ring of grain ports that had served Rome, Constantinople, and Istanbul for millennia. Or, as economist Avner Offer wrote, "the British urban fringe ran through the suburbs of colonial and American towns."[20] As with Theodosia, Tanais, or Caffa, the British Empire in North America sought deep water and built long docks. And just like in those regions, further processing of grain and shipping built up primitive urban industries. Developmental economists refer to the developmental contributions of any staple—like grain, rice, or cotton—as linkages. Backward linkages are industries that contribute to producing and marketing of the staple: for grain this means agricultural machinery, storage, and transport services. Forward linkages are opportunities for further processing of staples: for grain this means flour mills, bakeries, and even stockyards. Pigs and cattle can be seen as forward linkages because they eat the middlings from grain in the countryside, can transport themselves to ports, and are then "converted" into barrels of beef and pork. From the perspective of developmental economists, cities assembled themselves out of rope works, sailmaker's shops, shipyards, granaries, stockyards, flour mills, and slaughterhouses.[21]

After the American Revolution, the fledgling cities on the coast followed a slightly different version of Catherine's physiocratic strategy by expanding their provisioning trade to service even more tropical colonies in the Spanish, French, Danish, Dutch, and Swedish West Indies.[22] Slave regimes and food provisioning remained compatible: Virginia and Maryland produced much of America's exported wheat, while coastal South Carolina provided rice. Yet the northern fringes of the slave regime—Delaware, Pennsylvania, New Jersey, and New York—also found ways to feed the Caribbean. After the American Revolution, in the Delaware, Hudson, and Ohio valleys, enslaved people challenged chattel slavery, pointing out that it violated the frequently stated cause of the Revolution itself. Pushed in part by lawsuits brought by enslaved people against the institution, slavery was legally abolished in the North American states, though full emancipation took as long as thirty years in New York and New Jersey.

North America's flour barrels occasionally made it all the way across the Atlantic, particularly during European wars. But the risk of selling flour was always great since the price and condition of flour barrels could change drastically during a stormy two-month journey across the Atlantic. Even still, the former colonies' love affair with grain never faltered. From 1793 to 1815, continuing wars between Republican France and Europe provided opportunities for the Americans to provision the ships, as well as the tropical islands, of Britain, France, and Spain. In those years the country exported an average of a million barrels of flour a year at an average price of nearly $10 a barrel. "Our object is to feed and theirs to fight," quipped Secretary of State Thomas Jefferson in 1793 after news emerged of France's expanding war with the European powers. "We have only to pray that their souldiers may eat a great deal." The French Revolutionary Wars drove wheat prices so high in Europe that American ships could occasionally feed ports in Spain, Italy, and Britain.

Thomas Jefferson and Benjamin Franklin, in the time they spent in France, absorbed physiocratic ideals, though they drew slightly different conclusions from them. For Jefferson, like Catherine, expansion through space, in western land settlement, would prevent the country from expansion through time, a rapid economic development along English lines, which would create a country full of dark, Satanic mills with child labor and social unrest. As for Catherine, he saw "free trade" not as meaning a bar on taxes on foreign goods but rather as the free export of agricultural goods without hindrance. Another contentious physiocratic principle was the "single tax" on landowners. Because physiocrats viewed farmers as the primary creators of wealth, they saw landlords as a drain on the national balance sheet. As a result physiocrats argued that taxes should rest on landowners. In both the United States and Russia, powerful landed interests (enslavers and serf owners) strongly rejected this principle.[23] Spending to boost agriculture, however, they strongly supported. As a result both landed empires imposed minor taxes on imported manufactures, because taxing goods at a few ports was simpler than collecting income or land taxes. Physiocratic principles stressed building roads and canals, deepening rivers, and supporting public education. Both Russia and America aimed to construct the broadest, widest route to promote agricultural sales on an international market. The French Revolutionary and Napoleonic Wars, in making Europe hungry, benefited both empires at Europe's margin, American and Russian.[24]

Provisioning flour to cities at war was as risky for the United States as it was for Russia. American shippers had to be especially inventive in defying British and French blockades. They introduced the concept of the "broken voyage" in which a shipper would bring sugar from a French colony, stop for a day in Baltimore to pick up grain, and then ship out again for France with a new ship manifest that declared all the goods to be American. Whether merchants practiced intentional physiocracy or not, selling grain past imperial blockades built merchant fortunes and expanded the international market for American flour, which fed the US Treasury before it had even erected a building. After the war America's grain-trading exploits, like the stories of *The Iliad* and *The Odyssey*, were spun into adventure stories such as John Frost's *The Young Merchant* and Washington Irving's *Astoria*. Wistful stories of privateering and fraud became anthems to American's commercial probity.[25]

After the American Revolution, as slavery ended in New England, a grain-based strategy of farm expansion and a cotton-based strategy of plantation expansion created distinctive landscapes, increasingly following different grooves of trade. Contemporaries blamed the cotton gin.[26] In the South, slavery surged in importance after the invention and cheap reproduction of the cotton engine, or cotton gin for short. The gin allowed the rounded boll in short staple cotton to be separated easily from its heavy seeds, then packed into bales for delivery to English cotton mills. The gin lowered the cost of postharvest separation by over 800 percent. Because growing cotton required what Alexis de Tocqueville called "unremitting attention," thus year-round care by men, women, and even children, enslavers found it profitable to enslave entire families to grow and tend cotton on larger estates. If cotton needed care, every farmer knew that wheat could mostly be ignored after planting. Because wheat could be "seeded" in one month and "garnered" in another without year-round labor, some enslavers regarded wheat as incompatible with slavery.[27]

But America's initial plan of expansion through wheat exports could not last. In 1784, Britain imposed Foster's Corn Law to ratchet up Irish grain imports over Russian and American grain. The danger, as the English Crown and Parliament saw it, was that spending foreign exchange on wheat would pull gold and silver out of Britain. Subsidizing grain fields just offshore was a classic imperial move, one that Julius Caesar would have applauded but that physiocrats abhorred. Britain expanded those corn laws in 1815 after Napoleon's defeat. The United States responded with the American Navigation Acts of 1817 and 1818 to block selected British manufactures. Britain responded in turn with the Free Port Act of 1818, one of the most important and understudied acts in American history. Proclaimed in August 13, 1818, it blocked American ships from entering British ports, with the exception of the distant Canadian ports of Halifax, Nova Scotia, and St. John, New Brunswick. Once a Canadian buyer took grain and other provisions, that merchant could only use British ships to carry this American grain into the Caribbean.[28]

The result in America was a 50 percent drop in the price of flour and the American panic of 1819, perhaps the severest panic in nineteenth-century American history. Land prices dropped 40 percent, particularly along the Mississippi River. The US Land Office and the Second Bank of the United States seized thousands of acres for defaulted loans. In the sixteen years between 1803 and 1819, the total value of American wheat and flour exports had averaged $10 million, about the same as cotton exports. By 1820 American wheat and flour had shrunk to one-fifth the value of cotton exports. By the 1830s it had sunk to one-tenth. Cotton replaced wheat as America's most valuable export. A Catherine-style policy of expanding by grain export appeared on the decline, at least relative to the growing empire of cotton.[29]

American grain still found a way into the Caribbean, however, though at higher prices. A brisk trade in New York, Pennsylvania, and Ohio grain took place across the Great Lakes into Toronto and Montreal, where the Canadian legislatures simply failed to tax any grain that arrived by riverboat and bateau. Flour mills there turned mostly American wheat into bonded "Canadian" flour that could then be sold down the Saint Lawrence River to British plantations in the Caribbean.[30] This costly, snaking path from American grain farms through Canadian mills to Caribbean plantations caused Caribbean food prices to double, however. As early as 1822 many wealthy London investors began to divest themselves of Caribbean plantations. The high cost of provisions, paired with slave revolts and a growing antislavery movement, contributed to the push for emancipation in the Caribbean colonies.

The special exemption for American trade to the Caribbean via distant Canadian ports pressed wheat production north so that after 1820 wheat became somewhat more associated with northern states and freedom. Because wheat, as a weed, can grow almost anywhere, while cotton then required two hundred frost-free days to fruit, Americans planted cotton in a corridor of rich soil and long summers that stretched from Richmond, Virginia, to Macon, Georgia. After the Louisiana Purchase of 1804 and after American participation in the slave trade ended in 1808, enslavers bought men, women, and children from declining wheat farms in Maryland and Virginia as well as failing rice estates in Charleston, South Carolina. They would be "sold down the river" to Georgia's piedmont and to the even more fertile Mississippi Valley. Over the 1830s and 1840s, the tightly integrated economies of slavery and freedom diverged. Wheat and flour still came from slave plantations in Missouri, Kentucky, and Virginia, but the newest farms for planting wheat emerged north of the Ohio River. Cotton, meanwhile, could hardly be planted north of Charlotte, North Carolina, or Nashville, Tennessee.

And so exports of American cotton prevailed over American wheat for forty years from 1820 to 1860. In 1857, with an enslaver's characteristic hubris, Senator James Henry Hammond of South Carolina imagined a world where the South stopped growing cotton for three years: "England would topple headlong and carry the whole civilized world with her, save the South. No, you dare not make war on cotton. No power on earth dares to make war upon it. Cotton *is* king." Yet its hold was not uncontested. The rediscovery of ancient grain-storing secrets, combined with new ship technologies, suggested that the United States might invade Russia's position as the provisioner of Europe and the world and one day dethrone King Cotton.

A crucial innovation for grain shipment came from the results of French archaeological expeditions made during the reign of Napoleon, who sought to discover the lost secret of how ancient Romans stored grain underground. The secret of Persephone, who remained untouched by yeast or other fungi, was one of the closely guarded secrets in the Eleusinian mysteries. Though we will probably never know the entire ritual, it must have involved slightly heating and drying wheat grains to preserve them, though not enough to prevent replanting. The secrets were lost some time between AD 300 and 1400. As French agronomists well knew, European farmers in the Middle Ages had reverted to primitive open-air drying of their grain, which preserved it for a season but did not allow for long-term storage or long-distance transport. These agronomists also knew from the stories of Alexander the Great that grain could be safely stored for more than three months, which allowed Alexander's competitors to defend themselves for years against sieges. If Persephone's secret could be rediscovered, grain might travel farther for the long-term supply of armies. The French invasion of Italy allowed Napoleon's chemists to investigate what the French called "Caesar's vaults" to figure out the mystery.[31]

Around 1810 chemist Jean-Antoine Chaptal found Persephone's secret. After visiting numerous ancient ruins in Italy, he successfully reverse-engineered the ancient process. Excavations showed sand and dried grass around the edges of the walls of ancient *horrea*. Chaptal discovered a process that involved drying grain and sealing it without oxygen in a nonporous shell. The discovery remained France's state secret, though Napoleon could not share it with his army in time before sending the troops off to invade Russia, where they starved in 1812. After Napoleon's banishment,

Chaptal published the vital discovery. By 1817 Italians could store Black Sea grain for years at a time using the ancient secret. These discoveries were translated and published in Boston in 1839, and the first successful hermetic grain container in America came to Buffalo around 1840. It was a copy of the French "silo" and labeled, confusingly, the "elevator."[32]

The discovery of how to store grain lingered without a cheap method of long-distance delivery. American wheat became American flour in Baltimore and Richmond. That cheap bounty could continue to feed enslaved people relatively nearby: in Cuba, Brazil, and even the American South. In fact, cheap flour from the mid-Atlantic and Midwest probably helped prop up King Cotton for forty years, not just in Brazil and Cuba but also on the southern frontier regions of Mississippi, Louisiana, and Texas.[33] But delivering American grain to Europe remained challenging. Once hermetic grain storage was rediscovered in France, the New England shipping industry devoted years to improving the nautical qualities of ships that could send cleaned and dried grain across the Atlantic. The famous American clipper ship had shortened the crossing to as little as two weeks by 1850, though the clipper's sharp profile in the water meant that space in the hold was small. Nevertheless the shape, weight, and density of American grain ensured that it paired well with the export of slave-grown cotton. Bags of wheat are heavy and dense (forty cubic feet per long ton) as well as moldable, which made them attractive for stabilizing the bottom and edges of a ship. The lower grain portion of a cargo hold could be covered with lighter, less dense, and more valuable cotton. A shipowner who wanted his ship to be full of goods and low in the water wanted his cargo to be both "full and down": cotton made it full, and wheat held it down.[34] As French observers noted by 1850, this combination of grain sacks and cotton bales ensured that America would have a greater share of the Atlantic trade, with ships that topped one thousand tons in capacity.[35] Nevertheless while the United States still fed Caribbean colonies and briefly fed European cities in times of war, it would only be a bit player in the Atlantic wheat market until the Civil War.

AFTER CATHERINE DIED in 1796, Odessa became crucial to Napoleon as his power over France and then Europe expanded. The young artillerist turned general, then first consul of the French Revolution, knew his bread. France had broken because of bread. When the physiocrats had taken control of the French grain trade, eliminated internal taxes, and allowed the price of grain to float, conspiracies circulated. France's artisans persuaded themselves that the physiocratic attempt to remove fixed prices for grain was a "famine pact," designed to raise the price of their food.[36] Rapidly increasing bread prices had led to riots in Paris in 1789; the failure of the French version of the Russian assignat helped end the monarchy and introduce the Directory. Then, as his militias seized control of Paris and overturned the Directory, Napoleon built an army and an empire of his own. As a young artillerist, Napoleon both feared and admired the physiocratic empire Catherine had created in Russia, declaring that her expansion was so fast that in fifty years all of Europe would be either republican or Cossack.[37] But he recognized that his greatest enemy would always be England, with its powerful men-of-war and its bread-gobbling imperial city, London.

Catherine was dead by the time Napoleon's armies expanded east across Europe, adding up victories and bodies, crushing baronies and kingdoms. Understanding the physiocratic principle that food was power, he did his best to close off every European grain port to English commerce. He did so by seizing towns along the Baltic, North Atlantic, and Mediterranean coasts and inventing nearly a dozen tributary republics to control them, with every republic sworn to block British trade. Britain responded to this "Continental System" with orders in council that blockaded every one of Napoleon's ports. No neutral state, according to the British orders in council, could use a port that blocked British commerce. This was warfare, in part, through bread: Britain couldn't buy grain in European ports, but France couldn't easily carry bread over water to feed armies. Bread brinksmanship of this kind would be repeated in World Wars I and II. By 1807, when it came to bread, the British and the French had checked each other. Britain could not buy flour abroad, and Napoleon's armies would have to lug their food overland along vast army corridors with tree-lined vistas that are still visible in Europe today.[38]

France's bloody expansion across Europe proved the long-term value of Catherine's physiocratic system a decade after her death. Only one place was exempt from the power of the two-empire standoff between Britain and France: the Black Sea. The Ottoman Empire had controlled its gates at Istanbul since 1453, and the Turks would never allow military ships to enter. As a result, as soon as the Russians built Odessa, no competing empire could block grain ships without facing the Ottomans first and the Russians second.

While France's physiocratic actions had helped contribute to a revolution, the governors Catherine had appointed before her death in 1796 turned her physiocratic utopia into a reality. All neutral powers, including Revolutionary France and monarchical Britain, could pass through the strait at Istanbul and freely buy grain in the safe zone of Odessa. Odessa had just a few houses in 1800, but after 1807 the city became the international market for European grain while Europe was at war. The paths had already been laid out centuries before by the *chumaki*. Hundreds of thousands of oxcarts would soon fill the black paths, all filled with grain, all destined for parts unknown, but mostly Europe. Grain-growing colonies quickly spread across the arid steppes, earning a fortune for Odessans and the Russian Empire. Greek shipowners in the Ottoman Empire had unique advantages in this trade, having ancient footholds in Istanbul and the Greek islands and on the Black Sea. Intensive grain growing crossed from the right bank of the Dnieper to the left, while Catherine's standing policy of free land to settlers attracted emigrant German farmers to establish colonies throughout the new territory.[39]

Before Odessa, the Russian Empire had expanded slowly and defensively, one line of forts at a time. After Odessa, Russia—just like the United States—possessed foreign exchange and could expand dramatically. Wheat exports allowed the Russian Empire to fund its foreign wars, and so it surged into Poland, across the Caspian Sea, and toward China. Nothing seemed capable of stopping the yeasty, kvassy expansion of the Russian Empire. In fact, the spread of a different invisible creature, an invisible water mold, would further entrench Odessa as Europe's city of wheat.

By the eighteenth century, the Russian Empire, modeled partly on the medieval Byzantine Empire, used new technologies, including national banking facilities, to repeatedly invade lands controlled by the Ottomans, then to colonize them, and finally to build up grain-producing colonies on the steppe. It reached again and again for the strait at Istanbul, though it never got there. The empire's wealth, crucially, would not be hoarded at the empire's center but would be most impressive at its edge. An analysis of taxable estates determined that by 1905, outside Moscow, most of Russia's wealth was concentrated on its western edge, in the grain corridor from the Baltic to the Black Sea, and on its southern edge along the Black Sea.[40] In this way South Russia (now Ukraine) resembled the North American colonies, whose wealth was also concentrated at its seaports. For North America this was true because Boston, Philadelphia, Baltimore, and Richmond made the nation's income provisioning the British Caribbean. Imperial planners in previous centuries would have regarded these two empires, with their wealth hanging out on their edges, as peculiarly vulnerable to attack.

With its grip on grain, tsarist Russia soon became the biggest land empire in the world. The United States, locked into cotton for its export crop after 1820, struggled to compete. After Napoleon's defeat, European empires bought cheap, steppe-grown Russian wheat. Landowners imposed "corn laws" in 1784 and 1815 to weaken the effects of cheap Russian grain on their domestic producers. Cheap food threatened landlords whose tenants grew grain, and cheap grain from abroad could lead to an outflow of an empire's silver and gold. But then a water mold arrived in Europe, and that little parasite changed everything.

Four

P. INFESTANS AND
THE BIRTH OF FREE TRADE
1845-1852

YERSINIA PESTIS HAD harried and redirected empires as it stretched across the trade corridors of Eurasia, devouring rats and people from within. In 1845 a different parasite, this one infesting food, created its own pathways, enabling it, unlike *Y. pestis*, to float easily over bastions, redoubts, and borders. While *Y. pestis* had forced empires to shrink, move to land corridors, or expand by imposing quarantine, this new parasite forced crabbed empires to join together or face famine and revolt. Because it grew inside and destroyed a subsistence crop—the potato—it helped to internationalize wheat. Wheat would travel farther, much farther, to counter this pestilence. In attempting to put down revolutions in the countryside, empires helped summon a new international *aristoi*. A new set of multilingual traders would roam the fringes of the Black, Aegean, Mediterranean, Atlantic, North, and Baltic Seas. Odessa stepped in to heal the wound this new parasite caused by pouring wheat through the strait of Istanbul. After 1845 this wheat would accumulate in what Parvus called consumption-accumulation cities, which mushroomed in size, accumulated capital, and produced a new kind of bank that would scour the world for places to invest. And once again, just as in the days of the ancient Athenian kingdoms, the world would fill up with oceans of grain.

But first we must understand how the potato became the European subsistence crop, however untrustworthy, that was paired with European grain. In roughly 7000 BC, South American hunter-gatherers began selecting and modifying nightshade plants for their fleshy roots. They created what we call the potato, though in the region that became the Inca Empire, hundreds of different varieties emerged, with dozens of different names. *Phytophthora infestans* coevolved as the potato's parasite, an invasive water mold that colonizes, reproduces inside, and then devours potatoes, their living host.[1] After Europeans encountered the Americas, they transplanted American potato tubers throughout western Europe, between roughly 1700 and 1840. The potato's dry and dormant transmission over the cold Atlantic appears to have temporarily rescued the plant from its well-evolved, invisible freeloader.

Though it took many decades for European growers to adjust to the food, the fleshy, bulbous, white potatoes soon became a crop for farmers, peasants, and their neighbors, most famously in Ireland but also throughout continental Europe. An underground crop that required work to bring up from the ground, potatoes were relatively safe from the depredations of a different kind of freeloader: imperial soldiers. Potatoes, unlike wheat, do not have a Persephone stage of dry safekeeping. Locking up a potato for long-range transmission to an imperial capital is difficult. Thus wheat-growing peasants began to grow potatoes for themselves and for those who lived near them. Because these vegetables traveled short distances on farmers' trucks, Americans have called them "truck crops." Within a few generations a social hierarchy emerged in Europe that resembled the Incan hierarchy. In the Inca Empire potatoes fed agricultural workers, while the dry, transportable starches—quinoa and other grains—were locked up and delivered to the elite.[2] In Europe, too, Irish, German, and Hungarian peasants planted and harvested transportable wheat for London, Hamburg, and Vienna while eating potatoes themselves.[3] Likewise, Polish and Ukrainian peasants ate potatoes and rye, while valuable wheat moved into Moscow and Saint Petersburg or along the Baltic Sea to northern Germany, Finland, and Sweden. Bulgarian and Romanian peasants ate potatoes, while wheat traveled to Istanbul to pay an imperial grain tax that had existed for time beyond reckoning.

Fortunately for *infestans*, but unfortunately for Europeans, most farmers cultivated the fat, white potato—the lumper—by replanting its tubers rather than planting its seeds. This made every lumper genetically the same. Between 1700 and 1845 a hundred million nearly identical potatoes had spread across the European, British, and Irish countryside, making a perfect monoculture for *infestans*'s rapid invasion of Europe. Then, in the late summer of 1845, a container of potatoes crossed from the Americas into Belgium on a fast-moving ship. The ship bore along with it a breeding pair of *infestans*.

As a water mold, *infestans* needs a continually moist climate, but it does not need to travel in the intestines of an animal host, as *Y. pestis* does. In fact, *infestans* can travel airborne over short distances. As a result, once it landed in Belgium in 1845, *infestans* needed neither oxen nor horsemen nor plague ships to find homes in millions of European potatoes. The warm, wet fall of 1845 allowed birds, insects, and the wind to bear *infestans* rapidly across European farms. It first appeared as brown marks on potato vines, evidence of its feeding colonies. The colonies then dropped from the leaf into moist earth and devoured the potatoes underground. Potatoes stored in moist conditions could become a breeding ground for billions of *infestans* once a few spores attached to a single potato in a storage pit or container. By mid-September 1845, *infestans*'s lightning spread along pathways of its own making caused what we call the Irish potato famine, which killed nearly a million people in Ireland alone.

Though Irish farmers felt it worst, the destruction of potatoes and the loss of life due to famine and related diseases extended all the way across Europe between 1845 and the early 1850s. Thus began the period in Europe called the "hungry forties." According to plant pathologist J. C. Zadoks, the *infestans* invasion of Europe led to "intestinal infections, dysentery, typhoid, typhus, and tuberculosis."[4] London newspapers reported that "insurrectionary movements" in Polish Galicia and Russian Poland had broken out while "bands of starving peasants" had crossed from the Polish provinces into Prussia.[5]

Infestans threatened to destabilize the British Empire first. Irish landlords continued to export grain and cattle to England, while their peasants—deprived of their main source of nutrients—starved. British prime minister Robert Peel might have directed shipments of grain to Ireland's peasants—who were, after all, British subjects—but that was expensive. Seeking a cheap food substitute, Peel chartered shipments of American maize from the United States. While Americans ate maize regularly, it was so unfamiliar as food in Ireland that the landless rural laborers in Ireland referred to it as "Peel's Brimstone," presumably because it would be fed to him in hell.[6] Maize did little to stop the famine, so in 1846 Peel appealed to Parliament. The only response to the growing humanitarian crisis in Ireland was to suspend and later repeal the English "corn laws," which taxed foreign wheat (called "corn" in England). Free trade would cheapen the price of foreign grain and make it easier for the Irish to buy their way out of starvation. Peel's call for free trade was decidedly defensive: "Let us effect reforms," he told the Parliament, "that we may escape revolutions."[7]

Conflict in Peel's cabinet meant that it took nearly six months for the partial repeal of the corn laws to take effect. His Conservative government's membership, mostly landlords, opposed allowing cheap Russian grain—available in Livorno and Marseilles since the days of Napoleon—to enter the English market in competition with their own. Even worse for the government, Peel's repeal of the corn laws had the perverse effect of sending grain *out* of Ireland because news of the potato blight had caused international wheat prices to rise in 1846. Irish landlords took advantage by sending boatloads of grain to those countries that would pay the most for it. Observers reported nine grain ships leaving Irish ports for every famine relief ship that arrived.[8] As economist Amartya Sen has demonstrated, freer markets can actually exacerbate famines in rural areas, particularly, as was the case in Ireland, where agricultural laborers are not entitled to a share of the crops they plant and harvest.[9]

But *infestans* changed more than prices and wages; it created its own pathways to potatoes that made feeding people impossible. The *chumaki*-like pathways of empire itself ensured that. In the case of Ireland, the British Empire's dry grain infrastructure was designed as a wheel. Grain was collected from the middle periphery and brought into urban areas, just as in every empire before it. This meant that rural areas lacked the credit instruments and the distribution networks of flour mills and bakeries that imperial cities had. Just as importantly, Irish laborers did not legally possess the land that produced the wheat they harvested; farmers owned or leased the tiny plots of boggy land where potatoes would grow. Reversing the flow of food in the British Empire proved nearly impossible.[10]

After Ireland, central and eastern Europe suffered the most from *infestans*'s invisible invasion, especially western Germany, Prussian-controlled Poland, the dominions controlled by Austria, and Polish lands controlled by Russia. Food shortages and riots surged across these regions after 1846, but even France saw food shortages and riots.[11] Though a decent grain harvest came in the fall of 1847, the so-called Revolutions of 1848 followed in the wake of the famines and food riots. European free trade liberals led these movements, in Germany and Poland, for example. In other countries, notably France, liberals allied with anti–free trade conservatives to put down these revolutions by force of arms: the

July Monarchy (1830–1848) became the Second Republic, shortly to be replaced by a new monarchy. When the Austrian Empire faced a revolt of Hungarians and Poles, the Russian tsar sent tens of thousands of soldiers across the Carpathian Mountains in 1849 to put a stop to it.[12]

Besides turning cavalry and cannon on civilians, European continental empires responded to the *infestans* infestation in the long term by lowering tariff barriers between the empires in a series of interlocking free trade treaties. Just as Peel noted, their incentive was more fear of disorder than dreams of economic growth.[13] Europe's interlocking treaties guaranteed that each initial signatory would benefit as a "most favored nation" for future trade agreements with other trading partners. In this way, an 1869 treaty with Austria-Hungary, rather than Britain's commitment to free trade, finally forced the island empire to suspend all taxes on wheat. Britain's path to free trade in grain would have been impossible without the spur of other European monarchs.[14]

Though *infestans* and Britain's slow response to it killed perhaps a million Irish people through starvation and its related illnesses, Britain's repeal of the wheat tax had a surprising and mostly unexpected long-term benefit at home: a surge of prosperity at the center of the British Empire rather than weakness or decay.[15] The British imperial core's continued safety from famine was the first sign. By 1847, British flour millers on the coast found they could cheaply buy their way out of any grain shortage.[16] In 1845, before *infestans* landed in Europe, just over one hundred sailing ships laden with Russian grain passed through the strait of Istanbul every spring bound for European cities. Most were Greek-owned vessels that traveled from Odessa to the Mediterranean ports of Genoa, Livorno, and Marseilles, where grain was dried and stored in coastal warehouses. Merchants there held it until bread prices grew high enough to export it over the tariff barriers to Britain, the Netherlands, or Belgium.[17]

Famine and revolution in the 1840s, though, burned new grain pathways from Russia into Europe. With *infestans* on the loose, bread increasingly replaced potatoes as poor peoples' food, most decidedly in European cities whose sizes had always been limited by the availability of food. By 1850, as many as four hundred ships per year carried grain directly from the Black Sea to European ports, providing food for Europe's urban workers.[18] This cheap Black Sea wheat altered the quality of bread that Europeans ate and, with it, Europeans' sense of divisions among social classes.

For centuries the color of the bread a family ate, as much as the clothing it wore, indicated its wealth and status. Before 1848 dark brown bread or porridge fed common laborers outside Britain's port cities. Only skilled workers, city merchants, and government employees could afford to cover their tables with lighter-brown loaves and rolls. And only aristocrats, lawyers, and the landed gentry could afford to have servants put white bread, cakes, and pastries on their plates, though few engaged in such luxuries daily.[19]

With the free trade in grain, white bread became workers' fast food from Liverpool to Hamburg to Naples and in cities on both sides of the Rhine and all around the Baltic and North Seas. The new fast bread of urban workers was a large, soft roll, called a "bap" in Ireland. Bakeries sprouted up between ports and mills, delivering breakfast breads at 8 a.m., hot loaf breads starting at 1 p.m., and hot tea cakes at 5 p.m. Bakeries became factories, with as many as four ovens operating continuously, with bakers working day and night in multiple shifts. Corner sellers added a strip of bacon, a dab of grease from beef and pork casks, and a sprinkle of sugar. "Half a bap with sugar on the tap" was a song that sellers cried out at dawn. It became the breakfast food of Belfast's mill workers, and the song became famous among the city's children.[20]

Cheap grain remade European food as well. In Hamburg rye did not disappear—a rye loaf was still half the price of white

bread—but fewer urban workers or clerks would touch it for breakfast anymore. White bread became the morning meal. Only supper became the refuge for rye bread, which was served with sour
cream or pickles.[21] According to a working-class London saying,
common workers throughout the country had by the 1850s lost
their teeth for brown bread. It was still sold, as every mill expelled
bran residues called biscuit, pollard, and bran, which bakers mixed
with flour to make brown bread. Doctors prescribed brown bread
for indigestion, while dentists suggested a dark loaf as a treatment
for bad gums and even as an alternative to brushing teeth. Because
a brown loaf lasted a little longer without drying out, draymen
carried it to feed their horses and themselves on long journeys.
But bran increasingly became food for cows, horses, and pigs, not
humans. Using the by-products as feed allowed more animals and
their meat to enter cities.[22]

Odessa's bounty allowed working families in the 1850s to buy
their bread white, which most people preferred, not recognizing
that the bran and endosperm in brown bread made it a health-
ier food because it supplied more protein and delivered indigest-
ible bits ("roughage") that scrubbed the sides of intestines. Urban,
working-class families got shorter over the mid-nineteenth century,
probably in part as a perverse side effect of the white bread upgrade
that the wheat fields around the Black Sea provided to working-
class diets.[23] While cheap bread may not have been healthy on
its own, its increasing affordability after 1850 allowed workers to
regularly buy additional foods for the first time. Fish sandwiches
emerged as a regular meal for workers in Britain around 1870 once
American grain arrived; a decade later this became fish and chips.
Cheap beef dried and canned in Hamburg could be made appetiz-
ing by adding a bap around it, producing the hamburger.[24]

Thus emerged what Parvus called the European consumption-
accumulation city. Labor and capital accumulated where food was
cheapest. Cheap food arriving by water meant that cities with the

deepest docks thrived. As emigrants and orphan children from nearby rural areas filled these dock cities, would-be manufacturers collected and deployed them. Reformers and capitalists huddled poor people fresh from the countryside into workhouses, where they assembled goods from foreign and domestic sources: matchsticks, pencils, hard candy, lead toys, wooden boxes, and combs, to name just a few. Near the docks, storage and further processing of food expanded. Far from the docks, inland processing of grain declined. Tens of thousands of inland wind- and watermills became historical relics within a generation. Dozens of inland towns competed for river, canal, and railroad access to these consumption-accumulation cities. The successful ones became cities by drawing cheap food from coastal ports and specializing in manufacturing. Capital increasingly accumulated at ports in the hands of middle- and upper-class families with too little land to spend it on.[25]

Between 1845 and 1860 the European consumption-accumulation cities of Paris, London, Liverpool, Antwerp, and Amsterdam more than doubled in size, their fastest rate of growth ever. European industrialization and urbanization had little in the way of European roots. It was fueled by foreign food. Before 1845 the industrial development of Europe had been taken out of workers' hides. Child labor, high rents in cities, and crowded conditions had lowered the average height of workers, increased infant mortality, and produced spectacular infirmities that had become characteristic of working-class life, including rickets, scurvy, cholera, tuberculosis, and typhoid fever. But as cheap grain began arriving from over the ocean, workers' average height rose, infant mortality declined, debilities decreased, and tea and sugar consumption increased, suggesting that cheap bread gave workers more disposable income to spend on more and better food.[26] Though foreign grain could feed a European city and help fill it with a million souls, citizens packed so closely together required apartment buildings, waterworks, subways, and sewers to accommodate them.

With cheap bread at hand, European empires determined to make further use of the Dutch financial revolution that had first helped Britain, then Russia and the United States. Empires would borrow to lay the foundations of truly metropolitan cities, latter-day models of the imperial cities of the ancient world. Louis Napoleon—Napoleon Bonaparte's nephew—had been elected France's president in 1848. He then took advantage of the revolutionary upheavals to seize power in a coup in 1851. With no monarch to precede him and none willing to come to the ceremony, he crowned himself Napoleon III, emperor of France. A self-proclaimed socialist in coattails, he baffled his numerous critics by appropriating, twisting, and occasionally granting a malformed version of their demands. After dissolving the National Assembly, he created an assembly of ministers that was, he told the press, politically diverse and therefore entirely above politics: "The Empress is a Legitimist; Morny is an Orleanist; Prince Napoleon is a Republican; I am a Socialist. Only Persigny is an imperialist—and he is mad."[27]

In the years when *Yersinia pestis* was spreading through Europe, the terms "socialist" and "imperialist" had different meanings than they would just a few decades later. Imperialists, before 1870, referred to those who supported a monarch's coup against a republic, not armed expansion across oceans. The opposite of an imperialist was a republican. In the 1840s a socialist supported socialized institutions but not necessarily equality or democracy. In the terminology of his day, then, Louis Napoleon could claim to be a socialist while his seizure of power was an imperialist act.[28] Becoming emperor allowed him to devote his days to retroactively legitimizing his coup. He started a four-volume history of Julius Caesar, a man who closely resembled himself. While few would think to update Julius Caesar's classic autobiography, Louis Napoleon's biography was so bad that he never finished the third and fourth volumes. This Napoleon then employed archaeologists and naval architects to excavate Roman ruins and build him replicas of a catapult and a war galley.[29]

Yet the vain and self-important emperor appreciated the socialist principle that banks could draw on the collective ownership of hundreds of small lenders. The socialized savings of many owners, gathered and invested, might provide the capital necessary to erect a Paris as grand as Rome. His ministers—Bonapartists all—were fascinated with efficiency and obsessed with engineers; like Napoleon III, they proclaimed themselves experts on everything. Imperial socialism relied on public advertisement, a fake-democratic appeal, and sales of bonds for public projects. Lots of bonds. Selling bonds to the public required democratic banks: Crédit Mobilier, Crédit Lyonnais, Crédit Foncier. In Germany they were called *Gründerbanken*, or founders' banks.[30]

Louis Napoleon's literary predecessors, the utopian socialists Charles Fourier and Henri de Saint-Simon, were an important influence in creating founders' banks in post-*infestans* Europe. Fourier argued, like economists before him, that bringing people and funds together into large groups increased productivity. To that end he proposed democratic banks that would organize people into cooperatives, which he called "phalanxes." Each phalanx would comprise just over sixteen hundred people, who would live in four-story apartment buildings, their numbers carefully organized around what he had calculated to be the 405 different temperaments of each sex. Every man and woman had work to do in this society. Cooking and child-rearing would be collective, and children would collect the garbage because they liked to get dirty. Poverty would thereby be eliminated. We take for granted huge apartment buildings, public parks, and cafeterias. In the 1850s few existed for a broad public outside the leather-bound folio volumes of utopian socialism.[31] They would be the lasting result of a Russian and then American bounty of cheap and abundant wheat.

Henri de Saint-Simon gave Fourier's plan a funding formula. Long-term futurist experts would draw the plans; visionary bankers would irrigate them using the capital of thousands of small investors. The crusty Bank of France, which provided only short-term lending, would be overshadowed by upstarts. New banks—Crédit Mobilier, Crédit Foncier, and Crédit Lyonnais—flourished under the sponsorship of the French crown. The entrepreneurial socialist bankers drew in customers with colorful advertisements plastered on subways and streetcars, city walls and taverns. Prominent manufacturers, engineers, and royal hangers-on endorsed these new institutions. Commercial investment banking had begun.[32]

And in a certain sense, it worked. For millennia, when farming families fed themselves, the clergy, and the local gentry, improved *land* was the most important investment for future generations, however entailed by the taxes of cities, counties, states, and empires. But after 1848, as free trade brought oceans of cheap grain from Russia, bread came cheaper and whiter in the cities, while agricultural land could easily fall in value. The families of the working class had no land and thus no easy place to store their wealth for their children and to provide for their retirement.

And so, a generation after Fourier, socialized savings converted France from a "country of smallholders" into a country of bondholders. This was particularly true in Paris. Over the following decades the storage of family assets in bank accounts, stocks, and bonds could and did lead to growing inequality. Yet French citizens' collective investments funded railways, subways, apartment buildings, theaters, and international exhibitions. These quasi-public institutions flourished, while French bankers watched the horizon for large industrial projects that would earn them more than 5 percent. While British investors tended to invest in their own empires, the French model of investing outside the empire was soon emulated in Germany (Darmstädter Bank) and Austria-Hungary (Austrian

State Railway Company and the copycat Credit-Anstalt). Still, no one invested more in foreign holdings than the French.[33]

Cheap bread drew workers into consumption-accumulation cities; urban dwellers accumulated capital and pushed their savings into banks, which furthered the boom in imperial centers. Public bond ownership allowed the city of Paris to demolish its medieval city walls and begin a massive reconstruction after 1860. Bankers in the Prussian and Austro-Hungarian empires followed suit, first with flotation banks (*Effektenbanken*) in the 1850s and then in 1870 with the founders' banks (*Gründerbanken*). Germans later called the period the *Gründerzeit*, or founders' period. The publicity, together with the spectacular construction, seemed to have the added effect of stabilizing and legitimizing the power of autocrats like Louis Napoleon and Prussian monarch Frederick William IV. Louis Napoleon, in speaking of his destiny as ruler of France, made a habit of noting how much capital had increased in the Crédit Lyonnais after his domestic or military victories.[34] A growing sense of nationalism surged in the wake of cheap grain, blossoming in consumption-accumulation cities and encouraging appeals to the public to apply their capital to the needs of the nation. This could be the nation-state's greatest strength and its greatest weakness.

Five

CAPITALISM AND SLAVERY
1853-1863

FROM THE 1700S until the 1860s, when Europeans thought about foreign wheat, whether from Russia or the Americas, they thought about serfdom and slavery. Indeed, much of the original justification for blocking cheap Russian wheat after Napoleon's defeat was that otherwise family farmers in Europe would have to compete with enslaved and enserfed agriculturalists. "In this vast area, which extends from the mouth of the Volga to the mouth of the Danube," thundered representative Adolph Thiers in the French Chamber of Deputies in 1851, "you can have a worker for ten or twelve cents a day." Lowering trade barriers in France meant inviting farmers to compete with serfs east of the Vistula River and slaves west of the Atlantic. "Everyone knows the condition of the Russian serf owners," he continued. "The serfs owe them four days of work a week and in exchange receive less food that is given to the blacks in our colonies." With free trade the Odessa serfs would "vomit destructive torrents of grain on the defenseless agriculture of England, France, and Belgium."[1] Then the newly liberal empires of Europe, which generations before had imposed slavery on the Americas, found themselves forced to open their markets because of a water mold. They found their dependence on the food produced by enslaved and enserfed people at the margins of their world to be abhorrent.

And then, almost simultaneously, forced labor ended in both Russia and the United States between 1860 and 1863. The two empires differed enormously of course. American grain farmers in the 1850s were often highly literate, had farms (or plantations) that yielded twelve bushels per acre, and produced more wheat while requiring fewer than half the seeds.[2] American yields rose in the 1850s in part due to the use of machinery that Russian farmers would not adopt for a generation.[3] Yet the serf regime in Russia and the slave regime in the United States were linked. Catherine the Great's reforms in 1785 drastically shrank the difference between Russian serfs and American slaves. American wheat growers, North and South, could not have expanded across the American plains without replanting seeds that came from wheat fields on the northern edge of the Black Sea. American farmers got better yields by importing Black Sea grain with unique properties like resistance to drought, cold, or fungus. These unique landraces of wheat allowed American enslavers to grow wheat in the Shenandoah Valley and the fields of Tennessee. The specialized grains that had evolved in arid farms on the Black Sea could suit the drier, colder climates of the upper Midwest. Without Red Queen and Turkey Red, wheat might never have arrived in Kansas or Nebraska.[4]

Like brothers from a different mother, both imperial Russia and the United States embraced family production of grain at nearly the same time. The free states of Illinois, Indiana, Wisconsin, and Ohio—each producing over ten million bushels of wheat a year—had surged past Virginia's production by 1860. Likewise the private estates in Ukraine, then called New Russia, produced most of Russia's exported wheat. The abolition of serfdom and slavery opened up new lands to farm families to grow wheat in Ukraine as well as Texas, West Virginia, and Missouri.[5]

Both the United States and the Russian Empire ended forced labor without full cooperation of the owners of human flesh. The two empires disowned manorial lords and enslavers in a cataclysmic end to slavery and serfdom with effects that reverberate to this day in Russia, Poland, Ukraine, and the American South. Historians have tended to laud imperial and nationalist heroes for the end of slavery and serfdom: Catherine the Great who professed to dislike the harsh punishment of serfs; "the liberator" Alexander II, who demanded that his Council of Ministers end bondage by shouting, "I desire, I demand, I command"; and Abraham Lincoln, who wrote in 1860 that he could compromise with slaveholders on other things but would "hold firm" against slavery's extension "as with a chain of steel." Certainly the language used to end slavery and serfdom dropped from their lips like sweet-smelling myrrh.[6]

As we shall see, the end of serfdom and slavery had little to do with the bold pronouncements of emperors and presidents, however. The shearing of bondage and wheat, of slavery and capitalism, was a complicated and bloody matter. It had much to do with how wheat grew, who harvested it, and how farmers expanded across the plains. The economics of railroad freight, the influence of foreign investors, and the impact of war contributed more to the rapid end of serfdom and slavery than liberal impulses and amber waves of grain.

IN THE MID-1850S a failed Russian campaign of southern expansion destabilized the seemingly invulnerable agricultural empire. The bountiful port of Odessa had made it possible for the Russian Empire to become provisioner and policeman of autocratic Europe. But then Russia overreached. The hard currency Tsar Nicholas I received for other people's grain only increased his hunger to seize productive lands around the Black Sea and its gateway on the banks of the Bosporus and Dardanelles. His hunger for new lands combined with arrogance. In 1833, after having defended the Ottomans against an invasion from Egypt, he was confident; in 1849, after helping put down the revolutions of 1848 in Europe, he was smug. Nicholas regarded the sultan as his vassal and the European empires as his luckless henchmen.

In early February 1853 he summoned the British ambassador in Saint Petersburg and announced that the time had come for him to carve up the Ottoman Empire, which he memorably called the "sick man of Europe." He offered Britain the crumbs in his plan for invasion. They could have Crete (then an Ottoman province) along with Egypt. "Speaking as a friend and a gentleman," he continued, "if England and myself can come to an understanding about this affair I care little what the others may think or do."[7]

In 1853, with an army of half a million serfs and a thousand cannon at its disposal, the Russian Empire began its ninth war against the Turks at the height of its powers. Betting everything on a rapid victory, Nicholas intentionally provoked Sultan Abdulmejid I. In the traditional story, Russian and Catholic priests had been squabbling over the keys to the church of the Holy Sepulcher in Jerusalem since 1846, leading the tsar to defend Orthodox honor in Ottoman territory. There was more to the story than a key, however. On the last day of February in 1853, Nicholas demanded that the Ottomans make him the protector of all Greek Orthodox Christians in Ottoman lands, an impossible demand that violated Ottoman sovereignty.[8] British spy and diplomat Laurence Oliphant called the war another in Russia's "succession of petty robberies, none of which has been of sufficient importance to rouse Europe to a sense of its insecurity."[9] But this petty robbery did rouse Europe. Russia's ninth invasion of Turkey ended rather differently than the previous eight. It started the first global war over bread since Napoleon, and its conclusion would, more than any other factor, contribute to the end of serfdom in Russia.

In the previous eight wars between Russia and Turkey, the British and French monarchies occasionally defended the Ottoman Empire against Russian and Austrian aggression, but Russian physiocratic expansion had mostly benefited those empires as it provided them with cheap grain. In part because France and Britain had fostered Ottoman independence movements in what became Greece and Egypt, they mostly they looked away as Russia and Austria alternated in carving off Ottoman-controlled regions along the Black Sea. But cheap bread, and Western European empires' dependence on it after 1845, kept the attention of Britain and France on the region. Both states worried about a Russian grain monopoly. European observers of grain exports argued that Russia had been intentionally disabling its competitors on the inland ocean. The most glaring example was that the Russians had been entrusted with ensuring that the Danube exited freely into the Black Sea, but for decades they had allowed it to silt up, weakening the export prospects for the independent states of Wallachia and Moldavia.[10]

For France and Britain, a Russian monopoly over Europe's breadbasket on the Black Sea was an existential problem, one that threatened both European power and European bread. After Nicholas's navy won a lopsided naval victory over the Ottomans at the Battle of Sinop in November 1853, informed statesmen worried that Russia's final assault on Istanbul might give Russia a monopoly on Black Sea grain and the most powerful port connecting Europe to Central Asia, Africa, and the Middle East. "Let Russia once become the mistress of the Dardanelles," warned Oliphant the diplomat, and her position "would insure to her the command of the Mediterranean, and invest her with supreme control of the destinies of Europe."[11] Perhaps just as importantly for Britain, a trade route to the East passed through the Bosporus Strait and over the Black Sea. English merchants who had been drawing riches from India for generations worried that Russia's seizure of the narrow passage between Europe and Asia might threaten Britain's power in the subcontinent. Contemporaries referred to European squabbles over pathways to Asia as "the Great Game."[12]

But chaos in Europe helped to force the hand of Britain and France. Russia made the hasty mistake of prohibiting grain exports on the day of its declaration of war against Turkey, probably to ensure the Russian army and navy could be cheaply fed. Within a week the price of wheat in the United Kingdom and much of western Europe soared from an average of just over fifty-three shillings per quarter to more than seventy-two shillings.[13] Bread riots followed in the southwest of England, the first such riots since the days of Napoleon. With grain still comprising half the daily diet of urban workers, a 35 percent increase in the price of bread raised the specter of the "hungry forties" all over again. The threat to Europe's food was not an invisible water mold but a tsar and an army of serfs with hands on the grain that fed Europe's workers. In March 1854, Britain and France joined the Ottomans to defeat the bellicose Russian tsar.[14] The British Admiralty planned to attack the naval headquarters at Sevastopol on the Crimean Peninsula, destroy the Russian fleet, and then begin a spring offensive on the Baltic. Nothing worked right at first.

Getting biscuits, crackers, and beef to soldiers on the Crimean Peninsula proved a nightmare. Both the French and British empires demonstrated their incompetence in supply. Steamships seldom arrived on time, and atrocious officering made matters worse. Trench warfare dragged the conflict on for months. Soldiers on both sides died by the thousands, often of dysentery and gangrene, both diseases well understood but poorly dealt with. British and French officers refused to make effective use of their Ottoman and Egyptian allies nearby, whom they regarded as cowardly. As a result an understaffed military campaign bottled up European troops in an eleven-month siege of Sevastopol.[15] Repeated failures and high costs forced both empires to inject subsidies into merchant shipyards: in France along the Seine, in Britain along the Thames and the Mersey. By the end of the conflict, both British and French steamship firms had, at considerable cost, introduced wide-bottomed, steam-powered ships that could quickly be fitted for supply, troop transport, or bombardment. They could maneuver in waters less than a foot deep. Perfecting the operation of these highly mobile steamships allowed provisioning of marine troops for long-distance invasions.

For Britain and France, the Crimean War acted as a testing ground for the new instruments that would prove vital for imperial expansion in the decades that followed. Crucially, the British navy demonstrated the ability of shipboard cannon on small, maneuverable, screw-powered steamships to get within range of field fortifications and then target even the thickest and best-defended walls. The British and French navies destroyed Russian forts in Odessa and elsewhere on the Black Sea as well as on the Gulf of Finland near Saint Petersburg. Only Sevastopol took time.[16]

The war against Russia improved the Atlantic empires' capacities and heightened their cupidity. The British navy and merchant marine used the same sorts of maneuverable steamships developed in Crimea along China's White River in the Second Opium War (1856–1860) as well as in support of British evacuation and invasion after the Indian Mutiny (1857–1859). In China, successful destruction of Chinese fortresses forced the emperor to allow the British Empire's opium into the interior. Steamships like these allowed the French to conquer Tunisia in 1881 and the British to occupy Egypt in 1882. British and French "explorers" used the same kind of armed steamboats to penetrate the Congo, Zambezi, Niger, and Orange Rivers in the so-called scramble for Africa in those same years. The British and French navies, ironically, remained obsessed with wooden frigates and ships of the line, most of which were finally scrapped by 1870. The European merchant marine, fed mostly by mail subsidies, made European imperialism possible even as European navies declined in relative importance until 1910. Then, in 1910, dreadnoughts finally absorbed the technological discoveries made after 1853 by Europe's subsidized merchant fleet.

If Russia's opponents took time to build up the mobile weaponry for foreign invasion, Russia's army of serfs was doomed to failure. In March 1855, shortly after the Russian army failed to capture the allied supply base at Eupatoria, Tsar Nicholas I died. Contemporaries suggested it was suicide; Russian historians have concluded it was simply heartbreak over his coming defeat. "I hoped to have left you a well-ordered Empire," he told his son on his deathbed, "but it has pleased God to order otherwise: I can only pray for you and for Russia."[17] Nicholas left his heir, Alexander II, with an empire on the brink of fiscal ruin and the ruble at risk of severe depreciation. The surrender in 1856 was a humiliating defeat for Russia. After three years of war, the state's budget deficit had increased nearly sixfold to 307 million rubles. The state had already resorted to doubling the money supply to 800 million rubles and then suspended gold payments, threatening Russia's import and export market. In a preliminary announcement before the Peace of Paris, Alexander II hinted that he would abolish serfdom to "let everyone . . . enjoy in peace the fruits of his honest labor," but he prepared no concrete plans for ending the institution. While the Crimean War may have saved the Ottoman Empire, it paid a terrible price for its victory against the Russians. To fight the war the sultan took out exorbitant loans from Britain and France. The loans would bankrupt the empire in two decades.[18]

Alexander, like nearly every tsar after Catherine, regretted serfdom, but the Russian failures in the Crimean War accelerated change. The empire's key financial advisor, Julius Hagemeister, faced three related problems that became intimately connected after Nicholas's abortive war for control of the Bosporus Strait. In the long term, according to Hagemeister, serfdom would always hold back full exploitation of the plains above the Black Sea. Having visited numerous farms and landed estates in that region in the 1830s, he felt that family ownership yielded more crops per acre and produced the cleanest, most sellable wheat. Serf estates, he had learned from grain traders, produced dirty wheat, filled with rocks and sand. As the wheat traveled inland, he continued, serfs had no desire to look after the grain and so often left it uncovered, causing it to spoil on its way to market and sell at a steep discount. In Russia, according to Hagemeister, wheat would always have a serfdom problem.[19]

Hagemeister's middle-term problem was that the largest land-owners had huge debts to the Russian Land Bank. The bank issued loans only to serf owners with large estates and only if they pledged the value of their human property. By 1860, 60 percent of these serfs had been collectively mortgaged for terms of twenty-eight to thirty-three years. Finally, the short-term problem for Hage-meister came with the cost of the Crimean War. The Russian Land Bank sought to take over Russia's costly short-term loans. To build up capital, it lowered fixed interest payments for deposi-tors. Thousands withdrew their savings, which then magnified the bank's problems. Foreclosure on the long-term loans to serf owners seemed imminent.[20]

Thus the empire's long-term problem was serfs, its middle-term problem was serfs, and its short-term problem was paying for its failed war against Turkey, France, and Britain—but also serfs. Hagemeister settled on an ingenious solution. The empire would end serfdom by turning some land over to serfs, who would pay the state bank on forty-nine-year mortgages. The bank would issue long-term bonds to serf owners in exchange for land they surren-dered to serfs. Crucially, the empire would *subtract* payments to any landowner who had outstanding loans. This was an instant foreclosure. Freed serfs by this scheme would pay off the loans the serf-owning nobility had taken out on them. Because of the way Hagemeister structured the payments, peasants paid more than the calculated value of the land. The empire's bank was the greatest beneficiary of the "liberation" of the serfs.[21]

This ingenious solution appeared to separate wheat from serf-dom while the Russian state paid nothing and gained the most.[22] The serfs would be free, but their land would be ransomed, and the need for rubles would send hundreds of thousands of former serfs across the steppe as harvest labor on other people's farms. Most of the world's grain, it appears, came not from small peasant holdings but from what American historians call "frontier estates" and what economist Nikolai Kondratieff called possessory (*vladel'cheskikh*) farms. In the United States these were farms of between five hundred and one thousand acres. In Russia most of them were similarly sized estates run by farmers, many of them former serfs, who used credit, hired labor, and machinery to clear millions of acres of grassland to produce grain for European cities.[23]

In 1861, shortly after Hagemeister completed this extraordinary plan for ending serfdom, Alexander II dismissed him from service. The reason, according to the tsar, was that he had spoken abroad about Russia's "imminent state bankruptcy."[24] In the end Alexander II's "liberation" of the serfs looked more like a shell game aimed at hiding the empire's debt to defend its credit. The redemption of the serfs funded the physiocratic strategy of having free serfs expel grain from the steppe lands above the Black Sea, though mostly as employees, not peasant farmers. Serfdom had already been severely weakened in the wheat-producing regions of Kiev, Volhynia, Podolia, and what is now Belarus. Grain and slavery would now be separated across all of Russia.[25]

The center of wheat production moved along black paths to suit the end of serfdom. Farmers increasingly planted wheat on the "left side" of the Dnieper River, north and east of Odessa. This expansion of settlement from west to east gave Odessa rival grain ports on the Black Sea, including Mykolaiv, Mariupol, and Rostov-on-Don.

Unlike in the United States, the formerly bound population of Russia actually received land, even if it took small farmers more than a generation to pay it off. No such redistribution took place in the American South after emancipation, a result that has hobbled the family fortunes of the formerly enslaved to this day. As in Russia, wheat production relocated when slavery ended in the United

States. After the American Civil War, grain came increasingly from the area around the Great Lakes rather than its former preserves in Virginia, Maryland, Missouri, and Kentucky.[26] The abandoned grain regions of the South would come to resemble Russia's former fiefdoms, with a decaying gentry class holding oversized plots of some of the most valuable land in the world.[27] While Russia's failure in the Crimean War provided an opportunity and a justification for ending its serfdom problem, the American South's continuing dependence on credit and its failure to redistribute estates would hinder the growth of southern food crops and lock the region even more firmly into the production of cotton.[28]

In Russia, new political structures grew up around grain as serfdom disappeared. To emancipate the countryside, the tsar created a new county-level structure informally called the *mir*. A *zemstvo*, a governing body composed of multiple *miri*, slowly and haltingly took on features of local government. Grain growing with family labor and through the *mir* gave peasant farmers a modicum of authority. Though tsarist rule remained in place, the *zemstvo* became a place for peasants to choose local leaders, air grievances, and demand relief. It helped forge a rural public sphere that existed in relatively few places in Europe. While the tsar considered giving serfs individual land ownership, the final draft of the plan dictated that the *mir* would collectively manage and occasionally reallocate the land over time.[29]

The peasant farms were not as successful at producing grain as the frontier estates. Over time, when the United States, India, Australia, and Canada entered the international market, those countries also did so with frontier estates: massive, privately owned farms, between five hundred and one thousand acres in size, that used a large labor force for the harvest. These were not the twenty-thousand-acre "bonanza" farms built and then quickly abandoned by railroads in the 1870s but large farms operated by wealthy families who settled, built fences, and hired migrant laborers. The frontier estates in what is now Ukraine relied heavily on the seasonal labor freed and forced into a cash economy by the redemption system.[30]

Nicholas's dream of capturing Istanbul with a serf army ended with a humbled, almost bankrupted empire in which his son, in a desperate attempt to stave off bankruptcy, abolished serfdom. The Peace of Paris in 1855 placed limits on Russia's expansive power. The treaty created an independent international body that took control of the Danube's grain route through the Black Sea. Within a few years, European powers would discover a way to blast out the Danube's exit and allow a new grain state, Romania, to emerge as Russia's miniature rival.[31] Finally the allies against Russia banned Russian warships from passing through the strait at Istanbul. With serfdom ending and Russian imperial expansion diminished, Britain and France felt they had tamed Russia.

RUSSIA'S IMPERIAL OVERREACH awoke a sleeping giant across the Atlantic, a collection of merchant princes who were also increasingly uncomfortable with bound labor. When the Crimean War nearly doubled grain prices in London and Liverpool, North American merchant princes like John Murray Forbes took notice. These aristocrats imagined the future of the steppe lands somewhat differently than the Russian tsar and his ministers did, but they too believed that slavery and grain export were incompatible, no matter how much flour Virginia exported in the 1850s. As Forbes and others saw it, the biggest threat to sending grain to Europe was not the sultan or the tsar but the growing political gulf between midwestern wheat farmers and southern cotton growers. Politically this was manifest in what they called the "slave power" in the South.[32]

They were right; there was a slave power in Congress. Through seniority, southern congressmen controlled most of the major committees of the House and Senate and thus the nation's purse strings. The merchant princes of New York and New England had little coherence before Europe's hungry forties, but by the 1850s they contributed strongly to the birth of the Republican Party, which would become the Western Hemisphere's standard bearer for physiocratic expansion along the model of Catherine the Great's utopian vision. The merchant princes increasingly demanded incentives that would put family laborers onto wheat farms on America's steppe lands. They helped craft a platform of free land in the West, federally subsidized interstate railways, a cabinet position devoted to agriculture, and land grant institutions of higher education that would promote progressive agriculture, thus increasing yields per acre. Their southern opponents had by 1854 determined that westward expansion was moving too quickly in the northern prairies and needed to be stifled.[33]

These railroad barons and grain traders would come to hold tremendous political power in the Republican Party. From California to Chicago, New York to Pennsylvania, many of the party's wealthiest supporters were not an industrial bourgeoisie but merchants and railway men interested in grain, as well as the lawyers who served them both.[34] The fundamental interest that tied them together was the grain pathways connecting East and West by canal and railroad.

Though called robber barons at the time, these people were more like what I would call boulevard barons. The medieval robber barons imposed tolls on grain passing near their fortresses. These boulevard barons sought to *decrease* the tollage, speeding and cheapening the delivery of western grain to European cities while charging fees for that rapid delivery. East-to-west traffic entailed providing western settlement with goods and credit; west-to-east trade required gathering grain for sale on national and international markets, as the region had once done in grain's heyday between 1700 and 1818. In the parlance of developmental economics, they wanted to promote the backward and forward linkages to midwestern grain. The Civil War, fought to prohibit slavery on a western railway corridor to California, became an opportunity to tune the state to the fundamental interests of boulevard barons devoted to lining and straightening grain pathways from the United States to European cities.[35]

DAVID DOWS, LIKE many other motive forces in the wartime Republican Party, started his career as a dry goods clerk in Albany, where he forwarded grain coming down the Erie Canal on its way to the Hudson River and New York City. At age nineteen he became a clerk for his older brother, a freight forwarder and commission merchant in Manhattan, and in that position David learned how to use credit. When his brother died in 1844, David Dows, then thirty, took his place. Using a network of correspondents along the Great Lakes, he prevailed during the downturn in the grain trade in 1846 and then again in 1857.[36]

Each bust and boom in the American grain trade to this point derived from volatile shifts in European demand for wheat combined with the problem of delayed information. News of the Irish famine in 1845 caused grain prices to shoot up for a year, but Robert Peel's partial repeal of the corn laws caused prices to drop again. The Crimean War, in closing European access to Russia's grain ports, saw a rapid rise in prices, which whetted the appetites of prominent Republican grain merchants. "Our Western Roads have been earning enormously," crowed John Murray Forbes in 1854 to his brother Paul, "& I think the richness of the Illinois soil & free import of grain into England will bring up all the *decent* Western Roads."[37] But the end of the war in March 1856 saw Liverpool grain prices tumble again that April, contributing to the American panic of 1857. Even still, the volume of trade was potentially enormous.

Dows, like the Forbes family, maintained family fortunes in the boom-and-bust cycle for American grain by diversifying from grain forwarding into all of grain's subsidiary industries, including railways, warehouses, ships on the Great Lakes, and marine insurance. While he improved delivery, he also taxed it. As early as the 1840s, Dows had identified railroad grain corridors as key to expansion. Railroads were intended not to replace canals and riverboats but to act as first-mile extensions to grain silos in territories, like Iowa, unreachable by ship.[38] In part by providing credit to farmers along the railroads spreading into the countryside, Dows had become by 1861 one of the most important grain traders in New York, a principal in the New York Produce Exchange, and one of the wealthiest men in the world.[39]

Through politics and trade, Dows was close to other merchant aristocrats in New York who became the boulevard barons who would cheapen travel across the plains. James A. Roosevelt of the Chemical Bank, for example, imported European plate glass but also provided credit to hardware vendors far in the American interior. He was an early investor in canals. William E. Dodge, another "merchant prince" of New York, was a hardware and import-export merchant as well as a fellow board member in Republican organizations like the Loyal Publication League. After the Civil War he too made his fortune in railroads. Jackson S. Schultz, one of the foremost exporters of leather, collected skins from stockyards far in the interior to be tanned in the "New York Swamp" on what is now the Manhattan side of the Brooklyn Bridge. Collecting, tanning, and exporting western skins became his source of wealth.[40]

John Murray Forbes had first made his fortune in the opium trade in China. But by the 1840s he was thoroughly involved in grain, having established control over the Michigan Central Railroad in the 1840s. By 1855 he was lending to, and then taking over, multiple railroads heading west from Chicago. When conflicts between free and slave-owning settlers in Kansas began in 1854, he was the principal funder of the New England Emigrant Aid Society, which sent well-armed New Englanders to Kansas to defeat proslavery southerners who sought to make Kansas a slave state.[41] By 1860 he was a member of the Secret Six that provided aid to John Brown in his attempt to foment a slave revolt in Virginia.

These Republican boulevard barons of New York and Boston shared numerous attitudes and interests: they resented banks for their outsized influence on credit, they had little interest in cotton—which they regarded as in the hands of banks—and they sought railway connections to western territories and towns where they could extend credit to local stores, collect grain and leather for urban centers, and expand their control over western railways that would provide a stable return. Railroads charged for freight, the back-and-forth trade with the backcountry. The freight paid off the loans required to build the roads. Bonds paid off with railway income provided a steady source of income, a rent on the transit of grain. By 1880, grain made up nearly three-fourths of all the goods sent east on trunk lines.[42]

The railroads existed as sovereign entities on narrow tracks, fifty yards across and hundreds of miles long. State and federal legislatures granted them eminent domain, which allowed them to seize land along the route that engineers deemed most energy efficient. Their sovereign powers would soon extend to having their own police.[43] They often needed lawyers like Edwin M. Stanton, Peter H. Watson, and a young Abraham Lincoln to recover debts, sue towns that sought to block their railway bridges, litigate land disputes with property owners, or unruffle the feathers of municipal leaders in towns bypassed when railways linked up just north or south of them.[44]

The privately owned railway was not just a technical marvel of the age but an ingenious legal device that could concentrate wealth. It held a monopoly on a low-friction corridor, though the black paths, as Indian roads and pathways, had long predated them.[45] The railway was built to collect a tax on distance, a seemingly intangible good.

Railways were peculiar in that they embodied the black paths, but the Indian traders, trappers, draymen, oxen, and horses that had previously carried goods over these paths were crowded out by a steam-powered monopoly: the railway engine and its cars. As historian Laurence Evans has suggested, the railway company, as both a road and the monopoly agent on that road, defied the logic of traditional economic models of supply and demand curves: "What is [the economist] to make of a good [like a railroad] that cannot be stored; that is dissipated forever if not used when it is available; that cannot be removed from the market except at substantial cost to the supplier; and that must be operated at less than maximal efficiency if it is to be of the greatest benefit to the market and the economy as a whole?" [46]

In many countries, the government response to the difficulties posed by this kind of monopoly pathway was to nationalize railway companies. As we shall see, a decade after the American Civil War brought cheap grain to Europe, Prussia and Russia assumed control of most railway companies, producing interesting, perverse incentives. Adjusting railway rates could sharpen or dull the effects of tariffs, encourage fiscal overreach, and make state capture by political elites more appealing.

Continued private ownership in the United States before the Civil War, however, produced a different set of incentives. Because of the intertwining of economic and political power, railroad trunk lines remained in the hands of the merchant princes, allowing them to multiply and diversify their assets. From the outset, these merchants' obsessive attention to the wants of the railroad's customers turned them into social engineers, for railroads could carefully calibrate the prices charged for every manner of good that passed back and forth. A minor change in railroad rates could promote or dampen incentives—crop by crop—for farmers, artisans, and manufacturers. For example, grain always traveled at the cheapest, fourth-class rate on a railroad through the midwestern plains, making grain growing an obvious first choice for farmers near its edge. Grain farmers thought twice about diversifying into crops that would be charged second- and first-class rates. Monopoly corridors, by favoring a single commodity with low shipping rates, helped strengthen monocultures: wheat in the Midwest and cotton in the South. Railway companies also operated coal and copper mines along their corridors and frequently charged higher rates to competing mines to strangle their earnings.[47] High rates for shipping manufactured goods to the West led rural people to manufacture their own substitutes, but by suddenly dropping the rate for imported goods, a railway company could destroy an inland manufacturer. American farmers on these monoculture railway lines did not despise capitalism; they despised the publicly favored, privately owned railway companies that—once built—charged rent on their every interaction with the outside world.[48]

Railroads, however, were phenomenally expensive—a risk for merchants who had plenty of other places to put their capital. Beginning in 1850, American railroad promoters had happened on an ingenious model of expansion that used the federal government to drastically cut back on the upfront capital required to build railways into the interior: the railroad land grant. Just like the bill of exchange and the assignat, the railroad land grant would transform the long-distance transit of grain. The property clause in the US Constitution had given Congress one of the biggest sources of capital in the world: all unregistered land in the West that was claimed from Native Americans in the interior. Under the first land grant act in 1850, Congress granted land to railroads in a checkerboard pattern along the route. Imagine a snake with a checkerboard for skin. Railroads kept the white blocks, and Congress got the black ones. Because being on a railroad approximately doubled the value of land, Congress lost nothing in giving away half this land.[49]

The ingenious part of the land grant railroad was how little upfront capital it required of railroad promoters. After just a few miles of building, the secretary of the interior would authorize federal land grants along the completed section. The railroad then sold these lands on four-year mortgages to emigrants from other states and especially from Europe. Railway land sellers blanketed the European countryside with flyers, newspaper advertisements, and pamphlets promising great wealth to settlers. The mortgages represented a future flow of payments. Once signed, these mortgages could be bundled together into railroad bonds that could also be sold in Europe. Put another way, mostly foreign lenders bought railway bonds that would be paid off by indebted farmers, many of them foreigners. This foreign capital allowed the Illinois Central to reach north from the southern tip of Illinois to the Great Lakes without incurring the high upfront costs of building a railway over plains of grass.[50] The plan worked brilliantly, contributing to a massive influx of European settlers into the state's wheat-growing prairie counties.

But in November 1852 slavery reared its head, and a group of southern congressmen known as the F Street Mess blocked all proposals for railroads into the western plains. These southern congressmen feared that the rapid expansion of emigrants into northern states would weaken the power of the slave states. In addition, one member of the Mess had personal and financial reasons for blocking western grants. In June 1852, Senator David Rice Atchison had sponsored a western land grant for a railroad corridor through the slave state of Missouri, the Hannibal and St. Joseph Railroad, but then, in October of that year, boulevard baron John Murray Forbes seized control of it.[51]

Slave owners' problem with railroads into the prairies was simultaneously economic and political. Land grant railroads like the Illinois Central attracted settlers and progressed rapidly; the same railroads in slave territory, like the Mobile and Ohio, did not. Albert Pike, a slaveholding lawyer in Arkansas, foresaw that railroad land grants would create "a cordon of free States carved in succession off from [free] territories, extending with a continuous and swarming population across the continent, giving such power to the Northern vote in Congress as has hitherto been only dreamed of, and securing to their road, the Nile of this new Egypt, aid from the National Treasury, and countenance and encouragement from the general government."[52] By November 1852 the F Street Mess, using their seniority in the House and Senate, placed a stranglehold on congressional bills for land grants into the plains, effectively blocking the boulevard barons, whom they labeled the "corruptionists."[53]

By January 1853, the F Street Mess would go even further, demanding that Nebraska, a free territory, be split into the Kansas and Nebraska territories, with Kansas opened up for settlement by slave owners. When Abelard Guthrie, representative of the antislavery Wyandotte Indians who owned land on the Kansas River, sought out federal sponsorship for Nebraska statehood, one of the F Street Mess told him frankly that "he would see the territory of Nebraska sunk into hell before he would vote for it as a freesoil territory."[54] Between 1854 and 1859, shooting conflicts in Kansas between slaveholders and nonslaveholders started the battles that led to the Civil War.[55]

The Republican merchant princes of New York, Boston, and Philadelphia understood intimately why a railroad through the slave state of Missouri would fail miserably. As we shall see, slavery helped produce a society with an insubstantial middle class of resellers and consumers of eastern goods. Impoverished enslaved people couldn't buy cloth, razors, plate glass, or hard candies. Without a sturdy middle class of consumers, no one would erect stores to sell eastern goods in interior regions. While it seems ironic that New York millionaires would resent slaveholders for their inordinate wealth, this was precisely the boulevard baron's problem with slavery. From the founding of the Free Soil Party and the Republican Party that followed, these important merchants hated slavery not on moral but on economic grounds, declaring that slavery degraded labor, slave and free, producing a society of extreme inequality.[56] Nonslaveholding communities had "populous, thriving villages and cities," according to Republican orator and Iowan James Grimes, but if southern congressmen forced slavery into productive territories like Nebraska, then the developmental possibilities of the West would be lost. "Shall unpaid, unwilling toil, inspired by no hope and impelled by no affection, drag its weary, indolent limbs over that State, hurrying the soil to barrenness and leaving the wilderness a wilderness still?"[57] Not if the Republicans could help it.

The Republicans viewed slavery in the same way that Julius Hagemeister did, as a barrier to the planting of wheat. As Republicans saw it, slavery had, by the middle of the nineteenth century, created a feudal oligarchy in the South that was just as problematic as that of the serf owners of Russia. Slaveholders limited economic opportunities for both white and black by stifling public schools, limiting free speech, and concentrating political power in slaveholding regions. Indeed, the three-fifths compromise, by counting three-fifths of the adult male slave population for representation's sake, strengthened the voting power of planters inside many southern states. Slave-owning counties had a large population of enslaved people and a tiny number of white voters with outsized representation.[58]

Republicans' economic case against inequality in the South was compelling.[59] Railroads established in slave states—whether under land grant or with state aid—struggled to make payments to their original incorporators. Charles F. M. Garnett, chief engineer of the Memphis and Charleston, remarked in 1851 that the number of passengers transported across Massachusetts in one year was more than five times the population of the region. "Why," he asked, "should not that which has taken place in Massachusetts happen here also?" After extolling a few Georgia towns that grew slightly with the arrival of railroads, he admitted that there "may be something in the institutions of the South less favorable to rapid growth of towns," though improvements might come "in kind, if not in degree."[60]

The tension between bondage and railroads, between slavery and capitalism, was more than just political. Most southern railroads faced a serious problem with backhaul: railway cars moved east with the slave-produced staples of cotton and tobacco, but the demand for hardware, dry goods, manufactures, and imports in slave states was minuscule. Railway cars returned from east to west mostly empty, effectively doubling the price of goods sent from west to east. As a result of what southern railroad directors called the backhaul problem, southern towns like Richmond, Charleston, and Savannah never built the substantial traffic that Boston, Albany, or New York City did.[61]

A survey of landholding based on the 1860 census suggests the enormity of the problem of inequality in the slaveholding South. The difference between mean and median landholdings among free households north and south is striking. For example, in Minnesota, the mean value of land was $871 in 1860. Thus, all the land owned in Minnesota, if divided equally by all the households, would give everyone an $871 homestead. The median landholding value was $500, suggesting that Minnesota had a middle band of households with landholdings close to the state's mean. There was a middle class. If we look at all the states that would remain in the Union in 1861, including states with hundreds of thousands of landless households like New Jersey and New York, we find the mean-to-median ratio of landholding to be 5.2:1. States in the upper Midwest were more equal and ranged from a high of 3.9:1 (Illinois) to a low of 1.7:1 (Minnesota). In the Confederate states, the ratio was an astonishing 10:1. In other words landholding in the Confederacy was so unequal that the middle band of white households had 10 percent of the mean value of land. In Louisiana the mean real estate value was an impressive $5,258; the median was zero.[62]

The grossly unequal landholding pattern among free white residents was well understood among Republicans in the 1850s, though slaveholding southerners in Congress challenged the numbers at the time. Historians have tended to diminish the Republican criticism of the southern economy as a fiction.[63] For the Republican merchant elite in New York, who followed land, transport, productivity, and railroad stock prices more closely than we can, the problem could be simply expressed. A scant ninety thousand slaveholders owned the vast majority of slaves in the South and most of its valuable land.[64] With this southern 1 percent holding so much wealth, there was no middle class of consumers outside New Orleans, Charleston, and Richmond. Southern defenders of slavery repeatedly pointed out that there were more landless people in the North than in the South. Of course, this logic works because after 1770 the South had a smaller population than the North. But the relative number of poor whites per acre in the southern versus the northern population was the crucial part of the problem merchants had with the South. Most white farmers were either landless or held so little land that they made poor consumers, and consumers were what the merchant kings wanted.

The Civil War, then, while a conflict fought over the issue of slavery, can also be understood as a war about capitalism and the menace of inequality. The South certainly had capital accumulation. But inequality in slaveholding regimes was so extreme that slavery's expansion into free territories posed an existential threat to profitable railroad settlement of the prairie lands of the Midwest.

The systematic use of canals and railroads in the upper Midwest had built colossal fortunes for these men, but the success of railroads depended on stable, balanced, back-and-forth trade that gave them access not only to raw materials but also to a large, stable class of consumers for the products they sold. Grain merchants, like David Dows, had found that stability in infrastructure investment could counterbalance the storms brought by up-and-down commodity prices. Put another way, the modern portfolio of a merchant capitalist required diversification from staple goods into provisioning, infrastructure, and insurance. In the 1850s and 1860s, the model that worked required free settlers who produced and consumed in greater quantities than the latifundial organization of the plantation South. For a brief period in the 1850s, the merchant princes found their interests allied with a household system of free labor. They wanted shoeless, hatless, middling farm families prepared to sell but also to buy.[65]

Why the difference in household income north and south? To some extent this reflected a difference in the staple regimes. Western canal and railway expansion in the North was built on planting grain and sending it to port cities in exchange for manufactured and imported goods. This made food cheaper in port cities, where flour mills and bakeries were located. Wheat germ, mixed with hay, could feed horses, pigs, and even cows, making meat cheaper.[66] Landless laborers who worked for their food might be more likely to settle in cities on the edge of food-transportation routes, particularly if rent was relatively low.[67] As a result, midwestern railroads tended to superheat city growth in the eastern port cities of New York, Philadelphia, and Boston.[68]

One could argue that western expansion based on household production of wheat, oats, and corn demanded a somewhat more equal society in western states, where grain was grown, while producing a somewhat more unequal society in eastern states, where grain was consumed.[69] New York and New Jersey had mean landholdings of just over $2,000, while the median landholding was zero. States dominated by ports had a proletarian majority drawn, in part, by the cheap food that would someday cross the Atlantic Ocean.

BY THE 1850S hungry European cities increasingly digested bread made of seeds harvested on the Russian steppe. Europe's port cities grew rapidly, becoming accumulation centers. Odessa was the primary port, the strait of Istanbul the potential pressure valve. Britain and France, understanding the threat of Russian monopoly on the wheat lands that surrounded the Black Sea, fought to block Russian control over the worldwide valve for the grain that would feed European cities. Inside the intestines of millions of European servants, soldiers, prostitutes, and silversmiths lay thousands of digested kernels of Russian wheat, wagoned into Odessa, shipped through the Bosporus, ground by the bagful in Europe's wind- and watermills, and soured and baked in a hundred thousand city ovens in two dozen of the largest cities in Europe. These grain-accumulation cities also became accumulators of capital, including the capital of smaller investors. The cities held more capital than could profitably be invested nearby, leading to the growth of international finance and investment in states that produced food. By the end of the 1850s, European banks in European cities were scouring the world for places to invest.

When the Russian tsar sought to control all the grain leaving the Black Sea, the British and French empires protested. Fearing monopoly, they came belatedly to protect the Ottoman Empire from the "ruffian burglar," Nicholas I.[70] As Russia suffered a protracted and humiliating defeat, the tsar's son, Alexander II, faced a fiscal crisis greater than any that had befallen Russia since the days of Peter the Great. The Council of Ministers ingeniously turned a doddering financial vehicle, the Russian Land Bank, into an agency for bailing out serf owners while parsimoniously doling out land to agricultural laborers. Using steamships and cannon, the combined forces of Britain and France had ended slavery in Russia, though quite unintentionally and almost absentmindedly, as they sought to prevent Russia from capturing Istanbul. This was no heroic capitalist effort to end an old form of bondage but rather an expensive, state-supported imperial struggle over black pathways to wheat that tempted a Russian Empire to exhaust itself in war, then break down bound labor in an audacious bid to rule another day.

The war between capitalism and slavery was somewhat more pointed in the United States, though no heroic capitalist class stood at the fore, destined to make its mark. Instead, a new rentier class of boulevard barons had found the slave labor aristocrats of the South to be a barrier to their plans to squeeze wealth out of a railway monopoly. They dreamed of a low-friction iron pathway connecting grain lands to the ocean and wheat to the world. Yet they were revolutionaries in their way. Their ideology of free labor directly pointed against slave owning and landed inequality in a way that horrified the unemployed aristocrats in the House of Lords, the Bonapartist charlatans in France, and the feckless Bourbon dynasty.

Russia's monopoly on life-giving grain was as dead as serfdom. A conflict over inequality and forced labor in the Western Hemisphere would alter the world's grain pathways. Once the South seceded and Confederate cotton was blockaded, the Union cabinet and Congress knew that it needed a new crop for foreign exchange in order to fight secession. And Americans in the War Department recognized that if the nation's roads could be refashioned to transport wheat more efficiently than the Ukrainian *chumaki*, they might turn Lake Michigan into another Black Sea and Chicago into another Odessa. The pathways of the world's grain might change again. In December 1863, Peter H. Watson and David Dows had created a new technology that would alter the flow of grain: a futures market that could bring oats and grain to soldiers stationed a thousand miles away. A new kvassy empire, built on the export of wheat, was in the making.

Six

"CERES AMERICANA"

1861–1865

I N 1863, PETER H. Watson's powerful, hefty frame and red, Amish beard made him an instantly recognizable figure in the War Department offices of Washington, DC. Before becoming assistant secretary of war, Watson had been a corporate lawyer who had briefly hired Abraham Lincoln for a patent dispute in 1855. Watson was known to be ruthless: he had artificially aged the wood on a manufactured reaper to make it appear that his client's design was older than it was. He was also arrogant, having allegedly dismissed the young Lincoln as a "railsplitter from the Wild West." Yet, when the Civil War began, he became wholly committed to destroying the Confederacy. Watson knew that the drafty offices of his newly expanded War Department were crowded with spies who worked for two kinds of people: Confederates and contractors. Both wanted to know the size, disposition, and direction of the Union's forces: the Confederates, to stop them; the contractors, to overcharge them when the army was in trouble. For reasons of security, then, Watson often worked out of a railway car that brought him from place to place along his and other firms' railroads. Most of his orders were communicated via telegram, which he had hand-delivered to his lieutenants or transmitted in code. Due to his fierce commitment to secrecy, the highest-ranking official to establish America's long-distance grain corridors to the world remains nearly unknown to historians.[1]

RAILROADS
1 New York Central
2 Erie
3 Pennsylvania
4 Baltimore & Ohio

Grant's "cracker line" connecting midwestern grain to Chattanooga, Sherman's March to the Sea, and the four trunk lines connecting midwestern grain to the Atlantic Coast, c. 1863

Kate Blackmer

At the end of 1863, Watson's most pressing problem was getting food to starving horses. The War Department owned more than two hundred thousand of them. They were scattered from Texas to New York to Florida, but most were quartered in Alexandria, Virginia, at the cavalry outpost in Gettysburg, Pennsylvania, and at the edge of the invading Union Army inside the besieged town of Chattanooga, Tennessee.[2] Long supply lines stretched from the main eastern depot in Alexandria and the main western depot in Jeffersonville, Indiana, through Confederate territory to hundreds of winter military encampments all over the country.

Union control of the natural fortress of Chattanooga, key to Union success in the war, appeared tenuous. The Union Army suffered defeat in September at Chickamauga, just south of the city, and was now recuperating at that strategic crossroads. Union general William Rosecrans, depressed, had been forced to surrender command to one of his corps commanders, George Thomas. Chattanooga's besieged Union forces had dwindled to a few officers. Confederates had cut off all supplies coming into the city, forcing those commanders to abandon dozens of horses and mules to die inside the city for lack of forage. One private described the city as nearly empty, nothing but "shoulder straps dashing around on hungry horses."[3] After the arrest of two corrupt officers in the US Army's Quartermaster Corps—Captains Colin Ferguson and William Stoddard—along with their coconspirators, Watson feared that he had too few supplies to relieve Chattanooga, that the Union would have to abandon it entirely, and that the war would be lost.[4]

Ferguson and Stoddard's crime was complicated and clever. As assistant quartermaster general of the army, Stoddard had devised a scam in which he received hay delivered by contract to the Alexandria depot and then condemned the load as unfit. His soldiers dumped the condemned hay at a nearby wharf until the draymen sent by the contractors had left. With Stoddard's approval, Ferguson then brought the shipment back in, ran it through a winnowing machine to clean it, rebaled it, and then accepted the lot, paying a local "contractor," Francis Rowland, who was actually his uncle, for the delivery. In other cases Ferguson adulterated the supplies that he or Stoddard later declared genuine. Because hay prices were low and oat prices were high, he'd purchase a tiny amount of oats, mixing them with large amounts of hay, then pay Rowland as if the mix were the nearly equal blend of hay and oats that the army required. Horses fed on mostly hay lacked energy and were likely to collapse if pushed.[5]

Tipped off to the fraud, on December 7 Watson had sent his newly created secret police force, called the National Detectives, to break into Ferguson and Stoddard's offices. There they found that each officer had hidden a secret safe containing signed contract forms, as well as currency and US bonds together totaling over $86,000.[6] Taking depositions and arresting those involved took over a week and recovered more than $175,000. But after the investigation was concluded, Watson's War Department had unfilled contracts for the 2.5 million bushels of oats required each month to feed the Union Army's horses.[7] Seeing the army's distress, contractors capable of delivering oats now demanded rates more than double those of the previous year. The acting commissary-general faced a crisis.

Watson's problem was as old as war: how to feed soldiers and animals deep in enemy territory. The long, brittle supply lines for horse fodder, food, and other supplies that his corrupt officers had co-opted had been designed to *reform* the existing contracting system. Before that, chaos had reigned. Between the outbreak of the rebellion in April 1861 and January 1862, under the *old* secretary of war, Simon Cameron, overlapping and competing state supply systems had allowed millions of dollars to pass through the hands of state governors and their friends and then to go missing.[8] Watson was in the midst of reforming the War Department, but a Republican Congress had already interfered, seeking to legislate its own solution. In June 1863, Congress had created a newly centralized, long-distance, national purchasing system. The Alexandria depot would serve the eastern armies; Louisville and neighboring Jeffersonville would serve the western troops. Sworn bids were required, with agreements signed in quintuplicate. Civilian contractors faced military court-martial if they failed to deliver. Watson used these 1863 laws to prosecute Ferguson, Stoddard, and their contractors, but the rigid, centralized system created by Congress ensured that relatively few bidders would be capable of delivery once the existing contractors were jailed.[9] Just like the sultan's army at Kagul in 1768, Union troops at the fortress of Chattanooga depended on long, uncertain supply lines with an enemy controlling the rivers and roads.

Whereas Catherine the Great had successfully issued assignats to pay for her war against the Ottoman Empire, Union-issued paper money had given Watson nothing but headaches. After February 1862, the War Office was paying for supplies with the US Treasury's legal tender notes—called greenbacks. Unlike dollars issued by prewar banks, these were not backed by gold or silver reserves. As a result they traded for as little as thirty-five cents to the gold dollar. Two prices were thus frequently quoted for commodities during the war: a low price for gold dollars and a higher one for greenbacks. The other problem for potential contractors was time: because the government paid its debts in greenbacks, signing a contract with the government could be risky if the value of the currency dropped by the time government auditors approved the purchase. Even worse, after mid-January 1863 the commissary-general's office had been paying contractors not with checks but with "certificates of indebtedness" that would be payable at a later, unspecified date.[10] Of course, if the Union won an important battle or two in the interim between billing and payment, the greenbacks would be worth more, sharply increasing the profits of a contractor.[11] This made the intelligence gleaned by spies in the War Department valuable. The rapid fluctuations in both the price of oats and the value of the notes paid for them made contracting with the government risky. The number of contractors willing to assume the risk shrank through 1863, and the prices of provisions rose.[12]

Watson knew that centralized distribution, the harsh requirements for contractors, and the ambiguity about payment would
continue to make conspiracies possible, even after the arrests of
Ferguson and Stoddard. Only about a dozen merchants in the
country could make a bid on ten thousand bushels of oats, the
standard size of a signed government contract.[13] "A large combination of men and money," as the assistant quartermaster general,
Captain Samuel L. Brown, put it, was "controlling the supply of
oats and corn then acceptable for supply of the Army." These dozen
merchants then "demanded increased (and constantly increasing)
prices for grain."[14] So in December 1863, when Ferguson, Stoddard, and their contractors were arrested and removed to Old Cap-
itol Prison, the ruling price for oats had more than tripled, from
under thirty cents to over a dollar per bushel, and the army's horses
still needed those 2.5 million bushels per month.[15]

Watson's long-distance supply lines for both horses and
soldiers—it was not just horses that needed to be fed—hampered
his army's effectiveness. Union rations were large and bulky, almost
double the rations of French soldiers. Confederates recognized the
Union's weakness in its supply lines. Mobile raiding parties under Confederate generals Earl Van Dorn, Nathan Bedford Forrest,
Joseph Wheeler, and John Hunt Morgan had routinely destroyed
Union stores, slowing Union forces in the first two years of the
war. Supply problems had delayed Union general U. S. Grant's
planned siege of Vicksburg for months. The same disruptions had
delayed Union general William Rosecrans's initial plan to capture Chattanooga. Western army troops had resorted more often
to "forage" by forcefully requisitioning needed supplies from the
local populace. But foraging obliged Union forces to remain in
the wealthier, productive parts of the South or near ports with
well-defended supply lines. A concerted movement through the
impoverished regions of East Tennessee and North Georgia required a stabler long-distance supply line for food.[16]

To break the power of the dozen merchants and to feed the army and its horses at a reasonable cost, Watson thus proposed a solution that would rewrite the history of the international grain trade. Whereas Catherine had used assignats and bills of exchange to enable long-distance supply and Nicholas I had issued more paper rubles, Watson would fracture bills of exchange into hundreds of tiny, enforceable contracts, each representing a thousand bushels.

On December 20, 1863, Watson ordered Captain Samuel L. Brown to an office building on 113 Broadway in New York City, a few blocks away from the New York Produce Exchange. Once Brown was ensconced at a telegraph station in New York, the grain trader David Dows assisted him in sending a series of coded telegrams to the Chicago Board of Trade.[17] Over a hundred contracts for oats acceptable to the US government were requested and agreed to, with a month of delivery fixed. A week later the War Department sent Brown a draft for $500,000 to make good on all these contracts. Dows then directed his agent in Chicago—probably Chicago merchant Nathaniel Fairbank—to pack the oats onto ships at the Chicago wharves for shipment across the Great Lakes, then by water all the way to the army's principal supply depot at Alexandria and to the forward depot at Fortress Monroe, Virginia. Other shipments made their way to Jeffersonville, Indiana, where the commissary-general there was authorized to write as many ad hoc contracts as he needed to feed the horses and mules in Chattanooga and in the entire western theater of the war.[18]

This solution fit within Congress's rules, if one interpreted them broadly. Congress had mandated detailed government contracts in 1862 but had authorized suspending the rules "when required by the public exigency" for an "open purchase or contract."[19] Both the assistant secretary of war and the acting commissary-general now certified the exigency as half-starved horses and the monopoly power of a dozen merchants. For Brown's part, he recognized the apparent sneakiness of his transaction. He declared in his report that Watson had ordered him to "forestall" the market for oats.[20] "Forestalling," a medieval term, means buying goods in order to re-sell them. A hundred years ago forestallers were placed in a pillory alongside cutpurses, forgers, and prostitutes.[21] But in forestalling for the army that day, Brown had entered into over a hundred of the world's first modern futures contracts. Neither Watson in his railway car near Washington, DC, nor Captain Brown at his tele-graph post in New York could have guessed that within decades slips of paper changing hands in Chicago would disrupt empires all over the world.

The futures contract was not entirely new. By the mid-nineteenth century, a forward contract for goods where parties agreed to fu-ture delivery, a fixed price, and a fixed quantity was well estab-lished and decades old. Parts of the process were centuries old. In 1859, a Baltimore commission merchant named Sackett with good references might enter into a contract with Mr. Tiller, a farm owner in Indiana, to take 253 bushels of his country wheat after harvest based on evidence of previous sales. Sackett would offer Tiller a cash advance for this business, which could be used to buy more land, pay for seed and provisions, or buy harvesting equip-ment. That contract might then be sold to a flour mill operator or a broker who collected such receipts or even sold to other brokers. A bank would certainly lend money to Sackett based on evidence of contracts in hand. Tiller and Sackett's contract might pass through four or five hands, and a speculator who knew of a coming wheat shortage might pay more for it. If prices were falling the specula-tor might sell it quickly to someone else. The final sale would take place months later in Baltimore, with Sackett taking a 5 percent commission. The final buyer would inspect either a sample or the whole package first with Sackett nearby. Mr. Tiller's name would be on the contract, Mr. Sackett's name would be on the sacks of grain, and the people who had held the contract would have en-dorsed its back on passing it on to a new buyer. After the final buyer accepted the grain in Baltimore, Sackett would send Tiller the amount paid for the contract minus the commission, cash advance, and shipping costs.

But the army's futures contract had new features: a fixed month of delivery; a fixed percentage paid by each party to guarantee the contract (the "margin"); a standardized *quality* based on third-party inspection; a standardized (and smaller) *quantity* (one hundred or one thousand bushels), which was called the "contract"; a third-party *arbiter* (the Chicago Board of Trade) that collected the margins; and the arbiter's *legal authority* to punish the buyer or seller for nondelivery. An Illinois state charter ensured the board's arbitration committee had authority over these contracts. The harshest sanction was expulsion from the Board of Trade.[22]

While Tiller and Sackett's forward contract had a few of these features, the entire package—which the Chicago Board of Trade first called "time contracts" in 1864—required new rule making between 1864 and 1865.[23] Immediately after the Civil War, merchants in Montreal, Liverpool, New York, and London took note of the Chicago futures contract as a distinct and puzzling entity, a bizarre and uniquely American form of banking that attracted capitalists to invest in long-distance food trading.[24] It took over a decade for merchants in those other cities to abandon the older "forward" contracts—where large shipments were bought and sold on the basis of a sample—and accept the virtues of Chicago's rigid method of futures contracts.[25] Eventually the New York Produce Exchange (1874) and the Liverpool Corn Exchange (1883) would adopt Chicago's rules for grain.[26] In 1884 the British Empire would design futures contracts for Bengal, Madras, and Bombay that were letterpress copies of the Chicago contract.[27]

For Watson, a key advantage of the futures market was that the buyer and seller could be anonymous. He relied on secrecy to hide the army's dire predicament. The Chicago Board took margins from buyer and seller and ensured the grade by its own standards.

In the Tiller-Sackett forward contract, by contrast, a buyer had to determine that Sackett was a legitimate dealer who represented a reliable farmer, and each had to enforce the contract.[28] A futures contract was "self-enforcing," making it unnecessary to judge the trustworthiness of individual trading partners. In the futures contract the only variables were date and price.

Economists have rightly pointed out that the futures market operates as a kind of bank for grain or any other commodity. For those involved in the grain trade, a futures contract provided a "convenience yield," comparable to a bank account balance, because unlike the Tiller-Sackett contract, this contract was instantly sellable in a liquid market. The futures market also provided protection for swings in commodity prices: Mr. Tiller could sell two or three one-hundred-bushel futures contracts to protect himself from price drops; flour millers could buy futures contracts to guard against price increases. Relatively small incremental "contracts" of one hundred bushels allowed speculators with fewer assets to bet on rises and falls based on their interpretation of all the news that might affect future prices. The increased numbers of buyers and sellers increased market liquidity, which, according to neoclassical economic theory, protected against wild swings in prices, improving everyone's life.[29]

Within a few years many more people would be buying grain this way, though the board's own history makes clear that in December 1863 only one entity was doing so: the US Army.[30] Eventually, what began as a series of ad hoc secret telegrams to suit a desperate Union Army operating thousand-mile supply lines became an opportunity to speculate on future supply and demand for grain. New trading methods emerged from the distinct features of the futures contract, including what is now called pillaring, strangling, and collaring.[31] These allowed multiplying the profit on a price rise, betting on volatility, or betting on a moderate rise while protecting against a drop.

The most radical feature of the futures market, signaled by its origin in telegraphic communication, is the way it squeezed the costs of delivery. Before the 1850s, information and goods traveled at roughly the same speed. With the development of telegraphs—like the one Brown used—prices between buyers and sellers could be negotiated before goods arrived. A time difference between negotiation and delivery hurt commission merchants, who often bought goods and held them in a warehouse for future sale, a process that entailed considerable costs that were passed along to the buyer. Just as importantly, the final price for any long-distance commodity like grain had always included sample inspection, warehouse rental, loading, unloading, shrinkage, insurance, and the merchant's own profit margin of 10 to 40 percent. But if price negotiation could precede delivery, the ship, or later the railroad car, could become the warehouse, allowing the prearranged buyer to take possession of the goods on the day of arrival.[32]

The dozen merchants who were driving up the price of oats for the army appeared to have been thwarted, but opportunities for market influence existed elsewhere on the grain pathways. Controlling a large warehouse of grain still mattered, of course. A sharp operator could sell more receipts than he had grain available in his warehouse when prices were high and quietly buy them back when prices dropped.[33] A "combination of men and money" had led Watson to persuade the Chicago Board to generate a bunch of identical, standardized contracts. Now any shopkeeper or small-time buyer with enough warehouse receipts had a silo in his pocket and might sell it when the price rose slightly. The dozen merchants' power over a market might be more easily broken, but a single large buyer or seller might be invisible to everyone else in the market.

This futures market, which would have a lasting impact on international trade, would not have worked without important changes in grain pathways brought by the war itself. The first vital change was the Confederacy's closing of the Mississippi River from 1861 to 1863, which drastically redirected American trading patterns. Confederate fortifications at New Orleans, Vicksburg, and Memphis cut the grain-producing states of Illinois, Indiana, and Ohio off from their southern markets, as well as from routes to international markets through New Orleans. The blockade initially forced most of the grain trade to the Great Lakes, so that between 1859 and 1862 the amount of grain received in Buffalo tripled.[34]

In the early days of the war, the beneficiary of the closing of the Mississippi was a monopoly, a single railroad bound to the War Department. Just before the war, Pennsylvania senator Simon Cameron had acquired the Northern Central Railroad connecting Maryland to Pennsylvania. When named secretary of war by President Lincoln, Cameron placed the Northern Central under the control of the Pennsylvania Railroad, which by then could reach from Washington all the way to Lake Michigan. Cameron chose as his first assistant secretary of war—Watson's predecessor—the company's vice president, Thomas A. Scott. As assistant secretary of war, Scott set rates for shuttling troops and supplies; as vice president of the Pennsylvania Railroad, he collected them. Under the newly reorganized Pennsylvania Railroad, a single railway trunk line soon stretched its tendrils from Alexandria to wheat fields in Ohio, Indiana, and Illinois.

More corruption followed. A congressional investigation reported numerous cases of outright fraud by Thomas Scott, including the disappearance of millions of dollars, and charges were brought in Congress and in the Pennsylvania legislature.[35] In the wake of the scandal, Lincoln's choice for a new secretary of war was Peter H. Watson. Watson, however, refused the low-paying government position, suggesting lawyer and politician Edwin M. Stanton, his right-hand man. Watson persuaded Stanton that becoming war secretary was his patriotic duty. A few months after Stanton took the job, he told Watson the same thing, demanding that Watson replace the corrupt Tom Scott as his assistant. Watson grudgingly accepted.[36]

Watson's first task was to break Tom Scott's monopoly on rail transportation to the seaboard.[37] Stanton persuaded Congress to give the president the power to seize railroads as needed for war purposes. In a meeting with competing railway executives in late February 1862, the war secretary laid out a plan to strengthen and consolidate competing railways between the Midwest and the East, with a discount for military transportation.

The president's wartime authority included both the carrot and the stick. Railways would be required to give the government a 50 percent discount on published rates or otherwise risk seizure by executive order. In return, they had the War Department's authority to consolidate management, regularize gauges, and share cars. System builders could ignore all the state and local laws that—for twenty-five years—had hindered interstate consolidation between the Midwest and the ocean. By 1863, four extended lines had expanded under consolidated management: the Erie, the Penn, the New York Central, and the Baltimore and Ohio (B&O). All soon connected the midwestern grain states to eastern ports, though until 1873 most traffic still came through lakes and canals to New York City.[38]

The New York Central's Cornelius Vanderbilt, the Pennsylvania Railroad's Edgar Thomson, and the B&O's John Garrett have been credited with building interstate railroads after the Civil War. But the moving force came during the war. It was actually Peter Watson, along with Stanton and Dows, who represented the business end of the boulevard barons who came to power on the election of Lincoln and the subsequent secession of the South. Watson was one part architect and one part revolutionary. In 1837, when still a boy, he had been involved with his father Leonard in the Upper Canada Rebellion against Tory loyalists allied with the Crown. Crown officials jailed and then threatened to hang his father. When Tories sent ruffians to raid the family homestead, neighbors helped young Peter escape undetected to upstate New York.

Educated in Washington, DC, as a patent attorney, in 1854 Watson became chief counsel for J. H. Manny, a company that made wheat-harvesting equipment. It soon faced a lawsuit from a competing firm with a patent. The following year Watson engaged both Edwin M. Stanton and Abraham Lincoln to support him in the costly patent case. By then in his late thirties, Watson was conceited to the point of boorishness and rebuffed Lincoln as soon as he met him. Only after working with Lincoln on the months-long case did Watson change his opinion and advise Stanton to keep the young Republican attorney on retainer. Partly through Watson's influence and patronage, Lincoln soon became a successful railroad lawyer. Peter Watson was Lincoln's unacknowledged route to the presidency.[39]

The intimate connections between railroad barons, grain dealers, and the ambitious lawyers who represented them coalesced in the Republican Party. Together their power was undeniable. From California to Chicago, New York to Pennsylvania, many of the party's wealthiest supporters were merchants, railway men, and their lawyers. It was Watson who helped use presidential authority to consolidate railroads across state borders and put Samuel L. Brown into the New York telegraph office that would rewrite the international history of commerce.

THE PORTABLE UNION ration did not arrive unbidden in military camps in 1863. The previous two years of the Civil War had seen considerable failures in the Union Army's capacity for movement. In the Peninsular Campaign, organized under George McClellan, over one hundred thousand soldiers arrived on the Virginia Peninsula in the largest amphibious landing American forces had ever made.[40] The army included a printing press for publishing orders, nearly fifteen thousand horses, and over twelve hundred wagons for carrying furniture, food, and equipment.[41] But the massive host moved so slowly that it took more than three months for its forces to move forty miles up the peninsula. As military historians have regularly rehearsed, McClellan's campaign failed in large part because of its ponderousness. The Confederate Army's ability to move more quickly and reconnoiter more rapidly repeatedly stymied the Union Army's attempt to lay siege to Richmond. One of the key problems was the Union's unwieldy supply trains.

By the middle of 1863, just as Watson's federally supported east-west railroad corridors began to emerge, the general headquarters of the army reorganized each squad of eight soldiers into a "flying column," based loosely on the French model. Equipped with lighter knapsacks instead of haversacks, soldiers were required to forgo either a blanket or an overcoat and to carry—alongside a rifle and sixty rounds of ammunition—eight days' worth of salted meat, crackers, rice, and water. Most carried cooking utensils.[42] With commodities like wheat and corn arriving in Louisville and Alexandria, in addition to packaged vegetables and meats, the Union commissary-general could assemble and pack these rations to permit eight days of travel away from supply lines.[43]

Both Jeffersonville-Louisville and Alexandria had another important advantage for expediting the delivery of rations. They relied on the cheap labor of free Black men. These cities had grown exponentially during the war as slaves freed themselves by crossing Union lines. At first in the western theater, under General U. S. Grant, the federal government seized abandoned lands and then leased them again to former slaves in an effort to pacify the area around these supply lines.[44] In addition, tens of thousands of former slaves were employed as teamsters, railway trackmen, and day laborers.[45] They built and rebuilt the fortified railway corridors that ran from Louisville south into the heart of Confederate territory.

With freedmen available as workers in massive numbers, Grant could—when he consolidated the western armies in Chattanooga in October 1863—focus on building what he called the "cracker line" to ensure that his soldiers and horses would never go hungry. In an effort that entailed fortifying and defending every mile of river and railroad track from the central depot outside Nashville to what would become the forward base at Chattanooga, Grant relied on the broad powers given to Lincoln to seize, modernize, and reorganize every southern railroad the Union Army crossed. To do so, the US Military Railroad impressed eight thousand freedmen in the middle of 1863 to tear up and rebuild track on the Louisville and Lexington Railroad,[46] allowing continuous supply from the depots in Alexandria and Louisville deep into the Confederacy.[47]

But this was just the beginning. By September 14, 1863, Daniel McCallum, a railroad manager and engineer who had been named the superintendent of Union railroads, was given control of all railways in the federal government's possession as well as all railway construction and reconstruction in the Confederacy.[48] By the beginning of 1864, a total of twelve thousand regular employees worked in the US Army's Transportation Department, overseeing maintenance and normal operations. Six thousand more worked in the Construction Department, charged with surveying, building, and rebuilding track destroyed by Confederate forces. These divisions relined all the southern railways with track at a standard gauge of four feet, eight and a quarter inches, as well as bridging all connections through towns where there had previously been breaks in transportation.[49] By war's end this totaled 2,105 miles of track.[50]

In October 1863, New York newspaperman L. A. Hendricks described the army's virtual annexation of the railway corridor as an "unwritten chapter" of the Civil War. "The railroad," he wrote, "is the bowels of the army; the railroad is the channel through which the army is fed, nourished and kept alive; by means of the railroad the army lives and moves, and has its being. Cut off the railroad and the army dies."[51] The Alexandria depot, Hendricks noted, occupied a two-hundred-acre expanse. The depots at Nashville and Jeffersonville were of comparable size. By 1863 the Nashville depot held five million rations and was delivering three hundred thousand rations a day to Union soldiers, refugees, and freed people who worked on its grounds and its corridors. Western commissary-general Henry Clay Symonds declared that, from Nashville, he was also "running a cracker bakery with 400 barrels of flour a day; a bread bakery with 150 barrels of flour a day; a soldier's rest, with from one to five thousand meals a day (on one occasion [it] furnished 15,000 meals); three pork houses, each packing about one thousand hogs a day; a pickle factory, putting up six thousand gallons of pickles a day, and was receiving about one thousand head of cattle a day," in addition to "provid[ing] for twenty-one hospitals, with 20,000 patients."[52]

By December 1863 Symonds had a secured and provisioned corridor that ran from the Louisville-Jeffersonville supply depot to a forward depot in Chattanooga and from there to Union troops in the western theater. A similar line ran from the supply depot in Alexandria to forward bureaus in northern Virginia. Only after these cracker lines were completed would General William Tecumseh Sherman's famous "March to the Sea" between November and December 1864 become possible.[53] While many military historians—and textbooks—give the impression that Sherman cut his soldiers off from their supply line, forcing them to live off the land, in fact his soldiers commanded double rations for the entire March to the Sea and the campaign through the Carolinas.[54]

Shown at the beginning of this chapter is the route from the primary depot at Jeffersonville-Louisville to Chattanooga. A rail route from Bridgeport to Chattanooga, cut by Confederate forces in mid-1863, was restored using steamboats and pontoon bridges in October of the same year. Grant referred to this short line as his "cracker line"; I use the term to refer to the entire Union supply route.

Feeding the half-starved horses of the Union Army required a significant confluence of circumstances: a plugged Mississippi, an organized group of boulevard barons, an enemy in the South's 1 percent, and a new model of military logistics. These factors together allowed Watson to deliver tons of oats to the horses and then an ocean of wheat to soldiers in Chattanooga. This, more than anything, made Union victory possible. A futures market with a centralized depot system had unified command in the Union's eastern and western theaters. It allowed Sherman in the west and Grant in the east to surround, cut off, and finally engulf the Confederate Army. A waterborne east-west route in the American North, a futures market for supply, and railroad corridors extending into the southern interior allowed the Union Army finally to feed its soldiers and horses both, drastically increasing the mobility of military units.

Once the war was over, building a civil logistics pathway to furnish goods to the world became a political priority for the merchants and railroad directors who stood to inherit the Union Army's infrastructure.[55] Portable nitroglycerin was already being tested in California and Virginia for blasting tunnels through mountains and extending railways toward deepwater ports. By then, Peter H. Watson had exchanged one railway car for another and become president of the Erie Railroad, which he had helped bring into being.

In an 1873 speech before the Montreal Board of Trade, New York senator Roscoe Conkling, after referring obliquely to Union success in the Civil War, highlighted the greatest future concern of the United States. As the brother of a New York dry goods merchant, he knew his statistics.

Between the water-sheds of our continent lies a granary which holds the food of the world. . . . We have a basin 2000 miles long, and 1400 miles wide, and the cereals that grow there, and the cattle which may graze there, added to those which British America can produce, are enough to feed all Christendom. . . . Now we doubtfully contest the wavering balance of trade with Russia in respect to her supply to Great Britain. Why? Because to bring a bushel of wheat from Chicago to the Atlantic coast costs us thirty cents. Russia can do it equally cheap, including the cost of production. How can you and how can we change all this? By finding a route by the St. Lawrence, or by any other channel by which you can reach the sea-board for fifteen cents a bushel. Do this and Russia can no longer hold dispute in the markets of the world. . . . A ruthless rebellion rolled upon us a great debt which burdens our people, though they steadily and bravely melt it away. Show us how to transport cheaply the growth of the West into the port of New York and our debt vanishes like the shadow of a passing hour. Cheap transit is, indeed, the great material question of the hour.[56]

In other words, America might now challenge Russia as the grain center of the world if only the cost of shipping grain dropped.

As Conkling spoke, he did not fully understand that his dream was already being realized. By 1873, a cheap route already existed to bring "the food of the world" by rail from the Midwest through New York into Europe's inland ports. In fact, America was absolutely challenging "the wavering balance of trade with Russia," and all hell was breaking loose.

Seven
BOOM
1866

A FEW EUROPEAN cities would soon begin to use explosives to turn themselves into grain gullets for swallowing and processing American wheat to feed Europe's workers. Beginning in 1866 a Prussian logistical pathway, a copy of the Union Army's transportation corridor, quickly and somewhat inadvertently hooked itself to a firehose of wheat in Antwerp. Four years later it would allow Prussia to defeat France and consolidate a German Empire by annexing Alsace-Lorraine. After 1866 four grain-trading firms would come to dominate the grain carried on the ten thousand sailing ships that plied the waters between the United States and Europe. Let us consider this transformation from the unlikely port of Panama, in Central America, where we can hear the first signs of the chaos that cheap food would bring.

At 7 a.m. on April 2, 1866, the SS *European* steamed south into the bustling wooden port town of Colón, New Granada, on the Isthmus of Panama. Bound from Hamburg and Liverpool, the steamer pulled up to a four-hundred-foot-long pier operated by the Panama Railway Company. As the day progressed, the local freight was removed first. On the following morning, clerks, stevedores, and railway workers awaited the train from the West Coast inside one of the most attractive buildings in town, the slate and stone shed of the Panama Railway Company. The inbound train, however, was delayed. Anticipating its arrival, stevedores had already begun unloading the international freight. They carried hundreds of wooden crates from the steamer into the shed. After the train arrived and was loaded, the cars would exit the shed to the south, cross the isthmus, and be unloaded at the Pacific wharf where steamers bound for San Francisco and other Pacific ports awaited their arrival. But on this day, nothing went according to plan.

At around 7 a.m. that morning, one of the boxes apparently fell. Seconds later, the clerks and port officials in the southern part of town startled at the sound of a colossal boom, then dodged flying bits of iron as the *European* exploded upward and outward. The metal braces of the ship shot out in four directions, putting a two-hundred-foot circular hole in and through the wharf and knocking out the pillars of the freight shed. Outside the immediate perimeter of the blast, shrapnel spread hundreds of feet farther in every direction. An instant later, the slate roof of the freight shed collapsed, crushing more than twenty workers. Two clerks survived by running quickly under a doorframe, which buckled but did not break. The force of the explosion was so violent that it shattered windows in a church nearly a mile away. One observer called it a "noise as terrific as the thunders of Sinai," a reference to the biblical story in which God commands Moses and the Israelites to receive the Ten Commandments.[1]

Minutes later, as the Royal Mail steamship *Tamar* tried to pull the smoking ruin of the *European* away from the shattered wharf, the broken hull exploded a second time, causing the *European*'s skeleton to sink into the Gulf of Limón down to its smokestack. One reporter lamented that there were "mangled and lacerated bodies, or pieces of bodies, to be met with in every direction for a great distance." Identifying casualties proved impossible because most of the bodies were thrown into the water, where they were quickly—in the words of one Liverpool reporter—"picked up by the sharks." As was the case in similar incidents that week in San Francisco and New York and on the tracks of the Central Pacific Railway, the mysterious explosions were so instantaneous and so forceful that bystanders hundreds of feet away were pierced by shards of the bones of those killed at the moment of impact.[2]

The source of these explosions was sealed boxes of nitroglycerin poured into zinc tubes, sealed with wax, packed in sawdust, and carefully stowed in wooden boxes. These boxes were bound for the Sierra Nevada mountains outside San Francisco, where the nitroglycerin tubes would be used in controlled explosions. One tube, when shaken with sufficient energy, could in a few microseconds expel nitrogen at a pressure of 275,000 atmospheres. The best gunpowder, by comparison, expanded one thousand times more slowly and with only one-fiftieth the force.[3] Yet in 1866 the science was still poorly understood. When the Russian-trained engineer Alfred Nobel and his assistants carefully placed seals on the crates outside Hamburg that March, they had failed to account for gradual leakage. Once a teaspoon full of loose nitroglycerin collected into a small pool, intense heat and a sudden shock could cause a small explosion. If this took place close enough to the boxes, the little blast could exert force enough to cause all the zinc tubes to explode at once.[4] In April 1866, nitroglycerin—if not quite stable—had arrived to remake the modern world. "Nobel . . . has shown us," declared one dynamiter, "how to chain and guide the wild forces that once seemed too strong to control."[5]

These wooden boxes of wrapped nitroglycerin were destined to radically change humans' relationship to the lithosphere, the outermost shell of our rocky planet. Nitroglycerine stabilized in mud, patented as dynamite in 1867, ushered in what chemist and historian Vaclav Smil has called an evolutionary saltation, a leap forward in humankind's relationship with the natural world. A convergence of human understanding of the biological, physical, and chemical world between 1867 and 1914 engendered what he has labeled the "Age of Synergy." It led to discoveries ranging from the understanding of plant respiration to the creation of the periodic table and gave rise to technologies that are, even in the twenty-first century, foundational aspects of modern life, from the mechanics of antiseptic medicine to the long-term storage of food and especially the production of synthetic fertilizer, which would allow mankind to extract more food from the biosphere. This new understanding would end the physical constraints that produced famine and in our own time usher in societies beset with the problem of obesity.[6] Few of these changes derived from the understanding of chemistry were as profound as the perfection of portable explosives, and none made a bigger boom.

Using the force of nearly 275,000 atmospheres in nitroglycerin, humans could shatter molecular bonds in shale, limestone, or slate, bonds produced by planetary and interplanetary forces measured in millions of pounds per square inch. Civil engineers thought of it more viscerally: this new explosive could rip holes in the world's mountains and blast passages in rock, allowing the construction of railway tunnels through mountains and turning inland river towns into ocean ports. Small cities like Antwerp, Rotterdam, and Amsterdam would become the planet's grand gateways. Contractors exploded thousands of containers of nitroglycerin underwater in the five years after the accident in Colón. They had a dramatic effect on international trade by deepening ports, shrinking the distance between them, and allowing a radical realignment of grain pathways.

THE WORLD'S GRAIN-IMPORTING cities quickly became receivers and assemblers of cheap American grain. Antwerp, just across the English Channel from London, had had its glory days centuries earlier. For much of the sixteenth century, the port city had been western Europe's center for trade. A meeting place for English woolens, Spanish American silver, Indian pepper, and Caribbean sugar, the wharves along the Scheldt River were a docking port and provisioning station for the galleons of Charles V's Spanish Empire. Antwerp, with over one hundred thousand residents, was one of the wealthiest places in Europe, sponsor of the art of Rubens and Brueghel.[7]

But wars of religion and imperial rivalries between the Spanish, French, and Dutch empires made poor Antwerp both prize and battlefield for three centuries thereafter. Sieges in the sixteenth and eighteenth centuries cut the population in half. The city foundered. During the Napoleonic Wars (1792–1815) Napoleon Bonaparte had used Antwerp to build a fleet aimed at smashing the British Empire. Because Antwerp was just across the channel from London, he called it "a pistol held at the head of England."[8] After Napoleon's defeat, the European allies at the Congress of Vienna decided that the pistol of Antwerp was too important to be held by any land-based empire. Antwerp and its immediate hinterland—its source of food and its destination for manufactured goods—would become the independent state of Belgium, pried from Holland. Holland then locked Antwerp's deepwater ports behind physical barriers and high tariffs to prevent entry by any more armadas, whether Spanish, French, or German. But as *Phytophthora infestans* brought down tariff barriers after 1846, Antwerp planned to rebuild again for the third time. In the 1860s it would become ground zero for America's cheap grain invasion.[9]

The merchants of Antwerp understood better than most how cheap grain could reshape Europe. After the American Civil War, the Antwerp Chamber of Commerce used Nobel's new explosives to widen and canalize the Scheldt River, then tore down the historic city walls to erect a continuous wharf space nearly three miles long. Antwerp became an ocean port large enough to service deep-draft ocean vessels from anywhere in the world. "The big city," to quote Parvus, "discards national egg shells and becomes the hub of the world market."[10] Antwerp became a consumption-accumulation city. For centuries agricultural goods from its hinterland, like flour, milk, eggs, and cheese, had arrived in the city to be traded for tropical commodities from the Americas. Before

P. infestans, however, food prices in Antwerp were still higher than in the countryside. The high cost of tollage, or "teaming work," as Rhode Island legislators called it, ensured that a farmer with horses and a wagon had to deliver food over difficult roads, increasing the price of grain every mile away from the cities. The high price of food had provided a natural limit to city growth, counterbalancing the opportunities offered by city work and discouraging potential migrants.

But by the 1860s, as both slavery and serfdom ended and the United States cranked up to expel the cheapest commodity grain in the world, the balance shifted. To accommodate the flood of cheap wheat, Antwerp's merchants began chartering small, broad-bottomed ships called lighters to hold excess grain that could not be milled. These lighters remained moored in the Scheldt for months or years at a time, to the irritation of many traditional grain merchants. Cheaper than warehouses, the lighters of Antwerp allowed large steam or sailing ships to quickly offload hundreds of tons of wheat and flour and then instantly find new cargo before setting out again. The lighters drastically shortened turnaround time, making Antwerp the preferred destination for a ship filled with grain, especially when prices were low. Rivers and snaking canals gave Antwerp water access into the heart of both France and Germany.[11]

The new competition from Antwerp prompted the Dutch government to hatch its own Antwerp. It spent over three million Dutch guilders to blast through the "Hook of Holland," to turn the inland town of Rotterdam into a seaport city for steamships. Once the route opened to steamship travel in 1871, Rotterdam—with easy access to hungry German cities along the Rhine—vied with Antwerp for the status of biggest grain port in continental Europe.[12]

It is difficult to overestimate nitroglycerin's effect in refashioning cities into grain devourers. Because ocean delivery was at least thirty times cheaper than land delivery with horses, a deepwater port allowed an inland city like Antwerp to expand its hinterland far past its own borders in Europe. The thirtyfold increase in the size of a hinterland made port building irresistible to city boards of trade. With a deepwater port, a city's artisans, wholesalers, and factories could assemble commodities and reach a drastically larger market. They could undercut the prices demanded by smaller cities and smaller firms. Cheap food fueled industrialization in tiny Belgium and put Dutch merchants closer to the center of the Atlantic market.[13] In European cities grain prices would drop about 40 percent between 1870 and 1900, the greatest long-term drop in the price of food in recorded history.[14]

For ports accepting grain, the relative cheapness of the so-called last mile further multiplied this cheap-food benefit. During the Middle Ages, the term "last mile" referred to the end of a journey or to death. Beginning in the 1970s, military suppliers and Bell Laboratories engineers redefined it. In their quest to minimize delivery costs, they identified the last mile as the longest and most expensive part of any delivery. Whether one delivers electricity, water, or bread, the last mile will consume up to 80 percent of the total cost of getting the product to the consumer. It includes things like storefront rent, hand delivery, physical connection, and billing to a house, all of which are distinct and particular. They require people, negotiation, and settlement of bills. Last-mile costs are the reason rural areas in the United States were the last to receive telephones in the nineteenth century, electricity in the twentieth century, and broadband internet in the twenty-first century.[15]

If we include grinding and baking in the last mile of grain's delivery, a loaf of bread in your hand costs over one hundred times the price of the grain that goes into it. Yet, because the last mile was such a large part of the price, cheapening the long, narrow end of the supply chain had a profound effect: cheap grain made cheaper bread, especially in deepwater ports. A four-pound loaf of bread in the city of London cost an average of 8.5 pence in the 1850s but just over 5 pence by 1905.[16] For new consumption-accumulation cities like London, Liverpool, Antwerp, and Rotterdam, consumers inside the last mile got the lowest prices. For wage workers, who for centuries paid half their wages just for food, cheap food in port cities became irresistible magnets after 1868. Irish and Scottish families moved to Liverpool and London; Antwerp drew dockworkers from rural Belgium, the Netherlands, France, and Germany. Just as American railroads from the 1830s to the 1850s allowed a surge in the size of the American port cities of New York, Philadelphia, and Baltimore compared to midsize American cities, so these European ports—favored by free trade and built by controlled explosions—began to grow more dramatically than other European cities. Antwerp's population was just over 88,000 in 1846; by 1900 it was 273,000.[17] American grain ships gave Antwerp international reach.

These new cities digested grain as the so-called forward linkages of grain exploded. Flour mills erected in Leuven, near the wharves of Antwerp, could churn out flour cheaper than that produced by wind- and watermills along the Rhine.[18] European cities quickly adopted innovations to cope with the flow of cheap grain, in part because bakers could not keep up. In 1873, to cope with the slowness of this last mile of bread delivery, an engineer in Stuttgart, one of Antwerp's tributaries on the Rhine, patented the "kneading machine." This improved the most laborious process in bread making: the diffusion of yeast cultures through moistened flour to allow yeast to digest it. This allowed a city baker and his apprentices to produce more bread in a day.[19]

Another last-mile cost was the oven. Mass baking of bread came next. A mechanical oven with steam pipes, a narrow heating element, and a movable plate—called a traveling plate—allowed a small group of workers to evenly bake roughly one hundred loaves in just over an hour. This so-called Borbeck oven, first purchased in 1883 by the Socialist Party of Belgium, served as the central device for a consumer cooperative—called the *Vooruit* (forward). It too cheapened the labor-distance from commodity to dining table: the cooperative could provide cheap food to workers, feed workers on strike, and even use the surplus to fund socialist newspapers. Recognizing the power of breaking bread together, the Belgian cooperative bread movement helped fuse together craft unions that had previously been suspicious of one another.[20]

Between 1864 and 1884, connected to the firehose of cheap American wheat, Antwerp's trade increased sixfold.[21] For arrivals by sea, the city went from insignificance in 1860 to the busiest port in continental Europe by 1880.[22]

International grain made Antwerp a gullet, a city that could digest and reexport cereals for much of Europe. Antwerp millers built flour mills near ports to buy cheap foreign wheat in the grain. All the leftover products from milling grain into white flour, called bran and middlings, could feed pigs and cows. Agriculturalists in Antwerp and along the Rhine and its tributaries traded their plows for pigpens, fields for pastures, and plants for animals, becoming porci- and boviculturalists. Belgian pigs and cows acted as mobile reprocessors of cheap American fodder. Within a decade Belgium became famous in Europe for producing cheap, shelf-stable commodities whose partial American origins were obscured inside the flesh of Belgian herbivores. European workers began to consume foods only the wealthy had eaten before, including butter, bacon, cheese, and chocolate. Rural dwellers in the suburbs of London, Liverpool, Rotterdam, and Hamburg did the same. Quite unknowingly, millions of European workers absorbed animal flesh composed of biologically reassembled American grain.

These gullet cities, according to Parvus, reorganized classes in Europe. A substantial trading and service class grew up in a grain port city; outside the city a grain-eating working class expanded in neighboring factory towns along the Rhine. Economists call this industrialization, as if factories somehow produced themselves, but those in the grain trade understood mechanization as the result of a burst of cheap calories circulating through corridors, pathways that brought cheap food to Antwerp's ocean port. Canals and railways brought grain and animal products to densely populated regions like Alsace-Lorraine, Westphalia, and the Rhineland. Industries emerged in the places where raw materials were abundant, food was cheap, and manufactured commodities could flow backward in the railway cars and ships that brought in food. Most disturbing to German and French landlords was that cheap American grain threatened to drive down rural rent in the European countryside. The explosion in 1866 was an accident, but the long-term effects of nitroglycerin on the black paths connecting growers and eaters of grain would, in just a few years, bring agrarian crisis to Europe.[23]

INFESTANS AND THEN dynamite brought food sources closer to population centers in Europe. Often rapid technological change—like the arrival of cheap transport and cheap food—can bring plenty, but for the many grain merchants of Europe, the rules changed too rapidly. For centuries merchants stored grain in port cities, banking it for a future rise in price. Others, who owned sailing ships and had connections in Odessa, could buy grain confident that it would earn roughly 20 percent over the purchase price. Private capitalists and commercial banks allowed buyers to issue six-month bills of exchange to pay for grain in Odessa, with final payment settled when the grain arrived.[24] The private bill of exchange had been, since the late Middle Ages, the foundation of capitalist trading networks in the Western world. The six-month bill of exchange, however, was on the chopping block, just as nitroglycerin was widening ports around the world.

Two things together killed the six-month bill of exchange, which had backed ocean voyages since the days of the Genoese. One was the underwater telegraph and the other was the Suez Canal. The long-term financing of delivery of staples like coffee, cotton, and sugar had for two centuries relied on a club of well-known traders who chartered ships or portions of ships, men who could buy and sell ten thousand pounds of sugar over a handshake. They did so in private mercantile exchanges like London's Baltic Exchange. These men knew each other intimately. Members had ships at sea in every ocean in the world, knew each other's specialties in commodities or ships, and could rely on the exchange itself to winnow out confidence men. Entrance into the Baltic Exchange, for example, could cost £10,000 or more. Similar exchanges sat in what were generally called bourses on the European continent in Marseille, Amsterdam, Hamburg, and Odessa. After the handshake, a trader who was buying would send out a runner to a nearby bank to borrow £10,000 or more on a bill of exchange, payable in whatever city the selling merchant required. It was understood that the bill of exchange relied on the trader's standing with his bank, but also that the bill represented coffee or sugar or wheat moving from one port to another. In case a trader defaulted, the underlying commodity was the security; the goods would belong to the last person who brought the bill of exchange to his bank. The last holder lost something in a default but not everything. These six- and nine-month bills of exchange had consumed most of London's circulating capital since before 1600, perhaps even centuries before that.[25]

During the American Civil War, the credit available in the London money market had doubled, partly because textile manufacturers in Lancashire now sat on what traders called a "plethora of unemployed capital" once Confederate cotton was blockaded. London banks, as a result, voted in the Bank of England to lower the standard interest rate. High interest rates in bad times like these, bankers understood, discouraged borrowers and forced gold into banks, where it earned nothing. But then, to take advantage of low interest rates in the money market, the London bank Overend, Gurney & Company hatched a scheme to use that market in a "sinister" way, according to traders, in what were called "pig-upon-bacon bills."

A pig-upon-bacon bill was a fake bill of exchange often used to make a dubious investment. Overend, Gurney & Co. issued six-month bills of exchange to other branches of its own firm and then sold these bills at a slight discount to other banks. The bills, which looked just like regular bills of exchange, did not represent any goods on the move. The bank was borrowing from itself—pig traded for bacon—with no goods en route. When the old bills came due, the firm traded them for new ones. The process resembled running up a debt on a low-interest credit card and then transferring the balance to a new card every few months. Overend, Gurney relied on the clubbish trust in the long-distance trade market that had sustained commodity traders for several centuries. Borrowing millions of pounds using cheap, short-term credit, Overend, Gurney bought shares in what were essentially front companies that never operated: the Metropolitan Railway and the Atlantic Royal Mail Packet Company were two examples. Actual railways and packet companies, which often held monopolies over particular trade corridors, feared firms like these, however suspect their founding documents seemed, and would buy them out to prevent their ever operating. The front company's stock prices would go from a penny to a pound in the days before the stocks were bought and canceled. Overend, Gurney made huge profits by selling their stock, then sought out new opportunities to create fake companies. A year after the American Civil War ended, the transatlantic telegraph was completed. Traders shortened their accounts, the old bills became increasingly unnecessary, and interest rates briefly rose. Overend, Gurney & Co., which had millions in merchant bills circulating, could not cover its massive debt. The firm failed.[26]

For ten weeks afterward, interest rates on bills of exchange more than doubled from 4 to 10 percent. This brought down at least six other major banks, many of which had been engaging in the same operation. In 1866 the failure of Overend, Gurney & Co. brought down twenty-two multinational banks that had been discounting bills of exchange for international trade. Economist Chenzi Xu estimates that the Overend, Gurney & Co. crash represented a loss of about 12 percent of British mercantile credit abroad, hindering numerous import-export relationships for decades.[27]

Nitroglycerin helped speed the decline of the six-month bills that had once kept commodities afloat all over the world. The most memorable change wrought by nitroglycerin was the creation of the Suez Canal, which opened a route between the Indian Ocean and the Mediterranean that bypassed the Cape of Good Hope on the southern tip of Africa.[28] After its completion in 1869, ship travel times from London to Calcutta dropped from six months to less than thirty days.[29] A continuous journey could also supplant both the overland Silk Roads and the two-part passenger journey that required changing ships in Egypt.

In these ways the Suez Canal broke traditional merchant pathways apart, radically altering international routes and time distances. In 1869, when the canal officially opened for business, the Horn of Africa replaced South Africa as the ocean corridor for world trade between Europe and Asia. Ottoman control of the Black Sea's eastern ports shrank in significance, while the Ottoman-controlled Horn of Africa suddenly mattered a great deal to traders between Europe and Asia. European powers had less desire to strengthen the Ottomans against Russian expansion and more desire to weaken their monopoly over the vital Red Sea pathway.

The Suez Canal had a surprising effect on the American grain trade. Most importantly, sailing ships could not use wind to travel through the narrow strait of Suez. The largest sailing ships—East Indiamen, Blackwall frigates, and windjammers—had been the core vessels for the tea and spice trade. According to British merchant Charles Magniac, the creation of the Suez Canal "virtually destroyed" them and their £2 million of carrying capacity.[30]

Magniac spoke too hastily. The Suez Canal did not destroy four- and five-masted sailing ships. In 1869 the tea and spice trade shifted to steamers that could pass through the canal, but steamships could not dominate the Atlantic trade. For long distances, sailing ships were more efficient until almost the end of the century. A coal-powered steamship in the 1860s consumed at least one hundred tons of coal a day at $15 a ton. The coal on a steamship counted for roughly half the weight capacity of any ship fitted for the Atlantic trade; the engine occupied half the ship's total volume.[31] As coal disappeared into the boiler, steamships had to take on water just to "stay in trim" to maintain speed and stability. A sailing ship, by comparison, had a smaller cost and a much longer reach. Until the 1920s sailing ships were still used to bring coal to island coaling stations.

Grain suited an Atlantic sailing ship because grain's high density stabilized the journey across the deep ocean. While the Suez extinguished the need for millions of pounds of carrying capacity between Europe and Asia, the same sailing ships moved into Atlantic and Pacific grain trading, where speed was less important. While grain *could* travel by steam, attempts by American railroads to establish steamer lines failed again and again because of steamers' poor efficiency over long distances and the low-cost competition of underemployed sailing ships. Between 1850 and 1874, British steamship tonnage increased tenfold from 190,000 to 2 million tons, but the tonnage under sail still rose from 4 million to nearly 5.5 million tons in the same period.[32]

Why did speed not matter to grain ships? The underwater telegraph, once completed and running reliably in 1866, perfectly complemented grain delivery by sail; combined with the futures contract, it simply changed the way that goods were ordered and paid for. As Walter Bagehot pointed out, "The telegraph enables dealers and consumers to regulate to a nicety the quantities of commodities to the varying demand." A grain dealer could order grain in New York and either sell it before it arrived or have the skipper wait until the ship docked at the Isle of Man to determine if it would go to Hull, Liverpool, London, Antwerp, or Rotterdam.

More disturbingly for London merchants, however, once grain was afloat, granaries became unnecessary in expensive cities of demand. If grain prices shrank, grain could wait in cities of supply like Chicago, Minneapolis, and Milwaukee. Thousands more bushels "on the float" at sea heading toward Europe could be ordered in transit. Just as wartime Cincinnati grain and oat dealers could be outfoxed by the Union Army's use of futures markets and telegraphed orders, so English dealers were bypassed by a large-scale grain trader who could use the telegraph to order a hundred thousand bushels on the Chicago Exchange and—on the same day—sell it for future delivery in London or Liverpool. Buying and selling on the same day effectively eliminated the risk of a change in prices. Between 1866 and 1873, the "margin"—the difference between the buying and selling prices—for grain traders shrank from 20 percent to 1 or 2 percent for vastly larger quantities of grain. For a trader this meant that a loan for a six- or nine-month journey was unnecessary. Established grain traders who had already sold what grain they bought had less need to borrow.[33]

SO MUCH GRAIN on the float not only turned cities into grain pumps but altered the rules of warfare. Young and ambitious military officers in Prussia understood wheat too and hoped that railways might allow armies to move more rapidly. They were deeply impressed by how American railroads and steamships during the Civil War could deliver carloads of grain and oats to warehouses near an army's front. The Union had planted inland depots on river ports like Jeffersonville, Indiana, to feed rapid, land-based campaigns like William Tecumseh Sherman's "March to the Sea." Prussian military experts sent officers to America to collect information. When General Daniel McCallum released his final report on the lessons the Union Army had learned about using railroads in the American South, the Prussian army instantly translated it. Scores of Prussian technical papers—many of them top secret—followed McCallum's report. The Prussian military created a Field Railway Section in 1866 to mimic the Union Army's Military Railroad Construction Corps. While the American version had been staffed with mostly African American pioneers carrying axes, the Prussian section would employ German youths with rifles. In the brief war with Austria in 1866, these pioneers quickly arrived in Austria, seized its railway stations, and captured all the engines and cars they could find, crippling Austria's ability to respond to German invasion.

While the Prussians succeeded in their brief war with Austria, the army could not actually deploy the Austrian trains they had seized to deliver food to troops, in part because they could not operate the engines.[34] They revisited the American plans. On August 10, 1869, a Prussian royal decree created separate corps of railway troops: the *Eisenbahntruppen*. These troops would even more closely resemble the Union Army's Railroad Construction Corps: they included construction engineers, pioneers, railway men, and auxiliary helpers who would both build and destroy tracks, then operate captured trains to bring forward troops and supplies.[35] Railroads would allow the empire to march with seven-league boots. Prussian officers created what they called the Etappen System, borrowing from the French word for "steps." Coordinated Etappen "lines" had "stations" staged 80 to 120 miles apart, reaching from the seat of war back to the *Kommandanturen*, the command headquarters at mile marker zero in Berlin. Each Etappen station had commissioned officers, a depot with warehouses, traffic coordinators, and telegraph stations.[36]

The opportunity to test Prussia's upgrade of the Union's transport system came with Prussia's famous war against France, the Franco-Prussian War of 1870 to 1871. Germany's imperial chancellor, Otto von Bismarck, began the conflict by goading the French emperor to declare war. Prussia's army, using the Etappen System, mobilized more rapidly and moved more quickly. French armies deployed a mostly state-controlled railway system to assemble troops, but provisioning proved a nightmare. Terrible traffic snarls emerged in France as soldiers traveled long distances to their units only to discover that uniforms, weapons, and food had not arrived. When the two armies met near the border, an armed and fully provisioned German force faced less than a quarter of the French army. Quickly outmaneuvered, the largest portion of the French army retreated to the ancient fortified castle of Sedan.[37]

But as Prussia's commandant had famously said, no plan survives first contact with the enemy. The transport world had fully changed by 1866, and internal supply lines did not always work. By the time Prussian troops moved into France in 1870, the Prussian army had to revise its Etappen System. Though Prussia had food in the east, an army's food requirements outweighed its need for all other materials by a ratio of nearly 100:1. Because grain and troops moved in the same direction, food and fodder got delayed on their way to the Etappen stations. Meat and flour rotted at train stations all along the pathway into France. Germany's invasion of France threatened to be a replay of the British and French supply problems in the Crimean War.

But after 1866 the ocean looked different. Within weeks, quick-thinking German generals disobeyed their orders. Rather than waiting for German grain to come east along the Etappen route, they ordered hundreds of thousands of tons of American grain to come west from neutral Antwerp. Antwerp grain imports nearly doubled in 1870, then nearly tripled again in 1871.[38] Imported grain went from Antwerp by canal up the Rhine to the Etappen stations closest to France, where it was baked and then transported down the Prussian army's railway supply corridors to troops.[39] One source of the Prussian army's food supply was the same as for Sherman's army: Illinois. Given the thirtyfold advantage of seaborne delivery, sending Illinois grain to German soldiers outside Paris may have cost only slightly more than sending it to Union soldiers inside Chattanooga.

In short, the Prussian army had become dependent on international grain pathways to win its war, a situation the Prussians abhorred, for it made grain traders vital to their success. "The purveyors of the several divisions of an army sent out their agents," recalled Baron von Goltz. "They flocked together in great numbers at the same place. . . . The state thus created for itself the most dangerous competition . . . and so the most fashionable hotels in the large towns were filled with persons who would be otherwise unknown there. . . . What impediments stood in the way of making contracts and of controlling their due execution need not be dwelt on."[40]

Prussia's need for foreign grain to fight a war was visible to everyone, and that stung. Men without titles, otherwise unknown because they lacked a "von" in their name, knew the dispensation of Germany's forces. No German officer could order these footloose grain traders in fashionable hotels to work any more quickly. With thousands of ships at sea carrying grain, war had changed. Supply lines often became external to empires, internal lines were no longer always the most efficient way to feed an army, and news of an army's victory or loss determined the price it paid for its food. Grain at sea made it increasingly possible for French, British, Italian, German, and Belgian armies to invade other places without worrying overmuch about finding local supplies or using costly, fuel-inefficient battleships to supply food. European imperialism after 1866, thanks in part to American grain, became easier for European empires to imagine.

If foreign grain helped make a saltwater invasion easier, it also made that invasion everyone's business. "Newsrooms" in the spacious trading halls of grain-receiving ports—London's Baltic Exchange, Liverpool's Corn Exchange, the bourses in Le Havre and Marseilles—kept abreast of every army at war, becoming the information gatherers of Europe. Traders received telegrams with the freshest news, well before it reached newspapers or general staffs. The grain exchanges accumulated stories of storms, revolutions, delayed soldiers, failed campaigns, droughts, and the high prices that resulted from these events.

These traders, while unknown to von Goltz, knew everything. They traded on armies' successes or failures, buying and selling boatloads of grain before it arrived in port. Warfare summoned pulses of grain, and the lack of grain could halt it. European cities competed with armies on the same exchange. Cities relied on fresh news and international markets to ensure their food supply, empires and soldiers be damned. This was the world that grain traders knew and the Prussian army despised. The London Baltic Exchange, the Berlin Bourse, and the *burzha* in Odessa received many of the same newspapers and magazines. These had been the multilingual centers of the world's news for centuries, the true centers of power, the nerves of the world. Within a few years the Prussians would desperately need men in the grain trade, though this irked military officers to their core.

While Prussian military companies relied on the international grain exchanges to feed themselves, hardened food corridors became one of their greatest advantages. Few locations mattered more than these new external supply lines, in this case from Antwerp to the front. In northern France in 1870, just like East Tennessee in 1863, the army stationed military companies on every mile of track and placed prominent local citizens on supply trains to discourage guerilla attacks.[41] The secured cereal corridor from the docks at Antwerp allowed Prussia to quickly cut off the eastern edge of the French Empire in Alsace-Lorraine. When Louis Napoleon surrendered, Bismarck demanded France surrender the French portion of the new Etappen corridor that extended from his newly created German Empire. Alsace-Lorraine, fed from

Antwerp, would become one of the German Empire's most important industrial hubs. Access to grain had helped to make the newly created German Empire a great industrial power at France's expense, provided it could feed the hungry industrial workers who lived along the Rhine.

THE TRANSATLANTIC TELEGRAPH, combined with the American futures market, lowered the need for port warehouses in Liverpool, London, Antwerp, and Amsterdam, and while it limited the gap between American and European prices, it did not entirely eliminate risk. Indeed, it contributed to the concentration of the grain trade in the hands of a few grain traders. Firms with offices in most of the major receiving ports could—using code—coordinate purchases based on future prices on multiple markets. Numerous snags could trap the unwary. Liverpool and Antwerp buyers, for example, accepted the grading standards of American shippers, but the London market required that a sample be submitted to an independent board. The risk of a drop in the grade required specialized insurance. Antwerp contracts differed slightly from London contracts, which differed considerably from Amsterdam contracts. Contracts might involve multiple languages and multiple international tribunals for adjudicating disputes. Thus, while margins shrank and volumes grew, relatively few firms had the detailed knowledge of multiple markets to succeed with smaller margins. Out of this breaking up of old markets and refusing of new ones, a few firms prevailed.[42]

A new group of international grain traders—known today as the ABCD grain traders—made use of this difference in trading norms across the Atlantic to gain a measure of control over the longest, largest, and most profitable shipments of the long-distance grain trade. They used the American futures market for purchases but then sold by sample in London or Amsterdam. These became the most important grain-trading families in the world: André in Lausanne, Bunge in Antwerp, Continental in New York City, Cargill in Minneapolis, and Dreyfus in Paris.[43] With one exception, these are still among the most prosperous (mostly private) firms in the world. They are operated by some of the wealthiest families on the planet.

The ABCD grain traders soon had their fingers on the pulse of the world's trade. Bunge, Continental, and Dreyfus got their start on the Rhine near the grain funnel at Antwerp but also had warehouses in Odessa that provided credit for grain from the Russian steppe.[44] Given problems of peasant illiteracy and the paucity of railroads, two or more intermediaries often stood between farmer and warehouse. These intermediaries were mostly Jews who—with Alexander II's peasant reform of 1860—had been driven out of the market for postal delivery and the operation of postal houses. Not being nobility, these local traders had little access to banks but relied on credit from the warehouses of Bunge and Dreyfus, credit that allowed them to advance money for grain in interior farms. According to Jewish lawyer and editorialist Ilya Orshanksy, the "haughty, puffy, but otherwise lazy and incompetent landowner despised Jewish traders to the depths of his soul but could not make a step in his economic affairs without them." The mostly Jewish inland grain traders resembled the line companies, though without a futures market, they had no way to cope with a drastic fall in price. If they advanced too much money and prices fell, they might have to extend the loan to the landowner or try to use the courts for bankruptcy proceedings. Greek merchants, who had previously made their fortunes between 1791 and 1861 controlling the grain supply chain from Odessa to Livorno to Liverpool, found themselves outmaneuvered by the warehouse shippers, who outspent them, and the Jewish traders, who had better contacts with farms in the interior.[45]

In this way, terraforming with nitroglycerin, dramatic technical changes in communication, the sudden appearance of thousands of underused sailing ships, and opportunities to profit from small differences in price helped bring a new *aristoi* to the fore. Between the 1870s and the 1970s, the ABCD grain traders dominated but never controlled the grain trade on the Atlantic Ocean. To operate effectively, according to journalist Dan Morgan, they ran "intelligence services all over the planet—private news agencies that never print a word."[46] They invested in what developmental economists call the backward and forward linkages of grain: elevators, refineries, and processing plants. With everything to lose and much to win with the slightest changes in grain prices, they invested millions in collecting information. European imperial leaders, by comparison, struggled to keep up and often overreacted to the little information they possessed. Because armies would increasingly depend on floating food to fight wars, news arrived faster in the grain-trading newsrooms of Liverpool, Antwerp, New York, and Odessa than it did in the imperial capitals at Whitehall, Saint Petersburg, Berlin, Vienna, and Paris. This made empires paranoid and inclined to see conspiracies everywhere.

Eight

WHAT IS TO BE DONE?
1866–1871

I N THE ANCIENT world the high cost of grain could encourage apocalyptic thinking. Even as grain became more abundant after the 1850s, both radicals and reactionaries on both sides of an Atlantic Ocean filled with grain could not avoid rehearsing, revising, and rethinking apocalypse. When would the black horse—famine and high prices—bring the pale horse, death? After 1866 new apocalyptic political movements, some quite small, began to use pistols and then nitroglycerin to try to break up empires. The threat of these "terrorist" movements led imperial leaders to invest in secret agencies to ferret out these small, conspiratorial organizations. At around the same time, new economic theories, including revisions to Marxist theory, flowed from attempts to mathematically calculate the causes and limits of the agricultural plenty that came to Europe after 1846. In 1871, a revolution in Paris would split communists from other social democrats and encourage secret agencies to devote time and energy to eliminating these radical groups too, searching for the threat that would end imperial rule. Neither socialists nor communists were terrorists, but the increasing infiltration of these agencies forced socialist movements to respond by toughening their edges, policing their boundaries, and searching for the secret agents that empires placed in their midst.

ON THE SAME day as the nitroglycerin explosion in Colón, Dmitry Karakozov, a twenty-five-year-old university student, entered Tsar Alexander II's Summer Garden in Petrograd, where the tsar was having his afternoon walk in the park. Karakozov was in disguise: underneath the plain red shirting of a peasant, he wore the fine white linen of a nobleman's son. The young man apparently attracted attention, sweating and shaking in the presence of onlookers. When the tsar turned to enter his carriage, Karakozov suddenly pulled out a flintlock pistol and leveled it at him. A shout from a policeman led a hatter standing nearby to knock the pistol aside as it fired. As people rushed to seize the young man, the tsar allegedly asked him, "Are you a Pole?" The tsar and his private police imagined that his highness had no enemies among the Russian people and only a Polish nationalist, angered by the Russian Empire's brutal crackdown on an independence movement three years earlier, would try to kill him.

After days of torture, Karakozov broke, and the police found their worst fears realized. The young man had joined a secret society devoted to reorganizing Russian society into a group of autonomous communes in the style of the revolutionary novel *What Is to Be Done?* The novel, written in 1863 by an ex-seminary student, largely focuses on a woman, Vera Pavlovna, who escapes an arranged marriage, abandons her privilege, and devotes her life to self-denial, an open relationship with others in a commune, and revolution. It also describes a relatively minor character, an ascetic revolutionary man named Rakhmetov, who has disappeared but will return in 1866 when it is necessary for him to be in Russia. The novel also refers to Isaac Newton's alleged prediction that 1866 would be the year of apocalypse. Karakozov, who had read the novel in university and then had been expelled for revolutionary activities, apparently decided to fulfill the novel's prophecy by killing the tsar and then swallowing strychnine. In this way he thought he might bring about the thorough reorganization of society that he hoped for.[1]

Whether Isaac Newton prophesied apocalypse and revolutionary change in 1866 is an open question, but the story had been repeated for over a century by this time. In the last decades of Newton's life, he did closely read the biblical books of Daniel, Paul, and Revelation.[2] Arriving at the date 1866 requires some dubious hermeneutics whereby 1,260 is added to 606. Getting 1,260 is the simple part. In the book of Revelation, the last book of the Catholic, Orthodox, and Protestant bibles, an angel describes the end of the world to a man named Paul. In the vision God holds a scroll or book with seven seals, each associated with a tribulation or judgment to be visited on the earth. The white horse of conquest and the red horse of war will bring the black horse that demands a costly penny for only a measure of wheat. In its wake the pale horse will bring death. The sixth of seven tribulations appears as the reign of the Whore of Babylon, who rides a horse with seven heads and holds a cup containing the blood of martyrs. During the sixth tribulation, two witnesses with God's authority will testify against her for 1,260 "days," but they will be clothed in sackcloth and mostly ignored. A stray line in the book of Daniel suggests that a day might be reckoned as a year.[3]

Starting the reign of the Whore of Babylon in AD 606 requires some mental gymnastics as well. Since well before the 1600s, Protestants had decided that the Catholic Church was the Whore of Babylon and seen themselves as witnesses against her. For centuries, radicals, including urban guilds in Germany, hermit messiahs, Martin Luther, Oliver Cromwell, Quakers, Rangers, Diggers, Fifth Monarchy men, and Isaac Newton, spoke of the Roman Catholic Church as the Whore of Babylon, though they differed about how to interpret the signs that followed.[4] Russian Orthodox believers translated the works of some of these Protestants, Newton in particular. If the Whore were the Catholic Church, then one could argue that the Whore's reign began in the year 606, when the Byzantine emperor Phocas declared the Catholic pope in Rome to be supreme over the Orthodox patriarch of Constantinople, effectively splitting the church into the powerful western and the weaker eastern branches.[5]

Thus the year 606 plus 1,260 years of struggle led some Protestants (and some members of the Russian and Greek Orthodox churches) to expect this tribulation to come to its terrible climax in 1866. According to the book of Revelation, there would be earthquakes, the moon would turn red, and stars would fall, while "every mountain and island were moved out of their places." Rich and mighty men would hide in their mountain "dens," calling on the rocks to hide them; yet all would face "the wrath of the Lamb." Just as a few Protestants saw end times in the violent explosions in Colón in 1866, to Russian observers Karakozov clearly had ties to the Whore of Babylon—the Catholic Church—through Jesuits and Polish nationalists. Forced confessions had led to an even more disturbing revelation: Karakozov was part of a secret revolutionary group that called itself "Hell."[6]

Movements to unseat the tsar had existed since the days of the Decembrists in 1825, but a well-funded secret police in Russia had driven these movements underground. Underground, the opposition to the tsar had formed numerous, diverse adherents: an interesting combination of Russian Orthodox nobles, Old Believers, Ukrainian Protestants, and Russian Jews. Some of the earliest— including nihilists, revolutionary anarchists, Narodnaya Volya (People's Will) populists, and later the Socialist Revolutionaries— formed underground movements that sought to destroy the monarchy by assassinating the monarch.

After 1871 radical intellectuals learned how a mechanic with chemical skills, using detailed instructions, might manufacture nitroglycerin for purposes besides deepening canals and building grain ports. He might build a more efficient handheld bomb that, properly placed, could kill an emperor. Handheld bombs were not new, but truly effective ones were. Two technologies—nitroglycerin and the revolutionary cell—would find their union in a series of explosions in the 1870s and early 1880s that killed landed gentry, British members of Parliament, and imperial rulers.[7]

The threat of radical intellectuals of all stripes forced both empires and radicals to change their tactics when Russian police finally determined that Karakozov was no Pole but a university-trained intellectual bent on changing the world with a handheld device. The intelligence agency, secret imperial tribunals, the assassin, and the radical intellectual were at least as old as the Second Crusade, but 1866 saw important changes to apocalyptic thinking in both the critics and supporters of empire.

Before 1866 the biggest threat to empires had been not intellectuals but *carbonari*, secret members of military orders bound by oath and capable of organizing, planning, and overthrowing an emperor.[8] The revolutions of 1848 had seen secret orders who helped to start revolts, occasionally successful ones. Their written plans and preparatory drilling made them easy to spot. The Giuseppe Mazzinis, Józef Bems, Lajos Kossuths, and Giuseppe Garibaldis of the world had pamphlets but also military training, organized armies, and schemes (sometimes fanciful, always involved) for the overthrow of imperial rulers. But the Karakozovs of the world, by comparison, had a novel, a mission, and a handheld device—a pistol or bomb—that could wipe out one or more heads of state in the blink of an eye. They were devoted to acceleration: the spectacle of execution that would shatter sovereignty and lead to change. "The aim of such activity is to break down the prestige of government," declared Narodnaya Volya in 1879, "to raise in that way the revolutionary spirit of the people."[9] Empires now feared not princes but rather college students and dissident communities.

To deal with the threat of amateur assassins like Karakozov, empires formed large, expensive intelligence agencies devoted to reading the novels, pamphlets, and articles written by imperial critics. It read mail, sent spies into meetings, and developed long and complex dossiers of would-be Rakhmetovs. They subsidized counterrevolutionary novels by the likes of former radicals like Fyodor Dostoevsky. These agencies tested intellectuals against new and evolving models for detecting threats. Who would provide the next model for revolutionary violence? Whose novels and articles should be suppressed? Who should be bought off? For the next fifty years, a complex dance emerged between radicals and empires. Empires developed reading strategies for weighing threats. The secret agent and the detective followed intellectuals and their groupings: the intelligentsia. Novelists in European states made threat readers into heroes like Sherlock Holmes. These agencies followed radical agents around the world, seeing themselves as the white blood cells that could contain the virus of anarchists seeking to fulfill apocalyptic missions, which anarchists called "propaganda by the deed."[10]

Apocalypse after 1866 meant something different. The four horsemen story was arguably about the lack of bread, as conquest led to war, high grain prices, and finally death. By the 1850s, however, the fear of famine had declined in Europe and North America. Yet apocalyptic threats appeared to blossom both among revolutionaries and in the imaginations of empires that sought to prevent revolution. Diverse radical groups adopted apocalyptic language as a way of mobilizing peasants, farmers, and workers to destroy Babylon. Empires saw horsemen, broken seals, and demonic conspiracies all around them.

BETWEEN 1848 AND 1870, Karl Marx and other social democrats seemed less of a threat to empires compared to anarchists, nationalists, and rural revolutionaries. The mixture of radical students, professionals, and artisans that Marx and his followers helped draw together seemed respectable to newspaper editors and book publishers, even if the Russian tsar and his council despised them. This was, after all, a group of intellectuals who rejected nationalism, argued for free trade, and advocated for shortening the workday. Some of their most dangerous ideas were their views about women. Like the characters in *What Is to Be Done?*, Marxists rejected traditional family life for its enslavement of women. A diverse and constantly squabbling group, they made inroads into working-class communities, particularly among skilled workers and professionals. Marx, in his ambitious, world-spanning histories, hoped to establish a model for the entire world economy that explained multiple things at once: the alienation of workers, the tyranny of husbands, class hatred by elites, the failure of religion, the solution to poverty, the brutality of states and empires, the horrors of child labor, and the evils of slavery.

Marx's understanding of the world and the future flowed from his understanding of Ricardo's paradox. David Ricardo, a classical economist and Whig, had marveled at improvements in grain production. In the 1820s Ricardo sought to establish a mathematical formula to explain these changes. Some improvements, like enhanced crop rotation and the use of manure, allowed more production on less land. Other improvements, like better plows and threshing machines, required less labor.[11] But a paradox left Ricardo puzzled. Landlords used these improvements, he said, but improved efficiency would probably hurt them collectively. Land-saving improvements meant that less land was needed to grow food. All things being equal, this would cause rents to fall. Labor-saving improvements were bad too. Because fewer workers would be needed, landlords would not have to borrow as much to hire workers. So interest rates ("money rent" in his phrasing) would also fall. Here was trouble. Improvements in agriculture provided short-term benefits to a single landlord but hurt landlords collectively as renters of land and lenders of money.

While the math is somewhat dodgy, Ricardo was onto something. Technical improvements in agriculture, grain storage, and delivery would lower rents on agricultural land in Britain and much of Europe after the corn laws were rescinded. There were problems with Ricardo's theory, though, because as workers flowed into cheap-food cities after 1845, the rents did not go down everywhere. Property in ports and cities, for example, generally rose in value. Economists in the Liberal Party, who favored higher taxes on land, pointed to rising rents in cities as proof that something was wrong with Ricardo's model.[12]

While other economists after Ricardo dismissed these concerns, Marx built a whole theory on Ricardo's paradox. Radical improvements that bettered people's lives—and they were everywhere—might motivate individual landlords and capitalists. But ultimately landlords were gonna landlord, Marx thought. Technical improvements would threaten the "rentier class" that made money on rents. Then Marx made a massive, but interesting, logical leap. Ricardo's paradox, Marx posited, drove human history. A kind of landlord dominated each stage of a society's development. In ancient societies, this was the slaveholder; in serfdom, this was the lord; in capitalism, this was the capitalist. The "forces of production," according to Marx, advanced in each stage of a society's progressive development: ancient slavery became medieval serfdom, which became modern capitalism. In each case the forces of production hit their peak, after which point existing property relations became oppressive. Then social change came through "contradictions": slave uprisings, peasant revolts, and workers' struggles against employers. If the forces of production were the new techniques that bettered everyone's lives, the "relations of production" were the hierarchy and robbery—the rent—that lay at the heart of each social form. But throughout history, a new, higher-tech society had waited in the wings. Workers' protests drove the change that ended one society and started another. The last social form would end the need for capitalists and the rentier class entirely.

The growing effects of cheap American food in Europe appeared to fit Marx's model, as new productive forms of food production and delivery did promise freedom from want. After around 1860 the condition of workers improved in large part because the cost of bread dropped, giving them resources to buy more goods. Until he died in 1883, Marx was sure declining rents (the falling rate of profit) would lead to crisis. The revolutionary transformations that brought cheap food to Europe seemed to point a way forward. Marx reported on both the Crimean War and the American Civil War. He saw both as the triumph of a rationalizing bourgeoisie against a reactionary class. Catherine the Great and Thomas Jefferson certainly had utopian ideas about the future of family production under wheat. So did Marx and his followers. They viewed the American Civil War as a great revolution of a righteous, forward-looking bourgeoisie against an entrenched, semifeudal slave-owning class. Many Marxists idealized the United States as an expanding society of family farms.[13] Few realized that the most productive American wheat farms were large estates of five hundred to a thousand acres that together used millions of migrating laborers during the harvest.[14] Few saw the parallel between the land acquisition during America's westward expansion into Indian territory and the brutal seizure of the steppe land of the Kazakhs and Kalmyks north of the Black Sea in Russia's southern and eastward expansion. Few thought to compare the Russian dispossession and genocide of Muslim Circassians in 1862 with its American form in the Trail of Tears between 1830 and 1850. Marx recognized the robbery of native lands, calling it "primitive accumulation of capital," but he tended to idealize grain production, particularly in his earlier writings.[15]

Marx and many Marxists lived in cities and so did not know a lot about agriculture. They understood that a revolution in grain production was reshaping the plains of Russia and the United

States but not that the same revolution would soon be changing Argentina, Australia, and India. Yet they could see and feel the revolution that cheap grain had brought to cities. The lowered price of food enticed farm families to urban centers and made industrialization possible.

The consumption-accumulation cities of Europe became an ideal place for Marxist thought to spread. A polyglot collection of workers was assembling. The lowered cost of living after 1860 allowed workers to organize into unions and fight for shorter hours. For workers in Britain and industrial Europe, the period from approximately 1860 to 1890 really was a golden age.[16] Shorter hours gave workers time to read and helped create a class of autodidacts who collected in consumption-accumulation cities. Shorter hours provided an opportunity for workers to band together in collective institutions and see a new world emerging that was not another bloody empire or racially exclusive state. The coherence of Marxist theory as a model for the history of the world and its future helped draw in both women and men, as well as democrats, socialists, utopian planners, engineers, and refugees from broken empires. While he rejected assassination, Marx suggested that the end to all the broken institutions would require a violent cataclysm. This prediction was millennial in a way that resembled the books of Daniel, Paul, and Revelation. The very coherence of Marxist theory made fragile empires regard Marxism as an existential threat.

After 1871, some of those social democrats who called themselves Marxists became even more threatening to empires. Louis Napoleon's September 1870 surrender in the Franco-Prussian War ended the Second Empire, but it did not end the war. France then became a republic whose government faced a four-month siege in Paris. The central problem for Paris was the route to bread. Cut off by the Prussian army from the rural countryside, Parisians faced the hard question that ancient societies came up against in sieges: Where is the grain? Parisians, out of bread, were forced to eat their horses, their zoo animals, and finally the city's dwindling population of rats. The French Third Republic was forced to surrender to Prussian forces in January 1871.

After the republic surrendered, the war had still not ended, and this would cause an important split in Marxist ranks. The Parisian National Guard—radicalized by the conflict—combined with working men and women of Paris to constitute itself as the Paris Commune. They occupied the Tuileries Palace and most of central Paris. But the Commune, controlling a capital without food, did not last long. Surrounded by a combination of French and German troops in May 1871, the radicalized National Guardsmen made their last defiant act the destruction of the Tuileries using petroleum and gunpowder. In the bloody week after the surrender, thousands of Communards were lined up against a wall in a cemetery and shot. Many liberals applauded. The legend of the Commune and the martyrdom of the Communards helped define a new group of radical social democrats, followers of Marx who called themselves communists.

That legacy has lasted. Parvus chose to have a column from the burned Tuileries transported to his front yard in the Wannsee district outside Berlin. The wrecked column simultaneously symbolized the end of the French monarchy, the martyrdom of the Commune's revolutionaries, and the birth of a new kind of politics. Parvus believed that a talented intellectual, centered in capitalism's world markets, might bring about international revolution and the collapse of empires. Vladimir Lenin, too, when he died, asked to be wrapped in a shroud that was the flag of the French Communards.

THE DANGEROUS AND destructive actions by the Russian secret police (first called the Third Section in Russia and later renamed the Okhrana) forced radical organizations to evolve, even those who despised assassination, for every critic of empire could be dragged into the net and potentially exiled or killed. Radicals who survived formed themselves into cells and used code names, drop points, secret messages, and invisible ink. By the 1880s most revolutionaries had abandoned terrorism, but the long, apocalyptic shadow of anarchists and Russia's Socialist Revolutionaries forced them underground. They maintained the organization by cell, each knowing a part of the larger plan but no more, each knowing some fellow members but not all of them.

Russian imperialists regarded all social democrats—communist or otherwise—as threatening for they espoused a doctrine that rejected the foundations of autocracy and predicted its imminent demise. Constant infiltration by imperial agents who identified, arrested, and either executed or exiled them forced the Russian social democrats to develop a unique language that would quickly identify them to one another. The specialized terminology of Marxism became this hidden vernacular: "contradictions," "dialectics," "forces of production," "relations of production," "organic composition of capital." Disciplined self-scouring of the organization to root out spies encouraged a constant, anxious threat assessment that could weaken socialists' founding principles of democratic brotherhood and strengthen tendencies toward defending a self-policing vanguard.

Lenin believed that a small, coherent, self-scouring group of intellectuals needed to educate workers—leading them from trade union consciousness to political consciousness. He laid this out in a 1902 pamphlet that took the name of the famous revolutionary novel *What Is to Be Done?* Intellectuals with sufficient resources could create a viral package to overwhelm and then replace an empire with a workers' movement, then surrender control to workers after concluding a temporary dictatorship. The dictatorship would purportedly stay around only long enough to determine that a similarly organized collection of monarchists, factory owners, generals, or counterrevolutionaries would not take advantage of the instability to destroy the installation and expansion of a workers' international. Leon Trotsky posed a slightly different model for the survival of the revolutionary cell, "permanent revolution," arguing that international revolution could only succeed with constant expansion of internationalist ideology through every neighboring empire. Revolution aimed to overthrow empire, but to survive it needed to constantly expand.

The communist model for the distribution of revolution was different from the anarchist model. Marxists sought to educate workers in Marx's theory about how advancing forces of production (like dynamite, deepwater ports, and steamships) might destabilize existing property relationships, lead revolutionaries to overthrow them, and end empires entirely. Rosa Luxemburg, for instance, who, like many Russian and Polish radicals, saw the world changing around her, began with the same populist foundation that anarchists, socialists, and the Socialist Revolutionaries began with: the novel *What Is to Be Done?* For her, the novel was about a woman who rejected bourgeois conventions to form a radical commune and communist family. Rejecting assassination, she and thousands of others like her joined the social democratic movement. The anarchist revolutionaries in the populist movement, for their part, rejected a socialist political movement that sought to educate workers. "Socialism bounced off people like peas from a wall," wrote the terrorist Stepnyak Kravchinsky to his former comrade Vera Zasulich. "They listen to our people as they do to the priest."[17] Though communists and anarchist revolutionaries took different paths, both were forced underground by the threat that assassins posed to empires.

In March 1881, a faction of the Russian populist movement Narodnaya Volya finally succeeded in killing Tsar Alexander II, fulfilling the apocalyptic vision of Karakozov, though it did not inspire revolution. Instead, reaction followed, and the Okhrana grew more and more powerful as it promised to destroy radical cells around the world. In about 1883, Parvus, the revolutionary student, joined a competing faction of the movement devoted to overthrow of the tsarist state through education and worker organization rather than assassination. But because of the way that assassins and empires had evolved together, agents of the tsar, seeking to kill him, would hound him for the rest of his life.

The apocalypse of 1866 foreseen by Protestants and Orthodox Christians never came. Newton was right about gravity but not about the book of Revelation. A small cell succeeded in assassinating Alexander II, but the longer-term threat to the empire in Saint Petersburg came not from a man with a pistol but from an explosion thousands of miles away. The violent explosion at Colón suggested that no rock or spit of land was safe from radical terraforming. Shortened pathways between the world's ports would destroy Russia's power over the world's grain markets. Mountains would tremble and islands be moved out of their place, and only then would the tribulations begin.

Nine

THE GREAT GRAIN CRISIS
1873–1883

I N 1873 A dramatic financial crisis developed when Ricardo's paradox fell with particularly heavy force in Europe. As nitroglycerin, the transatlantic telegraph, the Suez Canal, and the futures market reshuffled the world's hierarchy of grain ports, the margins of cultivation warped. Wheat fields in Kansas became closer to London than farms in Cracow or Kherson. The merchants' borrowing market, a relatively stable balance wheel for four hundred years, became unbalanced as grain-trading patterns around the world shifted. London's attempts to reel in credit as trade lines crossed destroyed edgy banks around the world, bringing financial chaos. The financialization of food production changed as a futures market partly replaced a centuries-old system of mercantile credit. A new "line system" of credit extended from a futures market all the way to farmers' gates. Parvus was an infant when intense competition from this new system of credit and the grain it brought struck Belarus, Kherson, and Odessa. His understanding of how the tangling of international trade lines could cause crisis led him to revise Karl Marx's theory. He altered it, adding to it a deeper understanding of global trade corridors and how their cheapening could produce tremendous surpluses and make workers' lives easier. As he moved through Switzerland and the German Empire, hounded by secret police in Russia and Germany, he refined his argument in newspapers written for a popular working-class audience. His theory would help form the groundwork for Rosa

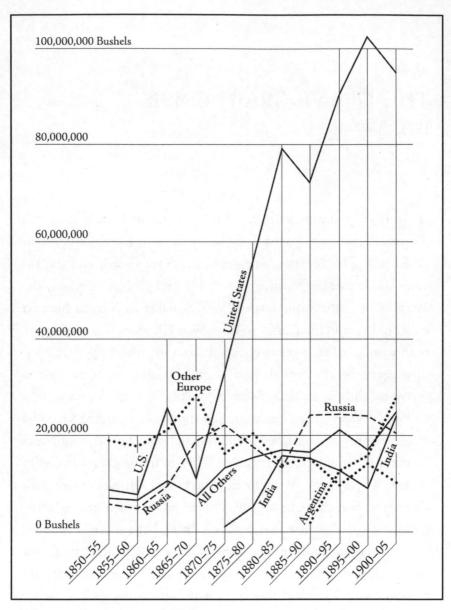

Average annual imports of wheat and flour to the United Kingdom in bushels (flour converted to wheat)

Kate Blackmer

Luxemburg's theory of an economic "world system," Vladimir Lenin's theory of imperialism, and Leon Trotsky's theory of combined and uneven development. Parvus's later elaboration of this theory would suggest how radicals might turn a war into revolution.

THE 192 STEEP Odessa steps lead down to the sea. Today, just to the east of the steps, twenty-first-century trains can drive directly to the open bays of ships. The grain in the cars might be bound for a mill in Qatar or Livorno, though it could easily go to Hong Kong, South Africa, or Tokyo. The efficiency of the layout now is breathtaking. Standing just east of the Odessa steps is like standing in the back of a massive spaceship organized for the export of millions of tons of anything. For tourists, of course, the view of crane gantries crowded over railroads and ships makes Odessa a little less romantic than it once was. Most of this construction was completed after 1991. Odessa is prepared again for the world's trade.

But in the 1860s, the Russian grain port of Odessa was poorly prepared for how portable nitroglycerin would change the world's grain pathways. For just over seventy years, sailing ships had drawn up to its wharves to buy Russian, Polish, and Ukrainian wheat. Besides the grain warehoused in Odessa proper, barges on the Dnieper, Dniester, and Southern Bug Rivers held thousands more "puds," thirty-three-pound sacks of grain waiting for sailing ships. But the newly built "great cargo steamships" that navigated short distances after 1866 found Odessa an awkward mooring space. The steamships—with compound engines, screw propellers, and capacities of approximately twenty thousand tons—found the choppy waters and cramped harbor outside Odessa challenging.[1] Even sailing ships faced difficulties in Odessa. Shipmasters there complained about delays imposed by the workmen's guild, the customshouse bureaucracy, and the Odessa banks.[2] British trade officials, stationed in Odessa to help shipmasters, gave them little time or respect. "To few ports do a lower class of shipmasters come than to Odessa," complained British consul Eustace Clare Grenville-Murray in 1869. "Five out of six are uneducated colliers from Shields or Sunderland," he continued, and the worst were those "troublesome half-educated men known among sailors as a sea-lawyer."[3] Grenville-Murray was removed from his position, but the merchants of Odessa attested that shipmasters, whether knowledgeable about the law or not, faced numerous difficulties, including the inattention of the governor-general and negligent port officials.[4]

Other tribulations for shipmasters included the narrow passage at Constantinople, which the Ottoman Empire might block in case of war, famine, or revolt. The possibility of additional taxes or delays in paperwork at the strait had always given merchants pause.[5] For all these reasons, by 1869 the cost of moving a bushel of wheat from Odessa to a European port was at least twenty-five cents. The same quantity of wheat could be transported from the United States for less than twenty cents, even though the route from Odessa was shorter, took less time, and did not cross the deepest part of the ocean.[6] After 1870, then, cheap American grain and flour began to replace Russia's as the food of Europe's urban working class.

With so much grain coming from the United States, landed estates in Europe were the first to fall, just as predicted by Ricardo's paradox. As early as 1870, according to one observer in Berlin, "the newspapers were filled with advertisements of landed property for sale side by side with the announcements of new companies."[7] Agricultural land prices fell more rapidly in Sweden, Germany, Britain, and Ireland, where grain growing on marginal land was more important than in France, which had a more diverse agriculture and excellent canals.[8]

The problems lay not just in existing credit relations with cash-strapped farmers but with the banks as well. By November 1872 a number of banks were tottering in the capital cities of Berlin and Vienna. These banks faced the same problem that Britain had faced in 1866. Finance companies used bills of exchange to borrow for long-term debt projects, particularly in the booming real estate market in the capital cities. Industrial and railroad promoters too had been effectively borrowing on the money market in three- and six-month installments for long-term, sometimes speculative projects.[9] In both Germany and the United States, the firms that failed first were, in the words of twentieth-century accountants, "borrowing short and lending long." They operated much in the way Overend, Gurney & Co. had in 1866, borrowing on money markets that had been used for the grain trade since the days of the Genoese and Venetian merchants. If interest rates went up, their credit would run out.[10]

The Bank of England, fearing the instability of banks in Vienna and Berlin, doubled the effective interest rate on bills of exchange from 3.5 to 7 percent in three "shocks" in November 1872, June 1873, and October–November 1873. The first shock hit the Odessa banks hardest, the second shock brought down Berlin banks, and the third shock brought down American banks. Identifying specific causes is difficult: it appears that high interest rates were both a cause and an effect of these panics. The Bank of England, for example, blamed the rate hike on bank instability in Vienna and Berlin and justified it based on the risk of lending to a bank on the brink of default. But banks that borrowed on the money market to engage in long-distance trade argued that sudden rate hikes made it difficult to arrange the credit required to ship goods to a buyer. As their stock of goods languished in sending ports, they could not pay their bills. In either case, scores of bankruptcies first hit Odessa banks; then most of Vienna's banks and fully one-third of Berlin's banks failed between May and the end of 1873; by November of that year, two of New York's largest banks had failed. Within three years mercantile failures in the United States reached $650 million.[11]

These bankruptcies all over the world would forever change bills of exchange as the keystone of both the international food trade and interbank lending. Banker Walter Bagehot of the *Economist*, days before he died in 1873, suggested that the British Treasury create short-term Treasury bills to replace six-month bills of exchange.[12] It was too easy to create false "pig-upon-bacon" bills that allowed long-term borrowers to run up short-term debts and then hit a wall when interest rates rose.

Two years after the start of the 1873 panic, the merchant Charles Magniac summarized the problems grain merchants faced and how they led to the crisis: "the Suez Canal, in conjunction with steam and ocean telegraphy" made obsolete "all the old machinery—warehouses, sailing vessels, capital, six months' bills, and the British merchant, whose occupation [was] gone."[13] Sailing ships survived, but grain merchant warehouses and short-term bills of exchange did become outmoded. British bankruptcies in 1873 were concentrated first among these country merchants, then in speculative enterprises that depended on bills of exchange, including engineers and iron founders.[14] As the transmission of food and food prices changed between ports and cities, an entire global commercial infrastructure using bills of exchange was shaken to its foundations.[15]

The sudden drop in shipping prices brought by nitroglycerin's collapse of travel times helped usher in the period economic historians call the first wave of globalization, from 1871 to 1914. Colonial goods worth more than roughly fifty cents a pound, like coffee, sugar, silver, and cotton, had been traveling across the Atlantic since the 1600s. With free trade, instant sharing of prices by telegraph, and nitroglycerin's elimination of expensive barriers, shipping became cheap enough for bulkier, lower-value goods worth less than fifteen cents a pound, like wheat, beef, and kerosene. By the 1880s American and Ukrainian farmers were also using nitroglycerin to blow up stumps, break through rock, and generally flatten soil for the further expansion of wheat monocultures at the margins of cultivation.

It is difficult to comprehend the volume of grain that crossed the Atlantic. The first surge of wheat from the United States to Europe had come just before the Civil War. Between 1855 and 1859, the five-year average for wheat imports into Antwerp was a mere twenty thousand tons. Between 1860 and 1869, it nearly quadrupled to seventy-five thousand tons, mostly from North America. But then between 1870 and 1874, the yearly average nearly quadrupled again, averaging 276,000 tons a year. Nearly all the increase came from the United States. It had become clear, in the words of one historian of European transport, that "the USA could become Western Europe's abundant grain shed."[16]

The American surge swamped the Russian export market. Between 1871 and 1880, the value of all US food exports to Europe rose from $32 billion to $231 billion, a 611 percent increase. The largest commodity was wheat, which saw a tripling of yearly shipments from 31 million to 154 million bushels, or two bushels a year for every European living west of the Rhine.[17] The *Moscow Times* reported Russia's fate using two dates. In 1867, 44 percent of Britain's imported grain came from Russia, while only 14 percent came from the United States. In 1873, US export made up 44 percent of Britain's wheat, while Russia only exported 21 percent.[18] Economists and contemporaries have emphasized the elimination of European tariffs after 1845, the introduction of the gold standard across Europe, and the advent of steamships as factors in the American Grain Invasion.[19] They have generally missed the ecological and political background: the spread of *Phytophthora infestans* that cracked empires open, the impact of nitroglycerin on port placement, and lower transaction costs brought by the decline of bills of exchange and the rise of a futures market. All three introduced breakneck competition in European trade, shrank the warehousing margin for wheat, and created a global food market.

The cheapening of transport had important secondary effects beyond the financial and commercial ones. Most notably, two great human migrations followed in the backwash from oceans of grain. Over the next four decades more than thirty million Europeans crossed the Atlantic to the Americas.

In fact Europeans traded places with American grain. They rode back on the same boats that brought it, most traveling in the cheap "steerage" compartments, which were refitted from grain compartments when the ships arrived in Europe. Over the same period almost as many people left China and northern India to work in parts of Asia, the Pacific Islands, and the Americas (many as indentured servants). Europeans' movement from countryside to city was even larger than these movements across the oceans, in part because food was for the first time cheaper in cities than in the countryside. In this period, according to one historian, "out of every seven persons added to Europe's population, one went abroad and four or five went to the city."[20]

Mercantile credit, once based on bills of exchange, was usurped by what was called after 1873 the "line system" of grain credit, which relied on grain commission merchants who used the futures market. The Chicago futures market had been born to resolve problems associated with the Union Army's logistical problem: delivering food over long distances. The instability of the greenback dollar, combined with the War Department's commitment to a market-based solution, led the Chicago Board of Trade to create a futures market to allow buyers and sellers to guard against a rapid rise or fall of prices in a rapidly changing market. A buyer of crops could become a seller of futures; the seller of a crop could become a buyer of futures. These bets on the other side of a volatile market could, if placed properly, minimize the dangers of drastic price swings.

But the American futures market offered more than price security: it also became the foundation of the food-credit system that could finance the feeding of Europe. American railways had already taken on some of the features of a bank. Since the 1850s railways had provided mortgages for land along their roadbeds. By the 1860s railroads issued elevator receipts for grain that traded like currency. Then, by the 1870s banks, in collaboration with railroads, extended credit to "line companies" who sent "grain commission men" to farm gates to give loans to farmers in exchange for future grain.

Mercantile credit had for centuries been port to port. A second, more informal credit system extended from banks through country stores to farmers. That system was as old as the American colonies.[21] Beginning around 1873 a single credit instrument could extend from the port all the way to the farmer's gate. In a way, the line companies were like branches of a central bank. The central bank, which provided liquidity to the line companies, was the Chicago Board of Trade. Aspiring young merchants in the line companies resided in western towns, where they tempted nearby farmers with loans to be repaid in grain. In the first years of operation, they wrote a check to a farmer, exchanging it for a signed contract for future crops.

Line companies had tight relations with railroads. Each line company operated along a single railroad corridor, gathering grain for elevators that lined their tracks. Within a day of signing a contract, the line company would use it to sell an equivalent number of wheat futures on the Board of Trade, occasionally buying a smaller portion as a hedge. By the early 1870s, farming along the midwestern railways could operate in a financial loop, with scores of unknown lenders in European cities buying grain futures to pay thousands of unknown farmers to grow the grain.[22] The boulevard barons, dedicated to stimulating westward expansion and extending long-distance trade for farm goods, had figured out how to fuse a maritime financial instrument, a bank loan, and a store credit to create a single financial instrument to encourage farming. The line companies had the bank capital to induce farmers to grow grain for increasingly distant markets.

FEW WRITERS UNDERSTOOD this transformation better than Parvus. Around 1871 his family fled Belarus, victims of one of the region's first pogroms. A pogrom—the word derives from *grom*, Russian for "thunder"—generally began with a mob of Orthodox Christians carrying banners emblazoned with the images of saints, who would march into the narrow streets of cramped Jewish quarters. The thunder came from the sound of Cossack horses, for Cossacks, while claiming to keep the peace, often led the charge against Jewish residents. Four-year-old Parvus hardly understood the commotion, he wrote later, surrounded as he was by toys and his family. He later learned that the pretty lights he was admiring on his last night in Belarus were the flames kindled by the Orthodox Christians who drove all the Jews out, including his family.

Parvus's parents relocated first to the farming community of Kuban. But as Parvus wrote later, Jews were "politically persecuted . . . crammed together in a limited number of cities, their freedom of movement greatly restricted, deprived of many state and civil rights."[23] Quickly uprooted from Kuban the family moved to one of the few places available to Jewish refugees, the grain-trading city of Odessa, where his father had grown up. His father or older brother became, probably with the support of family in the grain trade, a grain trader. The family would have begun as *skrupchiki*, small traders who used credit from grain warehouses to lend money to farmers in the interior. They were similar to "grain commission men," though without a futures market, they assumed more risks if prices dropped.[24] Eventually the family settled to work on the exchange in Odessa. From their position in that city, Parvus's family, the Helphands, would thereafter follow the rhythms of international grain financing and distribution.

Residents of the Jewish district in Odessa had already survived a pogrom in the same year that the Helphands were attacked in Belarus. The Odessa pogrom began on Palm Sunday, March 21, 1871, when Odessa Greeks discovered a cross missing in a church and accused Jews of stealing it. These conflicts had many origins, but they were partly connected to grain. Jewish *skrupchiki* and warehouse operators had since the 1860s been displacing Greeks in the grain trade, even as the price for Odessa grain was dropping. That said, the Greek pogrom in Odessa targeted not grain traders but rather the poorest and most vulnerable Jews crammed into Odessa's Jewish quarter west and south of the city center. Other pogroms followed in the 1870s, which Parvus would have witnessed or heard about as a child.[25]

According to Parvus's contemporaries, the Helphands were well-off, though probably not yet rich. Most Jews in Odessa were poor, however, and poor Jews near the crowded city center were the chief targets of pogroms. Because Jews were "artificially isolated and heavily oppressed by the government," Parvus wrote later, they must have appeared unified to their enemies; "the feeling of solidarity," he wrote, "must appear all the more powerful." Parvus knew, however, that the divisions between working-class Jews and merchants like his father were in fact vast and deep. From an early age, perhaps as a teenager, Parvus identified with Jewish workers, not with his own family. "Among the Jews there is really a small percentage of moneylenders, manufacturers, merchants, masters, and similar exploiters," Parvus wrote, "but what a tremendous number of proletarians there are among themselves."

Though Parvus—like his father—came to see the globe through the lens of international trade, he identified with the landless workers attacked by the Orthodox Christian mobs, perhaps because his own family had been attacked in Belarus, perhaps because his friends were poorer Jews, perhaps because his family had once been proletarian. Like many other radical Jewish intellectuals, he came from the bourgeoisie. He enjoyed a good life and was highly educated; yet, like other radical intellectuals, he identified with people unlike himself: workers who suffered at the hands of the mob, Russian sailors lorded over by imperious Russian noblemen, and peasants impoverished by the empire's heavy taxes on farms. A fierce opponent of the tsar, Parvus soon became an international communist and among the most important intellectuals of the twentieth century.[26]

When the family arrived in Odessa, they saw firsthand the tumult that America's new railway corridors and the invention of nitroglycerin had brought to the international grain pathways from Odessa to the world. That worldwide change was the touchstone from which Parvus's understanding of international economics grew. Adjusting to the new competition from America required careful analysis of how and when to sell grain to the wider world, how to move it more cheaply, how to rapidly respond to minor price changes, and how to gather enough credit to sell quantities of grain so large that one could thrive on a 2 percent margin. Like David Dows and Peter H. Watson in the United States, his father mastered the trade, made successful gambles on the future, and succeeded. The political structure of Russia differed profoundly from that of the United States, however, and Parvus's commitment to radical change brought him into contact with different ideas about the world.

PARVUS'S EARLY EDUCATION took place in a gymnasium (preparatory school). But after Narodnaya Volya (People's Will) assassinated Alexander II, the so-called May Laws passed in 1882 forced almost all Jews out of Russia's schools. His relatives scrambled to find university-educated tutors to teach him history, literature, ancient languages, and mathematics.[27] Around the same time, in his teens, Parvus joined a different splinter group called Chernyi Peredel (Black Repartition).[28] "Black" referred to the black soil north of Odessa; "repartition" referred to Nicholas I's promise to redistribute the land to peasants. Chernyi Peredel argued that Tsar Alexander II's ministers had reneged on Nicholas's promise of emancipation by editing his final proclamation and thereby reducing peasant land allotments and increasing their redemption payments. We now know that this was true.[29]

After 1883 Parvus, then sixteen, was educated at home in the classics and economics by what he called "academically educated tutors."[30] A writer who knew him in the 1880s noted that the Helphand family was by then already wealthy, having speculated in the grain and tallow exported from Odessa.[31] Parvus worked hard to hide his origins. He admitted later that he was a child of the bourgeoisie, though he never explained what his father did.[32] His most vivid recollection of Odessa, he wrote later, was of the stereotypical Odessa merchant who wore a kaftan, had a rough bowl-shaped haircut, greased his hair with linseed oil, and smelled of *juchten*, a leather-curing oil that had become a kind of perfume in the city. Spending more than a few years among merchants like his father, he likely learned his first lessons in international trade from them.[33]

The revolutionists that Parvus joined sought to recruit workers into a movement against the tsar. In 1885, Parvus was tasked with organizing skilled laborers on the Odessa waterfront. He used anarchist revolutionary propaganda that, even as he mouthed its platitudes, he found himself doubting. A crackdown on revolutionaries in December 1887 led him and many others to flee the city. At age twenty Parvus crossed the border into Germany and, "to resolve [his] political doubts," as he put it, devoted himself to reading and understanding the economic world around him. Abandoning the rural-centered politics of the Black Repartition, he became a Marxist and a communist. His years in Odessa would have driven him to match up the abstract Marxist economics he read with the world of Odessa merchants, who followed the news of the trading world and tested their knowledge on the roads leading to Russia's grain, on the bourses where grain was traded, and at the warehouses where grain traders knew the daily international price.[34]

Parvus lived briefly in Zurich, then entered university in Berne at age twenty-one. He quickly moved into graduate study, beginning a dissertation in political economy at the University of Basel under Karl Bücher, a German scholar of ancient history, newspapers, the public sphere, and political economy. By then, the twenty-two-year-old Parvus had joined the Plekhanov circle, a group of Marxist revolutionaries who believed that Russia's working class, as small as it was in rural Russia, was the key to overthrowing the tsar. In Switzerland Parvus rummaged through every revolutionary pamphlet and book he could find.[35] He found himself departing somewhat from Karl Marx's understanding of the international economy. In Marx's unfinished, multivolume *Capital*, the German communist created a mathematical model of the economy with a single capitalist, a single workshop, and scores of workers bunched together to produce a commodity. Marx calculated that a worker toiled more than half a day producing enough wealth to feed the family and that the remainder of his workday was stolen by the capitalist. The capitalist's power came from owning the means of production: the factory in particular. Parvus mostly agreed.[36]

But Parvus thought Marx's model was incomplete. The dockworkers that Parvus knew in Odessa moved goods, usually sacks of dried grain, from warehouses onto ships. In the port of Odessa generally, delivering goods occupied the lives of most workers. This included those who fabricated or repaired locks, built warehouses, and repaired ships. Dockworkers would have been skeptical of Marx's claims about a single factory, for they knew firsthand that the cost of delivery could comprise half or more of the final price of commodities on an international market, particularly for cheap, bulky goods like grain. The largest measure of cost came from the *chumaki* caravans, the men whose oxen lugged grain over the ancient black paths from rural Kherson, Ekaterinoslav, and Taurov provinces into the warehouses of Odessa. As a Marxist, Parvus was committed to reorganizing Russian society, but as an organizer and an observer of the world, he was compelled by his "political doubts" to revise Marx's model of a single factory.

Only four years after he left Odessa, at the age of twenty-three, he submitted his doctoral thesis. He declared with brash certainty that the working world was organized spatially around pathways. In his view, workers produced hundreds of commodities; then entrepreneurs sought out these dissimilar objects ("membra disjecta" he called them) to funnel them into port cities. The objects were assembled as near as possible to their "circles of consumption" (*Consumptionkreise*). Beds of pig iron stood outside steelworks; clothing sweatshops clustered around a business district; bun bakeries waited at the gates of factories. Workers might assemble goods in a factory, but the creation of salable objects there was often only the first part of a worldwide distribution process. Parvus pointed out that Marx recognized commodity production was a global process but had not put transportation logistics into his model, and without them, the model did not work.[37]

The entrepreneurs who assembled the pieces, Parvus argued, might discover new ways to cheapen the *organization* or *delivery* of commodities over long distances. He developed on his own a story about what I have called "tollage" and which the United Nations and World Bank now characterize in terms of cent per ton-kilometer. He used an example from a contemporary anthropologist's description of enslaved workers in Ottoman-controlled Sudan to prove his point. The anthropologist noted that Mohammed, an Egyptian slaveowner, was obliged to pay a grain tax to feed Ottoman troops in Khartoum, which lay hundreds of miles north of his grain warehouse. To pay the tax, Mohammed sent a caravan of more than twenty slaves and oxen to deliver the grain.

173

To survive, the slaves and oxen consumed the food they carried. Over a long enough distance, noted Parvus, the grain would eventually disappear. Labor was cheap in Sudan, but the teaming work from grain to flour mill was stretched to its breaking point by the demands of the imperial officer in Khartoum. The vast tollage required inside the Ottoman Empire meant that slaveowners had to send considerably more grain to Khartoum than their slaves harvested, just to ensure that workers and oxen could deliver the goods and return.[38]

If the tollage in these pathways between intermediate commodities could be cheapened—with better wagons, a better road, a cheaper ship, a deeper wharf, or a shortcut through the Continent—the precious commodities available to society as a whole would vastly increase. This cheapening of tollage might not alter the labor process in the factory or mill, only the delivery of commodities running into it. Yet, if the international pathways could be shortened or straightened, then Marx's model workshops could expand, the division of labor would increase, and even more value would be produced. The question was still the same: Who benefited? And Parvus, like Marx, believed that workers did not get their fair share.[39]

Here was why the pathways in Parvus's mind mattered. If wheat, the food of Europe's working classes and the largest expense in their budgets, could be delivered more cheaply from imperial frontiers, whether from the steppes of Ukraine, the swamps of South Sudan, or the plains of Kansas, then society as a whole would benefit. The tollage from commodity to mill to bakery could be minimized using grain elevators, railroads, deepwater ports, or nitroglycerin blasts through mountains. Shortening the path for commodities provided a vast social benefit that could rescue millions from Marx's tragic single-factory model in which intensification of capitalist production impoverished workers.

Thus Parvus was a new kind of Marxist, one who studied a world system of commodity pathways around the world. He believed that this world system was older than capitalism. He also believed there was a bonus for everyone in shrinking the world, whether by lowering tariffs, improving grain-drying methods, building grain elevators, or deepening harbors. Cheaper bread, if the benefit could truly be shared, might save millions of workers from lives of endless toil. Having tried to organize workers in Odessa, he knew that their time mattered as much to them as money or more. He argued that the bounty realized from lowering the tollage in grain distribution should benefit everyone both in material *and* time. Shorter, tighter pathways might allow a shortening of the standard twelve-hour workday to ten hours, then eight hours. The international scope of Parvus's model was as vast as the steppe and as deep as the ocean; explained clearly, it could attract workers to an international movement. Indeed, it required an international movement; otherwise workers in one country might—in a workshop bonded together by trade routes—compete against workers ten thousand miles away.

Parvus's views on agriculture differed from those of many Marxists. While he believed that the Russian nobility should be dispossessed of the land they kept in the Black Repartition, he doubted that collective peasant ownership would solve Russia's problems. Instead, he knew that in Kuban, where he had lived as a boy, the most productive lands were those worked by farm families. This was also true in East Prussia, where he lived in his midtwenties. Farms larger than a hundred acres could use mechanical equipment to cheapen the harvest process, and this was revolutionizing international markets. He believed as a Marxist in collective ownership of factories. But he argued that when it came to grain, family labor on a relatively large estate could produce more efficiently than land managed by a landlord or a collective.[40] In this way Parvus learned from the revolutionary populism of his days in Chernyi Peredel, but he also felt that communal agriculture was not a workable way to produce grain, a subject he probably knew better than any other Marxist of his generation.

When Parvus came to Germany in the summer of 1891, he arrived with a handful of journalistic clippings from newspapers in Switzerland. His goal was to become a revolutionary newspaper editor. In the summer of 1894, he became editor of a popular working-class newspaper in Leipzig, assuming the pen name Parvus, Latin for "poor" or "little." His inspiration may have been "Parvus Johan," the medieval name for Little John, the enormous, scholarly monk who joined Robin Hood's revolutionary band of merry men. Parvus, like Little John, was a large man, tending toward fat in his later life, and he was certainly a scholar who read Russian, German, Ukrainian, Latin, a little Greek, and even Old Church Slavonic. He understood Yiddish and may have known Hebrew. He was also poor, according to his friends, throughout his twenties. Whatever the source of the name, Parvus devoted his life to a mission that combined understanding how grain moved around the world and inspiring workers to bring an end to empires and capitalism. Few people outside the trade union movement knew his true identity.

Like Little John of the Robin Hood fable, Parvus would be a fugitive most of his life. The Okhrana, the Russian secret police, learned of his escape from Odessa in 1887, but liberal Switzerland refused to prosecute him for leaving Russia and entering university, no matter his politics. When Parvus moved to Germany, however, the Okhrana shared its already fat file on him with Department V, the secret police branch in Berlin devoted to purging the city of radicals. The threat readers in Department V labeled Parvus a "literary ruffian" (*literarischer Raufbold*) and soon hounded him out of Leipzig, Saxony, Dresden, Bavaria, and finally Berlin.[41]

A NUMBER OF other writers followed in Parvus's footsteps. They too assumed pen names because they were fugitives from imperial Russia who could be threatened by the constantly expanding Russian Okhrana. Their pen names are more familiar. Rosa Luxemburg ("Junius"), Lev Davidovich Bronstein ("Trotsky"), and Vladimir Ilyich Ulyanov ("Lenin") were Parvus's closest companions between 1891 and 1917. When the German police expelled Parvus from Leipzig, he suggested that his close friend, the Polish-born Marxist Rosa Luxemburg, take his place. She began her literary career in Leipzig as an internationalist critic of Polish nationalism. She and Parvus traveled to meetings of the German Social Democratic Party in the 1890s, initially as left-wing outsiders to the movement. She would, like Parvus, make a name for herself as an interpreter of the news. Those who agreed with them thought of them as intellectuals; critics called them propagandists. Parvus believed that they had to be a little bit of both.[42]

Shortly after his arrival in Germany, Parvus read the work of Eduard Bernstein, the German Marxist who was close friends with Marx and Friedrich Engels. Parvus believed that just as the German Social Democratic Party had become legal again, Bernstein had distorted Marx's writings to push the party to find common cause with German liberals and nationalists on the issue of state reforms. Bernstein appeared to believe that workers' control of the machinery of the state could come about through voting. Detecting a German nationalism in Bernstein that they believed poisonous to an international movement, Parvus and Rosa Luxemburg attacked him in print. Parvus coined the term "revisionist" in the 1890s to attack Bernstein and others who, Parvus felt, had deviated from Marx's commitment to revolution and also failed to see the tightly connected international economy of grain that Parvus had seen from Odessa. German socialist politician August Bebel described the reaction to their harsh criticisms to a friend: "Parvus stuck in their throats like a fishbone. . . . You cannot imagine the animosity against Parvus and also La Rosa in the party."[43]

Lenin, three years younger than Parvus, first learned of his work through his sharp attacks on Bernstein. In 1899 Lenin stressed that social democrats needed to appreciate Parvus's description of how cheap grain was creating new kinds of European port cities and that Russia's agricultural problems could only be understood in relation to "the general development of world capitalism."[44] In this way Parvus, then Luxemburg, then Lenin, and finally Trotsky deviated from Marx as well, arguing that the greatest threat to the world was no longer simply capitalism but capitalism aligned with empire.

Marxists began to follow the lead of economic liberals in using and transforming the word "imperialism." Imperialism before 1872 had referred to the military seizure of power by a despot. Thus in 1848 English journalists called Louis Napoleon's seizure of power an imperialist act. In 1872, after British prime minister Benjamin Disraeli's Crystal Palace speech endorsing Britain's far-flung empire, English liberals used the word "imperialism" to criticize him and the Tories for their obsession with costly and unproductive imperial holdings across oceans. Britain's empire in India and the Caribbean, for example, were "imperialist" adventures that could not pay.[45]

"Imperialism," to the liberals who coined the term, described the ways that nineteenth-century societies borrowed the trappings of ancient empires without really operating like empires. They made no fiscal sense. Grain, after all, was no longer gathered from an empire's inner ring to both feed the imperial capital and its armies. Free trade had put an end to that. A worldwide capitalist division of labor in agriculture ensured that the world's food would be shared.

Parvus and the neo-Marxists who followed him extended the liberals' critique of imperialism, arguing that workers benefited from a world economy of grain. Competition between empires for dependent colonies across oceans was becoming unnaturally fused with capitalists' desire for foreign markets. The combination of capitalism and empire—into imperialism—led to pointless and costly wars, including wars against the Zulus and later the Boers in South Africa, for example. Their Marxist opponent Bernstein doubled down against this argument about the horrors of European imperial adventures in Africa, stating that "civilized people" had a duty to "uncivilized people" around the world.[46]

Parvus's account of an international grain economy also motivated Trotsky, initially an outsider among the Russian social democrats. Trotsky also came from Ukraine and had, like Parvus, begun his political education as an organizer in the dynamic grain port of Odessa. Ten years younger than Lenin and thirteen years younger than Parvus, he arrived among the Russian social democrats in 1902, a year after they had formed themselves around the newspaper printed in Parvus's apartments. Following in the wake of Parvus's analysis of agriculture, Trotsky made a name for himself in arguing that the progress of capitalism had fundamentally changed during the European scramble for empire and the intensive capitalization of agriculture on the Black Sea. Marx had been wrong to talk about a system of oriental despotism in which monarchs controlled Russia and China with an iron hand. Instead, a broken system of "combined and uneven development" defined Russia, China, Africa, and the Middle East. Imperialism fused with capitalism could produce regions of advanced commodity production that were ripe for revolution, like Ukraine, alongside backward rural sectors little changed since the Middle Ages, like the area around the Volga River.[47]

Whatever their differences over how the world was changing, Parvus was the economist whom Luxemburg, Lenin, and Trotsky most admired and on whom they drew for many of their positions. His most prescient argument was that European social democrats needed to stop fighting among themselves because a world of cheap grain meant that life could be easier for everyone. Aggressive European states would fight wars to control the paths to strategic assets like grain, oil, and other commodities. Like Parvus, Luxemburg, Lenin, and Trotsky closely followed the lopsided imperial wars pursued by the British, French, Dutch, and Belgian empires in the mid- to late nineteenth century. The European empires were carving up zones of influence in Africa, the Ottoman Empire, and China. As communists they believed this was only the beginning of what would become a worldwide catastrophic clash between those empires.[48]

Using what he understood of the revolutionary effects of the world's grain trade and the panic of 1873, Parvus hoped to contribute to the destruction of the Russian Empire and help build new revolutionary states—including the modern Turkish and social democratic states—on its ashes. Parvus revised Marx, but communists around the world came to view his revision as orthodox Marxism, in part because official doctrine in the Soviet Union would later absorb Lenin's interpretation and extension of Parvus's arguments. Parvus's understanding of the Agrarian Crisis of 1873 was foundational in what became Marxist theory, world-systems theory, and the theory of imperialism. He succeeded in bringing about political change, though not in quite the way he imagined.

Ten

THE GRAIN POWERS OF EUROPE
1815-1887

T HE SHIFT IN "great power" status in Europe between 1815 and 1914 has been described as comprising three seemingly unrelated shifts. The fragmented principalities of Germany and Italy coalesced into powerful states; the Ottoman and Austrian empires declined in influence; these reconfigured European empires then increasingly fought over imperial control of Asia, Africa, and the Pacific.[1] There have been many plausible explanations for these changes. Most dwell on European states, including the growth of ethnic nationalism, the inherent weakness of multinational empires, the impact of universal military conscription, the craftiness of visionary politicians, and the "backwardness" of southern and eastern Europe. But the rise of Germany and Italy, the decline of Austria and Turkey, and the European scramble for empire all have more to do with the injection of cheap foreign grain into Europe than most scholars have recognized.[2] The great powers did not operate in a vacuum. They were powered, in part, by grain. Their deepwater ports sucked in food from the Atlantic and Black Seas, freeing workers to enter cities and make industrialization possible along the European rivers and canals closest to Europe's gullet cities. Some European states adjusted to the new normal of abundance by taxing a portion of the food surplus, picking workers' pockets to build battleships. European empires stuffed on cheap grain would soon export manufactures, including manufactured food, to the rest of the world. Big port cities were simultaneously vital to the expansion of European empires and the biggest threat to them. This was how the world worked after *Phytophthora infestans*.

Schoolchildren and scholars believe they understand the world when they know the names of countries, capitals, and kings. Reading almost any map, with a color for each country, will persuade you of this. But the colored states on a map are a simplistic model of the world. For grain traders, understanding the world did not mean counting empires and capitals; it meant finding the big cities where food converged and working outward. The human fraction of the world is not colored blobs; it is, and always has been, the black paths, the food pathways between humans.

Seeing the world as a series of lines through oceans, rivers, and ports is difficult, but it is crucial for those who trade in grain. Parvus recognized the great powers' dependence on the flow of cheap calories from across the ocean and imagined a different realignment of Europe and its relationship to the rest of the world. In 1896 Parvus suggested that any international understanding of Europe had to start with the fact that the lines connecting Europe to the Atlantic passed by London, while the lines connecting Europe to the Pacific passed by the Balkan Peninsula. While the Suez Canal had shortened the line between East and West, Istanbul was still the gateway between western gullets and eastern grain, and as a result any major world conflict would start there.[3] European diplomats, a self-important lot, persuaded themselves that the world revolved around relations between the great powers, and too many historians have followed that logic. Parvus knew that there was no greater power than grain and no greater decider of power than control of its routes. Every European-centered history of World War I devotes pages to the trenches in Europe; Parvus knew that a true world war would be decided on the Bosporus. When World War I began in the Balkans and Ottoman control of the two straits near Gallipoli made it difficult for British and French cities to feed themselves, he was proved right.

THE NINETEENTH-CENTURY DECLINE of the Austrian Empire may be simplest to explain. Before *Yersinia pestis* arrived, Austria built its future on exporting flour to the rest of Europe. Austria, which had become Austria-Hungary in 1867, had crucial advantages. Grain grew well in the fertile Banat region of Hungary. It became flour in the multistory flour mills of Budapest and found a market among elite bakers and confectioners from Germany to Paris to London to Brazil. As late as 1879 Austria-Hungary drew millions in foreign exchange from its agricultural bounty, flour above all.[4]

The Budapest mills relied on a multistage grain-milling process introduced in 1820 that it guarded jealously. For twenty centuries before 1820, the world had used grist mills: two horizontal rotating millstones that cracked wheat, the rotation pushing broken grain along grooves into a hopper. The grooves quickly gummed up with grain and so needed constant cleaning; the stones needed regular sharpening.

Budapest millers found a way to eliminate the grooves. Loose grain was poured by hand between two long, counterrotating cylinders made of glass, ceramic, or iron. The closely spaced cylinders carefully and delicately snapped the grain into slivers rather than crushing it. Additional cylinders underneath the first, each closer and closer together, continued to gently pop open the kernels to separate them from their hard outer shells. Gravity pulled the popped kernels and their shells downward, while fans and sieves separated the white endosperm from the tan bran on the outside and the brown germ on the inside. The number of workers required to feed grain into cylinders and sift out the residue was massive. Properly sifted, the grains could be sorted into twelve different grades of flour: one for each of the distinct classes of Austro-Hungarian society. The whitest flour was called *Kaiserauszug*, or kaiser extract. The *Kaiserauszug* contained so little bran that it could travel all the way to Rio de Janeiro without spoiling, though its price was high. In 1878 the mills on the Pest side of Budapest were producing thirty thousand barrels a day for markets in London, Liverpool, and South America; they sold at fifty cents per barrel above the US price.[5]

But complex taxes on Austria's food as it moved through the empire weighed it down terribly. As Parvus put it, Austria was "so like a beggar's coat, consisting of nothing but patchwork. . . . [A] shapeless being, whose bloated body leaks into numerous atrophied limbs, but which has no head and no arms can neither walk nor stand nor act."[6] Every grain trader in Europe understood the "patchwork" and "bloated limbs" in the food delivery system of this agricultural empire. Trade between provinces was heavily taxed— grain was taxed when it came in, and flour was taxed on its way out—and grain traders could be arrested for usury if they made too large a profit. The internal trade lines for grain, even up the beautifully efficient Danube, were knotted and tangled by complex rules. An overbearing suspicion of Jewish grain traders, according to economist Victor Heller, strongly influenced Austria's internal trade regulations.[7]

Austria's "kaiser extract" fell before the kaiser did. By 1877, millers in Minneapolis, Saint Louis, and Racine, Wisconsin, were touring Budapest's factories and attempting to reproduce the Hungarian method—which required thousands of laborers—on an industrial scale using waterpower. Wisconsin senator Robert Hall Baker described his snooping in Budapest in some detail. In 1878 he found "one engineer here [who] showed my brother plans he had underway for a large mill in America," he wrote. "I presume," he noted darkly, "it is for Minneapolis."[8] Engineers first tried steam-powered grain mills in America, but they failed catastrophically. A sparking steam engine too close to flour dust could ignite into a fireball able to level a city block, as happened in the Washburn mills of downtown Minneapolis in 1878, killing eighteen workers.[9] By 1881, after a number of explosive failures around the country, Americans had created a semiautomated Hungarian process and were selling hundreds of thousands of barrels of flour in London and Liverpool. The prices were so low that both British and Austrian firms accused them of "dumping" it on the British market. By 1885 Europeans in consumption-accumulation cities had reverse-engineered the use of labor-saving machinery in new rolling mills created expressly for foreign grain. Hungarian-method port mills sprang up in Liverpool, Hull, and London, as well as in Antwerp, Leuven, and Rotterdam on the Continent.[10] The Hungarian secret was out, and the closely protected Austrian export industry flagged and stumbled. The Austrian state's continued injection of capital into its flour industry only turned Austria into "a beggar's coat." Austria-Hungary was indeed becoming a "shapeless being." The flour milling industry fully collapsed in 1905.[11]

The Ottoman Empire was an agricultural empire, like the Austrian Empire, and also taxed internal trade with fixed prices, police regulation of grain, and powerful flour millers' and bakers' guilds. But there were important differences between the two. Austria exported flour, while the Ottoman Empire kept its grain inside, exporting mostly tobacco and dates. Catherine the Great's innovative use of grain markets to defeat the Ottomans in the 1780s had led the sultan's financial advisors to abandon fixed prices on military purchases of grain. That said, the internal taxation of grain remained a key part of how the empire supported itself until 1911.[12] High food prices inside the empire weakened it. Cheap external grain smuggled into the empire continued to be a problem for the Ottoman Empire, particularly as railroads allowed cheap American flour to bypass internal customs agents and benefit entrepreneurial bread sellers.[13]

More significantly, the Ottoman Empire's decline had less to do with flour-making secrets than with its inability to control its own taxes. Its loss of autonomy had a more straightforward cause: the British Empire. Between 1838 and 1911, the Ottoman Empire had become locked in the fiscal orbit of Great Britain. The difficulties started in 1833, when Sultan Mahmud II faced a revolt by his Egyptian governor, Muhammad Ali, which threatened to end the empire. Only hasty Russian intervention prevented Ali's capture of Istanbul itself. Reeling from this threat, Mahmud II sought the support of the British navy. In 1838 he signed the unequal treaty of Balti Limani with Britain, which made Turkey a kind of fiscal vassal to Great Britain. British merchants received free access to Ottoman markets with no corresponding Ottoman access to English markets. In return for this enormous favor, Britain helped the Ottomans beat back Egyptian forces, most famously with the 1840 British bombardment of Acre in Jerusalem. Thereafter cheap foreign flour and textiles imported by English merchants continually weakened the Ottoman Empire's internal industries, which had no ability to slow down imports. The empire imported more than it exported for the rest of its days. To make up for the loss of tariffs, it increased taxes on the Balkan states, adding fuel to the fire of independence movements in Serbia, Bulgaria, Wallachia, and Moldavia. Britain's ability to bypass an empire's tariffs became a model for squeezing resources out of Asia, Africa, and the Pacific thereafter.[14]

Cheap grain from abroad, high internal grain taxes, and tax-favored foreign imports cannot explain everything about the fate of the Turkish and Austro-Hungarian empires in nineteenth-century Europe. Yet both agricultural empires suffered from competition, direct and indirect, as cheap grain arrived from the Black Sea in the 1840s and the Atlantic in the 1860s. As the ability to draw resources from their own grain trades declined, so did the power of their once mighty empires.

OTHER EUROPEAN EMPIRES learned to gorge on imported grain and became great powers. Germany and Italy built deepwater ports and subsidized internal railway networks that facilitated the inward importation and distribution of foreign grain and other follow-on foods that could take advantage of port mills (including pork, butter, and beef). Railroad building and low tariff barriers were explicit policies of Italian prime minister Camillo Benso, Count of Cavour. By the 1880s, however, to slow down the burden of Ricardo's paradox, the falling price of agricultural land, these states imposed tariffs on imported grain. Taxes on imported wheat slowed the fall in agricultural rent, though limiting foreign price competition may have weakened agricultural innovation in those states.[15] But taxing the vast quantities of foreign grain that came in after 1846 also engorged the national budgets of these and other grain-importing states.

While the physiocratic empires of Russia and the United States had most of their wealth on their edges, European states, like Germany and Italy, that consumed and taxed cheap grain strengthened and concentrated wealth in their capitals. The gullet cities that prospered from cheap food tried to fight back. Millers and other processors of grain inside European gullet cities resisted grain tariffs at first but then agreed upon a complex new system of exclusions and transformations for grain. The states introduced a "drawback" for all grain used to make exported flour. In France, for example, a miller who exported ten thousand sacks of flour to a French colony in 1892 received a drawback certificate for $2,900, which grain traders bought to reduce their tariff expenses. In this way a grain tax could be reduced if the resulting flour, bread, and biscuit produced in gullet cities could be exported to a hungry world outside Europe.[16] Grain tariffs helped build railroads and battleships. European states would fight over potential markets in Asia, Africa, and the Pacific. Processing food from across the ocean and selling it abroad became the new work of European states.

The intimate connection between grain and empire is sometimes difficult to see, though its milestones are everywhere. When Prussia moved its capital from Königsberg to Berlin in 1701, architects built a grand marble column. It was to be mile marker zero for the center of the empire. A marker like this one had deep historical resonance. In 20 BC, the emperor Caesar Augustus had erected an obelisk in Rome called the Milliarium Aureum: the golden milestone. Smaller obelisks—milestones—marked every mile to the empire's edge. All roads led to Rome because the armies built them that way. When Byzantine Roman proconsul Constantine saw Rome's decline in 330, he had a new column erected in Byzantium. The city was soon rededicated as Constantinople—Constantine's city—and called the new capital of the Roman Empire.

Almost a thousand years later, French and Prussian kings, each claiming the mantle of Rome, established markers like these in their capital cities, though they may not have fully understood their significance. Italy relied on the ancient milestones of Rome. France's stands in front of the Notre-Dame cathedral near the Tuileries, the imperial residence. Berlin's golden milestone was erected on a bridge near the remains of a fortified castle. In 1730 the court planted elaborate statuary there, renaming it Dönhoffplatz to honor Alexander von Dönhoff, a Prussian hero in the War of Spanish Succession (1701–1714) whose army had beaten back French forces under Louis XIV. Until 2000, Germany's state-drawn maps of Europe marked every city's distance from Berlin's mile marker. Battle plans for every major conflict in Germany relied on them. Only by 2000, well after German reunification, did the German government change its golden milepost to the Brandenburg Gate.

These latter-day emperors may have failed to understand that Rome's milestones marked the distance not from the seat of power but from the empire's golden harvest: its warehouses of grain. Public grain warehouses, called *horrea*, lay clustered around the golden milepost. A mile (*mille passus*) was originally one thousand paces of a Roman soldier, a pace being two steps. Ancient military strategists seldom used maps but instead planned strategy using a long list of outposts with mile numbers beside them. The endpoint marked the distance in miles from Rome's grain to the enemy. Just as in Parvus's story, grain slowly disappeared as it fed the slaves and the oxen transporting them. For this reason Rome's military strategists used milestones as a measure of the tollage required to get to a spot. The milestones simultaneously measured distance, labor, time, and the empire's outer limits, every outpost an increasingly expensive defensible position away from Rome's stored grain, its golden center.[17]

A welfare state emerged in ancient Rome as a way of minimizing the chaos that a trading city, filled with landless workers, could generate. Once a year hundreds of tons of grain pulsed into the Roman Empire, arriving at the central milestone. About a month after the harvest, at an event called the *annona*, the grain in the capital was measured. In the third century BC, all citizens and soldiers received a coin once per month and thereafter exchanged these coins for grain. By the second century AD, the empire was delivering the monthly allotment of grain as bread, free to Roman citizens. By then a general market had grown up around the mile marker for additional purchases. As the Roman Empire expanded its military roads to the capital (*capita viarum*), these highways bore soldiers, material, and food outward in wars of expansion. Berlin and Paris, despite pretensions to imperial greatness, lacked the pulse of grain and the proximity to ocean traffic that archaeologists and historians deemed vital for ancient empires like Rome.[18]

Prussia's milepost zero is now an overgrown, mostly forsaken park filled with rubbish. Modern Germans' abandonment of this golden marker is not hard to explain. In the 1930s, when the Nazis came to power, Adolph Hitler imagined a Third Reich that radiated outward from Berlin's golden milestone and so built the chancellor's headquarters a few blocks away from it.

With Hitler's defeat, Russian military forces rushed to occupy the center of the Third Reich. As Russia's "Iron Curtain" fell across Europe, the Soviets demanded that the Reich's mile marker stay on the Russian-controlled side of the city. The monument remained in the Soviet-occupied portion of East Berlin for forty years. By the 1960s the German Democratic Republic had removed all statues commemorating kings and princes. Then, after the Berlin Wall came down in 1989, the map of Europe changed again. A cracked sign next to the mile marker declares that when Berlin reunited, the Berlin Borough Assembly decided to keep the name Dönhof-platz for the square but rededicated the mile marker to a liberal dissident, herself a descendent of the Prussian officer. Countess Marion Dönhoff had left university when the Nazis came in the 1930s, may have participated in an attempt to assassinate Hitler, and after World War II served as editor of a liberal Berlin newspaper. A few of the old monuments came back to the square, but they were crammed together in a tiny space, giving the park the appearance of a cemetery whose sexton had absentmindedly moved the headstones around.

THIS DESIRE TO improve internal channels of grain delivery motivated the Prussian state from its very beginning in 1871. The Prussian army, once it took Alsace-Lorraine, had an embarrassing problem. Most of Alsace-Lorraine drew grain from Belgian Antwerp, which came in turn from the Atlantic Ocean. While recognizing that Germany at the moment of its creation depended on foreign grain, the army felt the state's continuity depended on slowing it down. Antwerp could feed German troops in 1870, but it was a fickle port city that could feed any army, even serving as the depot for a land-based invasion of the European continent. Britain understood this as well. Indeed, just as Germany's invasion of France began, Britain had announced to both parties that neutral Belgium, with its grain port at Antwerp, was off-limits and that thirty thousand British troops were prepared to land to keep the port open. If either Prussia or France invaded Belgium, Britain swore it would join the other side. Eighty years before, Napoleon Bonaparte had controlled Antwerp, the pistol aimed at the heart of Britain. This threat would not be repeated.[19]

Grain collection ports like Rome, Antwerp, Istanbul, and New York had the potential to capture massive amounts of grain, which made empires anxious about them. For European empires, a small state around the port of Antwerp was safe; a shrinking empire around Istanbul was also safe.[20] Historians of European empire have argued that the partition of Africa during the "scramble" for that continent in the 1880s obeyed this dictum: find a port city first, then its river. These could be the foundation of a powerful state. As a result, historians have argued, Britain and other European empires ensured that the rivers would be "free zones." No African state (or empire that claimed African territory) was allowed to control both a large agrarian region and both sides of a major river. After decolonization most rivers remained as dividing lines between rival states. Egypt was the lone exception.[21] So while the grain port of Antwerp was an attractive prize for a German Empire assembling itself in 1871, it was both a threat and a prize in the eyes of other empires, particularly Britain, France, Spain, and the Netherlands.

For landlords in the parts of Germany and Italy that had previously provided grain, the flood of cheap food from the Americas was a longer-lasting problem. A new international division of labor centered in the Atlantic Ocean lowered the international price for grain, driving down the value of European land and putting Prussian landowners and farmers in an impossible position. This was Ricardo's paradox: improvements drove down agricultural land prices. Landlords in eastern Germany sarcastically elaborated on the new normal after the Agrarian Crisis. It was said that every farmer in Brandenburg needed to learn a new crop rotation: "wheat, rye, mortgage, pistol."[22]

Landlords demanded taxes on imported grain and special rates on railroads. The German Empire attempted to respond to the difficulties posed by cheap Atlantic food by retracting inward like a turtle, supporting internal trade with cheap travel over nationalized railways while slowing and profiting from the flood of cheap food.[23] A new coalition of anti–free trade landlords created the German Conservative Party in 1876. Critics later mockingly called industrialists and landlords who built the new party a "union of iron and rye" because they taxed imported metal and grain, benefiting both manufacturers and farmers.

The most direct antagonists of a grain tariff were workers, particularly the social democrats, who strongly supported cheap food from across the Atlantic. Modern scholars tend to forget that Marxist parties all over Europe enthusiastically supported free trade and that only the most conservative trade unions supported tariffs. In 1878, using the excuse that anarchists had tried to kill William I, Germany's imperial chancellor, Otto von Bismarck—the first chancellor of the German Empire—banned the Social Democratic Party from campaigning, giving speeches, or operating newspapers. The banning of social democrats shifted the political balance in Germany, making it possible for Germany to tax German workers' food.[24]

The conservatives' plan to rebuild a German Empire centered on Berlin was carefully calibrated. Besides "providing the Empire with new sources of revenue," Bismarck said, a tariff on imported grain would be simple to enforce. His proposal: cover the entrances into the empire with tariffs, slow down foreign grain by imposing higher transportation costs on it, then subsidize the internal movement of food.[25] Truly slowing down food imports through the deepwater ports of Antwerp and Rotterdam proved difficult by 1878 because not just grain but also flour, refrigerated beef, and canned meats threatened European landlords.

In 1879 the newly formed center-right government intervened even more in internal trade. It simultaneously imposed tariffs on imported grain while nationalizing central railroad corridors. Privately owned railroads, the government argued, could never have the interests of the state at heart. Anti-Semites in both the liberal and conservative parties argued that Jews owned the most important corridors and had caused the 1873 depression.[26] "According to my opinion," declared Bismarck, "we are slowly bleeding to death owing to insufficient protection. . . . Let us close our doors and erect some barriers in order to reserve for German industries at least the home market."[27]

Conservatives in the empire also sought to improve grain production east of the mile marker in Berlin, but that part was sadly deficient. After extensive investigations into American grain farming and marketing between 1881 and 1883, the Prussian government created a Prussian Settlement Commission. It would buy up large Polish-owned estates east of Berlin. This was the area taken in the partition of Poland in the 1790s, in what is now Poland between Gdansk and Poznan. The estates would be broken up into farms of approximately thirty-five acres each, modeled on midwestern American farms, and parceled out to German farmers. This was a mistake; these were far too small for mechanization. The plan was to directly compete with American grain, building out an imperial middle ground that could send grain to Berlin from the east. The final cost by 1918 was over a billion deutsche marks, though the effect on the Prussian grain supply was laughably tiny.[28]

Conservative scholars in Germany then lined up to reinvent the history of ancient empires to suit the new doctrine of imperial self-sufficiency. Heinrich von Treitschke, a history professor and member of the Prussian Reichstag, crafted a history of the world's empires that justified Germany's turn toward high tariffs. In his influential lectures, later published as *Politics*, he stated that

Macedon had overrun the Greeks because the Greeks were too cosmopolitan. The Roman Empire had fallen afterward, he continued, because it imported cheap grain from Africa: "If protection against the import of corn from Asia and Africa had been introduced at the right time the old agricultural class would not have perished and social conditions would have remained healthy. Instead of this Roman merchants were suffered to buy the cheap African grain, thus bringing distress upon the peasants of Italy . . . which made a desert of the Campagna, the very heart of the country." Cosmopolitanism and international trade, he continued, threatened empires old and new. Treitschke reinforced his already shaky claim with outright anti-Semitism. The crucial corrosive force for every ancient empire was the Jews: "what a dangerous disintegrating force lurked in this people who were able to assume the mask of any nationality."[29]

Besides blaming Jews and free trade, German conservatives blamed the courier: privately owned railroads that supported themselves by bringing oceans of American grain into Europe's city centers. Merchants floated foreign grain up the Rhine from Antwerp, where railroads obligingly delivered this dangerous cheap food to industrial city centers, particularly in the western states in Germany's federal republic. Full national control of railroads, the conservatives hoped, would block the pressure of cheap grain from outside German borders and sustain the golden milestone in Berlin.[30]

Yet Germany's new taxes on grain, because of the most-favored nation agreements between countries, could not be easily or instantly applied. Taxes would have to be imposed, and foreign ministers would have to slowly revoke the tangle of bilateral agreements Germany had with foreign nations.

Taxing the flood of foreign grain was not just a sop to landowners. The tariff had important benefits for state building in filling federal coffers. Tariffs and railway charges together made up the two largest sources of revenue in the Prussian budget. Both kinds of grain taxes—tariffs and high railroad rates for foreign grain passing through Germany—gave the empire a fund to buy off the smaller federal principalities that resisted the German Empire's authority.[31] German economists at the time justified the military rather than the economic advantages of grain tariffs, though as economists they recognized that cheap food benefited everyone who was not a landlord. They noted that, by 1881, the "double danger" of cheap food and cheap transport had allowed England's agriculturalists to dwindle to fewer than 8.5 percent of the population compared to a European average of between 35 and 69 percent. Only by taxing cheap grain could Germany escape the threat of starvation in case of war.[32] Just as importantly, the tax on cheap grain from abroad allowed Germany and Italy to build up war budgets without raising taxes on land. Cheap grain built European states, but it also gave them the resources to kill people.

Prussian economists further emphasized that giving preferential rates to internal trade allowed a synergy to build up between industry and agriculture. And it is certainly true that industrial by-products and chemical fertilizers improved crop yields somewhat.[33] The revolutionary Haber-Bosch process, a further refinement of the human understanding of the nitrogen cycle, grew out of intense German research into crop yields.

But the theory that tariffs would help productivity falls apart on close inspection. It would be decades before the Haber-Bosch process could be used to produce higher yields. And even with nitrogen fertilizer, the sandy soil of Brandenburg could never be turned into the black soil of Kansas or Podolia.[34] Twenty-eight years after Germany's grain tariffs were erected, Parvus ruefully declared that by separating the empire from the world market, they delayed improvements in Prussian agriculture by a quarter century.

"Here we have a stark example," Parvus thundered, "of how the politics of the capitalist state contradict the interests of capitalist development."[35]

Turtling around golden mile markers had perverse effects outside Germany. Germany's grain tariffs did more to hinder grain exports from the other agricultural empires in Europe than they did from the United States. Shipments arriving by rail from Russian-controlled Poland or through German ports like Hamburg nearly ground to a halt after the grain tariffs, according to the chambers of commerce in Germany's port cities. Increasingly Russian grain was driven farther northeast and southwest of Germany, around the path of Germany's grain-blocking, nationally controlled railways.[36] Foreign wheat had fed the Prussian army that annexed Alsace-Lorraine and solidified Germany's empire in 1871. But once solidified, the Prussian state, like the legendary fool King Canute, tried to command the oceans to stop their tides. While the new taxes and railroad rates fed the national state, they increased tensions inside it, tensions that buyoffs could never fully soothe. Southern and western industrial regions liked the cheap grain from Antwerp, as it lowered labor costs. European landlords in grain-growing regions, mostly in the north and east, continued to complain that the grain never really stopped coming. Tariffs could hardly stop the waves of Atlantic food spilling into Prussia and only distorted the effects. The German tariff of 1879, first 10 percent of the grain's value, then upward of 30 percent, only slowed the influx.[37]

French farmers and landlords too resented the cheap grain from the Americas. The French tariff, established in 1881, started like Germany's at around 10 percent of the grain's value, then rose in 1885 and again in 1887.[38] By the end of the century, France, Italy, and Germany taxed foreign grain at just over one-third its price at the port. As in Germany, France used this foreign bounty to invest heavily in infrastructure. The so-called Plan Freycinet, launched by

French minister of public works Charles de Freycinet, guaranteed over four billion francs in bonds issued to build railways and canals to connect rural regions to French cities. As in Germany, the plan to tax American and Russian grain to improve the black paths connecting France's urban centers to its backcountry both strengthened the state and enjoyed strong support from rural regions.[39]

Grain power could fuel the national expansion of the great powers, but taxing imported grain could only prolong the effect of Ricardo's paradox. Land prices fell in rural areas in Europe, starting at the time of the grain invasion at the end of the American Civil War and lasting through the rest of the century.[40] Steam-powered grain mowers would continue to cut down the cheapest wheat on the steppe in South Russia, as well as in the northern plains of the United States and soon Canada, the Argentinian pampas, and the eastern and western edges of Australia. The greatest beneficiaries of the increasing technological sophistication of grain growing—and the resultant cheapening of food—proved to be workers between the 1840s and the 1870s and then, after the Agrarian Crisis of the 1870s, the so-called great powers of Europe. These "grain powers of Europe" increasingly poached this bounty to bind their nations to golden mile markers with tracks of iron, to subsidize connections between the countryside and the city, and to seek military adventures abroad.

THE GERMAN AND French tariffs after 1879 to 1881 strongly bent the world's grain pathways. The German state imposed high tariffs and charged higher railroad rates on grain coming across the border from the east. As Germany tried to force the benefit of cheap foreign grain into state coffers, the traders adjusted the black paths along ingenious routes that eluded Germany's exorbitant railroad rates for foreign grain. To escape these high prices, Russian grain traders increasingly moved grain north to Baltic ports, then over water to ports on the Baltic and North Seas. As a result the grain that had once fed Germany directly over the Russo-German border now rode on subsidized Russian lines, left Russian ports on the Baltic Sea, and then dipped back into German ports. The added distance over water would render Germany's food supply of Russian grain vulnerable in wartime.

In addition, besides providing the income to produce new and costly battleships, the new tariffs gave European states a perverse incentive to seize markets in Africa, Asia, and the Middle East. Because imported grain could avoid the German and French tariffs if millers and bakers reexported grain products, port-city millers jumped through this loophole. If European states could locate export markets for European flour, they could continue to import cheap grain. European exports of milled products—flour, biscuits, pasta, and cookies, for example—received a tariff drawback that exceeded the amount of grain that went into making them.[41] In this way grain that came into Europe either fed the growth of European military capacity (by tariff) or subsidized European adventures abroad by providing bounties to port mills and factories if they exported flour, biscuits, and pasta to imperial holdings. The beneficiaries were re-exporters of flour, a corrupt customs infrastructure, and the military arms of imperial states. Dreams of imperial markets flourished in chambers of commerce in the port cities of France, Germany, the Netherlands, Austria-Hungary, and Belgium.

Antwerp and Rotterdam's adoption of the Hungarian milling method compounded Germany's attempt to slow cheap grain coming from the Atlantic. By the 1880s these cities produced white flour vastly cheaper than flour coming from inside Germany or Austria-Hungary. As grain prices and rents dropped further, a "Second Depression" hit Germany beginning in autumn 1882. Both Germany and France had quadrupled their grain tariffs by 1885. Attempts to respond to low prices for grain led to an all-out tariff war between Germany and Russia, which heated up from

1885 to 1890. By 1887 German exports to Russia had dropped almost 50 percent from 1880 levels.[42]

Beginning around 1878, the empires lashed outward; the mile marker could not hold. European brutality in the desire for overseas colonies was not new of course, but after 1879 violence in the name of opening markets reached shocking levels, including in the Anglo-Zulu war of 1879, the French conquest of Tunisia in 1881, the Russian capture of the region east of the Caspian Sea from Iran in 1881, the British occupation of Egypt in 1882, and the continuing Dutch war against the Aceh in Indonesia. European states established brutal colonial governments throughout Asia, Africa, and the Middle East. This was the scramble for Africa, the scramble for Asia, and the Great Game in the Middle East. Prosperous European states battled one another for imperial markets.

The benefits of this scramble for empire appeared illusory, however. Free trade economist John A. Hobson made the case most strongly that the scramble for Africa, Asia, and the Middle East had few benefits and many costs. He estimated that in 1900 the total British trade with British possessions or dependencies in Africa, Asia, and the Middle East totaled only £9 million, "while the expenses connected directly and indirectly with the acquisition, administration and defence of these possessions swallow[ed] an immeasurably larger sum."[43] Imperialism in Africa, the Middle East, and Asia, considered as a whole, may have made little economic sense since Europe's best trading partners were the United States, Russia, and other European states, and he did not fully understand how the customs infrastructure created perverse bounties for imperial expansion.

If European empires found a way to respond to the promise and prospect of cheap food by cranking up armies and navies, the story was different for the Ottoman and Qing empires, which struggled against cheap foreign food that drained their empires of gold and silver. Subjects of the Qing Empire, especially in its port cities, bought enormous quantities of California flour and its products, leading urban diets to shift from rice or noodles to bread and cakes.[44] These two empires mortgaged their futures on international bond markets. To compete with the German, French, British, and Italian empires, the Ottoman and Qing empires issued bonds and laid impossibly long railroads, built deepwater ports, and funded trading fleets. They borrowed and borrowed with little oversight.[45] The Ottoman and Qing empires, to pay their ever-growing infrastructure bills, allowed international firms to take over their tax collection, a dangerous step. The Chinese Maritime Customs Service (founded 1854) was technically international, but nearly all its agents were British. Its officers taxed junks that crossed the Yellow Sea but exempted British-owned steamships. The Ottoman Public Debt Administration (OPDA), founded 1881, was an organization elected by British, French, and German bondholders, though, according to Parvus, the French administrators were strongest inside it. Each tax agency had its own internal police force and had nearly complete autonomy inside the state. The Ottoman sultan could inspect the books of the OPDA's salt and tobacco monopolies, and the Qing emperor could do the same for internal customs inside China, but neither could alter the manner and method of tax collection. They were effectively European-controlled tax-gathering entities—states within states—that guaranteed Ottoman and Chinese imperial bonds and slowly paid off the debts contracted by the agricultural empires. Parvus's later discoveries about the way the OPDA effectively controlled the Ottoman Empire and helped drive it to destruction became key to the arguments Rosa Luxemburg and Vladimir Lenin would make about the dangers of imperialism.[46]

The autocratic Russian Empire responded differently to the threat of cheap American grain. Like the Ottoman and Chinese agencies, the Russo-Chinese Bank, formed in the summer of 1895, would collect railway fares, freights, and customs on its expanding eastern possessions. While the bank was technically an organ of French bondholders in Russia's Asian provinces, the tsar demanded veto power over its actions, and Russian finance minister Sergei Witte ensured that all bank correspondence took place in Russian. Whereas the state-within-a-state functions arguably hindered the Russian and Qing empires, the Russo-Chinese Bank's agents succeeded in advancing Russia's imperial interests. The Russo-Chinese Bank helped orchestrate forcing Japan to give up territory it won from China in the Sino-Japanese War, the vital Liaodong Peninsula on the Yellow Sea.[47] But as we shall see, Russia's gambit of using powerful bondholders to push its interests forward in the Pacific would fail catastrophically. The Ottoman, Qing, and Russian empires endeavored to strengthen their internal logistical pathways for food, though by World War I these independent taxing entities had helped drive them to destruction. By 1914, these empires would collapse.

A SMALL GROUP of international revolutionaries, Parvus foremost, envisioned a different center of the world than the imperial markers in Rome and Istanbul, Berlin and Paris. Parvus's marker is located on a little island on the Havel River about thirteen miles southwest of the Dönhoff monument. Though not on any tourist map of Germany, it is an interesting, alternative, radical pole stuck in the heart of the world. While the marker is in front of Parvus's house, the signs near the monument credit a real estate developer who sold him the land. Even proving the obelisk is Parvus's is difficult because he destroyed his records before he died. But the marker in his front yard is nonetheless a monument in its own right, a column lifted from the French imperial residence, the Tuileries, which revolutionaries had occupied between 1789 and 1792, in 1830 and again in 1848, and finally between 1870 and 1871, when Communards burned the imperial palace to the ground. For Parvus, this ruined imperial foundation marked his golden milepost for world revolution and an end to the grain-powered "great powers" of Europe.

Parvus died hundreds of feet from his column in 1922, but not before having—more so than any French or German emperor—redrawn the world's nodes, ports, and capitals. He hardly did it himself, but he understood better than his contemporaries that because empires depended on invisible lines of imported grain, they were weaker than their boastful statuary suggested. The world's pivot points are not made by proclamations or even battles; rather they stand on the foundations that underlie the roads leading to and from every empire in the world; they mark out where the people's food is and how long it takes to get it to soldiers and citizens. Unless this basic logistical problem is solved, an empire will starve, and starving empires can be toppled or revolutionized.

Beginning with his 1891 dissertation and continuing with his 1895 article "The World Market and the Agrarian Crisis," Parvus argued that cheap American food had changed the world's food roads, bringing Europe its crisis in 1873. When he arrived in Berlin in 1892, he understood that these self-proclaimed empires were responding to these food roads by building battleships and submarines. The agrarian empires in particular—Russian, Ottoman, Qing, and Habsburg—might not survive in a world where oceans of grain could stream from Odessa, New York, or San Francisco to whatever ocean port had the gold to pay for it.

Eleven

"RUSSIA IS THE SHAME OF EUROPE"
1882-1909

B ETWEEN THE AGE of ancient empires and the age of imperialism, wars had depended on hoarded energy: first in *horrea*, then in banks, then in assignats, and finally in bonds. In the ancient Mediterranean, armies depended on the productivity of an empire's inner ring. Grain moved outward to armies and navies; grain moved inward to the *horrea*, the grain banks around the golden milestone. The golden milestone was the empire's center, which fed the imperial city's defenders in cases of siege. With the emergence of capitalist city-states in Italy, grain and banks were separated, and grain became increasingly abstract. Bills of exchange represented grain in motion. Merchants bought and sold them, their prices rising—and occasionally falling—in the weeks before the grain reached the warehouse. With Catherine the Great the assignat functioned as a new kind of currency, a bet on the success of Russian arms. Banks remained vital to empires, their notes circulating in cities, their promises representing energy that lay trapped, as kernels of wheat, in ports and on the ocean. By the latter part of the nineteenth-century, grain growing and state expansion became intertwined in the part of the grain-delivering world that surrounded Europe. In Russia, the harvest included famine and violence.

After cheap food began circulating around the world in the 1850s, and after serfdom ended in the 1860s, two of Russia's finance ministers forged new credit pathways for planting and harvesting Russian grain. Wheat farmers on large estates increasingly used plowing machinery to blanket the Russian steppe with grain and an army of peasant laborers to harvest it. These farmers needed credit, which they soon got from something akin to America's "line system" of credit that connected line agents, elevators, railroads, banks, and grain brokers. Independent agents, called the *skrupchiki* in South Russia, could offer credit for future grain to smaller farmers. For the grain farmers on the largest estates, credit for future sales came from city agents of the largest grain-trading firms. By the 1880s this line system provided Russia credit for expansion and cheapened the tollage needed to get grain to the ocean.

In around 1881, the Russian finance ministry attempted to improve, engulf, and control this line system. It issued credit to farmers nearest the railway hubs, sold railway and imperial bonds on international markets, and relied on extremely creative accounting to make this appear natural. A tightly wound grain-spitting apparatus improved Russia's competitive position in the grain markets of Europe. But the finance ministry's draconian tax system, which squeezed peasants' tiny reserves of capital, turned a drought into a famine along the Volga River in 1891. Parvus and other Russian social democrats devoted themselves to explaining and exposing the Russian state's autocratic grain-delivery apparatus even as the finance ministry began its boldest plan ever: to build a grain-powered railway through Siberia all the way to the Liaodong Peninsula. Crisis came when the Empire of Japan determined to check Russia's expansion. Japan's military intervention and Russia's humiliating defeat drove Russia into revolution.

CREDIT FOR RUSSIAN grain expansion came from the least likely place: Russia's former enemy, republican France. France's cooperative financial institutions were hungry to help. French cooperative banking did not protect the country from the German invasion and war in 1870, but it did ensure that France would quickly rebuild after the emperor abdicated and France became a republic again. The German Empire demanded reparations for the war it had started. French citizens quickly oversubscribed the bonds to pay them off. In 1870 almost 1.3 million French citizens held French state bonds; six years later 4.4 million citizens held them, a large proportion of them in the capital city of Paris.[1] The French Republic, largely through its own citizens' savings and investment banks, became, after its defeat, a powerful international force. A desire for revenge against Germany mattered in France, but alliance with a tsar curdled the blood of many French republicans. Excess capital mattered, and the French Republic could never absorb all of French citizens' passion for investment for long-term gains. In 1850 French investors' foreign assets amounted to 53 percent of the country's national income, a larger percentage of national income invested abroad than in Britain. By 1890 French investment abroad was 110 percent of national income.[2]

The Russian Empire despised the French Republic, but it needed the investment. In comparison to France, Russia had a tiny collection of private banks that struggled to raise capital for trade even before the Agrarian Crisis of the 1870s had caused the tsar to stop chartering new banks.[3] A grain market centered in Odessa had formed at the end of the previous century, but the protracted end of serfdom after 1861 restructured the market profoundly. The tsar's emancipation plan required serfs to pay for their freedom and their land in rubles, which forced peasants to sell grain or, more often, their labor. The beneficiaries of this transformation were a relatively small group of literate, mechanically minded agriculturalists who used hundreds of workers to reshape the landscape of the steppe.[4]

One such grain farmer was David Leontyevich Bronstein, a Jewish farmer in Kherson province who owned over 250 acres of steppe land and leased four hundred more from landowners nearby.

Decades later his son Lev would take the name Leon Trotsky. For the elder Bronstein, raising, harvesting, and marketing hundreds of thousands of pounds of wheat in a region with few skilled industrial workers required capital. Operating a machine shop was perhaps the largest single cost. His shop repaired tractors and sleighs, sharpened plows, and operated as the headquarters of a partially automated farm in the middle of what was a nearly pathless steppe when Trotsky was born. Few Jews were farmers, but David Bronstein's parents had taken up farming around the time of peasant emancipation. Many of Ukraine's prosperous farmers were newcomers in one way or another. Some were former serfs from farther north; others were "Russian Germans" who had escaped religious persecution in Germany a century earlier; others were Cossacks who moved from beekeeping and herding into planting and harvesting grain. South Russia (now Ukraine) was very different from the rest of Russia. Before emancipation in 1860, more than two-thirds of the peasant farmers on the steppe were already free.[5]

In some ways these farmers on the Russian steppe resembled the successful farmer-mechanics who built sod houses on the Great Plains. Because the Russian steppe had few trees, farmers surrounded by grass had to build without wood as well. Trotsky remembered that the Bronstein farm had "two enormous sheds hundreds of feet long, one [made] of reeds and the other of straw, built in the shape of a gabled roof resting directly on the ground, without walls. The fresh grain was piled under these sheds, and here the men worked with winnowers and sieves in rainy or windy weather. Beyond the sheds lay the threshing-floor. Across a ravine lay the cowpen, its walls built entirely of dry manure."[6]

Trotsky called his first home on the Ukrainian plains "Russian America" and farms like his father's "wheat factories."[7] The slang term for this class of prosperous farmers was *kulak*, the Russian word for "fist" or "claw." Russian imperial economists called them "economically strong peasants," as relatively few had ever had a title or owned serfs.[8]

These farmers also needed labor. Every year kulaks collectively employed hundreds of thousands of young peasants, including serfs who, after the redemption of 1861, were trying to pay off their own land. Their sons and daughters came with them. They left farms north of Kherson province every May, traveling for four months in the southern provinces to work the harvest. "Some of them," Trotsky recalled, "appeared at the head of a long family procession. They walked from their own provinces on foot, taking a whole month to make the journey, living on crusts of bread, and spending the nights in the market-places." Like landless laborers in the American Midwest, these human "reapers," as they were called in the United States, followed the grain as it fruited, cutting and binding it for distant markets.[9] The quarters for Russian "reapers" were decidedly temporary, according to Trotsky. "The open field was their home in fine weather, in bad weather they took shelter under the haystacks. For dinner they had vegetable soup and porridge, for supper millet soup. They never had any meat. Vegetable fat was all they ever got, and that in small quantities." The reapers staged frequent strikes, but Trotsky recalled their ineffectiveness. "Then my father would give them some clabber, or water melons, or half a sack of dried fish, and they would go back to work again, often singing. These were the conditions on all the farms," Trotsky wrote defensively. The reapers would then depart for their homes on October 1.[10]

To pay for machinery and laborers, kulaks increasingly relied on credit from financial intermediaries, including grain warehouses and banks, though Russia's banking infrastructure was minimal compared to the rest of Europe and the United States. Banking inside Russia continued to be informal, with multiple middlemen, in part because literacy in Russia was so low. Odessan moneylenders, or *skrupchiki*—many of them Jews—were the first part of the credit chain. They traveled into the South Russian countryside before the harvest to offer paper rubles for farmers' standing crops. The moneylenders paid for and oversaw the wheat's arrival in Odessa, Mikolaiv, Rostov-on-Don, or Sebastopol.

Owners of prosperous warehouses were the next link in the chain of credit. Warehousemen gave loans to the *skrupchiki*, taking warrants (*varranty*) for wheat ready for harvest or en route. These *varranty* resembled futures contracts but were much less uniform. Instead of trading them on an open floor, warehouse owners brought them to commercial banks for further loans, though the warrants were not made enforceable contracts until the 1880s. A particularly wealthy or literate farmer, like David Bronstein, would have bypassed the *skrupchiki* and dealt directly with a warehouse or, if he had many thousands of bushels of grain, a commission agent in Odessa.

Warehouses sold grain as ten thirty-three-pound sacks (collectively called a *chetvert*) to commission agents, who then sold them to grain brokers permanently stationed near telegraph stations at Odessa and other Black Sea ports. After 1865 many grain brokers, including Louis-Dreyfus & Co., J. Bunge & Co., and M. Neufeld & Co. of Berlin, bypassed both agents and warehouses by purchasing their own warehouses near cities.

The chain of buyers—broker, agent, warehouse, *skrupchiki*, farmer—was longer than in the United States, but enterprising brokers or agents could always bypass a step or two if prices were rising or quantities on hand were low. An adventurous agent might travel into the countryside to meet with the largest grain farmers. A broker occasionally acted as his own agent. Some part of these transactions passed through the Odessa bourse, or commodities market. While it helped establish prices for local contracts, Odessa's bourse was never an authority as powerful as the Chicago Board of Trade. Like the Chicago Board, it published a daily price

based on a hundred or more transactions, which allowed negotia-
tors to contract at a fraction above or below the day's listed price.[11]

This system of multiple buyers and sellers dispersed risks among
partners who depended on two things that, it turned out, could not
survive the breakneck competition of the 1870s: a stable interest
rate and a stable ruble. The Moscow Loan Bank, Odessa's largest,
had been making loans to landed gentry on the prospect of further grain sales. Prices plummeted in 1873, and it finally closed
its doors in 1875, leading to a cascade of bank failures throughout
the empire. The Moscow Loan Bank's most spectacular loss was
in its colossal loans to railway promoter Bethel Henry Strousberg,
who had partially completed a railway to pull grain from southern and western Russia north to the Prussian port of Königsberg
(now Kaliningrad). The Russian Empire, seeking a scapegoat for
the downturn, arrested Strousberg and tried him for the crime of
overstating his credit and publishing an improper balance sheet.
As news of Russian bank failures spread, the value of the ruble
dropped. Holders of negotiable instruments, either *varranty* or
signed agreements, failed when their deposit banks failed. Some
buyers of grain benefited by the decline of the ruble, but as the
ruble tumbled, those with wealth in Odessa hoarded gold, sucking
credit out of the Russian grain trade after the financial crisis and
leading the ruble to plunge in value for over a decade.[12]

Until the 1880s Russian banks had little of the sophistication
of American banks that acted as middlemen for crop loans. The
Bank of Russia was a central bank, but the banks chartered in
the 1860s in Russia mostly gave mortgages to nobles, a faintly ri-
diculous proposition given the imperial restrictions that prevented
the sale of noble land. Warehouses and agents could get credit for
bills of exchange, but kulaks were often left out of this credit system. The Bank of Russia's theory was sound enough: serfs would
pay for their emancipation, and nobles would use payments to ac-
crue capital in Russian banks, which they could use to improve

the land. In practice, however, noble landowners failed in biblical proportions through the 1870s and 1880s. Bankers literally nailed the dishonored notes of dozens of noble families to the doors of Russian banks. Thousands of estates changed hands after 1873. There was an active market for land despite problems with credit— land prices quadrupled between 1873 and 1890. In this reshuffling some farmers, like Trotsky's father, became holders of large estates. While new banks had appeared in Russia in the 1860s, most collapsed in the bank panic that began in Odessa in 1872 and spread to Europe in 1873.[13]

But then in 1883, just as the Agrarian Crisis reached its bottom, the man and the hour met. More precisely, two Russian academicians took over the finances of the Russian Empire in a way that provided credit to Russia's kulaks in Ukraine. After 1883 they were leaving their calling cards at the doors of French bankers eager to find bonds that earned more than 5 percent. The careers of Ivan Vyshnegradsky and Sergei Witte help us understand the Russian Empire's transition from financial calamity to rapid, if unstable, growth.

Ivan Vyshnegradsky was the first non-noble to become a minister of finance in Russia. Trained first in the seminary, he taught school, studied math and physics in Europe, and finally returned to Saint Petersburg to become a professor of mechanical engineering. With specialties in artillery, steam engines, and cargo loading, he became an indispensable adjunct to every major engineering project in the city.[14] In 1878 he joined the Southwestern Railway Company, where he met Sergei Witte, a tall, broad-shouldered nobleman, also trained in math and physics, who was then a junior manager.

As a nobleman, Sergei Witte had many advantages over Vyshnegradsky, including close connections to the tsar. During the Russo-Turkish War of 1877 to 1878, Witte moved General Mikhail Chernyayev's volunteer fighters (a Russian force disguised as a Serbian militia) through the steppe to Russian ports in the war against the Ottomans. Witte did not fight in the war but bent railway rules to hurry soldiers, then food, to the front. In doing so Witte won medals from the army and the tsar's attention. At the end of the war, Witte rose to become business manager of the newly formed Southwestern Railway Company, the private firm that inherited Strousberg's half-built corridor connecting Odessa to Königsberg and other Baltic ports. By 1881 Witte had become the Southwestern's managing director and thus controlled most of the grain leaving Russia by rail on both the Black and Baltic Seas.[15]

Together Vyshnegradsky and Witte made it possible for Russia to double down on grain exports to match the punishing competition from the United States. Just as American railways were aggressively lowering rates to force wheat out of the West and cotton out of the South, Witte learned to do the same by closely emulating the American and European railway planners, whom he called the "railway kings."

After 1881, with the assassination of Alexander II, chaos in the tsar's cabinet and the reaction that followed soon strengthened the hand of Vyshnegradsky and Witte. The "May Laws," first enacted as a "war measure" by the tsar in May 1882 and later made permanent, prevented Jews from moving into rural districts or engaging in trade without membership in one of the restrictive trading guilds. Shortly afterward the tsar limited Jewish membership in preparatory schools and universities to 5 percent of entering classes. Saint Petersburg and Moscow established a limit of 3 percent. In other ways large and small, the empire sought to exclude Jews from Russia's social and commercial life, often through devious interpretations of these laws that barred rural Jews from changing houses or giving rural land to their children.[16] The then minister of finance, Nikolai Bunge, at first stoutly resisted these changes, including conservatives' attempts to either roll back peasant rights or restrict the role of Jews in the economy. He even created a land bank to provide credit for peasant farmers. But then in 1887 Bunge proposed solving Russia's financial difficulties by taxing noble land. The conservative nobility in the tsar's cabinet forced him out of office. Vyshnegradsky was the perfect replacement. He first drew the attention of the conservative nobility in Saint Petersburg by strategically allying himself with the so-called kvass patriots, the conservatives who pushed for rolling back the peasant and Jewish emancipation of 1860. Conservatives appreciated Vyshnegradsky's argument that the peasantry should be taxed instead. Liberals appreciated his deep knowledge of railroads, engineering, and port construction.

As Vyshnegradsky moved into the ministry, Witte rose up in his place at Southwestern Railway. Witte provided steep discounts for long-distance grain shipments and reorganized the railroad schedules to speed grain to the border at harvest time. With 1,500 miles of track (just 10 percent of Russia's total), the Southwestern ran an astonishing 13,862 freight cars in 1883, perhaps half of all the cars in the Russian Empire.[17] As in the United States during the Civil War, the nexus of political power in Russia would shift from the executive (the tsar in this case) toward those merchants and engineers connected with the empire's logistic pathways. If Vyshnegradsky was Russia's corrupt wheeler-dealer Simon Cameron, Witte was its monopolistic system builder Thomas A. Scott.

The same laws that had forced Parvus and other Jews out of preparatory schools and universities also barred Jews from buying or leasing any new property in rural areas. Jewish lenders in the wheat trade could no longer own or even lease rural land, making it harder for them to secure future grain. Nor could Jewish merchants own or lease the crucial warehouses in towns along the railway's corridors. In 1883, following the May crisis, Witte wrote a famous article with the unattractive title "Principles of Railway Tariffs for Cargo Transportation." He argued that the Russian Empire could expand by leaving private railways like his alone. But if the empire moved control of shipping rates from the railway ministry to Vyshnegradsky's finance ministry, he continued, the finance minister could selectively modify railroad rates to boost Russian grain exports and hinder foreign manufactures. It was a model that worked in America and Prussia.

In 1884 Witte further increased the railway's control over the wheat supply chain by attempting to displace the Jewish *skrupchiki* in the countryside. First, the railroads began providing direct loans to growers of grain, directly competing with the *skrupchiki*. He thus aimed to replace the credit chain that trembled during the Agrarian Crisis by consolidating in the railway the role of moneylender, grain merchant, and carrier.[18] In the United States, by comparison, competing warehousing facilities sprang up at supply centers like Chicago, Milwaukee, Grand Rapids, and Buffalo. Cutthroat competition created grain elevator kingpins like George Armour and Ira V. Munn at the competitive points. In some places, railroads triumphed; in other places, the ABCD grain traders won out; in others, entrepreneurs who knew their grain and how to preserve it carried the day. Witte, by comparison, mostly succeeded at closing out possible competitors. Witte's anti-Semitism combined with his cupidity: he regarded seizing this cereal corridor extending from the Russian steppe to the Black Sea as a patriotic duty. As early as 1870, more than half the foreign exchange that arrived in Russia came through Black Sea wheat exports; another substantial portion came from grain that moved north toward the German Baltic Sea port of Königsberg. As managing director, Witte controlled both routes.[19]

Witte's reorganization of the Southwestern Railway shortened the world's grain pathways connecting Europe to Russia's western and southern provinces. It recentered the Russian Empire in the rich fields of Ukraine: well-organized railway corridors eliminated friction, shrinking the tollage between farms and ports, an autocratic facsimile of the American system of grain export. The Southwestern Railway provided credit to grain growers, used specialized railway cars for unloading grain, and placed grain elevators at the major ports.[20] By the 1880s Witte's only real competitors were Louis Dreyfus & Co. and Bunge & Co., which had their own grain elevators and contracts deep inside Ukraine. Witte had created a Russian spine that partly followed the Varangian Way, a fifth-century pathway between the Vikings and the Greeks. Witte's route was a lazy *S* from Odessa through Kiev and then Brest-Litovsk to Königsberg in Germany and Libau in Russia. The Volga River, the old central food corridor that had defined Russia between the eleventh and eighteenth centuries, would diminish in importance by comparison.[21]

Witte's plot to control the Russian Empire's grain exports was not quite a coup, but it nonetheless moved with the calculated precision of a railway schedule. In 1887, Vyshnegradsky, as finance minister, lowered grain freight rates in order to fix Russia's embarrassing budget problems. The empire then had a deficit of fifty-two million rubles stemming from the Agrarian Crisis and the 1877–1878 war against Turkey. While his predecessor had argued for increasing the shockingly low property taxes paid by the nobility, Vyshnegradsky increased taxes on peasants and cities. He applied new tariffs on alcohol, tobacco, naphthene, and stamps, along with requiring new commercial licenses and levying new city property taxes. Over the protests of his own finance committee, he paid to deepen Russian ports on the Baltic to substantially increase exports.[22]

Vyshnegradsky also drew from the American and German example of using tariffs to build up state funds. He increased tariffs on imported pig iron, the coke used for steel, and on ships. These tariffs were too high, however. They blocked cheap industrial goods from Britain and Germany but produced little revenue because they also slowed down imports. Then, by the middle of 1888, Witte's credit system and Vyshnegradsky's tweaking of railway rates had started to work: a flood of grain exports led to a surge in railway revenues.[23] In two years the Russian state's embarrassing and costly deficit gave way to a surplus of almost fifty million rubles.[24] The Russian government would soon be buying up the railroads it had sold off in the 1870s.[25]

Witte continued to use the levers of state power to squeeze Russia's grain outward to buyers. In 1889 the Russian and German empires terminated all cheap-freight agreements between German and Russian railroads, forcing grain through Russia's own ports on the Baltic and Black Seas. As the Russian deficit became a budget surplus, the ruble temporarily stabilized, giving Witte time to put Russia on the gold standard. Together Witte and Vyshnegradsky had turned the Russian Empire's railway-based grain export system into a faucet, producing a fantastic stream of wheat flowing in two directions and new revenue flowing back along Russia's new pathway, its new spine, the Southwestern Railway.[26]

The German and English empires were horrified by Russia's new tariffs, though Germany—with high industrial and agricultural tariffs of its own—had little cause to complain. In 1887, in response to Vyshnegradsky's iron tariffs, German chancellor Otto von Bismarck struck back by closing the Berlin capital market to Russia. Russia could sell neither railway stocks nor imperial bonds on the public exchanges in Berlin or Hamburg. This fateful decision severed many investment ties between Russia and Germany. It has been called the single most important financial step leading to the tensions that would explode in World War I.[27] This choking of imports, flushing of exports, and attempt to suppress competing warehouses worked splendidly for a few years until the winter that started in 1890. And then, along the Volga River, the winds came.

WINTER WHEAT ON the Russian plains usually survives under a blanket of snow that protects the seeds for two months, but in the winter of 1890 a drought limited snowfall, while harsh eastern winds blew away the snow cover. This "winterkill" was followed by a spring drought. The drought was especially harsh because in most years the winter melt combined with rain to feed wheat and rye plants both for the spring and the winter plantings. The combination of a harsh, dry winter and a spring drought hit hardest in the region along the Volga River, Russia's older trade pathway. Crop yields in those central Russian *gubernia* saw an astonishing 50 to 75 percent decline compared to previous years.[28]

And here, Witte's capture of the credit and grain storage facilities in the western regions exacted a terrible cost. Traditionally, large landowners in the east were required to save as much as 10 percent of the crop each year to cope with poor harvests and to prepare for planting the following season. But after the spring harvest of 1891, warehouses along the Volga River had been emptied of their wheat and rye, their bounty loaded onto steamships heading north to Baltic markets. Much of the grain was sold to pay loans, the new Vyshnegradsky taxes, and the redemption payments demanded of serfs. Given control by Witte's railroads of the largest warehouses in the western spine of Russia and the May Laws barring Jewish ownership of warehouses, there were few financial incentives to store grain and many barriers to doing so. Most Russian warehouses in the ancient Russian communities of the east were empty, without enough to even provide for the next season's planting.[29]

Witte and Vyshnegradsky initially responded to the barren fields as tsars had for seven centuries: with offers of loans and tax abatements for stricken areas. Witte suggested lending rubles, however, rather than grain, causing local rye prices to rise faster than international prices. This caught peasants and rural laborers in what are called price scissors. Because peasants along the Volga River traditionally planted wheat for sale and rye for home consumption, the poor harvest shrank income, while the decline in rye stores made rye prices skyrocket. This effectively tripled the cost of food for most rural workers in 1891.[30] By the spring of 1891, peasant families were pulling down their thatched roofs to feed their horses, pushing their children to beg in the city for bread, and finally eating their own horses. The ancient solution to poor harvests was to pull up the *lebeda* weeds (known in English as orache) that grew among rye. In small quantities *lebeda* weeds could be ground up with rye to produce a dark, filling, but unappealing loaf that frequently irritated the stomach. Eaten more than a few days in a row, it led to diarrhea, weakening immune systems. Cholera followed in the wake of hunger. Of the thirty-five million people living in seventeen provinces, half a million died from direct and indirect causes, causing a population drop so profound that it was visible in the national census.[31]

Blame found a dozen fathers. Some blamed deforestation, others the deep plowing of the black soil. Count Leo Tolstoy, who saw the famine firsthand, blamed the railroads. He argued that railroads took nature's bounty from the peasant cultivators who kept grain in their sheds, giving it to railway industrialists who kept grain in railway cars. Censors prevented publication of his story in Russia and abroad.[32] In the end Vyshnegradsky received most of the blame for the 1891 famine. The newspapers blamed not his new taxes or the ruble-based relief—both solid explanations—but his waiting too long before blocking Russian rye exports. In the cruelest irony, the fast-talking Sergei Witte usurped his former patron by telling the tsar that Vyshnegradsky had suffered a stroke and was incapable of continuing service. Witte proposed that only additional imperial borrowing could fix Russia's mess. He would succeed where others failed, he said, in "kindling a healthy spirit of enterprise."[33]

Witte proposed approaching the banks of France for new loans to railroads. Rather than relying on imperial bonds, which had been on shaky ground since the Crimean War, the empire would

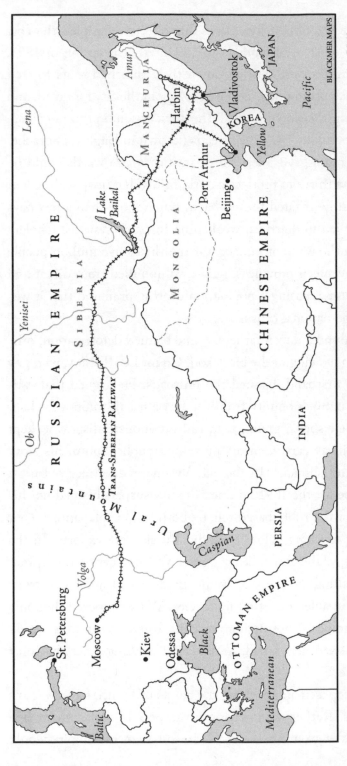

Russia's costly plan to sell grain to the world: 5,500 miles (9,000 kilometers) from Moscow to the deep-sea port in the Yellow Sea, c. 1905

Kate Blackmer

issue railroad bonds on the Crédit Mobilier model in which the imperial seal (the tsar's "bond") was no longer needed. Bonds had forever changed after the American defaults of the 1840s and Russia's near default after 1854. Instead, corporate "bonds" meant that the physical assets of rail, rolling stock, and enginehouses would act as collateral for loans. This had succeeded in raising millions in the United States for the Union Pacific and Central Pacific railroads, had generated millions in the French plan for the Suez Canal, and appeared to be succeeding in a French Panama Canal (though French engineers never completed it). In each instance the empire was no longer the guarantor. Instead, the underlying assets of the corporation itself somehow acted as the promise or seal.[34] Witte proposed a trans-Siberian railway, like America's newly finished corridor to the Pacific, which could open Siberia to grain growing and create a warm-water export port in Vladivostok and, possibly, Manchuria. The French public, hungry for debt that would act as retirement funds for city pensioners, would be sure to buy up Russian imperial, Russian railroad, and Russian bank bonds. When bond prices faltered, Witte followed the same path that Crédit Mobilier had in New York and the southern railways had in the South: he bribed financial newspapers to place puff pieces about the future prospects of his firms. His payoffs to financial reporters in Paris were tallied in the millions of francs.[35]

HERE PARVUS REENTERS our story. Parvus recognized that to create a revolutionary response to starvation in Russia, revolutionaries would have to shape the news of events. He had been a student of Karl Bücher, a scholar of political economy and the media. From Bücher, he had learned that reporting on the news was an ancient practice. According to Bücher news was probably first transmitted in ancient Rome when senators asked their literate slaves to attend meetings of the Senate and then summarize important information in private notes. In time, slaves read these notes aloud in the provinces, effectively retransmitting the information to other senators and citizens. This gave the slaves who retold the stories in the Senate considerable power. Julius Caesar, hoping to control this passage of information, had created public notice boards, erecting the first in Rome and later others in the provinces. Caesar hoped an official account of the transactions of the Senate would drown out the observations made by slaves.[36]

Here the "intellectual," the Roman slave, acted as a translator first but also—a bit—as a legislator himself, transmitting the news of Senate conflicts but also shaping it into a story. While some scholars have argued that the Enlightenment saw a shift from "intellectual as translator" to "intellectual as legislator," Bücher would have argued that there was never such a line.[37] Mobilizing political forces through the distribution of the news was as old as the Romans. Who were the legislators in the Russian system? Obviously the tsar. But who strengthened the capacities of the empire and became its leading light? Sergei Witte. And what was the weakness of the growing imperial system built on railways? The news.

Parvus's finger was on the pulse of Witte's central weakness. For, as Parvus put it, the "pompous display of absolutism, which draws the eyes of the whole world on itself" was a fragile thing; with a single crisis, "the mighty tsar and all his gold-drenched garbage [could] be instantly wiped away."[38] Witte needed to control the news about Russia that reached the Paris Bourse, particularly the bond market. Tens of thousands of French investors' appetite or distaste for Russian railway bonds directly affected the interest rate Witte would have to pay for each new issue. Any doubts that his "gold-drenched" bonds were not good, and the interest rates on them would climb. "The great famine," Parvus declared, "was not an accidental phenomenon, but the conclusion of a long-lasting process of destruction and decomposition."[39] Parvus became, after the Russian famine, a master at organizing, interpreting, and explaining the news about Russia, the Ottoman Empire, and all of Asia to hundreds of thousands of increasingly literate workers.

In early 1895, Parvus traveled to Leipzig to become a reporter and then editor for the *Leipziger Volkszeitung* (Leipzig people's paper), a daily paper funded by the Social Democratic Party. Within months he was lured away to the *Sächsiche Arbeiter-Zeitung* (Workers' newspaper of Saxony). He brought working-class readers an understanding of the economic world outside Saxony, framed in a lucid, vivid, approachable style. Whereas drab descriptions of trade union meetings had filled previous newspapers, Parvus explained how international capitalism had evolved since the American grain invasion of the 1860s. He did so with a gripping story of capitalism lashed to empire. It became the first discussion of international economics that would become world-systems theory. As later elaborated by Immanuel Wallerstein, world-systems theory proposed a world system of capitalism in which a European capitalist core profited by somehow producing powerful, autocratic states in the economic periphery that abused workers and produced "underdevelopment."[40]

Parvus's story about Russia's inevitable collapse as a ruthless exploiter was more dramatic, and more concrete, than this world-systems theory. The American competition for grain, he wrote, and the Agrarian Crisis that followed had hampered Russia's rapid industrial development. The costly Russo-Turkish War of 1877 to 1878 had only worsened the problem. But then the assassination of Alexander II in 1881 had forced his heir, Alexander III, to form an alliance with industrial interests, Witte in particular. Witte harmonized the interests of tsar and bourgeoisie, driving both toward an aggressive railroad expansion into Asia that would ultimately fail. Just as the British, French, and Prussian empires had been tied to their industrial bourgeois classes in wars of expansion that we call the scrambles for Africa and Asia, so would Russia. When

Nicholas II took the throne in May 1896, he became "the emperor of the bourgeoisie." And for this reason, Parvus assured his readers, Russia was a short way from collapse. The end of all Russia's heedless expansion could only be war. He disagreed with Karl Marx that capitalist crises necessarily ended in revolution. First would come war, then revolution.[41]

Parvus quickly picked up German barnyard idioms using comical but clear language. An agricultural program to buy up farm mortgages was too boring to even "attract a dog behind a stove."[42] Poland, he wrote, could have blocked Russia in the eighteenth century, but because it never connected from "sea to sea," it had "friendly neighbors" that would "gobble it up."[43] The Russian Empire, he joked, "always pulled Austria along, but it could not prevent Austria from occasionally biting its calf."[44] Tsars Alexander II and III had always turned up their noses at the bourgeois "up-and-comers from the grocery, the tavern, and the butchery." Only Nicholas II listened to them, and his alliance with the bourgeoisie would be his downfall.[45]

Parvus was not just a comical writer who could describe the capitalist world in memorable quips. He was also disturbingly prescient. Writing in 1896 he assured his readers that Russia's expansion on the backs of a peasantry that was "totally disintegrated, disheveled, ruined, divided into classes and burdened with the ballast of millions of dispossessed" meant that the ship of state would sink.[46] The Russian Empire's drive to build railroads in the direction of Asia would end disastrously. Furthermore, the Russian Empire's bottomless desire to capture Istanbul would lead to an international war in the Balkans.[47] Parvus's writing style was bombastic—the German Social Democratic Party called its tone unpleasant and vulgar—but it sold papers.[48] He offered his working-class readers an understanding of the struggles between empires over what Parvus understood to be the deeper conflict: the ebb and flow of the world's trade as it made and remade cities.

Instead of pointing a finger at Jews or foreigners, he blamed the empires themselves for their woes.

Parvus's writing attracted the attention of a young Vladimir Ilyich Ulyanov, who called Parvus the "gifted German journalist" who had figured out the cause of the Agrarian Crisis of 1873. Parvus's criticism of small-scale German landowners fit with Lenin's own critique of the Russian Narodniks, who believed that collective ownership of the land would solve everything, and the kulaks, whom he believed to be exploiting the peasantry.[49] Parvus also attracted the attention of the secret police in Austria-Hungary, Germany, and Russia. The Russian Okhrana reported that Parvus, along with his wife and eleven others, "attended local anarchist and social democratic sessions, read social democratic magazines such as *Forward* and *Socialist* and spoke at the meetings to stir up the masses."[50] German conservatives called his writing radical propaganda, and because of his papers' success in flaying the monarch and the Prussian Parliament, the German state hounded Parvus from city to city, expelling him as a noncitizen.

His first analytical writings explored international agriculture. In 1895 he declared that the German social democrats could not rescue, and should not ally with, German peasant voters who were destined to fail in an international market that Russia and America were flooding with grain. Peasants wanted a tax on foreign grain, but this strategy would merely delay the inevitable. Only with the lowering of rents could the development of capitalism allow successful family farms to buy up smaller, less efficient ones. Only these farm families could mechanize grain-production methods along American lines. While he did not love wealthier farmers, a political alliance with small farmers was a losing proposition because their holdings were too small to benefit from automation.[51] When the Royal Government of Saxony forced him out of the state in September 1898, Parvus persuaded the Social Democratic Party to appoint a new editor to his paper, an editor whose

German citizenship, albeit based on a sham marriage, would make her harder to deport. Her name was Rosa Luxemburg, and she later became famous for critiquing the Polish labor movement for its obsession with Polish independence.[52] She too declared that markets were international and nations were an illusion.

In 1899 Parvus directly attacked Russia's monarchy when he reported from the famine-stricken regions along the spine of old Russia on the Volga River. He argued that Witte's system of public finance, which he called an elaborate con game, had caused the famine. In a series of articles and then a book published in 1900 as *Starving Russia* (*Das Hungernde Russland*), Parvus looked closely at the public debt figures Witte had published and demonstrated that they had been faked. Witte had bought up railroads for the Russian Empire, then moved all railroad freight charges onto his balance sheet as earnings but included none of the sunk costs in the railroads or the costs of purchase as capitalized costs. With almost no costs on the balance sheet, showing a profit was easy. By not calculating wear and tear on the railway as a future debt, Witte grossly overestimated the railway's future prospects. Witte's scheme to build a railroad all the way to Manchuria, as Parvus famously put it, was "feeding the dog with bits of his own tail," rapidly spending French investors' dollars to pay off old interest on previous loans, while spending only a fraction of the capital on tracks leading to Asia.[53]

Parvus was no slave, but like the ancient Roman reporter of antiquity, he could deliver a persuasive story about the origin of Russia's famine. In *Starving Russia* he recognized that the problem was logistical and described the old Volga River grain route as destined to fail. But he also told the tragedy of the famine as a story about the tragedy of international capitalism lashed to empire that would ultimately lead to collapse. His words would, in less than two decades, become a self-fulfilling prophecy. As a financial analyst writing in popular newspapers, he could reach more readers over longer distances than Witte or any of the empire's mouthpieces, who could only buy positive press in French journals. Parvus, like Rome's slaves, was translator and interpreter. Knowing Russian and German, but also balance sheets and the grain trade, he could delineate the pyramid schemes, false promises, and self-dealing at the heart of Witte's enterprise.

In Parvus's mind, Witte's scheme encapsulated what he believed were the failings of international capitalism, an international system that was, he assured his readers, destined to fail. Between 1899 and 1910 he extended his analysis of the 1891 Russian famine into a general theory of global capitalism that encompassed cosmopolitan accumulation cities, trade breakdowns, and imperial wars. He declared as early as 1894 that the twentieth century would pit the grain-producing regions of southern Russia against the American Midwest. Russia and America would come to blows, he said, while Europe would simply be its battleground. Rosa Luxemburg, then Vladimir Lenin, then Leon Trotsky would extend this analysis into an account of world capitalism. It was an analysis of grain, empire, railroads, and international debt that would change the world.

THE RUSSIAN EXPANSION into Siberia, Central Asia, and Manchuria did not appear to be a particularly rational response to the world of grain. By 1890 more agricultural empires would join in a worldwide competition to supply the globe with food. The Ottoman breakaway states of Egypt, Serbia, Bulgaria, and Romania had begun exporting grain in considerable quantities. Argentinean and Australian farmers grew grain enough to warm the hearts of any physiocrat. Even more disturbingly France, Germany, Italy, and Austria-Hungary began to erect tariff barriers on wheat and flour in the 1880s that would have further dampened international prices. Russia's efforts to sell wheat to pay off loans and balance imperial budgets would lead it to behave more and more recklessly.

In March 1898, the Russian government persuaded the Qing Empire to lease Dalian (then called Port Arthur) and space for a railway corridor on the Liaodong Peninsula. This southern "branch" of the China Eastern Railway—called the South Manchuria Railway—gave Russia what it had long desired: a deepwater port in the middle of the Yellow Sea. In time the Chinese government fully ceded military and civil control of the region.[54] The Russo-Chinese Bank, which acted as the funding vehicle for the railroad, took full control of customs going in and out of Port Arthur.[55] When the British complained about the secret deal, the Russian government was belligerent: "Every other great maritime power had a naval station on the Chinese seas, and why should not Russia, whose fleet was very considerable and whose territory was coterminous."[56] The China Eastern Railway then established its headquarters in Harbin, near the juncture with the South Manchuria Railway—first occupying an old distillery on the Sungari River. Within months Harbin became a boomtown as Russian promoters located untapped lumber and coal deposits. A flour mill completed Harbin's status as an important inland city, a competitor to Chicago or Milwaukee.[57]

Russian military authority backed up its claims to financial control. Witte admitted that he used "subterfuge" to create a railway guard composed of retired soldiers and others "temporarily retired" from military service. In 1898 these disguised Russian troops expelled Chinese and Manchurian people living near the expanding town of Dalian.[58] In collecting customs from the deepwater port of Dalian, the Russians aggressively rejected the authority of the British-controlled Maritimes Customs Service, which had previously demanded customs payments for all goods flowing across the Yellow Sea to repay the Qing Empire's foreign loans.[59] The presence of Russian troops on what was technically still Chinese soil helped expand the ambit of an anti-foreign social movement whose adherents Europeans called the Boxers. This rapidly growing movement got started in the German-controlled region of Shantung Province, where it recruited young men at public boxing grounds into a group called the Boxers United in Righteousness. By July 1900 the movement had crossed into Manchuria. Organizing quickly, this self-proclaimed citizen militia—wrapped with charms to ward off bullets and believing themselves temporarily possessed by the heroes of popular Chinese literature—fought back against Russian dispossession by seizing and burning railway terminals, tearing up track, and finally capturing and beheading railway engineer Boris Verkhovsky.[60] The Russian government responded by sending more regiments into China's Kwantung Province.[61] By the end of the month, Cossack regiments had begun something like a pogrom against Chinese men, women, and children. With rifles and clubs they drove Chinese residents—mostly the families of the workers who had built their railroad—into the Amur River, telling them to "swim back to China." Russian soldiers drowned somewhere between three thousand and nine thousand Chinese civilians over two days.[62]

At about the same time that tracks were being laid to the Yellow Sea, in December 1900, a popular movement against Russian expansion was emerging. Parvus's apartment in Munich became the center of a revolutionary project to bring news of empire and revolution to Russia's small but growing working class. A new newspaper called *Iskra* (The spark) would transmit Parvus's understanding of the deeper framework of international capitalism upon which empires and states struggled with one another. Parvus provided the mechanical press, with other friends of the revolution in Russia providing funding. Vladimir Ulyanov, assuming the name Lenin, acted as the editor. By the end of 1902, the South Manchuria Railway was running cars all the way from Lake Baikal to Port Arthur on the Yellow River. Chinese exports included pottery (clay and terra-cotta), forest products, kerosene, and tea. A flour-milling industry in Harbin hoped its products would compete with the ubiquitous flour sacks from America.[63]

Beginning slightly earlier, in December 1898, Parvus's closest associate, Rosa Luxemburg, began to extend Parvus's argument about a world system of trade and the irrelevance of states in a series of articles later collected in her 1913 book *The Accumulation of Capital*. Both argued that the economy had broken through nations, that booms came when new territories were added to the world market, like Russia or America, Africa or the Far East, and that busts would follow when the quantity of manufactured goods greatly exceeded demand. Both postulated that economic crises would become more serious.[64] Parvus's partner in 1905, Lev Davidovich Bronstein, under the pseudonym Trotsky, extended Parvus's argument about accumulation to posit what he called "permanent revolution," arguing that the bourgeoisie in places like Russia could not be trusted to improve capitalist development and that an alliance between workers and peasants might bring revolution, though this would require the revolution's continuous expansion into new regions.

Lenin's first public writings in Russian appeared in *Iskra*. There Lenin attacked peasant expropriation in the grain-producing regions of southern Russia and fiercely criticized Witte's system of land distribution along the railways in Siberia. Lenin argued that the exclusion of Jews and non-Russians, along with the favor shown the nobility, would doom Witte's railroad to failure.[65] Lenin's 1916 pamphlet titled "Imperialism: The Highest Stage of Capitalism" repeated the argument laid out by Parvus and Junius.

In widely published writings, Parvus, Junius, Trotsky, and Lenin described the brutality of European empires—a theme common to many other writers, liberal and socialist—as well as how international capitalism was distorting the Russian, Qing, and

Ottoman empires. In Russia they called attention to the falsified balance sheets and undocumented debt that Witte relied on to build his railroad-based cereal-exporting empire. By 1904 the cost of the railway to Manchuria had made Russia the most indebted empire in the world, with billions of gold francs' worth of bonds in the hands of French investors misled by Witte's promises.

In July 1903, when Witte's railroad reached China's Port Arthur in Manchuria, Japanese socialists and liberals became incensed. The Japanese had previously captured and claimed Port Arthur and the entire Liaodong Peninsula at the end of the First Sino-Japanese War (1894–1895), only to cede it back to China when France, Germany, and Russia together forced them to renounce those claims. In response to the triple intervention that blocked its empire, Japan began its own borrowing spree. It amassed a sizable fleet using state-of-the-art warships built by Vickers & Co. in Britain.[66] Though some funds came from reparations that China paid after the Sino-Japanese War, the Japanese Empire raised most of the funds for this fleet by selling bonds to New York investors. Promoters included prosperous Jewish firms in New York that abhorred the Russian Empire's expansionist policy and its treatment of Russian Jews. With this fleet, the Japanese navy and army were prepared to defend Japan's empire against the Russians.

"Russia is the shame of Europe," declared the largest-circulating newspaper in Japan in February 1904. "We need to defeat this nation in the name of civilization, in the name of peace, and in the name of humanity."[67] That month Japan broke off diplomatic relations with Russia and launched a surprise attack on the fleet of ships that Russia had parked at Port Arthur. The fleet was quickly destroyed. The land-based conflicts seemed to favor Russia at first, but between April and December 1904, attempts by Russia to call on reserve troops led to 123 separate disorders, mostly in opposition to this distant foreign war.[68] The Japanese siege of the Russian citadel at Port Arthur lasted from August 1904 to March 1905. In May 1905 the Russian Atlantic fleet finally arrived at Port Arthur. It took the Japanese navy only three days to destroy it.

The Russian minister to Tokyo, Baron Roman Romanovich Rosen, pointed out (with the benefit of hindsight) that with Russia finally forced to surrender the port, the billions of francs spent on a railway across Siberia could never be repaid. The Russian Empire's "sacrifices in blood and treasure" were already enormous, and it would have to default on its long-term debt for a road to nowhere. Russia was essentially bankrupt. This futile, costly railway expansion and the surrender that followed, Rosen argued, spelled the end of the Russian Empire.[69]

In January 1905, Father Georgy Gapon led a procession of mostly loyal workers to present a petition to the tsar to end the war, improve working conditions, and establish an eight-hour workday. Before the crowd had even entered the square in front of the Winter Palace, soldiers opened fire on them, killing perhaps two hundred people.[70] By mid-October 1905 a strike by printers had become a general strike in Saint Petersburg and Moscow. By late October, a nationwide rail strike led by the Union of Railway Employees and Workers appeared to be in the offing. Given the prospect of a broader revolution, Trotsky and Parvus traveled to Saint Petersburg, where they produced the first Russian two-kopeck daily, *Izvestia*. The inexpensive newspaper became the organ of an organization calling itself the Soviet of Workers' Deputies, which increasingly sought representatives from all the unions on strike. The soviet, with crucial financial support from the Railway Union, made some headway in bringing multiple unions together under one umbrella.[71] This was largely Parvus's plan, to create a new kind of state power around soviets, which Lenin at the time opposed.[72] Civil unrest by ethnic minorities convulsed and nearly split the new spine of the Russian Empire that Witte had helped to create, particularly in the Baltic and Russian Poland, as well as Ukraine.

The government lost control in Warsaw, Riga, Baku, and many other cities.[73] On October 12, the tsar's ministers determined that individual revolts among reservists had turned into a "general ferment" and that Russian troops could not put down the conflict inside the empire.[74]

After the Saint Petersburg police arrested the first chairman of the soviet, Parvus became its new chairman. As the last chairman of the Petersburg soviet, his most spectacular activity was to issue the "Financial Manifesto." It warned workers, factory owners, and merchants throughout Russia that the Russian Empire was bankrupt and that the bonds it was issuing were making interest payments on debt that could never be paid. "The government is on the brink of bankruptcy. It has reduced the country to ruins and scattered it with corpses," he wrote. He told peasants to stop all land-redemption payments, suggested workers accept only "full-weight hard cash" for pay, and advised all citizens to "withdraw deposits from savings banks and from the state bank, demanding payment of the entire sum in gold."

His manifesto nearly destroyed the banks in Russia; Sergei Witte quickly stifled it and destroyed every press that had received a copy.[75] The tsar then issued the October Manifesto, which appeared to promise civil rights and the creation of a Duma, or parliament. Order appeared to reemerge between October and December, as army units began to use artillery on workers still on strike in Saint Petersburg. In December the ministry sought out social democrats and social revolutionaries in particular, and a rapid series of trials and summary executions began. Trotsky and Parvus were arrested in the latter half of December 1905. Transported to Peter and Paul Fortress in Saint Petersburg, they were almost certain to be executed. Parvus escaped eight months later by bribing his guards.[76]

Twelve

ORIENT EXPRESS, ARMY OF ACTION
1910–1914

R USSIA, FRANCE, AND Britain feared a German railway corridor through Istanbul to the Middle East. The threat
this corridor posed would lead all three nations into an uneasy
alliance, starting in 1914, as the Allied Powers. Tensions in Istanbul between 1908 and 1914 would lead a new group of military
officers, called the Young Turks, to rebuild a Turkish army and
state inside the Ottoman Empire. This state-building campaign
was peculiar and would become a model for revolutions around the
world in the twentieth century, particularly in Russia in the years
after the Russian Revolution. The Young Turk method involved
turning the army into a hybrid military-educational structure, an
organ for simultaneously politicizing, educating, and indoctrinat-
ing young men. Crucially, an overseer military structure inside
army regiments would ensure that the newly forming ideals of the
revolution would be sustained, preventing an officer-led defection.
This method of military organization, combining newspaper and
educational propaganda with practical education in mathematics
and engineering, allowed Turkey to rebuild itself in the midst of
the Balkan Wars and then defeat the combined forces of Russia,
France, and Germany at Gallipoli during World War I.

Parvus was drawn to the Young Turks' revolution as it was beginning in Istanbul in 1908. He arrived two years later to share
his financial acumen and understanding of how to mobilize a mass
audience. Once the Balkan Wars began, his influence expanded

beyond his initial hopes. Between 1910 and 1914 the Young Turk Revolution would beat back an alliance of Balkan states that sought to destroy the empire. As the Young Turks learned how to command the city with artillery mounted on automobiles, Parvus helped supply the Turkish army with modern munitions and reorganize Turkey's pathways to give it a modern, flexible grain supply. When he first arrived in Istanbul in 1910, he was an intellectual with big ideas. By 1914, after he had watched the Young Turk revolution unfold, he would have the capital and connections to plan even more audaciously and consider how a world war might start a revolution in Russia.

WHEN PARVUS, THEN forty-three years old, arrived in the Ottoman capital of Istanbul in November 1910, he almost certainly came by train from Vienna on the famed Orient Express. It was the fast passenger service on the partially completed Berlin-Baghdad railway, with connections from the North Sea port of Hamburg through Austria-Hungary, Serbia, Bulgaria, and Turkey, over the strait at Istanbul, all the way to Konya at the base of the Taurus Mountains in Asia. This railway corridor, Parvus knew, haunted diplomats and kings in Paris, Petersburg, and London for it appeared to give Germany an all-rail route through a crucial chokepoint for the world's trade. Germany's rapid commercial expansion by railway into revolutionary Turkey seemed apparent and persuaded Parvus that an international crisis was brewing. He knew, as he had known since he was a boy, that a German connection to Turkey, fabled gateway to the Black Sea, was the key to ending the "political shipwreck" that was the Russian Empire.[1]

Because Parvus was wanted by agents of the Russian secret police, the Okhrana, he arrived under a Czech alias with a false address. With little cash to spare, he rented a room across the Bosporus Strait on the Asian side of Turkey, in the slums of Scutari (Üsküdar).[2] He had almost certainly shaved his trademark goatee and hidden his Russian great coat, though he would never have abandoned his immaculate suit or polished shoes.

In a literal sense the city was more lock than key. Like the founders of empires that preceded it, the Ottomans did not build from scratch. They simply rearranged long-distance transportation lines between cities and farms that traders had established in times beyond reckoning. Its walls were assembled from the fragments of the ancient capitals that preceded it. Properly defended, it could strangle the Russian tsar. Russia's ambitions since the days of Catherine the Great depended on using grain lands to expand across the planet. Grain-based physiocratic expansion, however, required international markets. Now that Russia had lost its deepwater port in Manchuria, everything depended on the Black Sea's outlet to the world.[3]

Parvus arrived in Istanbul to seek out the Committee of Union and Progress in Turkey, a group of reforming officers and intellectuals who sought to reorganize the Ottoman Empire in a way that would create a "Turkish" national identity devoted to defending a Turkish homeland on what was left of the shrinking Ottoman Empire. A faction among these Unionists, led by a small and slender young officer named Ismail Enver, sought alliance with the German Empire.[4] Trained in the prestigious Imperial War College under German officers, Enver had helped recruit Muslim military bands on the empire's frontier to collaborate with his Ottoman Third Army against Turkey's enemies. Those plans for state building seemed ephemeral at first. When Parvus arrived, the Ottoman capital must have appeared as fragile as it had in 1453. In 1908, fires had spread across the city, destroying hundreds of crowded, ramshackle wooden structures that had housed tens of thousands of Muslim refugees west of the city. Hounded away from former Ottoman lands by nationalist movements, they had been made refugees a second time by the fires. But in that year Ismail Enver—then given the honorific Enver Pasha—had, together with other officers, enacted the Young Turk Revolution, which forced Sultan Abdul Hamid II to reinstate the General Assembly in the hope that it would turn the Ottoman Empire into something like a constitutional monarchy.

Enver Pasha's group of Unionist officers were a modern army built inside the imperial Ottoman Empire like an alien force. They comprised a sort of *carbonari* of highly trained revolutionaries with plans to defend the empire against its enemies, including the Balkan states that hoped to expand by picking it apart. Like the Italian and Russian *carbonari*, the Unionist officers like Enver swore one another into a conspiratorial brotherhood. Elaborate rituals of entry involved a blood oath to defend the state against all threats foreign and domestic.[5] These Young Turks were, like Enver, mostly *mektepli*, officers trained in new methods of fighting and state building in the Imperial War College. They understood how new technologies like machine guns, automobiles, and airplanes might allow a relatively small force of well-trained soldiers to hold off a substantially larger force.

But the Ottoman army needed soldiers, and the Unionists' pressure to expand enlistment provoked a crisis. These new *mektepli* officers opposed the old-fashioned *alayli* officers who had risen through the ranks in the empire outside the Imperial War College and thus owed obedience to the sultan. The Young Turks blamed Turkey's military weakness on Anatolian youths who had been enrolling in *madaris* (singular *madrasah*), schools for Islamic instruction. The Young Turks argued that most *madaris* were not schools at all. Roughly one-third of Anatolian men were *madrasah* graduates and thus exempt from military service, but most, according to the Unionist officers, could not even read. After the revolution began in July 1908, the Unionists proposed a simple literacy examination for *madrasah* graduates: those graduates who failed an Arabic literacy test would be drafted into the army and educated and would defend the empire. The Young Turks' demands for rapid expansion and reorganization of the army provoked a revolt composed of Anatolian soldiers, Islamic religious leaders, and *alayli* officers. Sultan Abdul Hamid II had inspired and possibly provoked them to rise up. Their opposition crystallized around allegations that the Unionists had hired assassins to kill opposition newspaper editors. This counterrevolution against the Young Turks begun in 1909, called the 31 March Incident, threatened to break up the General Assembly, put the Young Turks in prison, and restore Abdul Hamid to the throne.[6]

The Unionists responded by destroying opposition newspapers and encircling the city with a new kind of urban assault vehicle, automobiles with armored machine-gun turrets in the back. After the Unionists seized power, they sent Abdul Hamid into exile in Salonica. The new sultan, Mehmed V, would be a figurehead. The Unionists doubled down on newspaper propaganda, increasingly binding the army directly to the nation, the defense of the state, and, most importantly, the education of citizen-soldiers,[7] which would be taken away from the Islamic schools of instruction and conducted by the army itself. Turkey would be a "nation in arms" (*Volk in Waffen*), to quote the German general who had designed the training regimen for officers in the Imperial War College. After 1909 Unionist officers would be teachers as well, training soldiers in engineering, mathematics, and nationalist propaganda to support a nation in peril.

Through friends in the socialist Left, Parvus made contacts in Istanbul. Just as he had as a youth in Odessa, he sought to organize dockworkers. They had already built a powerful boycott movement, initially aimed at punishing Austria-Hungary for its expansion into Ottoman territory. In 1910, in the name of Turkish nationalism, these unions expanded their boycotts on goods coming from Austria-Hungary, Greece, and other enemies of Turkey. They refused to unload goods with waymarks from those places and enforced boycotts of firms owned by Greek citizens of the empire. Parvus's continuing ties to dockworkers would give him considerable influence in Turkey's ports and allow him to displace the Greeks who had long-standing trading networks there.[8]

Parvus next connected with the most extreme nationalists among the Committee of Union and Progress, which by 1910 was a government within a government. The Unionists controlled much of the bureaucracy, though a large and complex alliance of opposition parties was aligned against them, making the party just one voice among many in the General Assembly. Few believed the Ottoman Empire could survive the separatist movements that threatened to tear it apart. And Parvus knew that the Imperial Russian Navy was already plotting to seize Istanbul as the Russian Empire's western port.[9] "Russia can wait now," he had written back in 1897, "for Russia is sure of its prey. . . . [I]n time Constantinople must fall in its hands, since it cannot fall to anyone else."[10]

Parvus shared with the Unionists his considerable expertise in using newspapers written in an easily accessible language to reach workers and soldiers. Within a year his apartments would be the headquarters of a new magazine that would help form a mass ideology designed to unite Istanbul's workers and soldiers around a shared sense of national destiny. Unlike the *Iskra* newspaper that had helped bring an internationalist movement to life in 1900, *Türk Yurdu* (Turkish homeland) sought to build a strong nationalist movement, doing so from the Ottoman Empire's center. Adapting his arguments to the new environment as he saw it from Üsküdar, he wrote articles for *Türk Yurdu* that shaped Turkish grievances about foreign control, national bankruptcy, and military defeat into an economic strategy for national rebirth. In helping to organize *Türk Yurdu*, Parvus became a central part of the campaign to educate soldiers in the new ideology of the Turkish revolution. Parvus began to see in Istanbul the use of the military as a simultaneous agent of politicization, indoctrination, and education. As the Young Turks reorganized the military after the 31

March Incident, they built an overseer structure inside each unit. Each regiment had younger *mektepli* officers with direct control over senior *alayli* officers. Military discipline continued but with the younger political officers having a veto power over their older military counterparts.

PARVUS'S ARRIVAL AT the end of 1910 was fortuitous, for the Ottoman Empire soon faced catastrophe. In September 1911 Italy invaded North Africa west of Egypt in what is now Libya. As soon as a large portion of the Ottoman army was away in North Africa, a "Balkan League" hurriedly formed to invade and seize all Ottoman land in the European part of the empire. Here, in the slow-motion collapse of the Ottoman Empire, World War I began.[11]

Parvus was ready with a prescription for the empire's malady. As he did in his book *Starving Russia*, he performed in 1911 a forensic accounting of empire in a series of articles in *Türk Yurdu*. He examined how it contracted debt, how interest rates were set, and how foreign-controlled institutions ensured payment. The Ottoman Empire's debt problems had begun with the Crimean War, he concluded, after carefully studying its accounts. In seeking to save Istanbul from invading Russia, Sultan Abdulaziz had borrowed heavily, and as debts came due, his successors had gradually turned over the empire's most valuable monopolies—in tobacco, for example—to European states. Parvus calculated that the European-controlled Ottoman Public Debt Administration (OPDA) had probably already collected all the taxes necessary to pay off Ottoman debts. Yet it continued to control tax collection in the empire and could easily disguise its prodigious bounty by (for example) expanding the OPDA printing, publishing, training, and foreign relations apparatus while counting those as expenses recouped directly from the tax. The Turkish Empire would always be on a short leash so long as the foreign-controlled OPDA collected its most valuable internal taxes on tobacco and salt and allocated the benefits to its growing infrastructure. This was the same system of external taxation on an empire's internal trade that Britain had imposed upon China with the Maritime Customs Service.

Parvus pointed out that cheap grain from America had crippled agricultural empires after 1865. Grain prices were halved between 1860 and 1890, he noted, benefiting the more "industrial domains" like Germany, France, Britain, and even Italy, while hurting the more "agricultural domains" like Russia, Turkey, and China. This was the Agrarian Crisis that began in 1873.[12] When industrial states then imposed tariffs in the 1880s to protect European farmers from cheap wheat and build up their status as great powers, the agricultural empires suffered the worst, hit by the combined effect of American competition and European tariffs. The only way to improve the Ottoman Empire was to radically improve agriculture by abolishing slavery, ending serfdom, and performing a complete survey of population and agricultural land.

Internally, Parvus continued, the Ottoman Empire needed reforms to strengthen its supply lines, its backward and forward linkages. It had to build railroads through promising but remote agricultural lands, as Britain, France, Germany, Italy, and the United States had done. Workers had to be educated to use modern agricultural machinery. Railroads from Turkish ports into the grain country could multiply the internal traffic inside the empire. Russia, by comparison, had overspent on the railroad to the Yellow Sea with an overly optimistic plan for the region's agricultural potential. Empires, just as they had from the days of Julius Caesar's milestones, needed cheap, fast, efficient paths that delivered food to cities and brought a backhaul of manufactured goods to the countryside. The sultan had spent too much on railroads that could move armies over mountains. This made the Ottoman Empire's logistical pathways expensive and prone to breakdown. Parvus worried that these costs could never be recouped.

Parvus was making a case not for traditional economic nationalism and tariff barriers but rather for a grain-to-city infrastructure, protection of private agricultural property, expanded loans to farmers, a currency exchangeable internationally, and higher taxes on farmland that would force agricultural improvement. Bulgaria had once been a poor part of the Ottoman Empire, Parvus pointed out. But once it gained independence, it exported much more grain than it ever had in the Ottoman domain and could thus pay higher taxes.[13] Parvus's observations must have puzzled orthodox Marxist readers of his Turkish articles. His Marxist-inspired development strategy, emphasizing private property in agriculture combined with a mix of public and private control of industry, had been his prescription for the Prussian state as early as 1895. The same strategy would transform China and Vietnam a century later, though without his direct influence.[14]

He collected his 1911 writings into a 1914 book titled *Turkey's Financial Imprisonment*, which became a textbook for military students and is still taught in courses on modern Turkish history. Its central argument that a world system of capitalism forced peripheral states to produce primary commodities, allowing core states to produce industrial goods, would long outlive him.[15] As Parvus saw it, the Young Turks needed to understand that the Ottoman Empire's biggest problem lay not in its position as a target for the Russians, nor in its frequent fires, nor in its colossal debt. Its biggest problem lay in how it funded, produced, taxed, and distributed the grain that passed from its farmers' fields, to its ports, to its capital on the narrow strait of the Bosporus.[16]

The Americans, he told the Young Turks, had faced the same crisis that the Ottomans faced now and managed to win the Civil War using grain. By 1900, however, the American contribution to the world's wheat supply was dropping because American cities were increasingly consuming the grain produced on the nation's prairies. This would briefly move the balance wheel back eastward.

With America's forty-year grain onslaught waning, Istanbul might put its finger once again on the pulse of Europe's food supply. The city on the Bosporus Strait had the power to starve Russia, France, and Great Britain in the Great War that was on the horizon.

America had filled the world with wheat, Parvus wrote, by applying "big capital" (*büyük sermaye*) to food production and distribution. The Turkish state needed to emulate the Americans.[17] He proposed a drastic reform of imperial taxation. Taxes on luxury items like tobacco were important but had been completely surrendered to the British, French, and Dutch through the OPDA. Control and taxation of grain as it entered the Bosporus had been the go-to formula for centuries, but the empire needed to abandon this. Millers in Istanbul were importing cheap grain into the city and underpricing the flour that flowed from Ottoman lands through Istanbul's granaries, then to its flour and bread guilds. Taxing the diminishing supplies of grain was pointless, Parvus argued. The Turkish state needed to encourage settlement of underused land by building railroads, subsidizing farming in these regions, and taxing transport. The American version of this process was the Homestead Act and the transcontinental railroad. But the Ottomans needed to minimize all restraints on imported grain because cheap bread would provide food for Ottoman slaves and serfs who could be liberated to work in factories.

The Young Turks' defeat of their opponents after the 31 March Incident in 1910 put them more directly in power. They mostly embraced Parvus's radical suggestions for how to save Turkey. At this crucial point Parvus purchased rapid-firing artillery for the Ottoman military.[18] As a contractor for the Turkish army, he apparently gained the power to direct all Ottoman grain transport on the Black Sea, while modernizing the shipment of grain into the city. Parvus also improved trade importing western sources of grain into Istanbul. The Balkan War of 1912 to 1913 had lost Turkey the grain it had drawn from European territories, now all taken by

Bulgaria, Greece, and Serbia. He replaced the old *horrea*, whose physical structure still resembled the ancient Roman and Byzantine grain banks (one still stands in Üsküdar), with American-style grain elevators. Parvus was not the first to understand that Turkey needed to provide loans to grain producers. Under Sultan Abdul Hamid II, the empire had used its Ziraat Bankasi (Agricultural Bank) to advance cash to growers of wheat. But this overburdened bank also taxed the empire's grain, and the empire routinely raided the bank to provide funds for military projects.[19]

Parvus also acted as a purchaser for the city's grain on international markets. Some of the grain came from his home city of Odessa, where he still had family contacts in the grain trade. A great deal also came from America. By 1912 he had established grain terminals on both sides of the Bosporus. He also established a grain terminal, a bank, and a palatial private residence on one of the Princes' Islands on the Mediterranean side of Istanbul. Hostile Russian observers called his network of control over this trade a "mafia" and suggested that in concert with his grain-trading family and connected with his role as a military contractor, he used the valve at Istanbul to establish some sort of monopoly on Black Sea grain between 1911 and 1914.[20]

Parvus later wrote that he made his substantial fortune "before the Turkish declaration of war [in October 1914] delivering food from Anatolia and elsewhere to Constantinople."[21] He neglected to mention that he was also running guns to the Ottoman Empire and (according to some accounts) her sometime-enemy Bulgaria during the Balkan Wars. By the end of the Balkan Wars, in July 1913, Parvus—the Bolshevik—was a multimillionaire.[22]

Thirteen

A WORLD WAR OVER BREAD
1914-1917

S TORIES ABOUT THE Great War of 1914 to 1918 often begin with an account of German aggression. But the war's cause also had roots in the cheap grain cast upon the waters every spring and summer to feed Europe's working classes. The Turkish-German alliance threatened European gullet cities: it combined the grain-bottling Bosporus, which could block Russian grain, with Germany's ship-destroying U-boats, which could block grain from Argentina, Australia, and America. Together Turkey and Germany could starve Europe.

Grain was key to almost every stage of World War I. Fearing the threat to its grain exports, imperial Russia helped provoke this global conflict. During the war the British underestimated the threat of Istanbul and overestimated their ability to overcome it. As the conflict dragged on, Germany, also suffering from a dearth of cheap bread, found a unique path to Russia's bountiful harvest. German success in 1917 and most of 1918 would rely on the unlikeliest of allies: a communist grain merchant with an ax to grind.

World War I has been characterized as a "great powers" conflict with Germany as the aggressor. A Serbian assassin killed Archduke Franz Ferdinand, heir to Austria-Hungary's throne, leading that empire to declare war on Serbia. Russia backed Serbia, mobilizing its army near the Austro-Hungarian border. Germany, itching for conflict, supported Austria-Hungary and demanded that Russia demobilize. When Russia refused, Germany invaded

Belgium to attack France—Russia's ally and financial backer. In the same month the Germans and Austrians attacked Russia near Tannenberg, wiping out the Russian First and Second Armies. England joined the side of the Franco-Russian Allies after Germany invaded Belgium. The Ottomans only joined the Austrian-German Central Powers two months later.[1]

That's an oft-told story, but for scholars of the pathways of grain around the world, the war's history begins a little earlier and much farther east. In 1911, Italy invaded what would become Libya, taking it from Turkey. The day after the fighting stopped, Greece, Bulgaria, Serbia, and Montenegro took advantage of the conflict to invade Turkey. Then, crucially, Turkey closed the Bosporus and Dardanelles Straits to commerce, blocking all Russian grain and oil exports. Russians, fearing that Bulgaria or Greece might capture Istanbul, put both their army and the Black Sea fleet on alert. Russian agriculture minister Alexander Krivoshein, who then dominated the tsar's council, reorganized the Russian cabinet in 1914 to prepare for a global war. From the cabinet's perspective, this coming conflict would be the seventh Russo-Turkish war since the reign of Catherine the Great, yet another attempt to protect Russia's precious grain-export trade.

Krivoshein saw in Istanbul an existential threat. He recognized that Germany, in helping build up Turkey's military, was drawing Istanbul into its orbit. The paranoid Russian cabinet saw signs of this German-Ottoman alliance everywhere. German officers had been training the Ottoman army since 1883, and Prussian officers organized the placement of the artillery that Parvus had purchased on city walls in Istanbul and Adrianople. Most concerning was that, in July 1914, the Turkish state would receive its first dreadnought: a costly state-of-the-art ship from the English firm Vickers & Co., with other ships on order. This dreadnought was a massive upgrade from previous generations of battleship, with more guns on board than any ship afloat. Russia feared a repeat of its defeat in the Yellow Sea: a single Japanese battleship had led a small armada that destroyed Russia's eastern and then its western fleets. A single Turkish dreadnought, with a small escort of torpedo boats, might wipe out the Russian navy on the Black Sea. Such one-sided battles had become familiar. The Americans had done the same to Spain in the Spanish-American War in 1898, Italy had done it all over North Africa in 1911, and the Greeks had done it to the Ottomans in the Balkan Wars in 1912 and 1913. If a Turkish dreadnought passed through the Dardanelles, wrote Russia's naval minister, the "Turks would have undisputed mastery of the Black Sea."[2]

This account, most associated with Russian historian Sean Mc-Meekin, puts Russia as the primary aggressor in World War I. Fearing a rapid Turkish buildup on the Bosporus Strait, the Russians sought the earliest-possible opportunity for a conflict with Turkey. They feared that the combination of new harbor defenses and a dreadnought would make the passageway to the Black Sea impregnable and threaten Russian trade. The assassination of Franz Ferdinand provided Russia, already prepared for conflict, a perfect pretext to assemble troops on the border. The Russians had little interest in defending Serbia but knew that massing troops at the border would provoke Germany and Austria-Hungary to declare war first, and if war was declared before the Turkish dreadnought arrived, Istanbul might be easy prey for Russian ships. Russia hoped that a hasty German attack would provoke Britain. A too-rapid attack on Turkey, however, risked revealing the Russian dagger: the deep desire to take Istanbul.[3]

Parvus was of course at the center of Turkey's growing power, both in its increasing access to credit and grain and in its fortifications. Numerous sources suggest that Parvus was also the Turkish representative for both Vickers & Co. and Friedrich Krupp & Co. in Istanbul, arranging long-distance credit.[4] He helped make Istanbul impregnable.

In this Russia-focused view of World War I, Germany and Britain came to the party late. France had early signaled to Russia that it would follow Russia's lead. Russia, France, and England feared that Germany's power in Istanbul could starve Europe. Secondarily, German railways connecting Turkey to the Middle East threatened Russian, French, and German routes to the Arabian Peninsula. World War I, by this view, began as a war over Europe's control of the Middle East. The Russian Empire saw the threat first and mobilized to start the conflict.[5]

Statesmen saw the alignment of colored blobs on a map; Parvus saw lines of wheat. American grain exports, which had surged for fifty years, had already shrunk by 1910 as booming American cities consumed more grain. The Ottoman Empire was positioned at the important juncture point between Russian grain and the gullet cities to the west that would manufacture gunpowder and munitions. Romanian grain could not get to France without going through the Bosporus either. At the strait, Parvus knew, lay the world's tipping point. Properly defended, Istanbul could bottle up the Black Sea wheat that might otherwise feed France and England. He knew those countries had been grinding Russian grain into flour since 1794. A blockade at Istanbul could also prevent the arrival in Russia of crucial military supplies, crippling the Russian mobilization.

But Germany's food supply was almost as vulnerable as Britain's.[6] Germany, to be sure, had plenty of munitions and impressive state-controlled railway logistics: the Etappen System. Yet western Germany depended on the Atlantic for food, brought in mostly through Antwerp and Rotterdam. Its own grain supply would be in danger if Germany were entirely encircled. Railways through German-controlled Poland hardly existed, and grain from the Baltic might slow or stop if Russia and Britain could block the Baltic trade. From the days of the Hanseatic League, the Baltic still carried grain that supplied eastern Germany. German tariffs did not stop that grain but only ensured that much of Russia's grain traveled to Germany by water. Germany had spent a billion deutsche marks in the last thirty years trying to improve its path to German-controlled Poland with little effect. With the Etappen System it could fight quickly but not for very long.

And so, Germany's ultimatums to Russia to disarm went unanswered, and war was declared. We are used to thinking of World War I in terms of trenches in Europe, but Parvus knew that war would be fought over grain. Whoever won on the Black Sea and the straits connecting it to the Mediterranean would win the war.

England at first relied on a simple naval strategy: keep Germany under lock and key by patrolling and mining the North Sea. If Germany was likely to invade Belgium on its way to France, it was unlikely to seize and control Antwerp in time. Without Antwerp and Rotterdam, western Germany could starve. Britain explicitly used Abraham Lincoln's expanded strategy of blockade, blocking any goods that might supply Germany, food above all. Britain would prevent Belgian and Dutch merchants from selling grain to Germany by demanding exorbitant bonded guarantees that any grain bought in Belgium and Holland would not be re-sold to Germany. After six decades of Europe's reliance on oceans of grain, which military alliance would starve first?

As principal economic advisor and military provisioner to the Unionists in Turkey, Parvus would have been directly involved in the delicate negotiations that pushed the Ottoman Empire into its alliance with Germany between August and October 1914. Later German communications suggest that Parvus had strongly supported Germany's position. Other communists made it clear that they would support neither side. They all wanted revolution and understood that the colored blobs would not do the fighting. They believed nationalism was an illusion and workers would be the cannon fodder for this imperial war.

Parvus thought differently. He knew that in Russia, privation during and after the Russo-Japanese War had provoked Russian soldiers, workers, and peasants to reject the tsar. Indeed, the unwillingness of Russian soldiers to fight had forced the tsar to sign the October Manifesto creating a Duma. He knew that the Russian military was itself a powder keg: tensions between gentry officers and common Russian soldiers had flared up in 1904 on the Manchurian peninsula and in 1905 in Moscow and just outside Odessa, most famously on the battleship *Potemkin*.[7] The hierarchical, gentry-dominated Russian military was Russia's greatest weakness because—as Friedrich Engels had shown—modern war with rifles and infantry quickly educated workers about their own deprivation and gave them a sense of their own power. Parvus strongly believed this and quoted Engels on this topic frequently. Parvus's experience in Istanbul taught him that the Russian army might also be swayed with a proper Young Turk–style infiltration of the ranks of junior officers.[8]

It might be difficult to separate Parvus's understanding of the war as a communist from his own financial interests as a grain trader and arms dealer. His former friends certainly thought so. By 1915, Parvus's German newspaper, *Die Glocke* (probably funded by Germany), warmly supported the German war, arguing that a German victory was best for the working class because any support of Russia propped up tsarism. This pro-German position led Leon Trotsky to publish Parvus's obituary, titled "Epitaph for a Living Friend." Directly addressed to Parvus, it accused him of national chauvinism. His former comrade Clara Zetkin called him a "pimp of imperialism."[9] Rosa Luxemburg, Vladimir Lenin, and most other communists said the same and thereafter would have nothing directly to do with him. But Parvus knew where the grain was going. He only needed time and hunger to do his work for him.

Britain recognized that a dreadnought might be a threat to grain that came from the Black Sea. Even before the Ottoman Empire had declared its side, Winston Churchill violated Ottoman neutrality by forcing Vickers & Co. to surrender the Turkish dreadnought to England before it could get to Istanbul. Churchill later lied about his reasons for seizing the ship. In retaliation, two German destroyers steamed to Istanbul. Threatened at sea by the English navy, they were hastily promised to the Ottoman Empire. Days later the same officers and soldiers, dressed in the uniform of the Turkish navy, moved into the Black Sea to bombard Odessa.[10] The bombardment of Russia's grain entrepôt was the first evidence that Turkey had joined the war on the Austrian-German side.

Britain fatally underestimated Istanbul. Believing the Ottoman army and navy to be weak, the British quickly organized an amphibious expedition to clear the vital path connecting the gullet cities in France and England to grain waiting on the Black Sea. They also worried that Russian oil in Baku would be inaccessible if Istanbul held the strait. The Triple Entente (Russia, France, United Kingdom) believed a fleet of destroyers and amphibious forces would make quick work of the Turkish army. In 1916, the Entente promised to turn Istanbul over to Russia at the end of the war.

But the allies learned the ancient lesson that Byzas knew when he founded Byzantium long before the city became Constantinople or Istanbul. Destroyers, submarines, machine guns, and artillery could not change a single word of that lesson. Parvus had learned it as a teenager. The pinch point of the world's trade was an impregnable fortress, and properly defended it could not be won without decades of careful planning. The Triple Entente tried to land at Gallipoli, just south of Istanbul. Wave after wave of British, Australian, and New Zealand troops came onto the beaches but faced a well-supplied Turkish army that commanded the heights above. After nearly a year of fighting, from February 1915 to January

1916, allied troops failed to capture "the city" or open a sea route to Russia. France and England would increasingly rely on American grain. In 1915 European grain prices doubled.

England and France soon faced shortages of food due to the threat posed by new German submarines that plied the Atlantic and the North Sea. A World War I submarine could destroy a ship with a torpedo from underwater, but when it surfaced, it could be sunk with a single pistol shot. This meant, crucially, that a U-boat could never safely capture a ship. As a result submarines could only destroy food and other materials, and submarine attacks on American supply ships risked bringing the United States into the war.

Germany would soon be hungrier. In 1914 the German war machine proved decisive in its rapid march through Belgium and its rapid assault on the Russians at Tannenberg. But just as in the American Civil War during the Siege of Petersburg, soldiers settled into a ground war in trenches. By 1916 the allies against Germany had coordinated multiple, continuous attacks from the east and west. This forced Germany to fight on both fronts at the same time. In January Russia attacked the Ottomans and took the cities of Erzurum and Trabzon, as well as Mush and Bitlis in the south. A Russian advance against Germany failed miserably in March, but the massive Brusilov offensive in June proved more successful. Germany's "Turnip Winter" began in 1916. It saw near starvation, plunging morale, and food riots.[11]

In the short term, Germany suffered most from the Brusilov offensive. But the costly series of battles may have fully destroyed Russia's future grain as it cost Russia perhaps a million peasant soldiers. According to economist Nikolai Kondratieff, these soldiers were taken directly from the "reapers" who had been harvesting grain in Ukraine's "possessory estates" for decades.[12] In the trenches in France, hundreds of thousands of the young sons of workers and farmers died, draining France and Great Britain. But Germany also suffered a loss of food.

Parvus understood Germany's need for speed and for grain. At some point before January 1915, he approached a top-secret organization operating inside Germany's Foreign Office called Enterprises and Incitements Against Our Enemies (Unternehmungen und Aufwiegelungen gegen unsere Feinde). It is not well understood, but the organization apparently aimed to bring about revolutions among the allies, including in Ireland, Russia, the United States, and the Middle East. Every empire had what the Germans called "reptile funds," which had no budget line and could be used to bribe political supporters inside an empire while fomenting divisions outside it. Once the war started, the German Foreign Office had an extremely large fund, in the tens of millions of deutsche marks, with rather extravagant designs for fomenting revolutions among Germany's enemies. Some of these plans, like Germany's Middle Eastern operation, were almost comical in how much money was spent and how little was realized.[13] But Parvus had a much more extensive network among revolutionaries, and money given to him was better spent. In January 1915, when more than a few hundred thousand marks were required, State Secretary of Foreign Affairs Arthur Zimmerman had to directly connect Parvus to Foreign Secretary Gottlieb von Jagow. In Zimmerman's letter of introduction, he notified the foreign secretary that "the well-known Russian Socialist and publicist, Dr. Helphand, [was] one of the main leaders of the last Russian Revolution." He continued that Germany's interests and the revolutionaries were almost identical: "the total destruction of Czarism and the division of Russia into smaller states." Zimmerman continued that Parvus believed that even after the war, Germany would always be vulnerable "if the Russian Empire were not divided into a number of separate parts."[14]

Between January and March 1915, Parvus composed a twenty-page memo titled "Preparations for a Political Mass Strike in Russia." He included little detail about exactly what would happen in

Russia besides blowing up railway bridges and oil fields, organizing strikes among railway workers and soldiers, and forcing the army to retreat to Saint Petersburg and Moscow. More broadly, he promised that secessionists in Finland and Ukraine were prepared to rise up against Russia if Germany could only fund a propaganda war inside those states. A wireless telegraph would be required to coordinate communications between the revolutionaries, Parvus, and the German Foreign Office. Most importantly, antiwar socialists in Russia could sow discord in the army and break the Russian war machine if their radical publications could be printed in neutral Switzerland and then smuggled into the hands of Russian soldiers. A revolution in Russia would disorganize the war on the eastern front, allowing Germany to concentrate its forces in the west and end the war before the United States entered the conflict. By December 1915 the state secretary of the Treasury, who was finally notified of all this spending by the Foreign Office, authorized an additional million rubles to support Parvus's plan for an independence movement in Ukraine and Finland, as well as for propaganda inside the Russian army, but complained, "There is a great deal of fantasy in his plans." Parvus's first attempt to start a revolution in February 1916 failed.[15]

But Parvus's plan was no fantasy. Impossible as it is to believe, Russia's grain would vanish.

Fourteen

GRAIN AS AUTHORITY

1916–1924

D URING THE WAR, Alexander Krivoshein's Agriculture Ministry sought to alter the grain supply infrastructure, but he only interfered with Russia's black paths and drove up prices. His desire to replace grain markets with state entities undermined imperial grain delivery to Russian cities and contributed to instability and revolution. After the February Revolution, three groups—the new Provisional Government, railroad workers' committees, and grain-delivery agents—struggled to bring order to the black paths. Bolsheviks undermined both the Provisional Government and the workers' committees in their attempts to deliver grain. The harvest would be chaos, even after the Bolsheviks seized power.

When World War I started, Krivoshein's ministry determined that feeding the army and navy was the empire's highest priority. Unwilling to work with contractors, he marked the most productive grain regions along the Black Sea as supply zones, reserved for military purposes. He permitted private sales from granaries but only after government requisitions had been met. Immediately after the Agricultural Ministry claimed and then set a price for grain in warehouses for the military, the civilian prices for the grain that remained shot up as owners tried to compensate for the artificially low prices imposed for the army and navy. By October 1915, more than 500 of Russia's 659 cities reported food shortages. Krivoshein's grain-supply plan to support Russia's military starved its cities.[1]

Between provinces in Russia, competing civilian institutions sought to replace the existing grain-trading and credit network that fed Russia's cities. A governmental agricultural organization called the Union of Zemstvos simultaneously created a department of supply, a stockpiling commission, a warehouse commission, and a transport commission, all designed to coordinate supply and set prices, yet with overlapping roles. These competing organizations continually overruled one another.[2]

In the latter part of 1916, the Union of Zemstvos then sought to establish a single grain monopoly. Monopoly prices on grain without monopoly prices on industrial goods further aggravated tensions between the grain-producing regions in the south and east and the grain-consuming regions in the north and west. The grain-consuming cities of Moscow and Petersburg verged on riot.[3]

By 1916, Russia's grain prices had risen more quickly than prices on the world grain market, an astonishing transformation for a country where grain had been so cheap and that had exported half of its grain before the war. In response to the rapid increase in grain prices, a black market in grain trading emerged. Governors then imposed tariffs and finally embargoes on grain exports from their regions. Soon governors and tsarist militias were competing to block and sideline grain cars bound for Russian cities. While grain prices had doubled around the world, including in the grain-rich United States, in Russia the price of bread increased more than tenfold between the spring of 1916 and the spring of 1917.[4]

Then on March 8, 1917 (February 23 on the Russian calendar), protests over food rationing in Saint Petersburg led to a riot. Instead of suppressing the unrest, as it had in 1905, the army turned against its officers. Within days Tsar Nicholas II abdicated. Parvus, who had predicted much of this in his twenty-page memo, suddenly drew intense interest from the German war ministry, which he admonished not to extract a price from Russia's ruling Duma or break Russia into pieces. Both actions would now only embolden the Russian opposition and maintain the war, he wrote.[5] He also knew these actions would strengthen the authority of nationalists, liberals, and manufacturers. For Parvus, who remembered the fate of communists in the Paris Commune and his friends executed by Russia in 1905, this would be unacceptable.

Instead, Parvus said, the German government needed to spend much more, perhaps an additional fifty million deutsche marks, to send a sealed train of Bolsheviks and Mensheviks to the Finland Station outside Saint Petersburg. The Germans would have to follow up with delivery of pistols, dynamite, and medicines. He could arrange for grain deliveries to Germany from Russian warehouses on the Baltic. His agents in neutral Denmark would contact agents in Petersburg and elsewhere on the Baltic by wireless telegraph. He already controlled neutral ships with Danish and Swedish flags.[6]

The Bolsheviks and many of the Mensheviks, Parvus promised, would embrace defeat. Some Russian socialists supported the war. These Social Patriots, Russian socialists who supported Russia's side in the conflict, needed to be defeated with counterpropaganda. He promised that the Bolsheviks and Mensheviks would permit an independent Ukraine and an independent Finland and would surrender on the eastern front.[7] His new trading agencies between Copenhagen and other Baltic ports would have the support of socialist dockyard workers and permits to trade on the Baltic. Russian grain would be traded for German munitions and medicines.[8] It was much like the trade Parvus had organized in the Black Sea during the Balkan Wars. The German army would have bread, the measure of victory; Russia would have revolution.

Between fifty and two hundred million deutsche marks flowed from Germany to the Bolsheviks in 1917. Parvus multiplied that aid with his efficient smuggling operation. Much went to the delivery of newspapers. The Bolsheviks' access to machine guns and artillery by mid-1917 gave them the military capacity to defend themselves against the Duma and the counterrevolution under General

Lavr Kornilov, just as the Young Turks had defended themselves against a counterrevolution by the sultan in 1909. In mid-1917 the Duma tried to put Vladimir Lenin, Leon Trotsky, and others on trial as German agents. Prosecutors announced in the newspapers that they had considerable evidence of telegraphic communication between Lenin and Parvus through third parties that showed how German money was funding the Bolsheviks. The October Revolution prevented the trial, and the documents have disappeared.[9]

BOLSHEVIK SUCCESS WAS not primarily about machine guns. "Peace, Land, and Bread" was the Bolshevik slogan, and success had much to do with bread and the control of the new grain pathways inside Russia. As Russian grain flowed from ports along the Baltic to the German army in 1917, the revolution changed.

Cheap and abundant newspapers became the crucial method by which the Bolsheviks presented their side of the story of Russia's continuing problems. In the February Revolution of 1917 (March 8 on the western calendar), after Tsar Nicholas II abdicated, the Duma became Russia's official government. Yet the Duma shared power with the soviets, the workers' councils promoted by the Bolsheviks and Mensheviks. The soviets had more authority in the cities, including police authority, as well as a much more active press.

The press was crucial to Bolshevik authority. When Lenin arrived by train in April, for example, he delivered his "April Theses," which declared that the government was bourgeois and that all power should go to the soviets. He called for "revolutionary defeatism," declaring that Russia had more to gain in defeat than in victory. He called for nationalization of all of Russia's banks and for the army and navy to be abolished. In June German state secretary Arthur Zimmerman assured the state minister in Bern that the Bolshevik newspaper *Pravda* was already printing three hundred thousand copies.[10] Parvus's press in Stockholm reproduced Lenin's articles. The German government then smuggled Lenin's

April Theses through confidential third parties to Russian soldiers on the front.[11] In the "July Days" soldiers, sailors, and workers joined armed demonstrations against the Duma that broke down the unstable balance of power that existed between it and the soviets. State Secretary Richard von Kühlmann bragged to the foreign ministry liaison officer that this "Bolshevik movement could never have attained the scale or the influence which it has today without our continual support. There is every indication that the movement will continue to grow."[12]

But grain was also a crucial part of the story of the Bolshevik victory. Even before February, as grain delivery inside Russia faltered, workers' cooperatives and urban associations began sending men into the steppe region in the south and west. They brought rubles, silver, and even manufactured goods to trade for bags of flour from rural towns that operated flour mills. These *mesochniki* (baggers or sack-men) then brought their flour sacks back as luggage on trains.[13] In a way the sack-men were like twentieth-century *chumaki*. They brought the fixings for bread with them—though in concentrated form as flour. And they traveled much more quickly as passengers on railroads. Yet the *mesochniki* retraced the paths taken over the previous seven or more centuries by their ancestors, the *chumaki*, who first bound the nation together along black paths. The *mesochniki* even traveled armed—though with pistols instead of sharp sticks—to defend themselves against robbers or militias. The ability of these urban sack-men to feed workers' cooperatives helped strengthen the power and autonomy of the soviets against the authority of the Provisional Government while also demonstrating the latter's inability to feed its own people.

The railway that delivered grain to the cities *was* the state, just as Peter Watson understood and Sergei Witte had planned. The state-owned railroad corridors connecting the empire together thus became an important battleground for authority among Bolsheviks, Mensheviks, and the Duma. Between March and July 1917, conservatives, liberals, and Mensheviks sought to improve the connection between Russia's grain-producing regions in the south and east (mostly in today's Ukraine) and the grain-consuming regions in the north and west. Much of the organizational energy came from the so-called revolutionary line committees that formed among Russia's railroad workers beginning in March 1917. Committed to supporting both the soviets and the Provisional Government, these yard and repair workers gradually took over the management of the railroad from tsarist officials who had been abandoning their posts after the tsar abdicated. The line committees emphasized breaking up the tsarist militias that had created roadblocks on the railroads in the previous year. They organized the rebuilding of railway engines by exchanging parts. They mostly succeeded.[14]

By May, however, the Bolsheviks increasingly sought to undermine the railway line committees, regarding them as a dangerous, competing center of political power. In particular George Plekhanov, a leading Menshevik and the so-called father of Russian Marxism, stood at the head of the line committees. Plekhanov, who knew his Marx better than Lenin did, strongly opposed Lenin's April Theses and publicly bruited about that Lenin's Bolsheviks had German funding through Parvus, though he had no concrete proof. His railroad line's close working relationship with Minister of Justice Alexander Kerensky (a Socialist Revolutionary whose party had once supported assassination of tsarist officials) and Provisional Government minister-chairman Prince Georgy Lvov (a liberal) suggested a cross-party unity that the Bolsheviks rejected.

To break the line committees' power as an alternative state authority, the Bolsheviks took advantage of internal fault lines inside the railway brotherhoods. They organized unions among track liners one rank below the yard and repair workers, criticizing the line committees as groups of arrogant and selfish yard and repair workers who claimed to represent all railroad workers. The Bolsheviks separately lobbied the self-important "ribbon unions" (engineers, brakemen, and firemen) who stood *above* the members of the line committees in the railroad hierarchy, arguing that these workers were advocating raises that benefited only themselves against more skilled workers. A series of crippling strikes against the line committees began during the July Days and lasted through October. These actions drastically cut the efficiency of the state railroads and slowed the delivery of grain to cities. While the factional hatreds between liberals, Socialist Revolutionaries, Mensheviks, and Bolsheviks may have been an insoluble problem in Russia, the Bolsheviks apparently also targeted the state railroads to undermine the Duma as well as the railroads as a competing source of state authority. As Russia's railroads devolved into chaos, the Bolsheviks' claim to provide a military solution to the problem of the grain supply grew more and more appealing.[15]

The February Revolution—a cooperative effort of socialists, liberals, Bolsheviks, and Mensheviks—was overturned by the October Revolution, which put the Bolsheviks in power. Some of the problems after the February Revolution may have also been insoluble. As economist Nikolai Kondratieff pointed out, Russian army deaths in the war ensured that reaping Russia's grain would be impossible without bringing millions of urban workers into the countryside. No grain-distribution system might have successfully fed Russia. That said, the October Revolution made a bad grain-distribution system worse.

The Bolshevik "Decree on Land" converted all land to state land and then declared that it would be redistributed. While the redistribution of land shrank the number of landless peasants, it also broke up the "frontier estates" that had been Russia's primary source of grain. For a variety of reasons, five-hundred- to one-thousand-acre estates may have been the most practical way to grow wheat. Larger plots may have been necessary for growing grain on the steppe for numerous reasons. Efficient grain plowing and harvesting on rugged, flat plains demanded heavy equipment;

the dry plains needed coordinated, long-distance irrigation; and the plains had long used a four-field rotation system that required leaving many acres unused each season.[16]

The revolution also apparently revealed other difficulties in relying on the peasant estates to produce more food. Russian agrarian economist Alexander Chayanov did careful measurements of peasant productivity immediately after the revolution. He noted, based on these close studies, that peasants didn't respond to the market the way one would think. Disagreeing with David Ricardo, he argued that land, labor, and capital were not three equally replaceable quantities for a peasant. Because peasant families employed *themselves* to work, their resistance to drudgery was exponential. As they got closer to the peak amount of work they and their families could do, their resistance to that drudgery got sharper and sharper. In that environment, if the price of grain increased, as it did in 1918 and 1919, a family might not apply more labor to produce more crops in order to get more capital or land. Instead, peasants might actually produce *less* grain when prices rose because no increase in capital or land could match the satisfaction peasants got from not working themselves so hard. He also found that peasants worked hardest when they had young children, then gradually lowered the total working hours on the farm when the children got older. The family life cycle, not prices, governed their behavior. A "frontier estate," by comparison, looked more like a capitalist firm in that a farmer could purchase extra land, labor, and capital when grain prices were high. Bolsheviks rejected Chayanov's assessment of the peasant economy because it appeared to favor kulaks and suggested that peasant agriculture could not save Russia. He was arrested in 1930 on made-up charges and exiled to Kazakhstan. In 1937 he was rearrested and shot on the same day.[17]

A MONTH AFTER the October Revolution, Parvus and the German government parted ways. Rebellions in the trenches in

France and Germany may have persuaded him that a workers' revolution was emerging there. Parvus pinned his hopes on the Third Zimmerwald Conference in Switzerland that began in September 1917, which he hoped would unite the social democrats of Europe and create a separate socialist-led peace. But the unity of socialists soon broke down with a sharp Bolshevik-Menshevik split. In Germany Parvus then sided with the German social democrats (who reservedly supported a war of defense) against the Spartacists (revolutionary communists who sought to create general strikes in the trenches and in Germany's major cities). To quell the Spartacists the social democrats made a fateful alliance with the army and the far-right Freikorps. The Freikorps rounded up and killed hundreds of Spartacists, including Rosa Luxemburg and Karl Liebknecht. Parvus had known where they were, the story goes, but would not give up their location. The Freikorps found them anyway, killed them, and threw their bodies in a canal.

When the Bolsheviks seized power in Russia in October, they sought an end to the war but lacked a common front with Mensheviks and the social democrats of other countries. Between December 1917 and March 1918, German-Russian peace negotiations at the railway hub of Brest-Litovsk proved a dismal failure for the Bolsheviks. The Germans demanded not only the withdrawal of Russian troops from Finland and Ukraine but also control of the entire Varangian grain corridor from Königsberg to Odessa. This area produced most of Russia's grain and included the new spine of the Russian Empire that Bethel Henry Strousberg had built and Sergei Witte had improved. The revolutionaries could only claim the old Volga corridor. When the German army began to advance on Russian positions in Operation Faustschlag, the newly formed Red Guards could not push the army back. Trotsky was forced to sign the peace. His mission at Brest-Litovsk was a failure.

Poland and Ukraine's separation from Russia had already started before Brest-Litovsk was over. The Ukrainian People's Republic signed a separate "Bread Peace" promising to sell food to the Central Powers. The German military took the peace as an invitation to invade and marched into Ukraine, seizing Kiev, Odessa, and most of the region's principal cities.[18] The separation of Ukraine and Poland ensured that Russia's most productive grain-exporting lands would be unavailable to anyone but the Central Powers. Here Catherine the Great's physiocratic strategy of edge expansion through grain production proved Russia's undoing. With all of Russia's wealth on its western and southern edges, Germany's usurpation of those edges made feeding Russia much harder.

When he returned to Russia's new capital in Moscow, Trotsky shortly became commissar of the Red Army, with a plan to recruit five hundred thousand soldiers. To cope with the seizure of trains by both local soviets and armed bands of former soldiers, Trotsky created "flying detachments" of soldiers, sailors, and unemployed workers to try to stop the "sack-men."[19] The newly created Commissariat of Food in Russia then declared a food emergency and went to the countryside to seize any visible agricultural surplus.[20]

IN THE ORGANIZATION of the Red Army, Parvus's discoveries between 1911 and 1913 in Turkey served as an inspiration. In 1918 Trotsky would adopt the Young Turks' hybrid military-educational structure when he assumed command. Senior imperial officers would be held in check by younger political officers called commissars. Trotsky spent over three years on a mobile railway car, and the Red Army itself became the agent of radicalization and politicization of the Russian military. The railway car had two engines, a printing press, telegraph equipment, and thousands of Russian primers, calendars, pamphlets on Marxism, histories of the French Revolution, and copies of a Bolshevik analysis of the progress of the Russian Revolution. Trotsky and Parvus's cheap newspaper, Izvestia, had been the primary instrument of propaganda and radicalization in 1905, but by 1918 the newspaper and educational propaganda became fused with the army's own military structure—just as it had in the Ottoman army.

And just as in the Ottoman army, the older, hardened officers of the Russian Empire were brought by the tens of thousands into the Bolshevik army, where young political commissars would oversee each imperial officer. Commissars could countermand military orders on the battlefield if they violated party principles. The message of a new Russian nation, just like that of the Turkish nation before it, would be transmitted along the black paths alongside food, fuel, and munitions. Russian soldiers and their officers would absorb a highly structured curriculum in Marxist thought. This military structure, which emphasized soldier education of a received Communist curriculum, is well known to historians of Russia.[21] Only Trotsky, Parvus's closest associate, would have known that the model borrowed heavily from the revolution of the Young Turks.

The period between 1918 and 1922 saw starvation, civil war, and chaos. The Soviet population dropped by seven million in 1920, eleven million in 1921, and thirteen million between 1920 and 1922. Only two million had emigrated, while five million had died of starvation alone. Most died from the consequences of diseases like dysentery and cholera that chased hunger, as in the European famines of the 1840s and the Russian famine of 1891. Those two famines had a smaller demographic impact than the five hungry years that began in Russia in 1918.[22]

The association between the black paths and state authority were nowhere more visible than during the Russian Civil War, a period in which all the European powers were making war on the Soviet Union. Powerful armies targeted grain corridors that could be broken off and serve as a sort of Etappen fragment. Alexander Kolchak's white army relied on a railway corridor in Siberia, as did the Czechoslovak Legion that fought against Bolshevik authority. With control over a railway corridor, each fragment could make its own state. White Russians on the China Eastern Railway operated as their own kind of White Russian state and lasted longer than almost any other faction against the Bolsheviks.[23]

The Russian transformation in the wake of World War I was a vast and complex story of revolution, counterrevolution, secession, and consolidation. The result was a complex standoff between multiple parties with multiple visions of a future without tsars, gentry, or the rawhide whips called knouts that landed gentry kept in their barns. Years later, revolutionaries would tell the tale as a simple drama. Bolsheviks abbreviated the history as a gripping tale of workers storming the Winter Palace in October 1917.[24] Parvus the multimillionaire had learned lessons forgotten by everyone else: that wheat fields were Russia's and America's greatest assets, that liberation from serfdom might be related to a civil war in America, that bank deposits were an empire's weakest point, that control of the chokepoints of the international grain trade was the pivot on which the First World War would depend, and that a revolution could be funded by a German Empire with nothing left to lose.

Yet Parvus, who had written the road map for the soviets' seizure of power not once but twice, was deliberately erased from the story. Trotsky was given credit as the leader of the 1905 soviet, even though Parvus was its chairman. Lenin publicly declared that he had no connection to Parvus and refused to let him enter Russia but privately wired him when the Bolsheviks needed more cash.[25] Parvus died in 1924, just as Trotsky was being displaced from the Soviet Union. An important charge against Trotsky was his connection to Parvus. Trotsky's firsthand recollections of the tensions inside the party during the years before the revolution—though he carefully avoided discussing Parvus—later seemed a threat to his political opponents. Trotsky's enemies used his own recollections of Russian social democracy to make the case against him, as evidence of "Trotskyism," a deviation from the true principles of Leninist doctrine.[26] Trotsky was deported to Turkey, where he settled in Parvus's former estate in the Princes' Islands outside

Istanbul. The key story of wheat, transportation, railroads, banks, and the conversion of imperial officers into Bolsheviks would merit not even a footnote.

As I see it, Parvus was not the key actor, but his understanding of the world shows us a deeper history about the growing of food, its recipes for salvage and transport, its prehistoric long-distance distribution lines, and the abstract instruments that made that trade possible. Now, just as ten thousand years ago, producers and consumers are bound together in a common world ecology that viruses, empires, and states have only ridden upon, bits of foam on a vast, invisible deep. Parvus saw the lines that bind us all together, the empire's fault lines, and their fatal weaknesses.

CONCLUSION

YEAST COLONIZES AND feeds on grain. People plant and harvest grain, selectively apply yeast to the harvested seeds, and so feed themselves. Empires seize people, capture trade routes, plant emporia to invade, and feed their expansion by taxing subjects. For thousands of years microscopic flora and fauna have found ecological niches in the trade routes that bind and connect empires. These microscopic colonizations impose new taxes in the food-trade-tax cycle, forcing empires to adapt. The bubonic plague forced empires to close or slow down trade; the potato famine forced them to open it. Whether to regard empires as symbiotes or parasites depends on one's perspective. I tend to see empires as parasites, but one could make the argument that imperially sponsored universities—in analyzing these food-trade-tax cycles—try to prevent starvation by altering those cycles in ways that promote "growth" inside the empire. Physics, biology, chemistry, economics, and history are all, in their way, data-processing systems for empires hoping to keep their subjects—us—alive so that they can rule another day.

Was the United States an empire like Russia? Until the 1890s, I would argue, it was only partially so. Certainly US colonial expansion involved naming a parcel of land as a territory, sending colonists, planting food, and all the while expelling, killing, or encircling the original inhabitants. The US settlement differed from imperial traditions in a few respects: territories with a sufficient population applied to be states and, once accepted, received direct representation in the empire itself. The Qing may be the closest analogue to the American Empire in seeking to capture, assimilate, and incorporate subject peoples on its borders and make them fully equal to subjects in other regions. The Ottoman and Russian empires, both modeled on Byzantine and Roman antecedents, drew a sharper line between metropole and colony. Janissaries or *kolonisti* could become generals, admirals, or governors, but the colonials who fed the empire had fewer rights. Of course, the parallel sovereignty granted within the United States did not apply to native peoples displaced or surrounded by these empires—including the American one. Most American Indians would have regarded this as a distinction without a difference.

The Ottoman, Qing, and Russian empires had forms of territorial representation—even benign neglect—but their centralized executives amassed considerable authority. Crucially, most taxing powers in the Russian, Ottoman and Qing empires were centralized. After the mid-nineteenth century, new, European-dominated institutions hijacked this taxing authority. They imposed and collected those taxes directly. These new fiscal institutions were the Chinese Maritime Customs Service (1854–1950), the Ottoman Public Debt Administration (OPDA; 1881–1914), and the Russian Department of Railway Affairs (1889–1917). The first two were largely foreign controlled, and the last one was a kind of shared sovereign. They certified bonds and gradually paid off ("serviced") the empire's debt directly. The new fiscal centers owed nominal allegiance to a crown but concrete allegiance to creditors foreign and domestic. Lenders closely inspected the mandatory, published imperial reports. The Chinese Maritime Customs Service and OPDA reports meant that empires had few sovereign secrets. A persuasive, negative assessment of those reports could sharply increase the interest rates at which empires borrowed and thus hinder their ability to build or expand. These institutions had the power to set the lion's share of the empire's internal taxes and external tariffs. To a great extent these fiscal agencies *became* the empire, especially as regards the crucial issue of food circulation.

In the crucible of a civil war over slavery and southern inequality, the United States drastically altered its position in the world economy. In production it directly competed with Odessa. In its governance of the grain trade, US officials introduced a "Republican" model: a futures market, with private, shareholder-owned, competing interstate railroads to the coast. In 1787, writing what came to be called *The Federalist Papers*, James Madison proposed in Federalist No. 10 that a large republic with many factions could be safer than a small republic because the many factions' competition with one another would prevent any single faction from taking power. The War Department's plan was, in a way, like a Federalist No. 10 for railroads. One railroad monopoly was bad, but four parallel monopolies that connected Chicago to the coast might be fine. A few grain traders who profited from war were unacceptable, but hundreds of grain traders who could profit might be all right. Other technologies like dynamite and the transatlantic telegraph reduced the cost to deliver grain from the American empire to the empires of Europe. After 1865 the United States would—alongside Russia—feed empires, republics, and states in Europe and around the world.

The American deviation from an imperial mold diminished considerably during and after the Civil War. First, as the Union moved into the seceding states, it borrowed an ancient Roman system of occupation with military governors and loyalty oaths. In 1866 Congress briefly seized control of that system from the executive branch and introduced birthright citizenship with the Fourteenth Amendment. But Ku Klux Klan–led battles for white-only control of southern states led to a "Redemption" in which one-party state governments disfranchised African American citizens. After 1877, the United States, like so many other empires, now had citizens and subjects. Freed people, just like Roman slaves, for instance, could not serve on juries and had diminished access to the law. Shortly after 1877 the nation further broke its constitutional, anti-imperial promises as it expanded. It became an empire by adding territories that would never get representation, including Puerto Rico, Cuba, the Philippines, and American Samoa.

The United States and Russia were not alone in feeding the world. By the 1890s Argentina, Australia, and India were doing the same thing. The new steel pathways from prairie to emporia were largely attempts by the British Empire to offset its dependence on external food, to prevent capital flight, and to stabilize the British pound. The Ottoman and Qing empires—lacking control of their own internal fisc—had less capacity to secure cheap food internally, though subsidized internal colonization in the Balkans and Manchuria provided food to cities once imperial railways were laid. Grain growers in these overtaxed territories rose up in the Balkan and Boxer rebellions.

By comparison Russia's fiscal agency—centralized and controlled by Sergei Witte—began an ambitious program of grain expansion into steppe lands east and west of Ukraine, east of the Urals, and into Manchuria. This billion-ruble railway-construction campaign, aimed at building a deepwater port in Manchuria, failed catastrophically in the 1904–1905 Russo-Japanese War. All three agrarian empires after 1905 faced the slowly building threat that all empires faced: dependence on external food, then capital flight, then financial instability, and finally revolution. After the Russian failure in the Russo-Japanese War, revolution started and failed in Russia in 1905.

In Europe, cheap American grain fed the working classes in cities and the countryside. The relationship between cities and states changed as deepwater ports improved the lives of workers by shortening the last mile between them and grain from the plains in America as well as Russia. Ricardo's paradox ensured that landlords in agricultural regions would face lower rents and a loss of their cheap labor. Millions of those agricultural laborers came to the United States in the same ships that had carried grain abroad. Russia created an autocratic facsimile of the American line system of credit, though its many weaknesses allowed competing firms like Louis-Dreyfus & Co. to operate along its edges. Witte's attempt to borrow from French bond buyers in a bid to expand the empire was more dangerous than he realized. Once Japan closed off Port Arthur from Russia, the empire—with no year-round deepwater export port—would have no practical way to pay off these loans. Russian minister Baron Roman Romanovich Rosen suggested that the loss of Port Arthur was really the end of the Russian Empire. The bonds would never be redeemed.

World War I, as a battle between European nations dependent on foreign grain, meant that the grain-powered great powers could only last so long. The allies' inability to break the blockade at Istanbul prolonged the war, leading to starvation in Belgium and long-lasting devastation in France. Germany endured longer in part through secret negotiations for Baltic grain that are still not fully understood. It is possible that only Parvus could answer the question of how much grain Germany got in its financial arrangement with him and, indirectly, the Bolsheviks.

For the Ottoman, Qing, and Russian empires, revolutions arrived in 1908, 1911, and 1917. World War I was an interregnum in which most of the world's empires fought for control of the food-trade-tax nexus. By 1917 Bolshevik revolutionaries had gained insights from the Young Turk Revolution into how to successfully topple the massive Russian Empire. Crucial to their success but contrary to their revolutionary program, the Bolsheviks redistributed land to peasants across the steppe in 1917. They learned that authority was constituted through the control of bread and that breaking up the grain-delivering power of the Duma, the revolutionary line committees, and even the *mesochniki* was critical to seizing power. The Soviet Union would continue to define itself as the monopoly holder and distributor of bread, just as the ancient Romans had done in the days of the *annona*.

Ukraine's absorption into the Soviet Union made the Soviet experiment possible again. Indeed, modern Russia's relative weakness as a great power now (in 2021) may still ultimately depend on its separation from Ukraine. Russia's gross domestic product is the now the size of Italy's. Ukraine has always been the greatest prize, as Catherine the Great well knew. After 1930, Joseph Stalin would create a new story about Ukraine, as a place of grain abundance that large-scale independent farmers—kulaks—had taken for themselves. His brutal attempt to collectivize the farms of Ukraine in 1932 and redraw the lines of delivery and trade introduced an artificial famine that killed millions more in Ukraine in what has been called the *holodomor* (hunger plague).

THE NAZIS WOULD soon garble Parvus's role in the events of World War I. He did not save the German army by simultaneously helping feed it and ending the war on the eastern front. Instead, he was the central character in a Jewish-orchestrated coup that defeated Germany. The Communist Party was imagined as invaders who infiltrated German regiments, sowed discord, and operated as a fifth column inside Germany, contributing to German defeat in World War I and thus impoverishing Germany for a generation.

Shortly after Parvus died, Joseph Goebbels bought and moved into his house. There Goebbels began to craft the propaganda for a new empire. Goebbels's propagandistic style of interpreting the world economy, use of barnyard idioms, and predictions about the future borrowed a great deal from Parvus. This Third Reich, Goebbels wagered, would reclaim the Ukrainian steppe in the interest of so-called lebensraum, a living place for an imagined Aryan people. This was hardly the first, nor would it be the last, plan to claim the vast and fertile plains across the Black Sea. The Nazis would murder hundreds of thousands of Poles and Ukrainians and millions of Jews who stood in the way of this new Etappen program. It nearly succeeded.

Parvus's first son, Yevgeny Gnedin, was born in Dresden in 1898 and grew up in Odessa. His mother took him there in 1902 after Parvus's affair with an actress had produced another son.[1] In the 1920s he was a journalist; by 1939 he had become press spokesman for the Soviet Embassy in Berlin. Parvus's second son, Lev Helfhand, named after Leon (Lev) Trotsky, entered diplomatic service in 1925, contributed to the Franco-Soviet rapprochement in 1927, and became right-hand man to Pavel Litvinov, people's commissar of foreign affairs, equivalent to the American secretary of state. During the 1930s Lev was stationed in the Soviet Embassy in Rome. In May 1939, when Stalin determined to sign a pact with Adolph Hitler's Germany, all high-ranking Jews in the Russian state service were rounded up. Yevgeny was captured, tortured, and exiled to Siberia. Lev managed to escape to the United States.

Lev took the name Leon Moore, became a translator for journalist Dorothy Thompson, and provided crucial information about the internal workings of the Soviet Union for the Office of Strategic Services (OSS), predecessor of the Central Intelligence Agency. As the United States strove to find a way to ally with the Soviets against Hitler, Leon suggested that the Black Sea was key. If the Nazis took the Black Sea, the Russians would be forced to destroy their fleet and would never be able to ally with Britain, France, and the United States to open up a second front. Leon knew Stalin well and reported that he was vain and would only respond to American overtures if someone with authority went to beg for his support. Moore regarded Henry Wallace and Wendell Willkie as possessing a rank that would "flatter the vanity of a dictator like Stalin" and get him to agree to an alliance and a second front. As the highest-ranking Soviet defector to the United States,

Leon Moore was a key asset in building the US-Soviet alliance. He continued to analyze Soviet doctrine for the OSS during and after the war.[2]

In private life Moore became an international grain merchant, made a fortune dealing in war materials, and ran a commodities arbitrage firm, the Intercontinental Exchange of New York, which he passed on to his wife and daughter. For their part, Leon's wife and daughter, who had escaped with him to the United States, became world-renowned exponents of the Stanislavski method of acting.[3] In 1955, after Stalin's death, Leon's older half brother, Yevgeny, was rehabilitated and returned to journalism in Russia, becoming a prominent dissident in the 1960s. Yevgeny's daughter, Tatyana Gnedina, became one of Russia's most famous science fiction writers, though little of her work has been translated into English.[4]

Tatyana Gnedina's *The Last Day of the Tugotrons* is about a boy with a magic bicycle who travels to a world where massive robots dominate the smaller humans who perform labor for them. The robots have muzzles that prevent them from deviating from the orders imposed by a single robot who controls them. The workers are starved because the robots throw bags of harvested wheat into the ocean, not understanding or caring that the grain is used to feed the humans. The boy takes a bag and unties it, sees the grain there, and instructs the humans to untie the bags to feed themselves. The boy then tells the humans to tie knots everywhere, because he has learned that robots cannot untie knots. Next he reprograms the robots with poetry that makes them spout nonsense and break down. In the end the grain is freed. All the workers celebrate the collapse of their robot overlords by eating donuts.[5]

One could read the novel as a story about a decadent technocratic West brought down by workers and intellectuals, and doubtless this is how she described it to her Soviet publishers. One could also read it as the story of a tsarist bureaucracy that filled the Black

Sea with oceans of grain to feed Europe and the collapse of that system as Bolsheviks learned to tie the tsarist transportation infrastructure into knots. After Stalin's death, that reading might also have been acceptable. Finally, of course, one could read it as an anti-totalitarian novel, and this is surely how millions of Russian children read it in 1964: as the story of a mechanistic police state that mismanages its production, muzzles its leadership, starves its subjects, and is brought down by human ingenuity and clandestine (*samizdat*) literature.

The wheat is one key to the story's tension, for a starved population is easily controlled. But when an intellectual shows revolutionaries how to tangle the ropes that bind tyrants to the rural countryside, then revolution can begin. Tatyana Gnedina's grandfather Parvus would have been proud that she remembered him.

APPENDIX

Value and Proportions of United States Wheat and Flour Exports

Date	Wheat & flour exports: thousands of dollars	Percentage of total export as flour
1800	6,557	100%
1801	14,572	98%
1802	10,687	97%
1803	9,310	99%
1804	7,100	88%
1805	8,325	100%
1806	6,867	85%
1807	10,753	96%
1808	1,936	82%
1809	5,944	100%
1810	6,846	96%
1811	14,662	100%
1812	13,687	100%
1813	13,591	100%
1814	1,734	100%
1815	7,209	100%
1816	7,712	70%
1817	17,968	100%
1818	11,971	99%
1819	6,109	98%
1820	5,297	100%

continues

Date	Wheat & flour exports: thousands of dollars	Percentage of total export as flour
1821	4,319	100%
1822	5,106	100%
1823	4,968	100%
1824	5,780	100%
1825	4,231	100%
1826	4,160	99%
1827	4,435	100%
1828	4,284	100%
1829	5,800	100%
1830	6,132	99%
1831	10,462	95%
1832	4,974	98%
1833	5,643	99%
1834	4,560	99%
1835	4,446	99%
1836	3,575	100%
1837	3,014	99%
1838	3,611	100%
1839	6,940	100%
1840	11,779	86%
1841	8,583	90%
1842	8,292	89%
1843	4,027	93%
1844	7,260	93%
1845	5,735	94%
1846	13,351	87%
1847	32,183	81%
1848	15,863	83%
1849	13,037	87%
1850	7,742	92%
1851	11,550	91%
1852	14,424	82%

continues

Date	Wheat & flour exports: thousands of dollars	Percentage of total export as flour
1853	19,138	77%
1854	40,122	69%
1855	12,226	89%
1856	44,391	66%
1857	48,123	54%
1858	28,390	68%
1859	17,283	84%
1860	19,525	79%
1861	62,959	39%
1862	70,108	39%
1863	75,120	38%
1864	57,020	45%
1865	46,905	59%
1866	26,239	70%
1867	20,626	62%
1868	51,135	41%
1869	43,197	44%
1870	68,341	31%
1871	69,237	35%
1872	56,871	32%
1873	70,834	27%
1874	130,680	22%
1875	83,320	28%
1876	92,816	26%
1877	68,800	31%
1878	121,968	21%
1879	160,269	18%
1880	225,880	16%
1881	212,746	21%
1882	149,305	24%
1883	174,704	31%
1884	126,166	41%

continues

Date	Wheat & flour exports: thousands of dollars	Percentage of total export as flour
1885	125,079	42%
1886	88,706	43%
1887	142,667	36%
1888	111,019	49%

Source: Export values reported in Timothy Pitkin, *A Statistical View of the Commerce of the United States* (New Haven: Durrie & Peck, 1835), 96–97, and Louis P. McCarty, *Annual Statistician and Economist* (San Francisco: L. P. McCarty, 1889), 200. For 1800 to 1820, the United States Treasury only recorded the bushels of wheat and barrels of flour exported, not their value. For those years flour barrels exported were multiplied by the average export price of flour barrels in John H. Klippart, *The Wheat Plant: Its Origin, Culture . . .* (New York, A.O. Moore & Co., 1860), 328–329. For the small quantity of wheat exported between 1800 and 1820, the average price of one dollar per barrel (consistent from the 1820s through the 1840s) was used. Pitkin reports that grain exports before 1820 can only be approximate given the large amount of smuggling. I report these numbers because they are either incorrect or incomplete in the *Historical Statistics of the United States*. As of 2021, according to Douglas Irwin, Cambridge University Press has no plans to update the published reports. This is unfortunate because the invisibility of wheat exports has led historians to overstate the role of cotton and understate the role of wheat in United States exports before the American Civil War.

ACKNOWLEDGMENTS

MY DEBTS ARE long and deep. Apologies in advance to friends I have forgotten to thank. My kids Ren and Eli Hahamovitch listened to more stories about grain than any grown children should have had to. Ren's comments on the proposal helped immensely, and his own dissertation research on the parallel histories of Russia and the United States makes me proud. Eli's patient visits to my office with his lizards cheered me up immensely. Jamie Kreiner, Susan Mattern, and Ari Levine read and corrected my ancient and medieval chapters. Ari, in particular, helped me to think broadly about the medieval world. I spent two fantastic hours on the Bosporus Strait with logistics professionals Rowan Kersten and Ömer Bekdemir, who taught me much about Istanbul, international logistics, and how to understand Mehmed II's throat cutter. Rob Ferguson read and pointed out flaws in my discussion of Russian imperial matters. Steven Krug and Annelle Brunson provided helpful feedback about the Civil War chapter. Bill Kelson shared notes, articles, and commentary about late-Qing commerce. Karyna Hlyvynska transcribed some obscenely grainy scans of Russian and Ukrainian documents that I could not parse. She translated the *chumaki* folk songs as well.

I first came to this topic through time spent at the Agrarian Studies Center, led by James Scott and managed by Kay Mansfield. Jim has strongly influenced my way of thinking about the world and a scholar's place in it, not least in finding connections between food, life, conflict, and the social. The enormous debt to his scholarship should be visible throughout, but it is his book *Against the Grain* that has been most influential in my thinking about ancient and modern wheat. I was just a hanger-on in 1999, but Gaston Gordillo, Rohan D'Souza, Jeanette Keith, and the other fellows welcomed me like a brother. Likewise in 2013 the fellows at the National Humanities Center welcomed me into their reading group. I particularly remember learning much, when I presented on dynamite and revolution, from Luis E. Carcamo-Huechante, Christian De Pee, Lynn Mary Festa, Julie Greene, Heather Hyde Minor, Andrew Jewett, Martha Jones, Elizabeth Krause, Anna Krylova, Marixa Lasso, Michael Lurie, James Maffie, Tim Marr, Charlie McGovern, Anna Christina Ribeiro, Jane Ashton Sharp, Noel Kimiko Sugimura, and Martin A. Summers. A Guggenheim Fellowship came at just the right moment in 2019, allowing me to finish the first draft of this book.

I cannot fail to thank Nicolas Barreyre, who was prepared to talk with me about bonds for longer than anyone I have ever met. He is that rare scholar who will, with a winning smile, challenge every bloated argument you toss around. His invitation to the École des hautes études en sciences sociales (EHESS) is one of the highlights of my life because he put me in touch with Russianists, Americanists, economists, and social scientists who think about the world completely differently than American historians do. I especially admire the way that French historians regard history as a science and defend it as such. There are so many sentences here that are more reliable because of challenges from Nicolas that I cannot name them all. Indeed, when I asked Nicolas to review a late draft of the manuscript, he gave me many pages of corrections both large and small. That I did not follow his advice in all cases is testament to my ignorance and pugnacity. Among the historians at EHESS who heard my talk about the mercantocracy, whose constituents I here call the boulevard barons, I remember especially challenging questions from Eric Monnet, Gilles Postel-Vinay,

Jérôme Bourdieu, Cam Walker, and Pierre-Cyrille Hautcoeur. The economists Françoise Daucé, Alain Blum, Marc Élie, Juliette Cadiot, and Thomas Piketty had sharp questions but also made me think that my observations on the broader shape of what American economists have narrowly called the "American invasion" were worthwhile. Among the Russianists who made me think more broadly about the Russian famine, I would like to thank Thomas Grillot, Yann Philippe, Romain Huret, and Emmanuel Falguières. A long lunch where Noam Maggor and I sparred about the question of industrialization helped me think through why I consider food so much more important than steel or copper in the American economy. Some day I will convince him.

Richard White and Branden Adams invited me to give an early version of this book's argument at the Stanford Approaches to Capitalism Workshop. The feedback there was invaluable, particularly from Richard, Branden, and Charles Postel. The Dirty History Workshop on Agriculture, Environment, and Capitalism at the University of Georgia (UGA) also let me try out my chapter on nitroglycerin. Richard Smith, at the University of Liverpool, corrected me about nitroglycerin's explosive properties. I recall especially useful criticism from Bryant Barnes, Bill Kelson, Matt O'Neal, J. P. Schmidt, Pablo Lapegna, Dan Rood, and Jamie Kreiner. Long talks with J. P. Schmidt helped me to think about the relationship between ecological and political change. Nancy Manley invited me to give an early version of Chapters 1 through 3 at the UGA Genetics Wednesday Seminar Series. Finally, Sarah Covert, an expert fungologist and scholar of ecology, corrected me in matters large and small about *P. infestans*. This included letting me call it *infestans*, though no self-respecting biologist would do so.

Andi Zimmerman and Fred Corney, with little notice, read the full manuscript at its most overheated and epigrammatic stage and pointed out my many infelicities and historical failings. A hundred thank-yous are due to them still. They are payable—if I'm being honest—in Belgian beer and frites.

I have never had an editor like Brian Distelberg. He took my draft—a scattered collection of observations as I see it now—and forced me to be blunter and more honest about my central argument. His first comments ran for forty-two, single-spaced pages. I quailed when he asked for a longer book. His suggestions for recasting this book were brilliant, even if most of what he said about my failures as a storyteller made me blush with embarrassment. The current organizational structure relies on him. I thought I was done; then Michael Kaler came back with five hundred annotations in Microsoft Word. He pointed out unclear passages, weak transitions, and places where I assumed knowledge about things no one else knows or cares about. That this is a book and not the posthumous ramblings of an obsessed scholar are thanks to both Brian and Michael. Copyeditor Jennifer Kelland gave my prose the final drubbing it deserved. Many thanks to her as well. Over the last twenty years agent Deirdre Mullane has always made me think bigger. She taught me that wandering, following quirky trails, and sweating the details were not character flaws but a path to my own voice and structure. Her poet's ear for language is astonishing. Thank you Deirdre for everything.

Cindy Hahamovitch read more early drafts of these chapters than has been fair for any human. Her guidance, comments, revisions, and suggestions are so deeply embedded in this book that I could not possibly thank her in each instance. I would have to double the footnotes. At so many points she was the one who helped me think clearly and prodded me to do better. This book is a product of her patience with me and my love for her. She believed I could write an impossible book, and that has made all the difference.

NOTES

INTRODUCTION

1. Scott Reynolds Nelson, "The Real Great Depression," *Chronicle of Higher Education*, October 1, 2008, www.chronicle.com/article/the-real -great-depression. Within the next few weeks, the article had been translated in Peru (*La Republica*, October 2, 2008), Spain (*Cotizalia*, October 7, 2008), Canada (*Le Devoir*, October 8, 2008), Hungary (*Port-folio*, October 13, 2008), Italy (*Il Foglio*, October 15, 2008), Switzerland (*Weltwoche*, October 15, 2008), and Greece (*Elefthrotypia*, October 26, 2008).

2. The change in the currency for international exchange was subtler. In April 2009 a Chinese think tank proposed an alternative central bank to the World Bank and the International Monetary Fund, which China regards as dominated by the United States and Europe. This became the Asian Infrastructure Investment Bank. Considerable resources were then invested in the Belt and Road Initiative, a series of rail-based "economic corridors" to Russia, Europe, Southeast Asia, the Middle East, and Africa. In nearly all cases, foreign lending for these projects was denominated in the renminbi rather than in dollars or euros. Cross-border trade denominated in renminbi peaked in 2015 at two trillion renminbi and then dropped after turbulence in the stock market. Elcano Royal Institute, "Renminbi Internationalization: Stuck in Mid-River, for Now—Analysis," *Eurasia Review*, July 9, 2018, https://www.eurasiare view.com/09072018-renminbi-internationalization-stuck-in-mid-river -for-now-analysis.

3. Scott Reynolds Nelson, *A Nation of Deadbeats: An Uncommon History of America's Financial Disasters* (New York: Knopf, 2012).

4. "Let Them Eat Baklava," *The Economist*, March 17, 2012, www .economist.com/middle-east-and-africa/2012/03/17/let-them-eat -baklava.

5. Memorandum of the Odessa Committee on Trade and Manufactures, 1873, translated in UK Parliament, *Reports from H.M. Consuls*

on Manufactures and Commerce of Their Consular Districts, BPP-C.1427 (1876), 438–439.

6. Parvus, "Der Weltmarkt und die Agrarkrisis," published serially in ten parts in *Die Neue Zeit* from November 1895 to March 1896.

7. Israel Helphand, *Technische Organisation der Arbeit ("Cooperation" und "Arbeitsheilung"): Eine Kritische Studie* (Basel: University of Basel, 1891), 30–34.

8. Helphand, *Technische Organisation Der Arbeit*; Parvus, "Der Weltmarkt und die Agrarkrisis," *Die Neue Zeit* 14 (November 1895): 197ff.

9. Parvus, *Die Kolonialpolitik und der Zusammenbruch* (Leipzig: Verlag der Leipziger Buchdruckerei Aktiengesellschaft, 1907), 78ff; this resembles, I think, one part of Brent Shaw's critique of Chris Wickham's contention that trade changes mattered more than imperial tax structures in creating the militarized classes rooted in microregions that Wickham sees as characteristic of the Middle Ages. Brent D. Shaw, "After Rome: Transformations of the Early Mediterranean World," *New Left Review* 51 (2008): 89–114. Shaw's article critiques Chris Wickham, *Framing the Early Middle Ages: Europe and the Mediterranean, 400–800* (New York: Oxford University Press, 2005).

10. Zbyněk Anthony Bohuslav Zeman and Winifred B. Scharlau, *The Merchant of Revolution: The Life of Alexander Israel Helphand (Parvus), 1867–1924* (New York: Oxford University Press, 1965); Boris Chavkin, "Alexander Parvus: Financier der Weltrevolution," *Forum für Osteuropäische Ideen-und Zeitgeschichte* 11, no. 2 (2007): 31–58; M. Asim Karaömerlioglu, "Helphand-Parvus and His Impact on Turkish Intellectual Life," *Middle Eastern Studies* 40, no. 6 (2004): 145–165. Other children and mistresses are discussed in a Russian popular history magazine; see Vadim Erlikhman, "Doktor Parvus, Kuklovod Revolyutsia," *Rodina* (March 2015); Elisabeth Heresch, *Geheimakte Parvus: die gekaufte Revolution* (München: Herbig, 2013).

CHAPTER 1: THE BLACK PATHS

1. Kvass-patriotism was first used by P. A. Vyazemsky in his "Letter from Paris to S. D. Poltoratsky," *Moscow Telegraph*, 1827. See Alexandra Vasilyevna Tikhomirova, "'Lapotno-kvasnoy patriotizm' i 'Rus poskonnaya': k voprosu o russkikh natsionalnykh predmetnykh simvolakh," *Antropologicheskiy Forum* 18 (2013): 334–339; R. E. F. Smith and David Christian, *Bread and Salt: A Social and Economic History of Food and Drink in Russia* (New York: Cambridge University Press, 1984), 77–79; Carolyn Johnston Pouncy, *The "Domostroi": Rules for Russian Households in the Time of Ivan the Terrible* (Ithaca, NY: Cornell University Press, 2014).

2. Amaia Arranz-Otaegui et al., "Archaeobotanical Evidence Reveals the Origins of Bread 14,400 Years Ago in Northeastern Jordan," *PNAS* 31 (2018): 7925–7930.

3. I am indebted to Paul W. Mapp for pointing out myth's role in training children about the dangers of the future. F. M. Cornford argues for summer storage and fall planting in "The Aparxai and the Eleusinian Mysteries," in *Essays and Studies Presented to W. Ridgeway*, ed. E. C. Quiggin, 153–166 (Cambridge: Cambridge University Press, 1913). The translation comes mostly from Helene P. Foley, ed., *The Homeric Hymn to Demeter: Translation, Commentary, and Interpretive Essays* (Princeton, NJ: Princeton University Press, 1994).

4. Ivan Jakovlevich Rudchenko, *Chumatskia Narodnya Pyesni* (Kiev: M. P. Fritsa, 1874).

5. Rudchenko, *Chumatskia Narodnya Pyesni*; M. Gustave de Molinari, *Lettres sur la Russie* (Brussels and Leipzig: A. Lacroix, 1861), 235–256. On medieval exports from the Black Sea, see William H. McNeill, *Europe's Steppe Frontier, 1500–1800* (Chicago: University of Chicago Press, 1964), chap. 2.

6. Ernst Kapp, *Philosophische oder vergleichende allgemeine Erdkunde als wissenschaftliche Darstellung der Erdverhältnisse und des Menschenlebens* (Braunschweig: G. Westerman, 1845).

7. I rely here on Keith Hopkins's classic article "Taxes and Trade in the Roman Empire (200 B.C.–A.D. 400)," *Journal of Roman Studies* 70 (1980): 101–125.

8. Thomas J. Booth, "A Stranger in a Strange Land: A Perspective on Archaeological Responses to the Palaeogenetic Revolution from an Archaeologist Working Amongst Palaeogeneticists," *World Archaeology* 51, no. 4 (2019): 586–601.

9. Andrew Sherratt, "Diverse Origins: Regional Contributions to the Genesis of Farming," in *The Origins and Spread of Domestic Plants in Southwest Asia and Europe*, ed. Sue College and James Conolly (Walnut Creek, CA: Left Coast Press, 2007), 1–20.

10. Mancur Olson, "Dictatorship, Democracy, and Development," *American Political Science Review* 87, no. 3 (1993): 567–576. I cannot endorse any of the stadial arguments Olson makes, but the term "stationary bandit" is helpful for understanding this change.

11. Thomas Carlyle, *History of Friedrich II of Prussia, Called Frederick the Great* (London: Chapman & Hall, 1894), 3:83.

12. This was also called the price for "teaming work." General Assembly, Rhode Island, "An Act to Prevent Monopoly and Oppression, by excessive and unreasonable prices for many of the necessaries and conveniences of life, and for preventing engrossers, and for the better supply of

our troops in the army with such necessaries as may be wanted," *Acts and Resolves at the General Assembly of the State of Rhode Island* (Providence: General Assembly, 1777), 18.

13. Correlation in UN Economic Commission for Europe (UNECE), "Assisting Countries to Monitor the Sustainable Development Goals: Tonne-Kilometres," UNECE, https://unece.org/DAM/trans/main/wp6/pdfdocs/SDG_TKM_paper.pdf (accessed July 27, 2021). The "road transport intensity" of economic growth has been a cause for concern because of its relationship to greenhouse gas emissions. Ana Alises, Jose Manuel Vassallo, and Andrés Felipe Guzmán, "Road Freight Transport Decoupling: A Comparative Analysis Between the United Kingdom and Spain," *Transport Policy* 32 (March 2014): 186–193; Jan Havenga, "Quantifying Freight Transport Volumes in Developing Regions: Lessons Learnt from South Africa's Experience During the 20th Century," *Economic History of Developing Regions* 27, no. 2 (December 2012): 87–113; Theresa Osborne et al., "What Drives the High Price of Road Freight Transport in Central America?" (World Bank Policy Research Working Paper 6844, April 2014).

14. Heinrich Eduard Jacob, *Six Thousand Years of Bread: Its Holy and Unholy History* (Garden City, NY: Doubleday, Doran, 1944), 23–34; Elizabeth A. Warner, *The Russian Folk Theatre* (Boston: De Gruyter, Inc., 1977), 27–28.

15. Brent Shaw, *Bringing in the Sheaves: Economy and Metaphor in the Roman World* (Toronto: University of Toronto Press, 2013).

16. James C. Scott, *Against the Grain: A Deep History of the Earliest States*, Yale Agrarian Studies (New Haven, CT: Yale University Press, 2017).

17. Parvus, "Türkische Wirren," *Sächsische Arbeiter-Zeitung*, September 10, 1896.

CHAPTER 2: THE GATES OF CONSTANTINOPLE

1. David W. Tandy, *Warriors into Traders: The Power of the Market in Early Greece* (Berkeley: University of California Press, 1997); Neal Ascherson, *Black Sea* (New York: Hill & Wang, 1996); [Pseudo-Aristotle], *Oeconomica*, trans. E. S. Forster (New York: Oxford University Press, 1920), Book II.2.

2. Ernst Kapp, *Philosophische oder vergleichende allgemeine Erdkunde als wissenschaftliche Darstellung der Erdverhältnisse und des Menschenlebens* (Braunschweig: G. Westerman, 1845); Lionel Casson, *Ships and Seafaring in Ancient Times* (Austin: University of Texas Press, 1994), chap. 9.

3. Lionel Casson, *Ancient Trade and Society* (Detroit, MI: Wayne State University Press, 1984).

4. Horace, *Epistles*, 2.1.156.

5. O. S. Khokhlova et al., "Paleoecology of the Ancient City of Tanais (3rd Century BC–5th Century AD) on the North-Eastern Coast of the Sea of Azov (Russia)," *Quaternary International* 516 (May 2019): 98–110; Askold Ivantchik, "Roman Troops in the Bosporus: Old Problem in the Light of a New Inscription Found in Tanais," *Ancient Civilizations from Scythia to Siberia* 20, no. 2 (July 2014): 165.

6. Bettany Hughes, *Istanbul: A Tale of Three Cities* (New York: Hachette Book Group, 2017).

7. Paul Erdkamp, *The Grain Market in the Roman Empire: A Social, Political and Economic Study* (Cambridge: Cambridge University Press, 2005).

8. William Lynn Westermann, "Warehousing and Trapezite Banking in Antiquity," *Journal of Economic and Business History* 3, no. 1 (1930–1931): 30–54; Jason Roderick Donaldson, Giorgia Piacentino, and Anjan Thakor, "Warehouse Banking," *Journal of Financial Economics* 129, no. 2 (2018): 250–267.

9. Anna Komnene, *The Alexiad*, trans. E. R. A. Sewter (New York: Penguin Books, 1969), chap. 6. For the association of Dionysus with the Strait of Hormuz, see Wilfred H. Schoff, ed. and trans., *The Periplus of the Erythraean Sea: Travel and Trade in the Indian Ocean by a Merchant of the First Century* (New York: Longmans, Green & Co., 1912), 32–34 and footnotes on 130–133.

10. Thanks to Jamie Kreiner for this reference. On the two kinds of grain delivery, *annona* and military requisitions, see Erdkamp, *The Grain Market in the Roman Empire*. Peter Brown, *Through the Eye of a Needle: Wealth, the Fall of Rome, and the Making of Christianity in the West, 350–550 AD* (Princeton, NJ: Princeton University Press, 2012), chap. 1.

11. *Procopius, with an English Translation by H. B. Dewing*, ed. and trans. H. B. Dewing (New York: Macmillan, 1914), 1: 464–469. On the fraught topic of when, why, and to what extent European trade with the East declined, see Michael McCormick, *Origins of the European Economy: Communications and Commerce, AD 300–900* (Cambridge: Cambridge University Press, 2001). McCormick has this trade beginning to decline around 550 and reaching its bottom around 700, though the reasons for this decline could include European tastes, for example. Arab overland and waterborne trade in the eighth century and afterward was associated with the rise of commerce, not its decline.

12. J. H. W. G. Liebeschuetz, *Decline and Fall of the Roman City* (Oxford : Oxford University Press, 2001); Lester K. Little, "Life and Afterlife of the First Plague Pandemic," in *Plague and the End of Antiquity: The Pandemic of 541–750*, ed. Lester K. Little (New York: Cambridge University Press, 2007). Alain Stoclet argues, in "Consilia humana, ops divinia, superstitio: Seeking Succor and Solace in Times of Plague, with Particular Reference to Gaul in the Early Middle Ages," in Little, *Plague and the End of Antiquity*, that the Justinian plague was a proving ground for competing rituals, including ancient Roman, Frankish, and Gallic ones that morphed into Christian traditions like the cult of Mary and the belief that Capetian kings had a touch that cured the plague. A similar justification apparently made the case for an Islamic tradition among the Abbasids compared to the secular Umayyads.

13. Jack Goody, *Islam in Europe* (Malden, MA: Polity Press, 2004).

14. Schoff, *The Periplus of the Erythraean Sea.*

15. Florin Curta, *The Making of the Slavs: History and Archaeology of the Lower Danube Region, ca. 500–700* (New York: Cambridge University Press, 2001), chap. 4; Jonathan Shepard, *The Cambridge History of the Byzantine Empire, c. 500–1492* (New York: Cambridge University Press, 2008), 324–327.

16. George Vernadsky, *The Origins of Russia* (Oxford: Clarendon Press, 1959), 242–263. Vernadsky suggests that the Virgin Mary story may refer to the Byzantine defeat of the Rus in 860–861 (213–226).

17. Nicholas V. Riasanovsky, *A History of Russia*, 6th ed. (New York: Oxford University Press, 2000).

18. Heinrich Eduard Jacob, *Six Thousand Years of Bread: Its Holy and Unholy History* (Garden City, NY: Doubleday, Doran, 1944).

19. R. E. F. Smith and David Christian, *Bread and Salt: A Social and Economic History of Food and Drink in Russia* (New York: Cambridge University Press, 1984).

20. Mark Wheelis, "Biological Warfare at the 1346 Siege of Caffa," *Emerging Infectious Diseases Journal* 8, no. 9 (September 2002): 971–975. On a possible alternate route, see Monica H. Green, "Taking 'Pandemic' Seriously: Making the Black Death Global," in *Pandemic Disease in the Medieval World: Rethinking the Black Death*, ed. M. H. Green (Kalamazoo, MI: Arc Medieval Press, 2014).

21. Monica H. Green, "The Four Black Deaths," *American Historical Review* 125, no. 5 (2020): 1601–1631.

22. Fernand Braudel, *Civilization and Capitalism, 15th–18th Century*, vol. 2: *The Wheels of Commerce* (New York: Harper & Row, 1982); Parvus, "Der Weltmarkt und die Agrarkrisis," published serially in ten parts in *Die Neue Zeit* from November 1895 to March 1896.

23. On Venetian central banking, see Stefano Ugolini, *The Evolution of Central Banking: Theory and History* (London: Palgrave Macmillan UK, 2017), 37–43. On the bill of exchange, see Sergii Moshenskyi, *History of the Wechsel, Bill of Exchange, and Promissory Note* (Bloomington, IN: Xlibris Corp., 2008).

24. Fariba Zarinebaf, *Crime and Punishment in Istanbul: 1700–1800* (Berkeley: University of California Press, 2010), 82.

25. Felicity Walton, "Ulster Milling Through the Years," in *A Hundred Years A-milling: Commemorating an Ulster Mill Centenary*, ed. William Maddin Scott, 125–131 (Dundalk: Dundalgan Press, 1956); Brinley Thomas, "Escaping from Constraints: The Industrial Revolution in a Malthusian Context," *Journal of Interdisciplinary History* 15, no. 4 (1985): 729–753.

26. [Mehmed Esad Efendi] in A. P. Caussin de Perceval, trans., *Précis historique de la destruction du corps des Janissaires par le sultan Mahmoud* (Paris, 1833), 2. Hereinafter cited as Esad, *Destruction des Janissaires*.

27. Alan L. Olmstead and Paul W. Rhode, "The Red Queen and the Hard Reds: Productivity Growth in American Wheat, 1800–1940," *Journal of Economic History* 62, no. 4 (December 2002): 929–966; Wilfred Malenbaum, *The World Wheat Economy, 1885–1939* (Cambridge, MA: Harvard University Press, 1953).

28. The Dniester flows south, so its right bank from the river's perspective is the western side.

29. Martin Małowist, *Western Europe, Eastern Europe and World Development, 13th–18th Centuries: Collection of Essays of Marian Małowist* (Chicago: Haymarket Books, 2012); cf. Robert I. Frost, *The Oxford History of Poland-Lithuania*, vol. 1: *The Making of the Polish-Lithuanian Union, 1385–1569* (New York: Oxford University Press, 2018), 242–261; Cyrus Hamlin, "The Dream of Russia," *The Atlantic* 58 (December 1886): 771–782.

30. Karen Barkey and Mark von Hagen, eds., *After Empire: Multiethnic Societies and Nation-Building* (Boulder, CO: Westview Press, 1997).

CHAPTER 3: PHYSIOCRATIC EXPANSION

1. Catherine believed that Great Britain didn't believe in free trade either in that it adjusted its tariff every year to promote its navy and build up particular industries. See William E. Butler and Vladimir A. Tomsinov, *Nakaz of Catherine the Great: Collected Texts* (Clark, NJ: Lawbook Exchange Ltd., 2010).

2. Richard Pipes, "Private Property Comes to Russia: The Reign of Catherine II," *Harvard Ukrainian Studies* 22 (1998): 431–442. Pipes

argues that what distinguished serfs from slaves was that slave owners produced for an international market while serf owners produced for local consumption. As we shall see below, this was never true, but especially not for those serf owners living near rivers, along the black paths, and on the coast of the Black Sea. The historian Cedric Robinson argues, in *Black Marxism: The Making of the Black Radical Tradition* (Chapel Hill: University of North Carolina Press, 1983), that the distinction between slavery and serfdom has been greatly overstated.

3. Some of this was land she seized from the Orthodox Church.

4. Though Revolutionary France's poor regulation of the assignat contributed to runaway inflation and contributed to the rise of the Directory and the terror.

5. Marianne Johnson, "'More Native Than French': American Physiocrats and Their Political Economy," *History of Economic Ideas* 10, no. 1 (2002): 15–31.

6. Marten Gerbertus Buist, *At Spes non Fracta: Hope & Co. 1770–1815* (The Hague: Martinus Nijhoff, 1974); John Brewer, *The Sinews of Power: War, Money, and the English State, 1660–1873* (New York: Routledge, 1989).

7. Esad, *Destruction des Janissaires*, 115.

8. A careful analysis of Russian and Ottoman military supply is in Brian L. Davies, *The Russo-Turkish War, 1768–1774: Catherine II and the Ottoman Empire* (New York: Bloomsbury, 2016), though Davies emphasizes Russian innovation in order of battle and tactics. In 1793 Sultan Selim III abolished official price regulation in grain and established a Grain Administration, which introduced *rayic*, or flexible, pricing, though it still did not eliminate the monopoly. Seven Ağir, "The Evolution of Grain Policy: The Ottoman Experience," *Journal of Interdisciplinary History* 43, no. 4 (2013): 571–598.

9. Esad, *Destruction des Janissaires*, 115.

10. After the failure of the campaign, the *arpa emini* (grain commissioner) in Istanbul was replaced by an organization called the Grain Administration, and the *miri* price was for some time replaced by a negotiated (*rayic*) price. On changes in Ottoman grain provisioning, see Ağir, "The Evolution of Grain Policy." On the financial instruments used by the Ottoman army, see Sevket Pamuk, "The Evolution of Financial Institutions in the Ottoman Empire, 1600–1914," *Financial History Review* 11, no. 1 (2004): 7–32. The army may also have used *suftajas*, which were more negotiable financial instruments, but these were still not as flexible as a bill of exchange. Esad, *Destruction des Janissaires*, 115.

11. Esad, *Destruction des Janissaires*, 32–36; Virginia H. Aksan, *An Ottoman Statesman in War and Peace: Ahmed Resmi Efendi, 1700–1783*

(Leiden: J. H. Brill, 1995), 141–143; Ali Yaycioglu, *Partners of the Empire: The Crisis of the Ottoman Order in the Age of Revolutions* (Stanford, CA: Stanford University Press, 2016), 36–38; William C. Fuller, *Strategy and Power in Russia, 1600–1914* (New York: Simon & Schuster, 1998), 139–176; Hew Strachan, *European Armies and the Conduct of War* (New York: Routledge, 2005), 32–33. On the efficiency of the Ottoman Empire in the seventeenth century, see Rhoads Murphey, *Ottoman Warfare, 1500–1700* (New Brunswick, NJ: Rutgers University Press, 1999).

12. John T. Alexander, *Bubonic Plague in Early Modern Russia: Public Health and Urban Disaster* (New York: Oxford University Press, 2003).

13. Virginia Aksan, *Ottoman Wars: 1700–1870: An Empire Besieged* (New York: Routledge, 2007), 151–154; Davies, *Russo-Turkish War*, 103, 145; M. Şükrü Hanioğlu, *A Brief History of Late Ottoman Empire* (Princeton, NJ: Princeton University Press, 2008), 44–45; Christopher Duffy, *Russia's Military Way to the West: Origins and Nature of Russian Military Power, 1700–1800* (New York: Routledge, 2015), 170–178; Christopher Duffy, *The Fortress in the Age of Vauban and Frederick the Great, 1600–1789* (New York: Routledge, 2015), 2:244–247; M. Gustave de Molinari, *Lettres sur la Russie* (Brussels and Leipzig: A. Lacroix, 1861), 234–235; Kelly O'Neill, *Claiming Crimea: A History of Catherine the Great's Southern Empire* (New Haven, CT: Yale University Press, 2017).

14. O'Neill, *Claiming Crimea*.

15. Patricia Herlihy, "Port Jews of Odessa and Trieste: A Tale of Two Cities," *Odessa Recollected: The Port and the People* (Brighton, MA: Academic Studies Press, 2018), 196–208; William H. McNeill, *Europe's Steppe Frontier, 1500–1800* (Chicago: University of Chicago Press, 1964); Alexander, *Bubonic Plague*.

16. Harold C. Hinton, "The Grain Tribute System of the Ch'ing Dynasty," *Far Eastern Quarterly* 11, no. 3 (1952): 339–354; Seung-Joon Lee, "Rice and Maritime Modernity: The Modern Chinese State and the South China Sea Rice Trade," in *Rice: Global Networks and New Histories*, ed. Francesca Bray et al., 99–117 (New York: Cambridge University Press, 2015).

17. Patricia Herlihy, *Odessa: A History, 1794–1914* (Cambridge, MA: Harvard University Press, 1986).

18. Translation from Timothy John Binyon, *Pushkin: A Biography* (New York: Vintage, 2007), 154.

19. Brooke Hunter, "Wheat, War, and the American Economy During the Age of Revolution," *William and Mary Quarterly* 62, no. 3 (2005): 505–526; Gautham Rao, *National Duties: Custom Houses and the Making of the American State* (Chicago: University of Chicago Press, 2016); Scott

Reynolds Nelson, *A Nation of Deadbeats: An Uncommon History of America's Financial Disasters* (New York: Knopf, 2012).

20. Avner Offer, "Ricardo's Paradox and the Movement of Rents in England, c. 1870–1910," *Economic History Review* 33, no. 2 (1980): 236–252.

21. Melville H. Watkins, "A Staple Theory of Economic Growth," *Canadian Journal of Economics and Political Science / Revue canadienne d'economique et de science politique* 29 (May 1963): 141–158.

22. Timothy Pitkin, *A Statistical View of the Commerce of the United States of America, Including Also an Account of Banks, Manufactures, and Internal Trade and Improvements* (New Haven, CT: Durrie & Peck, 1835), 119–130.

23. On this question in the United States, see Robin Einhorn, *American Taxation, American Slavery* (Chicago: University of Chicago Press, 2008).

24. On American adjustments of physiocratic theory, see Johnson, "More Native Than French." On expansion through space, see Drew McCoy, *An Elusive Republic: Political Economy in Jeffersonian America* (Chapel Hill: University of North Carolina Press, 1980).

25. Hunter, "Wheat, War"; Rao, *National Duties*; Nelson, *A Nation of Deadbeats*.

26. Pitkin, *A Statistical View*, 108–118.

27. For "unremitting," see Alexis de Tocqueville, *Democracy in America* (New York: Colonial Press, 1899), 375. For "seeded" and "garnered," see "Tobacco and Slavery," *Friend's Review* (June 6, 1857): 620; John J. McCusker and Russell R. Menard, *The Economy of British America, 1607–1789* (Chapel Hill: University of North Carolina Press, 1985). On the decline of slavery in the upper Chesapeake, see Max Grivno, "'There Slavery Cannot Dwell': Agriculture and Labor in Northern Maryland" (unpublished PhD diss., University of Maryland, 2007). On enslaved Virginia farms as a source of technical innovation in harvesting and milling, see Daniel B. Rood, *The Reinvention of Atlantic Slavery: Technology, Labor, Race, and Capitalism in the Greater Caribbean* (New York: Oxford University Press, 2017). On the question of slavery and grain, see Carville Earle, *Geographical Enquiry and American Historical Problems* (Stanford, CA: Stanford University Press, 1991).

28. F. Lee Benns, "The American Struggle for the British West India Carrying Trade, 1815–1830," *Indiana University Studies* 10, no. 56 (1920): 1–207.

29. Numbers from Pitkin, *A Statistical View*, 96–97, and L. P. McCarty, *Annual Statistician and Economist* (San Francisco, CA: LP McCarty,

1889), 199; Scott Reynolds Nelson, "The Many Panics of 1819," *Journal of the Early Republic* 40, no. 4 (2020): 721–727.

30. Jonathan B. Robinson to Robert Wilmot, January 27, 1822, in *Journal and Proceedings of the Legislative Council of the Province of Upper Canada [4th session, 8th Provincial Parliament, beginning 1821]*, 98–103; William J. Patterson, *Statements Relating to the Home and Foreign Trade of the Dominion of Canada, also, Annual Report of the Commerce of Montreal for 1869* (Montreal: Starke & Co., 1870).

31. John Antony Chaptal, *Chymistry Applied to Agriculture* (Boston: Hilliard, Gray & Co., 1839). On refinements of this technique after 1830, see Francois Sigaut, "A Method for Identifying Grain Storage Techniques and Its Application for European Agricultural History," *Tools and Tillage* 6, no. 1 (1988): 3–32.

32. Chaptal, *Chymistry Applied to Agriculture*; Charles Byron Kuhlmann, *The Development of the Flour Milling Industry in the United States with Special Reference to the Industry in Minneapolis* (Boston: Houghton Mifflin, 1929).

33. Here I find myself agreeing with Douglass North, *The Economic Growth of the United States* (New York: Prentice Hall, 1961), that the South relied on the Midwest for food, despite strongly worded objections in Robert E. Gallman, "Self-Sufficiency in the Cotton Economy of the Antebellum South," *Agricultural History* 44, no. 1 (1970): 5–23; Sam Bowers Hilliard, *Hog Meat and Hoecake: Food Supply in the Old South, 1840–1860* (Carbondale: Southern Illinois University Press, 1972); Joe Francis, "King Cotton the Munificent: Slavery and (Under)development in the United States, 1789–1865" (working paper, April 2021), https://joefrancis.info/pdfs/Francis_US_slavery.pdf.

34. Brysson Cunningham, *Cargo Handling at Ports: A Survey of the Various Systems in Vogue, with a Consideration of Their Respective Merits* (New York: Wiley and Sons, 1924).

35. Louis Adolph Thiers, *Discours de M. Thiers sur le régime commercial de la France* (Paris: Paulin, L'Heureux, 1851).

36. Steven Kaplan, *The Famine Plot Persuasion in Eighteenth-Century France* (Philadelphia: American Philosophical Society, 1982), chap. 2.

37. Monstuart E. Grant Duff, *Studies in European Politics* (Edinburgh: Edmonston and Douglas, 1866), 72.

38. I am indebted to Alexander Bucksch for pointing out these Napoleonic trails in Europe.

39. Stanley Chapman, *Merchant Enterprise in Britain: From the Industrial Revolution to World War I* (New York: Cambridge University Press, 2004), 153–166.

40. Peter H. Lindert and Steven Nafziger, "Russian Inequality on the Eve of Revolution," *Journal of Economic History* 74, no. 3 (2014): 767–798.

CHAPTER 4: *P. INFESTANS* AND THE BIRTH OF FREE TRADE

1. *P. infestans* is a parasitic oomycete. While initially considered a fungus, oomycetes differ from fungi in many ways, including having cell walls made of cellulose (like plants) rather than chitin (like fungi and animals). Eva H. Stukenbrock and Bruce A. McDonald, "The Origins of Plant Pathogens in Agro-ecosystems," *Annual Review of Phytopathology* 46, no. 1 (2008): 75–100.

2. Rebecca Earle, *Potato* (New York: Bloomsbury Academic, 2019).

3. William H. McNeill, "How the Potato Changed the World's History," *Social Research* 66, no. 1 (1999): 67–83.

4. P. M. Austin Bourke, "Emergence of the Potato Blight, 1843–1846," *Nature*, August 22, 1964, 805–808; Susan Goodwin et al., "Panglobal Distribution of a Single Clonal Lineage of the Irish Potato Famine Fungus," *Proceedings of the National Academy of Sciences* 91 (November 1994): 11591–11595.

5. "Foreign Grain Markets," *The Economist*, February 14, 1846; Jonathan Sperber, *The European Revolutions, 1848–1851* (New York: Cambridge University Press, 2005).

6. E. C. Large, *The Advance of the Fungi* (London: Jonathan Cape, 1949), 36.

7. "France," *[London] Daily News*, May 19, 1862.

8. Cecil Woodham-Smith, *The Great Hunger: Ireland, 1845–1849* (New York: Penguin Books, 1991).

9. Amartya Sen, *Poverty and Famines: An Essay on Entitlement and Deprivation* (New York: Oxford University Press, 1981).

10. Sen describes similar problems in the Bengal famine. Much of the literature on the Irish famine has focused on food availability and not entitlement.

11. Susan Elizabeth Fairlie, "Anglo Russian Grain Trade" (unpublished PhD diss., London School of Economics, 1959), 93–94.

12. J. C. Zadoks, "The Potato Murrain on the European Continent and the Revolutions of 1848," *Potato Research* 51 (2008): 5–45; Sperber, *The European Revolutions.*

13. At the same time, some states, like Prussia and France, also blocked the export of grain. Carl Johannes Fuchs, *Der englische Getreidehandel und seine Organisation* (Jena: Gustav Fischer, 1890), 11.

14. Fuchs, *Der Englische Getreidehandel*, 11.

15. Paul Bairoch, *Economics and World History: Myths and Paradoxes* (Chicago: University of Chicago Press, 1995), 21–22.

16. Graham L. Rees, *Britain's Commodity Markets* (London: Elek, 1972), chap. 6.

17. Gelina Harlaftis, *A History of Greek-Owned Shipping: The Making of an International Tramp Fleet, 1830 to the Present Day* (New York: Routledge, 1996); Fairlie, "Anglo-Russian Grain Trade"; Patricia Herlihy, "Russian Grain and Mediterranean Markets, 1774–1861" (unpublished PhD diss., University of Pennsylvania, 1963).

18. "The Prices and Stocks of Wheat in Europe," *The Economist*, March 9, 1850; Fairlie, "Anglo-Russian Grain Trade," 110.

19. Daniel C. Carr, *The Necessity of Brown Bread for Digestion, Nourishment, and Sound Health; and the Injurious Effects of White Bread* (London: Effingham Wilson, 1847).

20. Jack Magee, *Barney: Bernard Hughes of Belfast, 1808–1878, Master Baker, Liberal and Reformer* (Belfast: Ulster Historical Foundation, 2001); Edward J. T. Collins, "Dietary Change and Cereal Consumption in Britain in the Nineteenth Century," *Agricultural History Review* 23, no. 2 (1975): 97–115; John Burnett, *Plenty and Want: A Social History of Food in England from 1815 to the Present Day* (1966; repr. New York: Routledge, 2005).

21. Naum Jasny, *Competition Among Grains* (Stanford, CA: Stanford University Press, 1940), 41–51.

22. Jonathan Pereira, "Triticum Vulgare," in *The Elements of Materia Medica and Therapeutics* (Philadelphia: Blanchard and Lea, 1854), 2:119–125; Carr, *Necessity of Brown Bread*.

23. Max Rubner recognized that fewer urban workers were eating peasant bread but regarded this as advantageous; see Max Rubner, "Über den Werth der Weizenkleie für die Ernährung des Menschen," *Zeitschrift für Biologie* 19 (1883): 45–100. On changing bread habits in Britain, see Christian Peterson, *Bread and the British Economy, c. 1770–1870* (Brookfield, VT: Ashgate Publishing Co., 1995). The bread divide continued in the Austro-Hungarian Empire; see, for example, "The Returned Veterans' Fest in Salzburg," *Hours at Home* (November 1869): 30–34.

24. Burnett, *Plenty and Want*.

25. Israel Helphand, *Technische Organisation der Arbeit ("Cooperation" und "Arbeitsheilung"): Eine Kritische Studie* (Basel: University of Basel, 1891). The best current survey of migration in this period is Leslie Page Moch, *Moving Europeans: Migration in Western Europe Since 1650* (Bloomington: University of Indiana Press, 2003), chap. 4. My

understanding of a geography-centered account of industrialization relies on Phillip Scranton, "Multiple Industrializations: Urban Manufacturing Development in the American Midwest, 1880–1925," *Journal of Design History* 12, no. 1 (1999): 45–63. Unfortunately most accounts of European industrialization and urbanization see these transformations as independent causes, and not effects, of cheap food circulation.

26. Burnett, *Plenty and Want*; Charles H. Feinstein, "Pessimism Perpetuated: Real Wages and the Standard of Living in Britain During and After the Industrial Revolution," *Journal of Economic History* 58, no. 3 (September 1998): 625–658; Roderick Floud et al., *Height, Health, and History: Nutritional Status in the United Kingdom, 1750–1980* (New York: Cambridge University Press, 1990); Simon Szreter and Graham Mooney, "Urbanization, Mortality, and the Standard of Living Debate: New Estimates of the Expectation of Life at Birth in Nineteenth-Century British Cities," *Economic History Review* (1998): 84–112.

27. Blanchard Jerrold, *The Life of Napoleon III* (London: Longmans, Green and Company, 1882), 4:378.

28. Thanks to Andy Zimmerman for pointing out how socialism was used in the nineteenth century.

29. David Baguley, *Napoleon III and His Regime: An Extravaganza* (Baton Rouge: Louisiana State University Press, 2000).

30. André Liesse, *Evolution of Credit and Banks in France: From the Founding of the Bank of France to the Present Time*, 61st Cong., 2nd sess., Senate Document 522 (Washington, DC, 1909), pt. 2.

31. Theodore Zeldin, "Ambition, Love and Politics," in *France, 1848–1945* (Oxford: Oxford University Press, 1973); Steven Soper, *Building a Civil Society: Associations, Public Life, and the Origins of Modern Italy* (Toronto: University of Toronto Press, 2013), chap. 4. On exclusive restaurants before 1845, see Rebecca Spang, *The Invention of the Restaurant: Paris and Modern Gastronomic Culture* (Cambridge, MA: Harvard University Press, 2000).

32. John M. Kleeberg, "The Disconto-Gesellschaft and German Industrialization" (PhD diss., University of Oxford, 1988); John C. Eckalbar, "The Saint-Simonians in Industry and Economic Development," *American Journal of Economics and Sociology* 38, no. 1 (1979): 83–96; Liesse, *Evolution of Credit and Banks in France*.

33. Kleeberg, "The Disconto-Gesellschaft."

34. Jacob Riesser, *The German Great Banks and Their Concentration*, 61st Cong., 2nd sess., Senate Document 593 (Washington, DC, 1911); "Emperor's Speech at the Opening of the Session," *[Dublin] Freeman's Journal*, February 16, 1853.

CHAPTER 5: CAPITALISM AND SLAVERY

1. Adolph Thiers, "Discours de M. Thiers sur le régime commercial de la France" (Paris: Paulin, L'Heureux, 1851); M. Gustave de Molinari reviews these charges, quoting Thiers, in *Lettres sur la Russie* (Brussels and Leipzig: A. Lacroix, 1861).

2. Yields from I. M. Rubinow, *Russian Wheat and Wheat Flour in European Markets*, Bulletin no. 66 (Washington, DC: US Department of Agriculture, Bureau of Statistics, 1908). Yields were consistent in the United States across much of the nineteenth century. See Giovanni Federico, *Feeding the World: An Economic History of Agriculture, 1800–2000* (Princeton, NJ: Princeton University Press, 2005).

3. Raj Patel and Jason W. Moore, *A History of the World in Seven Cheap Things: A Guide to Capitalism, Nature, and the Future of the Planet* (Oakland: University of California Press, 2017).

4. I. M. Rubinow, *Russia's Wheat Surplus: Conditions Under Which It Is Produced*, Bulletin no. 42 (Washington, DC: US Department of Agriculture, Bureau of Statistics, 1906); Alan L. Olmstead and Paul W. Rhode, "The Red Queen and the Hard Reds: Productivity Growth in American Wheat, 1800–1940," *Journal of Economic History* 62, no. 4 (December 2002): 929–966.

5. James A. Blodgett, "Relations of Population and Food Products in the United States" (Washington, DC: Government Printing Office, 1903), 28–30; Rubinow, *Russia's Wheat Surplus*, 45–50.

6. Alexander Kornilov, *Modern Russian History* (New York: Alfred A. Knopf, 1917), chap. 22; Ted Widmer, *Lincoln on the Verge: Thirteen Days to Washington* (New York: Simon & Schuster, 2020).

7. Francis Henry Skrine, *The Expansion of Russia* (Cambridge: Cambridge University Press, 1915), 149–150.

8. Skrine, *The Expansion of Russia*, 151. See also Orlando Figes, *The Crimean War: A History* (New York: Metropolitan Books, 2011), chap. 3, arguing that "the threat of Russia to British interests was minimal."

9. Laurence Oliphant, *Russian Shores of the Black Sea in the Autumn of 1852* (London: William Blackwood and Sons, 1853), 36. Alexander Kinglake suggests that Oliphant was an *amateur* spy though he was assistant at the time for James Bruce, the Earl of Elgin. Alexander William Kinglake, *The Invasion of the Crimea: Its Origin, and an Account of Its Progress Down to the Death of Lord Raglan* (New York: Harper & Brothers, 1868), 2:57–60. During the Crimean War he acted as aide to Ottoman field marshal Omar Pasha.

10. C. W. S. Hartley, *A Biography of Sir Charles Hartley, Civil Engineer (1825–1915): The Father of the Danube* (Lewiston, NY: Mellen Press, 1989); "Danube, European Commission of the," in *Appletons' Annual Cyclopaedia and Register of Important Events* (New York: D. Appleton, 1884), 272–274.

11. Oliphant, *Russian Shores of the Black Sea in the Autumn of 1852*, 363.

12. On the growing British imperial interest in the support of the Turkish Empire, see Frederick Stanley Rodkey, "Lord Palmerston and the Rejuvenation of Turkey, 1830–1841: Pt. 1, 1830–39," *Journal of Modern History* 1, no. 4 (December 1929): 570–593; and Frederick Stanley Rodkey, "Lord Palmerston and the Rejuvenation of Turkey, 1830–1841: Pt. 2, 1839–41," *Journal of Modern History* 2, no. 2 (June 1930): 193–225. Rodkey overstates Ottoman "misrule" but captures well Britain's financial interests.

13. This average of 53 s. 2. d. per quarter ran from 1845 to 1873. John Kirkland, *Three Centuries of Prices of Wheat, Flour and Bread* (London: J. G. Hammond, 1917), 33–34.

14. "Free Trade Bread Riots," *Derby Mercury*, February 25, 1854; *[London] Standard*, January 11, 1854; John Burnett, *Plenty and Want: A Social History of Food in England from 1815 to the Present Day* (1966; repr. New York: Routledge, 2005), chaps. 2 and 7.

15. Mesut Uyar and Edward J. Erickson, *A Military History of the Ottomans: From Osman to Ataturk* (Santa Barbara, CA: ABC-CLIO, 2009).

16. On the naval battles, see Eric J. Grove, *The Royal Navy Since 1815: A New Short History* (New York: Palgrave MacMillan, 2005), chap. 2. On subsidies, see Yakup Bektas, "The Crimean War as a Technological Enterprise," *Notes and Records: The Royal Society Journal of the History of Science* 71, no. 3 (September 20, 2017): 233–262. On the significance of screw propellers, mail contracts, and superheated steam engines, see Freda Harcourt, *Flagships of Imperialism: The P&O Company and the Politics of Empire from Its Origins to 1867* (New York: Manchester University Press, 2006). John Penn's superheated steam engine and John Elder's double-cylinder engine were predecessors of the marine compound engine. On the protracted development of the marine compound engine, see Crosbie Smith, *Coal, Steam and Ships: Engineering, Enterprise and Empire on the Nineteenth-Century Seas* (New York: Cambridge University Press, 2018). Andrew Jamieson, in *Text-book on Steam and Steam Engines* (London: Charles Griffin and Company, 1889), explains that it took decades to determine that superheating's efficiency resulted largely from increased pressure and the use of waste steam.

17. Skrine, *The Expansion of Russia*, 162.

18. Parvus, *Türkiye'nin mali tutsaklığı*, trans. Muammer Sencer (1914; repr. İstanbul: May Yayınları, 1977), 29–32; Murat Birdal, *The Political Economy of Ottoman Public Debt: Insolvency and European Financial Control in the Late Nineteenth Century* (New York: I. B. Tauris, 2010).

19. Julius de Hagemeister, *Report on the Commerce of the Ports of New Russia, Moldavia, and Wallachia Made to the Russian Government in 1835* (London: Effingham Wilson, 1836). Hagemeister viewed the foreigners brought in by Catherine as the best farmers, while he viewed the Don Cossacks as wasting the lands they controlled: "The very constitution of their order presents the greatest possible hindrance to any thing like agricultural pursuits. The common right of property established amongst them, must for ever prevent those improvements on the land, which can result only from individual possession."

20. Steven L. Hoch, "The Banking Crisis, Peasant Reform, and Economic Development in Russia, 1857–1861," *American Historical Review* 96, no. 3 (1991): 795–820.

21. Hoch, "The Banking Crisis," 810–815.

22. The final result was more chaotic than that, however, as the Russian state had no surveys of land values. Some peasants paid too little, and some paid too much. Alexander Polunov, *Russia in the Nineteenth Century: Autocracy, Reform, and Social Change, 1814–1914* (Armonk, NY: M. E. Sharpe, 2005), 90–96; Steven L. Hoch, "Did Russia's Emancipated Serfs Really Pay Too Much for Too Little Land? Statistical Anomalies and Long-Tailed Distributions," *Slavic Review* (2004): 247–274.

23. Paul W. Gates, "Frontier Estate Builders and Farm Laborers," in *The Jeffersonian Dream: Studies in the History of American Land Policy and Development*, ed. Allan G. Bogue and Margaret Beattie Bogue (Albuquerque: University of New Mexico Press, 1996); Nikolai D. Kondratieff, *Rynok khlebov i ego regulirovanie vo vremia voiny i revoliutsii* (1922; repr. Moscow: Nauka, 1991).

24. V. M. Karev, *Nemtsy Rossii* (Moscow: ERN, 1999), 1:451–452.

25. On the severe "inventory regulations" that restricted serfdom in the wheat regions, see Kornilov, *Modern Russian History*, 1: 262–265.

26. Louis Bernard Schmidt, "Westward Movement of the Wheat Growing Industry of the United States," *Iowa Journal of History and Politics* 18, no. 3 (July 1920): 396–412.

27. J. J. Holleman, "Does Cotton Oligarchy Grip South and Defy All Plans for Diversification and Relief?," *Atlanta Constitution*, September 27, 1914. On the transition from labor lords to landlords, see Gavin Wright, *Old South, New South: Revolutions in the Southern Economy Since the Civil War* (New York: Basic Books, 1986).

28. Sven Beckert, *Empire of Cotton: A Global History* (New York: Knopf, 2014).

29. Isaac A. Hourwich, *The Economics of the Russian Village* (New York: Columbia College, 1892).

30. Gates, "Frontier Estate Builders"; Kondratieff, *Rynok khlebov i ego regulirovanie vo vremia voiny i revoliutsii.*

31. On the grain trade in Galați, see United Kingdom, Parliament, *Report by Her Majesty's Consuls on Manufactures and Commerce of Their Districts*, BPP-C.637 (1872), 1335–1340.

32. Alice Elizabeth Malavasic, *The F Street Mess: How Southern Senators Rewrote the Kansas-Nebraska Act* (Chapel Hill: University of North Carolina Press, 2017); Scott Reynolds Nelson, *A Nation of Deadbeats: An Uncommon History of America's Financial Disasters* (New York: Knopf, 2012); John Lauritz Larson, *Bonds of Enterprise: John Murray Forbes and Western Development in America's Railway Age* (Iowa City: University of Iowa Press, 2001).

33. Ariel Ron has argued that this agricultural leviathan was a grassroots project. While I would agree that farmer activists forged some of these appeals over a longer period and were crucially moved by them, I believe that much of the financial backing for this new party came from the people I am calling the boulevard barons. Ariel Ron, *Grassroots Leviathan: Agricultural Reform and the Rural North in the Slaveholding Republic* (Baltimore: Johns Hopkins University Press, 2020).

34. In this sense I am arguing for the power of what Robert Sharkey might call the William Pitt Fessenden wing of the Republican Party over the Thaddeus Stevens wing. See Robert P. Sharkey, *Money, Class, and Party: An Economic Study of Civil War and Reconstruction* (Baltimore, MD: Johns Hopkins University Press, 1959).

35. The Progressive School, following Charles R. Beard, saw in the Republican Party the rise of an industrial bourgeoisie. A modern version of this account can be found in Sven Beckert, *The Monied Metropolis: New York and the Consolidation of the American Bourgeoisie, 1850–1896* (New York: Cambridge University Press, 2001). Richard Franklin Bensel, in *Yankee Leviathan: The Origins of Central State Authority in America* (New York: Cambridge University Press, 1990), argues for what he calls a "market economy of competitive capitalism" (32), though he occasionally also refers, confusingly, to "expansionist industrial capitalism" (60). His argument does not explicitly link the Republican Party to grain and railroads, however.

36. "David Dows," in *America's Successful Men of Affairs: An Encyclopedia of Contemporaneous Biography*, ed. Henry Hall (New York: New

York Tribune, 1896), 200–203; "David Dows," *New York Times*, March 31, 1890; A[lexander] E[ctor] Orr, "To the Old Friends of David Dows This Short Sketch of His Active and Honorable Life Is Respectfully Dedicated, by A. E. Orr, Brooklyn, 1888," JohnShaplin, May 21, 2011, http://johnshaplin.blogspot.com/2011/05/david-dows.html.

37. See John Murray Forbes to Paul Forbes, November 26, 1854, Paul Siemen Forbes Papers, Forbes Family Papers, Harvard Baker Library Historical Collection, Cambridge, Massachusetts.

38. "Last-mile logistics" refers to the expense of delivering final goods. Logistics professionals occasionally refer to the route into a supply chain as the first mile.

39. The name changed between 1860 and 1868. Initially the "New York Produce Exchange Company" purchased the building, and the "New York Commercial Association" rented the second or main floor. In 1868 the Commercial Association assumed the name New York Produce Exchange. By 1872 the New York Produce Exchange had bought the building from the New York Produce Exchange Company. New York Produce Exchange, *Report of the New York Produce Exchange* (New York: New York Produce Exchange, [1873]), 17–18. This last mile is crucial to understanding the success of railroads and modern cable companies. Both erect infrastructure that connects hubs like Chicago to individual units, whether houses or grain stores. This is why Robert Fogel is wrong about railroads being unnecessary to American economic growth. His counterfactual model relies on a canal between New York and Chicago, but the railroads absolutely relied on the canal; their contribution to economic growth was accessing the places canals could not reach. Orr, "To the Old Friends of David Dows."

40. The above-listed men were the finance committee of the Loyal Publication Society, a Republican organization in New York devoted to publishing pamphlets to support the Republican Party during the conflict.

41. Larson, *Bonds of Enterprise*; Irene Neu, *Erastus Corning: Merchant and Financier, 1794–1872* (Ithaca, NY: Cornell University Press, 1960).

42. Nelson, *A Nation of Deadbeats*, chap. 8. On merchants blaming bank policy for the Panic of 1857, see James L. Houston, *The Panic of 1857 and the Coming of the Civil War* (Baton Rouge: Louisiana State University Press, 1987).

43. Sean Patrick Adams, "Soulless Monsters and Iron Horses: The Civil War, Institutional Change, and American Capitalism," in *Capitalism Takes Command: The Social Transformation of Nineteenth-Century America*, ed. Michael Zakim and Gary J. Kornblith (Chicago: University

of Chicago Press, 2011); Gerald Berk, *Alternative Tracks: The Constitution of American Industrial Order, 1865–1916* (Baltimore: Johns Hopkins University Press, 1994).

44. On Stanton and Watson's relationship to railroad firms, see Benjamin P. Thomas and Harold M. Hyman, *Stanton: The Life and Times of Lincoln's Secretary of War* (New York: Alfred A. Knopf, 1962), chaps. 3 to 5. Railroad owners did not always agree. One of Stanton's earliest railroad cases involved blocking a Pennsylvania railroad bridge that would have given a national toll road an advantage over the Erie Railroad.

45. Elliot West, *The Contested Plains: Indians, Goldseekers, and the Rush to Colorado* (Lawrence: University Press of Kansas, 1998).

46. Laurence Evans, "Transport, Economics and Economists: Adam Smith, George Stigler, et al.," *International Journal of Maritime History* 5, no. 1 (June 1993): 203–219.

47. Scott Reynolds Nelson, *Iron Confederacies: Southern Railways, Klan Violence, and Reconstruction* (Chapel Hill: University of North Carolina Press, 1999), chap. 8.

48. Richard H. White, *Railroaded: The Transcontinentals and the Making of Modern America* (New York: Norton & Company, 2011); Charles Postel, *The Populist Vision* (New York: Oxford University Press, 2007); Bryant Barnes, "Fresh Fruit and Rotten Railroads: Fruit Growers, Populism, and the Future of the New South," *Agricultural History* (forthcoming, 2022).

49. Ralph N. Traxler, "The Texas and Pacific Railroad Land Grants: A Comparison of Land Grant Policies of the United States and Texas," *Southwestern Historical Quarterly* 61, no. 3 (1958): 359–370.

50. Nelson, *A Nation of Deadbeats*, chap. 7.

51. August 14, 1852, Hannibal & St. Joseph's Railroad Co. Records, Chicago Burlington & Quincy Papers, Newberry Library, Chicago, Illinois; Larson, *Bonds of Enterprise*; Nelson, *A Nation of Deadbeats*.

52. Robert R. Russel, *Improvement of Communication with the Pacific Coast as an Issue in American Politics, 1783–1864* (New York: Arno Press, 1981), 165–166.

53. Malavasic, *The F Street Mess*.

54. "Atchison's Speech," *Missouri Courier*, July 7, 1853; Perley Orman Ray, *The Repeal of the Missouri Compromise: Its Origin and Authorship* (Cleveland, OH: Arthur H. Clark Co., 1908), 80.

55. Nelson, *A Nation of Deadbeats*, chap. 7; Malavasic, *The F Street Mess*.

56. Eric Foner, *Free Soil, Free Labor, Free Men: The Ideology of the Republican Party Before the Civil War* (New York: Oxford University Press, 1970).

57. Quoted in Foner, *Free Soil, Free Labor, Free Men*, 56.

58. Forrest A. Nabors, *From Oligarchy to Republicanism: The Great Task of Reconstruction* (Columbia: University of Missouri Press, 2017).

59. I differ here with Robert William Fogel, *Without Consent or Contract: The Rise and Fall of American Slavery* (New York: Norton, 1989), chap. 4.

60. Chief engineer's report, Memphis and Charleston Railroad Annual Report (1851), 14–15.

61. Nelson, *Iron Confederacies*, chap., 1; John Majewski, *A House Dividing: Economic Development in Pennsylvania and Virginia Before the Civil War* (New York: Cambridge University Press, 2000).

62. Data was crunched using the statistical package R and taken from Steven Ruggles et al., *Integrated Public Use Microdata Series: Version 6.0 [dataset]* (Minneapolis: University of Minnesota, 2015), http://doi .org/10.18128/D010.V6.0 R.

63. Historians have dismissed the so-called slave power as an example of the "paranoid style" in American politics. David Brion Davis, *The Slave Power Conspiracy and the Paranoid Style* (Baton Rouge: Louisiana State University Press, 1969).

64. Nabors, *From Oligarchy to Republicanism*.

65. On the sense that ending slavery would open up new ground for merchants and manufacturers, see Henry L. Swint, "Northern Interest in the Shoeless Southerner," *Journal of Southern History* 16, no. 4 (November 1950): 457–471.

66. A formal account of staple theory can be found in Melville H. Watkins, "A Staple Theory of Economic Growth," *Canadian Journal of Economics and Political Science / Revue canadienne d'economique et de science politique* 29 (May 1963): 141–158.

67. Laurence Evans, "Bread and Politics: Civil Logistics and the Limits of Choice," in *Maritime Food Transport*, ed. Klaus Friedland (Cologne: Böhlau Verlag, 1994); Laurence Evans, "The Gift of the Sea: Civil Logistics and the Industrial Revolution," *Historical Reflections* 15, no. 2 (summer 1988): 361–415.

68. Allan Pred, in *The Spatial Dynamics of U.S. Urban Industrial Growth, 1800–1914* (Cambridge, MA: Massachusetts Institute of Technology, 1966), emphasizes information circulation as the key variable in explaining why certain large cities tended to grow faster than their smaller counterparts between 1860 and 1914.

69. Simon Kuznets makes a similar argument, but it lacks this crucial geographical and staple dimension. Simon Kuznets, "Economic Growth and Income Inequality," *American Economic Review* 45, no. 1 (March 1955): 1–28.

70. "Necessity of Immediate Attack on Russia," *Reynolds's Newspaper*, March 12, 1854.

CHAPTER 6: "CERES AMERICANA"

1. William Émile Doster, *Lincoln and Episodes of the Civil War* (New York: G. P. Putnam's Sons, 1915), 126–131; E. D. Townsend, *Anecdotes of the Civil War in the United States* (New York: D. Appleton and Co., 1884), 79–81; Benjamin P. Thomas and Harold M. Hyman, *Stanton: The Life and Times of Lincoln's Secretary of War* (New York: Alfred A. Knopf, 1962), 152–164. For "railsplitter," see Charles A. Church, *History of Rockford and Winnebago County, Illinois* (Rockford, IL: W. P. Lamb, 1900), 322–324. I am troubled by Watson's absence in the standard military, railroad, and political histories of the war. He is mentioned frequently in the monthly reports of the commissary generals and of course in the Turner-Baker Papers, discussed below, as Levi C. Turner and Lafayette C. Baker reported directly to him in person.

2. Peter Cozzens, *The Shipwreck of Their Hopes: The Battles for Chattanooga* (Urbana: University of Illinois Press, 1994), chap. 1; Fairfax Downey, *Storming of the Gateway, Chattanooga, 1863* (New York: David McKay Co., 1960); Buell, *The Warrior Generals: Combat Leadership in the Civil War* (New York: Crown Publishers, 1997), 284.

3. James Withrow, diary, quoted in Wiley Sword, *Mountains Touched with Fire: Chattanooga Besieged, 1863* (New York: St. Martin's Press, 2013), 83.

4. Calculation from Mark Wilson, "The Business of Civil War" (PhD diss., University of Chicago, 2002), 490; Buell, *Warrior Generals*.

5. Rowland was his wife's uncle, making him harder to identify. Henry W. Hector, deposition, December 1863, Case Files of Investigations by Levi C. Turner and Lafayette C. Baker, 1861–1866 (microfilm), case file no. 3752 (rolls 107–119), M797, RG 94, Records of the Adjutant General's Office, 1780s–1917, War Department Division, National Archives, Washington, DC (hereinafter cited as Turner-Baker Papers). Ratio is specified in US War Department, *Revised United States Army Regulations of 1861 with an Appendix Containing the Changes and Laws Affecting Army Regulations and Articles of War to June 25, 1863* (Washington, DC: Government Printing Office, 1863), 166. The ratio for mules was fourteen to nine.

6. David F. Rowland, deposition, December 1863, Turner-Baker Papers. On the creation of the National Detectives, see Thomas and Hyman, *Stanton*, 153.

7. Erna Risch, *Quartermaster Support of the Army: A History of the Corps, 1775–1939* (Washington, DC: Center of Military History, United States Army, 1989), 381–382. On the amount finally recovered and the political figures involved, see Charles A. Dana, "The Lincoln Papers," *Fort Wayne Sunday Gazette,* June 14, 1885, 2; William P. Wood, "Wood's Budget," *Indiana [Pennsylvania] Progress*, November 26, 1885, 2.

8. Thomas and Hyman, *Stanton*, 126–146; Albert Churella, *The Pennsylvania Railroad*, vol. 1: *Building an Empire* (Philadelphia: University of Pennsylvania Press, 2013), chap. 8; Boeger, "Hardtack and Cofee [sic]" (unpublished PhD diss., University of Wisconsin, 1953), 83.

9. The new regulations are laid out in US War Department, *Revised United States Army Regulations of 1861*: on the oath, see pp. 534–535; on court-martial, see p. 538.

10. To Capt. E. D. Bingham, CS, Boston, Mass., January 13, 1863; Letters sent, volume 43; Records of the Office of the Commissary General of Subsistence, Record Group 192, National Archives Building, Washington, DC.

11. One benefit for contractors was that they could apparently receive US bonds, which had interest payable in gold rather than greenbacks. This is suggested by the fact that Ferguson's safe contained US bonds and checks rather than greenback currency.

12. Boeger, "Hardtack and Cofee [sic]," 212–213.

13. For the size of standard contracts, see "Lists of Proposals Received for Furnishing Forage," E. 1250, Vol. 1, Records of the Office of the Quartermaster General, Record Group 92, National Archives Building, Washington, DC.

14. Annual, Personal & Special Reports, 1865, Brown, Samuel L.; E. 1105, Records of the Office of the Quartermaster General, Record Group 92, National Archives Building, Washington, DC. Indeed, Ferguson and his assistant had been colluding with this very "combination of men and money" before including Alexander M. White, a contractor and brother of Pennsylvania state senator Harry White. "Wood's Budget," *Indiana [Pennsylvania] Progress*, November 26, 1885.

15. For total corn required, see US Quartermaster's Department, Report of the Quartermaster General of the United States Army to the Secretary of War for the Year Ending June 30, 1865 (Washington, DC: Government Printing Office, 1865), 165. For the fiscal year ending June 1865, the army received nearly 24 million bushels of oats; 10 million bushels were bought by contract, and an unprecedented 11.8 million were bought "on the open market." S. L. Brown reported that they were "procured in New York City, up to January 1, 1865, where the quantities

required under the exigencies of the service were such as to render it necessary to purchase in open market" (164).

16. Boeger, "Hardtack and Cofee [sic]," 102–195.

17. "David Dows," in *America's Successful Men of Affairs: An Encyclopedia of Contemporaneous Biography*, ed. Henry Hall (New York: New York Tribune, 1896), 201.

18. A[lexander] E[ctor] Orr, "To the Old Friends of David Dows This Short Sketch of His Active and Honorable Life Is Respectfully Dedicated, by A. E. Orr, Brooklyn, 1888," JohnShaplin, May 21, 2011, http://johnshaplin.blogspot.com/2011/05/david-dows.html. Boeger describes Dows's authority to use open market operations. Boeger, "Hardtack and Cofee [sic]," 290.

19. Article 41, Section 1048, in US War Department, *Revised US Army Regulations*: "When immediate delivery or performance is required by the public exigency, the article or service required may be procured by open purchase or contract at the places and in the mode in which such articles are usually bought and sold, or such services engaged, between individuals" (155).

20. Annual, Personal & Special Reports, 1865, Brown, Samuel L.; E. 1105, Records of the Office of the Quartermaster General, Record Group 92, National Archives Building, Washington, DC.

21. Arthur Barker, *The British Corn Trade: From the Earliest Times to the Present Day* (London: Sir Isaac Pitman & Sons. 1920), 10.

22. This rule on all contracts was adopted on March 27, 1863. See Harold Speer Irwin, *Evolution of Futures Trading* (Madison: Mimir Publishers, Inc.), 81.

23. The expression "time contracts" is confusing because in the 1850s New Yorkers used that term to describe forward contracts in cotton. Futures contracts as described here did not exist in cotton until about 1872, when the "basis" system was introduced to deal with deviations from a cotton grade. See Irwin, *Evolution of Futures Trading*, 84–85.

24. Banks in Montreal, for example, objected to clients using bank credit to make a "time bargain" on commodities. "Financial and Commercial: Monetary," *Chicago Tribune*, June 13, 1865.

25. The New York Produce Exchange changed to graded grain and delivery by certificates—namely, standardized grain contracts—in 1874. Richard Edwards, *Origin, Growth, and Usefulness of the New York Produce Exchange* (New York: New York Produce Exchange, 1884), 45–47.

26. Edwards, *Origin, Growth, and Usefulness of the New York Produce Exchange*, 45–47; George James Short Broomhall and John Henry Hubback, *Corn Trade Memories, Recent and Remote* (Liverpool: Northern Pub. Co., 1930), 34. Peter Norman argues that the first formal futures

market with central party clearing began in Liverpool in 1874 with the creation of the Cotton Market Clearing House. The American system, he argues, settled trades inside rings and so fails the test of a true futures market. But contemporary sources assert that the Liverpool futures market was created "after the American fashion." Individual traders bought and sold futures with each other using the grading imposed by the New York Cotton Exchange (founded with futures in 1870), but institutionalization of futures occurred through a series of changes between 1874 and 1882. See Charles William Smith, *Commercial Gambling: The Principal Causes of Depression in Agriculture and Trade* (London: Sampson, Low, Marston & Co., 1893), 6; Thomas Ellison, *The Cotton Trade of Great Britain* (London: Effingham Wilson, Royal Exchange, 1886), 272–280; "Commercial News," *Glasgow Herald*, August 6, 1870.

27. "Report from the Select Committee on East India Railway Communication, Together with the Proceedings of the Committee, Minutes of Evidence, and Appendix," *House of Commons Parliamentary Papers* 284 (July 18, 1884).

28. Cento G. Veljanovski, "An Institutional Analysis of Futures Contracting," in *Futures Markets: Their Establishment and Performance*, ed. Barry A. Goss (New York: New York University Press, 1986), 26–27.

29. The neoclassical case for futures markets, pitted against Keynesian theory, is laid out in Lester G. Tesler, "Futures Trading and the Storage of Cotton and Wheat," *Journal of Political Economy* 66, no. 2 (June 1958): 233–255. Milton Friedman, "In Defense of Destabilizing Speculation," is reprinted in chapter 13 of *The Optimum Quantity of Money and Other Essays*, ed. Michael D. Bordo (Chicago: Aldine Publishing Co., 1969).

30. Chicago Board of Trade, *Sixth Annual Report* (1864), 34.

31. For a description of pyramiding in futures, see Donna Kline, *Fundamentals of the Futures Market* (New York: McGraw-Hill, 2001), 19–23. On combining options with futures to strangle or collar, see Kline, *Fundamentals*, 193–218.

32. Joost Jonker and Keetie E. Sluyterman, *At Home on the World Markets: Dutch International Trading Companies from the 16th Century Until the Present* (The Hague: Sdu Uitgevers, 2000), chap. 4.

33. Elevator operator Ira Munn made a fortune this way, then failed when prices went in the wrong direction. See William G. Ferris, "The Disgrace of Ira Munn," *Journal of the Illinois State Historical Society (1908–1984)* 68, no. 3 (June 1975): 202–212.

34. Grain, including flour, counted in bushels went from 16.7 million in 1859 to 30.8 million in 1860, 52.0 million in 1862, and 63.0 million in 1863. *American Railroad Journal* 23, no. 45 (November 9, 1867): 1064.

By 1863 competition from Montreal and American railways began to stabilize these numbers.

35. Churella, *Building an Empire*, chap. 8.

36. Thomas and Hyman, *Stanton*, 152–153.

37. This resembles James Madison's case in Federalist No. 10 that competing factions will sustain a large republic. One merchant cabal in charge of Chicago to New York is bad. A minimum of four will prevent any one of them from dominating.

38. A fifth competitor existed in the Grand Trunk Railway, headquartered in London, which connected Montreal to Portland, Maine. Thomas and Hyman, *Stanton*, 152–154. Thomas Weber, in *The Northern Railroads in the Civil War, 1861–1865* (New York: King's Crown Press, 1952), chaps. 5 and 7, outlines the expansion of the trunk railroads during the war, as well as the legislation giving the president the power to facilitate continuous gauge and bridge crossing, but he does not connect the two.

39. Robina Lizars and Kathleen MacFarlane Lizars, *Humours of '37, Grave, Gay, and Grim: Rebellion Times in the Canadas* (Toronto: W. Briggs, 1897), 361–363; Church, *History of Rockford and Winnebago County, Illinois*, 322–324. When Stanton became attorney general for Democratic president James Buchanan in 1860, Stanton had Watson relay to President-elect Abraham Lincoln inside information about Buchanan's collapsing cabinet and the growing threat of Civil War. Thomas and Hyman, *Stanton*, 93–107.

40. Only D-Day was bigger.

41. Stephen W. Sears, *To the Gates of Richmond: The Peninsula Campaign* (New York: Ticknor & Fields, 1992), 21, 24.

42. Edward Hagerman, "The Reorganization of Field Transportation and Field Supply in the Army of the Potomac, 1863: The Flying Column and Strategic Mobility," *Military Affairs* 44, no. 4 (December 1980): 182–186.

43. Scott Reynolds Nelson and Carol Sheriff, *A People at War: Civilians and Soldiers in America's Civil War* (New York: Oxford University Press, 2008), 215–218.

44. Thavolia Glymph, "The Second Middle Passage: The Transition from Slavery to Freedom at Davis Bend, Mississippi" (unpublished PhD thesis, Purdue University, 1994), 92–95.

45. Nelson and Sheriff, *A People at War*, 88–91.

46. Thomas and Hyman, *Stanton*, 288–290.

47. James Arthur Ward, *That Man Haupt: A Biography of Herman Haupt* (Baton Rouge: Louisiana State University Press, 1973).

48. Construction had previously been under Herman Haupt. Robert G. Angevine, *Railroads and the State: War, Politics, and Technology in Nineteenth-Century America* (Stanford, CA: Stanford University Press, 2004), 136.

49. Edwin A. Pratt, *The Rise of Rail Power in War and Conquest, 1833–1914* (London: P. S. King & Son, Ltd., 1915), 17–21.

50. Pratt, *The Rise of Rail Power*, 136.

51. L. A. Hendricks, "Meade's Army," *New York Herald*, September 25, 1863.

52. Henry Clay Symonds, *Report of a Commissary of Subsistence, 1861–1865* (Sing Sing, NY: Author, 1888), 86.

53. See Boeger, "Hardtack and Cofee [sic]."

54. Symonds, *Report of a Commissary of Subsistence*, 129–134. Repetitions of Sherman's boast can be found in William Nester, *The Age of Lincoln and the Art of American Power, 1848–1876* (Lincoln: Potomac Books, Inc., 2014), 213. Robert A. Divine and R. Hall Williams, *America Past and Present* (New York: Longman, 1998), 467.

55. Carl Russell Fish, "The Northern Railroads," *American Historical Review* 22 (July 1917): 782.

56. "Transportation: Reception of the Committee in Montreal," *New York Times*, September 17, 1873.

CHAPTER 7: BOOM

1. *Hillsborough Recorder*, May 9, 1866.

2. *Reynolds's Newspaper*, April 29, 1866; *Manchester Courier and Lancashire General Advertiser*, May 1, 1866; *Lloyd's Weekly Newspaper* (London), April 29, 1866; "Terrible Catastrophe," *New York Herald*, April 21, 1866; "The Aspinwall Horror," *Daily Cleveland Herald*, April 23, 1866.

3. On packing method, see "The Nitro-Glycerine Case," *New York Herald*, April 26, 1866. On force, see George Ingham Brown, *The Big Bang: A History of Explosives* (Phoenix Mill, UK: Sutton Publishing, 1999), 101–102.

4. On the initiation of detonation, see Stanley Fordham, *High Explosives and Propellants* (Elmsford, NY: Pergamon Press, 1980), 25–28.

5. Testimony of Alfred Nobel transcribed in "The Nitro-Glycerine Case"; Henry S. Drinker, *Tunneling, Explosive Compounds, and Rock Drills* (New York: John Wiley, & Sons, 1878), 31.

6. Vaclav Smil, *Creating the Twentieth Century: Technical Innovations of 1867–1914 and Their Lasting Impact* (New York: Oxford University Press, 2004).

7. Anonymous, *Antwerp: Commercially Considered: A Series of Articles Reprinted from "The Syren and Shipping"* (London: Wilkinson Brothers Ltd., 1898); Fernand Braudel, *Civilization and Capitalism, 15th–18th Century*, vol. 3: *The Perspective of the World* (New York: Harper & Row, 1984), 143–157.

8. Edward Harris, Earl of Malmesbury, "Our National Engagements and Armaments," House of Lords, Parl. Deb. (3d ser.) (1871) col. 1376.

9. Matthew Simon and David E. Novack refer to the period from 1871 to 1914 as the American commercial invasion of Europe. Their choice of that latter date appears to depend on the shift in the US balance of payments. See Matthew Simon and David E. Novak, "Some Dimensions of the American Commercial Invasion of Europe, 1871–1914: An Introductory Essay," *Journal of Economic History* 24, no. 4 (December 1964): 591–605. J. C. Zadoks, "The Potato Murrain on the European Continent and the Revolutions of 1848," *Potato Research* 51 (2008): 5–45.

10. "Die Großstadt wirft die nationalen Eierschalen ab und wird zum Knotenpunkt des Weltmarktes." Parvus, "Der Weltmarkt und die Agrarkrisis," published serially in ten parts in *Die Neue Zeit* from November 1895 to March 1896. This article was published as a pamphlet in Russian in 1898 and received a glowing review from Vladimir Lenin in *Nachalo* in March 1899.

11. Jan Blomme et al., *Momentum: Antwerp's Port in the 19th and 20th Century* (Antwerp: Pandore, 2002); Fernand Suykens, G. Asaert, and A. De Vos, *Antwerp: A Port for All Seasons* (Antwerp: Ortelius Series, 1986); Edwin J. Clapp, *The Navigable Rhine* (Boston: Houghton Mifflin, 1911), 48–50.

12. Karel Veraghtert, "Antwerp Grain Trade, 1850–1914," in *Maritime Food Transport*, ed. Klaus Friedland (Cologne: Böhlau Verlag, 1994), 90; Van Ysselsteyn, *The Port of Rotterdam* (Rotterdam: Nijgh & Van Ditmar's Publishing Co., 1908), 45.

13. Laurence Evans, "Bread and Politics: Civil Logistics and the Limits of Choice," in *Maritime Food Transport*, ed. Klaus Friedland (Cologne: Böhlau Verlag, 1994), 581; P. N. Muller, "De Handel van Nederland in de Laatste vijf en twintig Jahr, 1847–1871," *De Ekonomist* (1875): 1–25; Frederik Bernard Löhnis, "Onze Zuivel Industrie," *De Ekonomist* (1884): 837–846.

14. On European food prices in ports, see Wilhelm Abel, *Agricultural Fluctuations in Europe from the Thirteenth to the Twentieth Centuries* (New York: St. Martin's Press, 1980).

15. On transport geography generally, see Jean-Paul Rodrigue, *The Geography of Transport Systems* (Milton Park, UK: Taylor & Francis, 2016).

16. John Kirkland, *Three Centuries of Prices of Wheat, Flour and Bread* (London: J. G. Hammond, 1917), 31–35.

17. Sarah Moreels et al., "Fertility in the Port City of Antwerp (1846–1920): A Detailed Analysis of Immigrants' Spacing Behaviour in an Urbanizing Context" (working paper, WOG/HD/2010-14, Scientific Research Community Historical Demography), accessed online March 28, 2021, https://core.ac.uk/download/pdf/34472007.pdf.

18. This occurred even when tariff walls went up. The so-called meal-trade exemption (*mehlverkehr*) allowed millers to avoid a tariff on foreign grain provided they sold a similar quantity of flour abroad. Inter-European flour sales involved a tariff, of course, but demonstrating that millers exported all the flour for the grain they imported proved nearly impossible, particularly as improved mills generated a larger quantity of flour for a given quantity of grain than the stipulated percentage. See Judit Klement, "How to Adapt to a Changing Market? The Budapest Flour Mills at the Turn of the Nineteenth and Twenties [sic] Centuries," *Hungarian Historical Review* 4, no. 4 (2015): 834–867; US State Department, Bureau of Statistics, *Extension of Markets for American Flour*, (Washington, DC: US Government Printing Office, 1894).

19. Paul Freyburger, Patent, E 170 a Büschel 1550, Patentkommission der Zentralstelle für Gewerbe und Handel, Landesarchive Baden-Wurttemberg, www.landesarchiv-bw.de/plink/?f=2-58962 (accessed November 3, 2020).

20. Carl Strikwerda, *A House Divided: Catholics, Socialists, and Flemish Nationalists in Nineteenth-Century Belgium* (Lanham, MD: Rowman & Littlefield Publishers, 2000), 78–81.

21. Wilfrid Robinson, *Antwerp: An Historical Sketch* (London: R. & T. Washbourne, 1904), 281.

22. Three million tons arrived by 1880. In Europe only London (6 million) and Liverpool (5 million) exceeded it; below it was Hamburg at 2.8 million and Marseille at 2.1 million. Paul Guillaume, *L'Escaut depuis 1830* (Brussels: A. Castaigne, 1903), 2: 370.

23. Parvus, "Der Weltmarkt und die Agrarkrisis," *Die Neue Zeit* 14 (November 1895): 197ff.

24. George James Short Broomhall and John Henry Hubback, *Corn Trade Memories, Recent and Remote* (Liverpool: Northern Pub. Co., 1930), 25–31.

25. R. C. Michie, "The International Trade in Food and the City of London Since 1850," *Journal of European Economic History* 25, no. 2 (fall 1996): 369–404; Baltico, *Life on "the Baltic," and Shipping Idylls for Shipping Idlers* (London: Ward Lock & Co., 1903); Hugh Barty-King, *The Baltic Exchange: From Baltick Coffee House to Baltic Exchange, 1744–1994*

(London: Quiller Press, 1994); Richard Malkin, *Boxcars in the Sky* (New York: Import Publications, 1951); Broomhall and Hubback, *Corn Trade Memories*.

26. "Overend & Gurney," *Glasgow Herald*, January 16, 1869. For the "pig upon bacon" maneuver, see [Anonymous], *Breach of Privilege: Being the Evidence of Mr. John Bull Taken before the Secret Committee on the National Distress in 1847 and 1848* (London: John Ollivier, 1849), 62–92.

27. [Walter Bagehot], "Commercial History and Review of 1866," *The Economist*, March 9, 1867, 4–5; [Walter Bagehot], "Commercial History and Review of 1867," *The Economist*, March 14, 1868, 2–3; [Walter Bagehot], "Commercial History and Review of 1868," *The Economist*, March 18, 1869, 6–7; Chenzi Xu, "Reshaping Global Trade: The Immediate and Long-Run Effects of Bank Failures," *Proceedings of Paris December 2020 Finance Meeting EUROFIDAI—ESSEC*, October 14, 2020, available at SSRN, https://ssrn.com/abstract=3710455.

28. Suez hard rock was removed at Chalouf using Lobnitz's rock dredger, not explosives, though the boulders generated by the dredger did require explosives to clear. "The Removal of Rock Under Water Without Explosives," *Engineering and Building Record*, October 12, 1889.

29. David A. Wells, "Great Depression of Trade: A Study of Its Economic Causes," *Contemporary Review* (August 1877): 277.

30. Wells, "Great Depression of Trade," 277.

31. Harold J. Dyas and D. H. Aldcroft, *British Transport: An Economic Survey from the Seventeenth Century to the Twentieth* (Surrey, UK: Leicester University Press, 1969), chap. 8.

32. William Henry Moyer, "PRR's Navy, Part V: Transatlantic Shipping Lines," *The Keystone: Official Publication of the Pennsylvania Railroad Technical and Historical Society* 44, no. 2 (2011): 18–69; Freda Harcourt, *Flagships of Imperialism: The P&O Company and the Politics of Empire from Its Origins to 1867* (New York: Manchester University Press, 2006), 181–190; Crosbie Smith, *Coal, Steam and Ships: Engineering, Enterprise, and Empire on the Nineteenth-Century Seas* (New York: Cambridge University Press, 2018), 364–365.

33. According to the family's retrospective on Dreyfus's life, he attributed his great success to his ability to use the futures market to manage risk. Louis Dreyfus & Co., *À l'occasion de son centenaire La Maison Louis Dreyfus & Cie rend hommage a son fondateur qui reste present dans son oeuvre* (privately printed, 1951).

34. Wilhelm Basson, *Die Eisenbahnen im Kriege nach den Erfahrungen des letzten Feldzuges* (Ratibor, Germany: V. Wichura, 1867).

35. Edwin A. Pratt, *The Rise of Rail Power in War and Conquest, 1833–1914* (London: P. S. King & Son, Ltd., 1915), 122–128.

36. [A Prussian General Staff officer], "German General Staff Railroad Concentration, 1870," reprinted and translated in *Military Historian and Economist* 3, no. 2 (April 1918), 161ff addendum at end of issue but with page numbers beginning again at page 1. I have not been able to locate the original German document. Martin van Creveld has sharply attacked the Prussian logistical system as inept. For a critique of this view, see Quintin Barry, *Moltke and His Generals* (Warwick, UK: Helion & Co., 2015), chapters 9 and 10.

37. Alistair Horne, *The Fall of Paris: The Siege and the Commune, 1870–71* (New York: Penguin Books, 1981), 64–67.

38. Anonymous, *Antwerp: Commercially Considered*; Robinson, *Antwerp: An Historical Sketch*, 281; Veraghtert, "Antwerp Grain Trade," 85; Colmar Freiherr von der Goltz, *The Nation in Arms: A Treatise on Modern Military Systems and the Conduct of War* (London: Hodder & Stoughton, 1914), 260–263. Martin van Creveld, in *Supplying War: Logistics from Wallenstein to Patton* (Cambridge: Cambridge University Press, 1977), chap. 3, sees these and other departures from the Etappen Plan as demonstrating that the German war machine was incompetent.

39. Dennis Showalter, *The Wars of German Reunification* (New York: Oxford University Press, 2004), 249–250.

40. Goltz, *The Nation in Arms*, 260–263.

41. Pratt, *The Rise of Rail Power*, 57.

42. In 1874 the New York Produce Exchange shifted to accepting graded grain certificates. Richard Edwards, *Origin, Growth, and Usefulness of the New York Produce Exchange* (New York: New York Produce Exchange, 1884), 45–47; London's unwillingness to use the American grading system is discussed in Aashish Velkar, "'Deep' Integration of 19th Century Grain Markets: Coordination and Standardisation in a Global Value Chain" (Working Paper No. 145/10, London School of Economics, July 2010).

43. André failed in 2001 but was replaced by Arthur, Daniels, Midland, preserving the ABCD abbreviation. Dan Morgan, *Merchants of Grain* (New York: Viking, 1979).

44. Morgan, *Merchants of Grain*, 30–34. The Fribourgs operated under the name Fribourg &c at first. Continental & Co. was formed from their business in 1921.

45. Ilya Grigorovich Orshansky, *Evrei v Rossii: Ocherki ekonomicheskogo i obshchestvennogo byta russkikh evreev* (St. Petersburg, 1877), 8–10, 71–90; quotation from p. 6. Orshansky's articles were written in the 1860s, but some, because of censorship by the governor-general, were not published in the Odessa magazine *Den*. On Orshansky's death, all the articles were published without censorship in the volume above. On

the fate of Orshansky's writings, see John D. Klier, "The Pogrom Paradigm in Russian History," in *Pogroms: Anti-Jewish Violence in Modern Russian History*, ed. John D. Klier and Shlomo Lambroza (New York: Cambridge University Press, 1992), 32.

46. Morgan, *Merchants of Grain*, 5.

CHAPTER 8: WHAT IS TO BE DONE?

1. *Lloyd's Weekly Newspaper* (London), April 29, 1866; Claudia Verhoeven, *The Odd Man Karakozov: Imperial Russia, Modernity, and the Birth of Terrorism* (Ithaca, NY: Cornell University Press, 2009). On his being Polish, see p. 45. On the three years, see p. 62. On the walk in the park, see p. 67.

2. Eugen Weber, *Apocalypses: Prophesies, Cults, and Millennial Beliefs Through the Ages* (Cambridge, MA: Harvard University Press, 1999), 96–98.

3. "And I will give power unto my two witnesses, and they shall prophesy a thousand two hundred and threescore days, clothed in sackcloth." Henry Forest Burder, *Notes on the Prophecies of the Apocalypse* (London: Ward & Co., 1849), 124–126, 187.

4. Burder, *Notes on the Prophecies of the Apocalypse*, 124–126, 187. On prophecy belief in the period of the English Civil War, see Paul Boyer, *When Time Shall Be No More: Prophecy Belief in Modern American Culture* (Cambridge, MA: Harvard University Press, 1992); Weber, *Apocalypses*.

5. Burder, *Notes on the Prophecies of the Apocalypse*, 123–132.

6. On Protestants, see Burder, *Notes on the Prophecies of the Apocalypse*, 124–126, 187. On the idea of a Catholic conspiracy linked somehow to a secular conspiracy, see Verhoeven, *The Odd Man Karakozov*, 50–54. A conspiracy that combines revolutionary anarchists and nonrevolutionary Catholics looks less paradoxical given the Orthodox reading of the Protestant interpretation of the book of Revelation in which the Catholic Church, in overpowering the Orthodox Church in 606, became the Whore of Babylon.

7. Frederic Zuckerman, *The Tsarist Secret Police Abroad: Policing Europe in a Modernising World* (New York: Palgrave Macmillan, 2003).

8. Eric Hobsbawm, in *The Age of Revolution* (New York: Vintage Books, 1962), chap. 6, talks about *carbonari* in the 1820s, including the Decembrists, though he sees 1848 as categorically different.

9. Ze'ev Iviansky, "Individual Terror: Concept and Typology," *Journal of Contemporary History* 12, no. 1 (1977): 43–63.

10. Richard J. Johnson, "Zagranichnaia Agentura: The Tsarist Political Police in Europe," *Journal of Contemporary History* 7, no. 1 (1972): 221–242.

11. David Ricardo, *On the Principles of Political Economy and Taxation* (London: John Murray, 1821), chap. 2.

12. Avner Offer, "Ricardo's Paradox and the Movement of Rents in England, c. 1870–1910," *Economic History Review* 33, no. 2 (1980): 236–252.

13. Parvus, Rosa Luxemburg, and Lenin, for example, tended to use American agriculture as a model for the critique of European landlord power. Marx's views on American agriculture changed a great deal between 1849 and 1870. See Kohei Saito, "The Emergence of Marx's Critique of Modern Agriculture: Ecological Insights from His Excerpt Notebooks," *Monthly Review: An Independent Socialist Magazine* 66, no. 5 (October 2014): 25.

14. Paul W. Gates, "Frontier Estate Builders and Farm Laborers," in *The Jeffersonian Dream: Studies in the History of American Land Policy and Development*, ed. Allan G. Bogue and Margaret Beattie Bogue (Albuquerque: University of New Mexico Press, 1996).

15. Saito, "The Emergence of Marx's Critique."

16. See Chapter 4 in this volume.

17. Franco Venturi, *Roots of Revolution: A History of the Populist and Socialist Movements in Nineteenth Century Russia* (New York: Knopf, 1960), xvii.

CHAPTER 9: THE GREAT GRAIN CRISIS

1. Ilya Grigorovich Orshansky, *Evrei v Rossii: Ocherki ekonomicheskogo i obshchestvennogo byta russkikh evreev* (St. Petersburg, 1877), 50–55; C. W. S. Hartley, *A Biography of Sir Charles Hartley, Civil Engineer (1825–1915): The Father of the Danube* (Lewiston, NY: Mellen Press, 1989), 190–193.

2. Memorandum of the Odessa Committee on Trade and Manufactures, 1873, translated in UK Parliament, *Reports from H. M. Consuls on Manufactures and Commerce of Their Consular Districts*, BPP-C.1427 (1876), 438–439.

3. "Papers Relative to Complaints Against Grenville-Murray as H.M. Consul-General at Odessa, and His Dismissal from Service," BPP-C.4163 (1869): 12–13.

4. Memorandum of the Odessa Committee, 437–450.

5. Yrjö Kaukiainen, "Journey Costs, Terminal Costs and Ocean Tramp Freights: How the Price of Distance Declined from the 1870s to 2000," *International Journal of Maritime History* 18, no. 2 (2006): 17–64.

6. I. M. Rubinow, *Russia's Wheat Surplus: Conditions Under Which It Is Produced*, Bulletin no. 42 (Washington, DC: US Department of Agriculture, Bureau of Statistics, 1906), 60.

7. Henry Vizetelly, *Berlin Under the New Empire: Its Institutions, Inhabitants, Industry, Monuments, Museums, Social Life, Manners, and Amusements* (London: Tinsley Brothers, 1879), 2:195.

8. Kevin H. O'Rourke, "The European Grain Invasion, 1870–1913," *Journal of Economic History* 57, no. 4 (December 1997): 775–801; Vizetelly, *Berlin Under the New Empire*, 2: 193–221; Avner Offer, "Ricardo's Paradox and the Movement of Rents in England, c. 1870–1910," *Economic History Review* 33, no. 2 (1980): 236–252.

9. This was frequently called the "accommodation market"; see "Continental Finance," *[Dundee, Scotland] Courier and Argus*, December 18, 1872; O'Rourke, "The European Grain Invasion," 775–801; Vizetelly, *Berlin Under the New Empire*, 2:193–221. Economists in the 1970s, focusing largely on industrial output, real prices, and freight rates, made the case that no depression began in 1873. Bank failures, farm failures, and total unemployment figures, for example, have no role in this intellectual exercise. See, for example, Samuel Berrick Saul, *The Myth of the Great Depression, 1873–1896* (London: MacMillan & Co., 1969).

10. On short-term borrowing by resellers like Fisk & Hatch, see McCartney, "Crisis of 1873" (PhD diss., University of Nebraska, 1935). On the failure of German firms engaged in the same activities, see Vitzelley, *Berlin Under the New Empire*, vol. 2, chap. 11, and Günter Ogger, *Die Gründerjahre: Als der Kapitalismus jung und verwegen war* (Munich: Droemer Knaur, 1982), chap. 9.

11. Jacobs, Freres & Co. in Antwerp and Russia blamed its failure on this increase in the rate for accommodation notes. See *[Memphis] Daily Avalanche*, December 19, 1872, and *Chicago Daily Tribune*, December 10, 1872; Report by Vice-Consul Webster on Banking in South Russia, UK Parliament, *Reports from H. M. Consuls on Manufactures and Commerce of Their Consular Districts*, BPP-C.1427 (1876), 450–457; Jeffrey Fear and Christopher Kobrak, "Origins of German Corporate Governance and Accounting, 1870–1914: Making Capitalism Respectable" (paper presented at International Economic History Congress, Helsinki, Finland, August 2006); Richard White, *The Republic for Which It Stands: The United States During Reconstruction and the Gilded Age, 1865–1896* (New York: Oxford University Press, 2017), chap. 7; E. Ray McCartney, "Crisis of 1873," 94.

12. "The security which you offer," Bagehot wrote, "should resemble as nearly as possible a bill of exchange both in form and method of negotiation." James Grant, *Bagehot: The Life and Times of the Greatest Victorian* (New York: W. W. Norton & Company, 2019), chap. 17.

13. Testimony of Charles Magniac in "Effect of the Suez Canal (1870–1874) on the Shipping Trade, and on the Commerce Between India and England and India and the Rest of Europe," *The Economist*, March 11, 1876, 48.

14. Numbers from "Money Market and City Intelligence," *[London] Times*, January 3 and 4, 1876.

15. On attempts to quantify this change, see Luigi Pascali, "The Wind of Change: Maritime Technology, Trade and Economic Development" (Warwick Economics Research Paper Series, University of Warwick, Department of Economics, 2014).

16. Karel Veraghtert, "Antwerp Grain Trade, 1850–1914," in *Maritime Food Transport*, ed. Klaus Friedland (Cologne: Böhlau Verlag, 1994), 82–84.

17. Calculated in 1913 dollars. See Matthew Simon and David E. Novack, "Some Dimensions of the American Commercial Invasion of Europe, 1871–1914: An Introductory Essay," *Journal of Economic History* 24, no. 4 (December 1964): 591–605; statistics on 599. While economists have written a great deal about shipping costs, they have not considered the annihilation of distance by tunneling.

18. "The Grain Trade," *Massachusetts Ploughman and New England Journal of Agriculture*, January 15, 1876.

19. Simon and Novack, "American Commercial Invasion of Europe, 1871–1914"; Antoni Estevadeordal, Brian Frantz, and Alan M. Taylor, "The Rise and Fall of World Trade, 1870–1939," *Quarterly Journal of Economics* 118, no. 2 (2003): 359–407; David S. Jacks, "What Drove 19th Century Commodity Market Integration?," *Explorations in Economic History* 43, no. 3 (2006): 383–412.

20. Robert Cedric Binkley, *Realism and Nationalism, 1852–1871* (New York: Harper & Brothers, 1935), 77.

21. Scott Reynolds Nelson, *A Nation of Deadbeats: An Uncommon History of America's Financial Disasters* (New York: Knopf, 2012).

22. A firsthand description of the line business is provided in Charles T. Peavy, *Grain* (Chicago: Charles T. Peavy, 1928).

23. Ignatieff, "Russisch-Jüdische Arbeiter uber die Judenfrage," *Neue Zeit* 6 (October 1892): 175–179.

24. Stuart Ross Thompstone, "The Organisation and Financing of Russian Foreign Trade Before 1914" (PhD diss., University of London, 1991), 145–146.

25. Simon M. Dubnow, *History of the Jews in Russia and Poland from the Earliest Times Until the Present Day* (Philadelphia: Jewish Publication Society of America, 1918), 2:191–192.

26. Leopold H. Haimson, *The Russian Marxists and the Origins of Bolshevism* (Boston: Beacon Press, 1971), chap. 2.

27. A photostat of the first and second draft of Parvus's outline of his education is reprinted in Elisabeth Heresch, *Geheimakte Parvus: die gekaufte Revolution* (München: Herbig, 2013), 38. He left fifth grade in 1882, the year of the May Laws. While Winifred Scharlau and Zbyněk Zeman assert that Parvus's father was a locksmith or mechanic, the anticommunist writer Mikhail Konstantinovich Pervukhin states that his family (*parenti*) were Odessa speculators in grain and lard. See Zbyněk Anthony Bohuslav Zeman and Winifred B. Scharlau, *The Merchant of Revolution: The Life of Alexander Israel Helphand (Parvus), 1867–1924* (New York: Oxford University Press, 1965); Mikhail Konstantinovich Pervukhin, *I Bolsceviki* (Bologna: N. Zanichelli, 1918), 99.

28. Parvus was closest to members of Chernyi Peredel, including Vera Zasulich and Paul Axelrod, who also fled Russia to Switzerland in the early 1880s.

29. When Adjutant-General Iakov Rostovtsev died, Count Viktor Panin replaced him and shrank plots while increasing redemption payments. Peasant allotments shrank 30 percent in Kharkov, Kazan, and Simbirsk provinces. Alexander Polunov, *Russia in the Nineteenth Century: Autocracy, Reform, and Social Change, 1814–1914* (Armonk, NY: M. E. Sharpe, 2005), 104–107.

30. Zeman and Scharlau, *Merchant of Revolution*, 9–10.

31. "I parenti de Helphand si specializzarono nell speculazoni con il grano e il lardo russo." Pervukhin, *I Bolsceviki*, 98.

32. Parvus, *Im Kampf Um Die Warheit* (Berlin: Verlag fur Sozialwissenschaft GMBH, 1918), 7.

33. Carl Lehmann and Parvus, *Das Hungernde Russland: Reiseeindrücke, Beobachtungen und Untersuchungen* (Stuttgart: J. H. W. Dietz Nachf., 1900), 189.

34. Parvus, *Im Kampf.*

35. Parvus, *Im Kampf.*

36. Israel Helphand, *Technische Organisation der Arbeit ("Cooperation" und "Arbeitsheilung"): Eine Kritische Studie* (Basel: University of Basel, 1891), 30–34.

37. Helphand, *Technische Organisation der Arbeit*, 30–49.

38. Helphand, *Technische Organisation der Arbeit*, 95n1.

39. Helphand, *Technische Organisation der Arbeit*, 55–65.

40. He did, however, believe that political bodies eventually ought to manage agricultural land. Parvus, "The Peasantry and the Social Revolution," in *Marxism and Social Democracy: The Revisionist Debate, 1896–1898*, ed. H. Tudor and J. M. Tudor (New York: Cambridge University Press, 1988), 196–204. In Parvus's debate with Bernstein, he argued that the largest landholders and Junkers needed to be displaced and that farmers on plots under twenty hectares could not purchase agricultural equipment or fertilizer. He refused to predict the future of agriculture but argued that the large farmers, the *Grossbauerntum* who farmed twenty to one hundred hectares, were more productive, were politically passive unless riled up by nationalists, and would become a vanishingly small part of European society.

41. Heresch, *Geheimakte Parvus*.

42. John Peter Nettl, *Rosa Luxemburg*, vol. 1 (London: Oxford University Press, 1966); Zeman and Scharlau, *Merchant of Revolution*; Parvus to Alexander Potresov, April 15, 1904, in Aleksandr Nikolaevich Potresov and Boris Ivanovich Nicolaevsky, comp., *Sotsial-Demokraticheskoye Dvizheniye v Rossii: Materialy* (1928; repr. The Hague: Europe Printing, 1967).

43. August Bebel to Karl Kautsky, September 4, 1901, quoted in Nettl, *Rosa Luxemburg*, 186.

44. Vladimir Lenin, "Review: Parvus, The World Market and the Agricultural Crisis," in *Collected Works*, vol. 4: *1898–April 1901* (Moscow: Progress Publishers, 1977), 65–66.

45. "Foreign Correspondence, from Our Paris Correspondent," *The Economist*, December 30, 1848; *Oxford English Dictionary*, 3rd ed., 2000, s.v. "imperialism, n."

46. Andrew Zimmerman, *Alabama in Africa: Booker T. Washington, the German Empire, and the Globalization of the New South* (Princeton, NJ: Princeton University Press, 2012).

47. Zeman and Scharlau, *Merchant of Revolution*, 57; Isaac Deutscher, *The Prophet Armed, Trotsky: 1879–1921* (New York: Oxford University Press, 1954); Leon Trotsky, *My Life: An Attempt at an Autobiography* (New York: Charles Scribner's Sons, 1930).

48. Parvus, "Die Orientfrage, 2. Ein geschichtlicher Rüdblid [sic]," *Sächsische Arbeiter-Zeitung*, March 13, 1897; Parvus, "Die Orientfrage, Bismarck's Borschubdienste an Russland," *Sächsische Arbeiter-Zeitung*, March 16, 1897.

CHAPTER 10: THE GRAIN POWERS OF EUROPE

1. Charles Tilly, *Coercion, Capital, and European States, 990–1990* (Cambridge, MA: Blackwell, 1990), 178–179.
2. Charles Kindleberger and others have an argument about cheap grain. This differs in many ways from theirs, as I don't see a Prussian road to capitalism.
3. Parvus, "Türkische Wirren," *Sächsische Arbeiter-Zeitung*, September 10, 1896.
4. Klement Judit, *Gőzmalmok a Duna partján: a budapesti malomipar a 19–20. században* (Budapest: Holnap, 2010).
5. Victor Heller, *Getreidehandel und seine technik in Wien* (Tubingen: J. C. B. Mohr, 1901); J. M. Lachlan, General Manager, United States and Brazil Mail Steamship Company, "United States and Brazil Mail Steamship Companies," in *Trade and Transportation Between the United States and Latin America*, 51st Cong., 1st Sess., Senate Exec. Doc 54 (Washington, DC: Government Printing Office, 1890), 207–208.
6. Parvus, "The Eastern Question," *Sächsische Arbeiter-Zeitung*, March 13, 1897.
7. Heller, *Getreidehandel*.
8. "Hungary: Hon. Robert H. Baker Tells What He Saw," *Racine [Wisconsin] Journal*, June 12, 1878.
9. Eugene Smalley, "The Flour Mills of Minneapolis," *Century Magazine* 32, no. 1 (May 1886): 37–47; John Storck and Walter Dorwin Teague, *Flour for Man's Bread* (New York: Oxford University Press, 1952), chap. 14. Millers continued to use waterpower over steam power in Hungarian-style mills, however, because the combination of coal-fired steam engines and airborne flour was more explosive than dynamite.
10. UK Parliament, "First Report of the Royal Commission Appointed to Inquire into the Depression of Trade and Industry," C. 4621 (1885); House, *Broomhall's Corn Trade Yearbook* (Liverpool: Northern Publishing Co., 1904), 7; Jennifer Tann and R. Glyn Jones, "Technology and Transformation: The Diffusion of the Roller Mill in the British Flour Milling Industry, 1870–1907," *Technology and Culture* 37, no. 1 (1996): 36–69.
11. "Hungarian Milling Depression," *Chanute [Kansas] Times*, December 22, 1905.
12. Sevket Pamuk, "The Evolution of Financial Institutions in the Ottoman Empire, 1600–1914," *Financial History Review* 11, no. 1 (2004): 7–32; Seven Ağir, "The Evolution of Grain Policy: The Ottoman Experience," *Journal of Interdisciplinary History* 43, no. 4 (2013):

571–598. On the continued use of fixed grain prices in the empire, see Margaret Stevens Hoell, "The Ticaret Odasi: Origins, Functions, and Activities of the Chamber of Commerce of Istanbul, 1885–1899" (unpublished PhD diss., Ohio State University, 1973).

13. Hoell, "The Ticaret Odasi."

14. Virginia Aksan, *Ottoman Wars, 1700–1870: An Empire Besieged* (New York: Routledge, 2007), 13, 388; Orlando Figes, *The Crimean War: A History* (New York: Metropolitan Books, 2011), chap. 2; Jeffrey G. Williamson, *Trade and Poverty: When the Third World Fell Behind* (Cambridge, MA: MIT Press, 2011), 103. Parvus discusses the model in Parvus, *Türkiye'nin mali tutsaklığı*, trans. Muammer Sencer (Istanbul: May Yayınları, 1977).

15. Kevin H. O'Rourke, "The European Grain Invasion, 1870–1913," *Journal of Economic History* 57, no. 4 (December 1997).

16. Henry C. Morris, "Consular Report, Ghent," in *The World's Market for American Produce*, ed. US Department of Agriculture (Washington, DC: US Government Printing Office, 1895), 57–59.

17. Susan P. Mattern, *Rome and the Enemy: Imperial Strategy in the Principate* (Berkeley: University of California Press, 1999).

18. In the nineteenth century, anthropologists, geographers, and historians of empire saw ancient empires as nodes for the concentration of resources. They noted that every ancient empire's center was near plains for grain, wood for mixed manufacturing, and navigable rivers for trade. Peninsular Rome was apparently unique among ancient imperial centers, however, in having unfettered access to the sea, making it an ancient crossroads for the division of labor and the mixing of cultures. On ancient Rome's reference point being the Tiber River, see Pliny [the Elder], *Natural History* (Cambridge, MA: Harvard University Press, 1942), book III, vol. 56, 42. On the uniqueness of Rome as a peninsular empire, see Carl Ritter, *Die Erdkunde im Verhältniss zur Natur und zur Geschichte des Menschen*, 2 vols. (Berlin: G. Reimer, 1817–1818). On access to the ocean as defining stages of civilization, see Ernst Kapp, *Philosophische oder vergleichende allgemeine Erdkunde als wissenschaftliche Darstellung der Erdverhältnisse und des Menschenlebens* (Braunschweig: G. Westerman, 1845). Kapp, a student of Ritter, introduced in 1845 three "ages" of man: the "Potamic or Oriental World," where China and India dominated; the "Thalassic World" of the Middle Ages, where Europe and other regions absorbed the discoveries of the East; and the "Oceanic World," opened circa 1500, when Spain, France, and England crossed the Atlantic.

19. The German Admiralty's solution to the consumption efficiency of an intestinal port city like Antwerp might have been to annex it. This

would have required a new mile marker zero, of course, and possibly a second capital city. But after Britain's proclamation, they understood that invading Belgium would have started a world war.

20. Parvus, "Türkische Wirren."

21. On the role of free river navigation in the Berlin West African Conference of 1884–1885 (arguably the starting gun for the scramble for Africa), see Matthew Craven, "Between Law and History: The Berlin Conference of 1884–1885 and the Logic of Free Trade," *London Review of International Law* 3, no. 1 (March 1, 2015): 31–59.

22. Lothar de Maiziere, "Pioneerarbeit," chap. 4 in *Ich will dass Meine Kinder Nicht Mehr Lügen Müssen: Meine Geschichte der Deutschen Einheit* (Freiburg im Breisgau: Verlag Herder, 2010). Thanks to Frank Müller, University of St. Andrews, for telling me about this story. On Prussian tariffs as a response to the agrarian crisis, see Cornelius Torp, "The 'Coalition of "Rye and Iron"' under the Pressure of Globalization: A Reinterpretation of Germany's Political Economy Before 1914," *Central European History* 43, no. 3 (September 2010): 401–427.

23. Rainer Fremdling, "Freight Rates and State Budget: The Role of the National Prussian Railways, 1880–1913," *Journal of European Economic History* 9, no. 1 (1980): 21–39.

24. Andrew Zimmerman, *Alabama in Africa: Booker T. Washington, the German Empire, and the Globalization of the New South* (Princeton, NJ: Princeton University Press, 2010), chap. 2. Then called the Social Democratic Party. A formal alliance was made in 1879 between the Central Association of German Industrialists (Centralverband Deutscher Industrieller) and the Agrarian Association of Tax and Economic Reform (Agrarischen Vereinigung der Steuer- und Wirtschaftsreformer), headed by Julius Mirbach, a prominent DKP member of the House of Lords. F. Stephan, *Die 25jährige thätigkeit der Vereinigung der Steur- und Wirtschafts-Reformer (1876–1900)* (Berlin: Verlag des Bureau der Vereinigung der Steur- und Wirtschafts-Reformer, 1900), 42. Conservatives blamed the Social Democrats for two attempts on the life of Kaiser Wilhelm.

25. Bismarck's 1878 instructions to the tariff committee of the Federal Council are described in William Harbutt Dawson, *Bismarck and State Socialism: An Exposition of the Social and Economic Legislation of Germany Since 1870* (London: S. Sonnenschein & Co., 1891), chap. 5.

26. On the role of the railroads as a substitute tax system for Germany, see Fremdling, "Freight Rates and State Budget"; Jeffrey Fear and Christopher Kobrak, "Origins of German Corporate Governance and Accounting, 1870–1914: Making Capitalism Respectable" (paper

presented at International Economic History Congress, Helsinki, Finland, August 2006).

27. Quoted in R. H. Best, "Our Fiscal System," *National Union Gleanings* 27 (July–December 1906): 277.

28. Zimmerman, *Alabama in Africa*; Robert L. Nelson, ed., *Germans, Poland, and Colonial Expansion to the East* (New York: Palgrave, 2009); Robert L. Nelson, "From Manitoba to the Memel: Max Sering, Inner Colonization and the German East," *Social History* 35, no. 4 (2010): 439–457. For 955 million, see Nelson, *Germans, Poland, and Colonial Expansion*, 56. Nelson's figures do not include railroad subsidies for grain going from east to west, which were quite large. Fremdling, "Freight Rates and State Budget."

29. Otto Julius Eltzbacher, "The Fiscal Policy of Germany," *Nineteenth Century and After* 317 (August 1903): 188; Heinrich von Treitschke, *Politics*, 2 vols. (New York: Macmillan Company, 1916), 1:408, 300–301.

30. Prussia, Ministerium für Handel, Gewerbe und öffentliche Arbeiten, "The Argument for State Railroad Ownership" (translated from German, original not found), *Railroad Gazette*, 1880.

31. The empire received tariff revenue while states received land taxes (which fell as land values fell); Dawson, *Bismarck and State Socialism*, chap. 5.

32. Hermann Schumacher, "Germany's International Economic Position," in *Modern Germany in Relation to the Great War*, ed. and trans. William Wallace Whitelock (New York: Mitchell Kennerley, 1916), 94–99.

33. Schumacher, "Germany's International Economic Position," 99.

34. Vaclav Smil, *Enriching the Earth: Fritz Haber, Carl Bosch, and the Transformation of World Food Production* (Cambridge, MA: MIT Press, 2004). On the problems of growing wheat in Germany's soil, see Naum Jasny, "Wheat Problems and Policies in Germany," *Wheat Studies of the Food Research Institute* 13, no. 3 (November 1936): 65–140.

35. Parvus, *Die Kolonialpolitik und der Zusammenbruch* (Leipzig: Verlag der Leipziger Buchdruckerei Aktiengesellschaft, 1907), 85.

36. Grain moved to Fiume on the Adriatic and to Ljublia (now Liepaja) on the Baltic. "The Returns of the German Railways for December," *[London] Guardian*, January 19, 1881. On the rapid development of the grain trade after the 1880s at Duisburg, Mannheim, and Basel, see Edwin J. Clapp, *The Navigable Rhine* (Boston: Houghton Mifflin, 1911). On complaints in the German towns of Insterberg, Konigsburg, and Tilsit, see Worthington Chauncey Ford, "The Commercial Policy of Europe," *Publications of the American Economic Association* 3, no. 1 (1902): 126–127.

37. James C. Hunt, "Peasants, Grain Tariffs, and Meat Quotas: Imperial German Protectionism Reexamined," *Central European History* 7, no. 4 (1974): 311–331.

38. John Nye, "The Myth of Free-Trade Britain and Fortress France: Tariffs and Trade in the Nineteenth Century," *Journal of Economic History* 51, no. 1 (1991): 23–46.

39. Between 1878 and 1892, according to Paul Bairoch, the average percentage of revenue France drew from its tariffs nearly doubled from 7 to 13 percent. Germany's share went from 42 to 36 percent, but the comparison is deceptive. German statistics only include federal government spending, with individual German states taxing land and providing services. France's national budget included much more of the income (land tax) and spending (municipal building) in French departments. If we parsed out these ancient local functions, the French central government would be shown to derive much more of its income from tariffs, mostly on grain. Paul Bairoch, "European Trade Policy, 1815–1914," chap. 8 in *The Cambridge Economic History of Europe*, vol. 8 (New York: Cambridge University Press, 1989); Theodore Zeldin, *France, 1848–1945*, vol. 1: *Ambition, Love, and Politics* (Oxford: Oxford University Press, 1973), 570–604; Robert M. Schwartz, "Rail Transport, Agrarian Crisis, and the Restructuring of Agriculture: France and Great Britain Confront Globalization, 1860–1900," *Social Science History* 34, no. 2 (summer 2010): 229–255.

40. Avner Offer, "Ricardo's Paradox and the Movement of Rents in England, c. 1870–1910," *Economic History Review* 33, no. 2 (1980): 236–252; Wilhelm Abel, *Agricultural Fluctuations in Europe from the Thirteenth to the Twentieth Centuries* (New York: St. Martin's Press, 1980), chap. 11.

41. The Hungarian milling method, by producing flour more efficiently than the grain-to-flour formula imposed by states, allowed millions of extra pounds of grain to enter European ports free of duty every year, something like half a pound of grain for each pound of flour exported. Merchants called this overproduction by indirect bounty. For Italian pasta, see Mack H. Davis, *Flour and Wheat Trade in European Countries and the Levant* (Washington, DC: Government Printing Office, 1909), 115–117. For complaints about this problem in Germany, see Davis, *Flour and Wheat Trade*, 118–123. On how drawback bounties for export contributed to overproduction, see Report by Mr. Scott on the Present Condition of Trade and Industry in Germany, in United Kingdom, Parliament, Royal Committee to Inquire into Depression of Trade and Industry, Second Report, C. 4715 (1886), Appendix II, 162.

42. The best discussion of the German-Russian tariff situation is Louis Domeratzky, *Tariff Relations Between German and Russia (1890–1914)*,

Tariff Series No. 38, Department of Commerce (Washington, DC: US Government Printing Office, 1918). Germany introduced a bounty system for exporting flour to the Netherlands, designed to push back the cheap American grain that became Dutch flour in Amsterdam. Davis, *Flour and Wheat Trade*, 118–123.

43. John A. Hobson, *Imperialism: A Study* (London: George, Allen & Unwin, 1902), 35–38.

44. Daniel Meissner, "Bridging the Pacific: California and the China Flour Trade," *California History* 76, no. 4 (1997): 82–93. The rapid expansion of American flour exports to China via Hong Kong after the Civil War is described in A. H. Cathcart, "Pacific Mail—Under the American Flag Around the World," *Pacific Marine Review* (July 1920): 53–58.

45. Parvus, *Türkiye'nin mali tutsaklığı*.

46. Murat Birdal, *The Political Economy of Ottoman Public Debt: Insolvency and European Financial Control in the Late Nineteenth Century* (New York: I. B. Tauris, 2010); Hans Van de Ven, *Breaking with the Past: The Maritime Customs Service and the Global Origins of Modernity in China* (New York: Columbia University Press, 2014). A revisionist account of the OPDA can be found in Ali Coşkun Tunçer, "Leveraging Foreign Control: Reform in the Ottoman Empire," in *A World of Public Debt: A Political History*, ed. Nicolas Barreyre and Nicolas Delalande (Cham, Switzerland: Palgrave Macmillan, 2020), 135–154. A harsher review of the Chinese Maritime Trade Association is in Dong Yan, "The Domestic Effects of Foreign Capital: Public Debt and Regional Inequalities in Late Qing China," in Barreyre and Delalande, *A World of Public Debt*.

47. Olga Crisp, "The Russo-Chinese Bank: An Episode in Franco-Russian Relations," *Slavonic and East European Review* 52, no. 127 (April 1974): 197–212.

CHAPTER 11: "RUSSIA IS THE SHAME OF EUROPE"

1. Worthington Chauncey Ford, "The Commercial Policy of Europe," *Publications of the American Economic Association* 3, no. 1 (1902): 119.

2. Thomas Piketty, *Capital and Ideology* (Cambridge, MA: Harvard University Press, 2020), chap. 7, numbers from figure 7.9. Foreign assets were calculated net of liabilities.

3. National Monetary Commission, *Banking in Italy, Russia, Austro-Hungary, and Japan* (Washington, DC: Government Printing Office, 1911).

4. Gregor Jollos, "Der Getreidehandel in Russland," in *Handwör-terbuch der Staatswissenschaften* (Jena: Gustav Fischer, 1892), 3:872–878; George Garvy, "Banking Under the Tsars and the Soviets," *Journal of Economic History* 32, no. 4 (1972): 869; I. M. Rubinow, *Russia's Wheat Surplus: Conditions Under Which It Is Produced*, Bulletin no. 42 (Washington, DC: US Department of Agriculture, Bureau of Statistics, 1906). David Moon, *The Plough That Broke the Steppes: Agriculture and Environment on Russia's Grasslands, 1700–1914* (Oxford: Oxford University Press, 2013), discusses the ecological dangers and the growing interest in understanding them.

5. Martin Gilbert, *The Routledge Atlas of Russian History* (New York: Routledge, 2007), 58.

6. Leon Trotsky, *My Life: An Attempt at an Autobiography* (New York: Charles Scribner's Sons, 1930), chap. 1.

7. Trotsky, *My Life*; Leon Trotsky, *1905* (New York: Random House, 1971), 26.

8. Rubinow, *Russia's Wheat Surplus*, 99.

9. Max Winters, *Zur Organisation des Südrussischen Getreide-Exporthandels* (Leipzig: Duncker & Humblot, 1905). On the yearly arrival of migrants to South Russia, see Trotsky, *My Life*, 24–25. On the role of Russian peasant migration in providing field labor in the south and agricultural labor in the north, see Trotsky, *1905*, 22–29.

10. Trotsky, *My Life*, 25.

11. On trade organization, see Winters, *Zur Organisation des Südrussischen Getreide-Exporthandels*, 7–19. On negotiation, see Eustace Clare Grenville Murray, *The Russians of To-day* (London: Smith, Elder, 1878), 80–89; Jollos, "Der Getreidehandel in Russland" (1892), 872–878. On incentives, see M. E. Falkus, "Russia and the International Wheat Trade, 1861–1914," *Economica* 33, no. 132 (1966): 416–429. On *varranty*, see Thomas C. Owen, *Corporation Under Russian Law* (New York: Cambridge University Press, 1991), 107. On getting grain into packets for water shipment, see Stuart Ross Thompstone, "The Organisation and Financing of Russian Foreign Trade Before 1914" (PhD diss., University of London, 1991), chap. 3. On Jews as financial intermediaries in grain after 1861, see Ilya Grigorovich Orshansky, *Evrei v Rossii: Ocherki ekonomicheskogo i obshchestvennogo byta russkikh evreev* (St. Petersburg: O. I. Baksta, 1877), 32–34.

12. On Russia in the 1872–1873 crisis, see Konstantin Skalkovsky, *Les ministres des finances de la Russie: 1802–1890* (Paris: Guillaumin, 1891), 147–170. On the ruble's effect on grain, see Carl Johannes Fuchs, *Der englische Getreidehandel und seine Organisation* (Jena: Gustav Fischer, 1890), 20–25.

13. Skalkovsky, *Les ministres des finances de la Russie*, 147–170.

14. V. L. Stepanov, "Ivan Alekseevich Vyshnegradskii," *Russian Studies in History* 35, no. 2 (1996): 73–103.

15. Sergei Witte, *The Memoirs of Count Witte* (Garden City, NY: Doubleday, 1921), 15–21; Francis W. Wcislo, *Tales of Imperial Russia: The Life and Times of Sergei Witte, 1849–1915* (New York: Oxford University Press, 2011), chap. 3.

16. Simon M. Dubnow, *History of the Jews in Russia and Poland from the Earliest Times Until the Present Day* (Philadelphia: Jewish Publication Society of America, 1918), chap. 26.

17. Mose L. Harvey, "The Development of Russian Commerce on the Black Sea and Its Significance" (PhD diss., University of California, Berkeley, 1938), 134.

18. Jollos, "Der Getreidehandel in Russland" (1892), 872–878; Gregor Jollos, "Der Getreidehandel in Russland," in *Handwörterbuch der Staatswissenschaften* (Jena: Gustav Fischer, 1900), 4:297–304; Rubinow, *Russia's Wheat Surplus*, 12–13.

19. Valerii L. Stepanov, "Laying the Groundwork for Sergei Witte's Monetary Reform: The Policy of Finance Minister I. A. Vyshnegradskii (1887–1892)," *Russian Studies in History* 47, no. 3 (December 2008): 38–70.

20. Robert V. Allen, *Russia Looks to America: The View to 1917* (Washington, DC: Library of Congress, 1988), 140.

21. Marika Mägi, *In Austrvegr: The Role of the Eastern Baltic in Viking Age Communication Across the Baltic Sea* (Boston: Brill, 2018), 94–104. On Louis-Dreyfus in Odessa, see Dan Morgan, *Merchants of Grain* (New York: Viking, 1979), 31–34.

22. Libau was expanded in 1888, tripling the vessels that could land compared to 1879. Nikolai Andreevich Kislinskim and A. N. Kulomzin, *Nasha zheleznodorozhnaya Politika po Dokumentam Arkhiva Komiteta Ministrov, Istoricheskiy Ocherk* (St. Petersburg: Kantselyarii Komiteta Ministrov, 1902), 102.

23. Valerii L. Stepanov, "I. A. Vyshnegradskii and S. Iu. Witte: Partners and Competitors," *Russian Studies in History* 54, no. 3 (July 3, 2015): 210–237.

24. Skalkovsky, *Les ministres des finances de la Russie*, 168–170.

25. On the Russian sell-off of railroads after 1870 and later repurchase, see Mikhail I Voronin and M. M. Voronina, *Pavel Melnikov and the Creation of the Railway System in Russia* (Danville, PA: Languages of Montour Press, 1995), chap. 9.

26. On tariffs and revenues, see Skalkovsky, *Les ministres des finances de la Russie*, 275–289. On terminated agreements, see I. M. Rubinow,

Russian Wheat and Wheat Flour in European Markets, Bulletin no. 66 (Washington, DC: US Department of Agriculture, Bureau of Statistics, 1908), 40.

27. Richard Tilly, "International Factors in the Formation of Banking Systems," in *International Banking, 1870–1914*, ed. Rondo Cameron and V. I. Bovykin (New York: Oxford University Press, 1991), 104–106; Jennifer L. Siegel, *For Peace and Money: French and British Finance in the Service of Tsars and Commissars* (New York: Oxford University Press, 2014), chap. 1.

28. Arcadius Kahan, "Natural Calamities and Their Effect upon the Food Supply in Russia (an Introduction to a Catalogue)," *Jahrbücher für Geschichte Osteuropas* 3 (1968): 353–377; Moon, *The Plough That Broke the Steppes*, 65–68.

29. Carl Lehmann and Parvus, *Das Hungernde Russland: Reiseeindrücke, Beobachtungen und Untersuchungen* (Stuttgart: J. H. W. Dietz Nachf., 1900), 170–191; Richard G. Robbins, *Famine in Russia, 1891–1892: The Imperial Government Responds to a Crisis* (New York: Columbia University Press, 1975), 24ff. Stephen G. Wheatcroft, in "The 1891–92 Famine in Russia: Towards a More Detailed Analysis of Its Scale and Demographic Significance," in *Economy and Society in Russia and the Soviet Union, 1860–1930*, ed. Linda Edmonson and Peter Waldron (London: Macmillan, 1992), 45–46, points out that Russia's net export in 1891 was actually higher than in 1889, another year of low production.

30. Wheatcroft, "The 1891–92 Famine in Russia," 44–64.

31. Lehmann and Parvus, *Das Hungernde Russland*, 170–191; Leo Tolstoy, *The Novels and Other Works of Lyof N. Tolstoi*, vol. 20: *Essays, Letters, Miscellanies* (New York: Charles Scribner's Sons, 1900), 271–275; James Y. Simms Jr., "The Crop Failure of 1891: Soil Exhaustion, Technological Backwardness, and Russia's 'Agrarian Crisis,'" *Slavic Review* 41, no. 2 (summer 1982): 236–250.

32. On deforestation, see Lehmann and Parvus, *Das Hungernde Russland*, 170–180. On Tolstoy's privately stated argument that the railroads were to blame, see Edward Arthur Brayley Hodgetts, *In the Track of the Russian Famine: The Personal Narrative of Journey Through the Famine Districts of Russia* (London: T. Fisher Unwin, 1892), 4. Tolstoy's published accounts of the famine were heavily censored, but he did point to the problem with *zemstvo*'s census in "Help for the Starving" and the censorship imposed by the *zemsky nachalnik* (land captains). See Tolstoy, *Essays, Letters, Miscellanies*. Following geologist and soil scientist Vasily Dokuchaev, David Moon argues, in "The Environmental History of the Russian Steppes: Vasilii Dokuchaev and the Harvest Failure of 1891,"

Transactions of the Royal Historical Society (2005): 149–174, that over-plowing led to drought, not deforestation.

33. Stepanov, "I. A. Vyshnegradskii and S. Iu. Witte."

34. Scott Reynolds Nelson, *Iron Confederacies: Southern Railways, Klan Violence, and Reconstruction* (Chapel Hill: University of North Carolina Press, 1999); Richard H. White, *Railroaded: The Transcontinentals and the Making of Modern America* (New York: Norton & Company, 2011).

35. Elie de Cyon, *Les finances russes et l'épargne française* (Paris: Chamerot et Renouard, 1895). On bribes in the west, see White, *Railroaded*. On bribes in the south, see Nelson, *Iron Confederacies*.

36. Carl Bücher, *Industrial Organization* (London: G. Bell & Sons), chap. 6.

37. Zygmunt Bauman, *Legislators and Interpreters: On Modernity, Post-modernity, and Intellectuals* (Ithaca, NY: Cornell University Press, 1987).

38. Parvus, "Eine Neue Äera [sic] in Rußland," *Sächsische Arbeiter-Zeitung*, July 9, 1896.

39. Parvus, "Eine Neue Äera."

40. Immanuel Wallerstein, who coined the term "world-system," suggests inspiration from four sources: a stadial theory of economic growth that grew out of European social sciences; Raúl Prebisch and Hans Singer's suggestion that economic development in Latin America produced underdevelopment through the unequal exchange of cheap primary products for expensive industrial goods; Maurice Dobbs's argument with Paul Sweezy about whether the transition from feudalism to capitalism was internal or external; and Fernand Braudel's Annalles School, which emphasized deeper economic sources of political change. See Immanuel Wallerstein, *World-Systems Analysis: An Introduction* (Durham, NC: Duke University Press, 2004). Though Wallerstein's understanding of how unequal development could be produced internationally closely tracks the arguments laid out by Parvus, Trotsky, and Rosa Luxemburg between 1891 and 1930, he regards world-systems as his own hybrid produced in the 1950s. While I do not doubt that Wallerstein came by his hybrid argument honestly, Dobb, Sweezy, and Braudel at least understood their arguments' deep relationship to an older tradition laid out by Parvus, Luxemburg, and Trotsky. But Dobb and Sweezy as "orthodox" Marxists would not have deigned to cite Trotsky, his predecessors, or his antecedents. Braudel knew Marxist theory but seldom discussed it in footnotes in *Civilization and Capitalism*. There are many failings of world-systems theory: its inability to explain how the core moves from Italy to the Netherlands to London and then to the United States;

its related incapacity to deal with how a semiperiphery like the United States can become a core; and its difficulty explaining the "Asian Tigers" of the late 1980s and then Chinese industrialization after the 1990s. These failings have led to many valuable revisions of world-systems theory, including the brilliant work of Harriet Friedmann, Giovanni Arrighi, David Harvey, and Jason W. Moore. I would suggest a reset of this theoretical framework that puts Parvus's analysis of the black paths, the Malthusian impact of food, the rise of gullet cities, imperial grain organization, the role of exchanges, and the role of news back into these debates. World-systems theorists tend to dislike cheap food for environmental reasons such as nitrification of rivers and the polluting costs of overseas shipping. These things are true, but cheap food benefits workers and other poor people. This was well understood and celebrated by Parvus and nineteenth-century Marxists. It is why Marxists supported free trade. This book is, in a way, a recognition of that boon to our grandparents' grandparents, who often starved before the advent of the changes I have described here.

41. Parvus, "Eine Neue Äera."

42. Parvus, "Zur Diskussion über den Agrarprogrammentwurf," *Leipziger Volkszeitung* (summer 1895).

43. Parvus, "Die Orientfrage, 2. Ein geschichtlicher Rüdblid [sic]," *Sächsische Arbeiter-Zeitung*, March 13, 1897.

44. Parvus, "Die Orientfrage."

45. Parvus, "Eine Neue Äera."

46. Parvus, "Eine Neue Äera."

47. Parvus, "Türkische Wirren," *Sächsische Arbeiter-Zeitung*, September 10, 1896.

48. Rosa Luxemburg notes that the press commission resented Parvus for "all the accusations against the unpleasant and vulgar tone of the paper." John Peter Nettl, *Rosa Luxemburg* (London: Oxford University Press, 1966), 1:160.

49. Vladimir Lenin, *Collected Works* (Moscow: Progress Publishers, 1977), 4:65–66.

50. Elisabeth Heresch, *Geheimakte Parvus: die gekaufte Revolution* (München: Herbig, 2013), 50.

51. Parvus, "Der Weltmarkt Und die Agrarkrisis," *Die Neue Zeit* 14 (November 1895): 197ff.

52. Nettl, *Rosa Luxemburg*, 109–110, 156–158.

53. "Starving Russia," *New York Times*, July 21, 1901, 30.

54. According to David Wolff, this agreement was worked out in April 1896, after Nicholas II's coronation, when China learned that Russia's

price for preventing Japan from taking the Liaodong peninsula was Russian control of the same peninsula. David Wolff, *To the Harbin Station: The Liberal Alternative in Russian Manchuria, 1898–1914* (Stanford, CA: Stanford University Press, 1999), 5.

55. C. Walter Young, "The Russian Advance into Manchuria," *Chinese Students' Monthly* 20, no. 7 (May 1925): 19.

56. Speech by Henry Labouchere, June 10, 1898, House of Commons, 1371–1372.

57. David Schimmelpenninck van der Oye, "The Immediate Origins of the War," in *The Russo-Japanese War in Global Perspective: World War Zero*, ed. John W. Steinberg et al. (Boston: Brill, 2005), 1:36.

58. Sarah C. M. Paine, "The Chinese Eastern Railway from the First Sino-Japanese War Until the Russo-Japanese War," in *Manchurian Railways and the Opening of China: An International History*, ed. Bruce A. Elleman and Stephen Kotkin (Armonk, NY: M. E. Sharpe, 2010), 13–36.

59. Young, "The Russian Advance into Manchuria," 18–20.

60. On the origins of the Boxers, see Joseph W. Esherick, *The Origins of the Boxer Uprising* (Berkeley: University of California Press, 1987). On their actions in Russia, see G. V. Melikhov, *Man'chzhuriya dalekaya i blizkaya* (Moscow: Nauka, 1991), 108–109.

61. Schimmelpenninck van der Oye, "Immediate Origins of the War," 34–36.

62. Andrew Higgins, "On Russia-China Border, Selective Memory of Massacre Works for Both Sides," *New York Times*, March 26, 2020.

63. [Tokuji Hoshino], *Economic History of Manchuria* (Seoul: Bank of Chosen, 1920), 41; Chinese Eastern Railway, *Ocherk kommercheskoy deyatel'nosti kitayskoy vostochnoy zheleznoy* . . . (St. Petersburg: A. Smolinsky, 1912).

64. Rosa Luxemburg to Leo Jogiches, December 12, 1899, in *The Letters of Rosa Luxemburg*, ed. George Adler et al. (Brooklyn, NY: Verso Press, 2011), 96–100.

65. Vladimir Lenin, "The Serf Owners at Work," in *Collected Works* (Moscow: Foreign Languages Publishing House, 1961), 5:95–100.

66. This included sixteen capital warships, twenty-three destroyers, and sixty-three torpedo boats at a total cost of 213 million yen. J. Charles Schencking, *Making Waves: Politics, Propaganda, and the Emergence of the Imperial Japanese Navy, 1868–1922* (Stanford: Stanford University Press, 2005), 84–85.

67. "Nihon kokumin to sensò," *Yorodzu chòhò* (February 28, 1904), quoted in Naoko Shimazu, "'Love Thy Enemy': Japanese Perceptions of

Russia," in *The Russo-Japanese War in Global Perspective: World War Zero*, ed. John W. Steinberg et al. (Boston: Brill, 2005), 1:366.

68. John Bushnell, "The Specter of Mutinous Reserves," in *The Russo-Japanese War in Global Perspective: World War Zero*, ed. John W. Steinberg et al. (Boston: Brill, 2005), 1:335, 339.

69. Baron Roman Romanovich Rosen, *Forty Years of Diplomacy* (New York: Knopf, 1922), chap. 17–23.

70. John L. H. Keep, *The Rise of Social Democracy in Russia* (London: Oxford University Press, 1963), 152–158.

71. Leopold H. Haimson, ed., *The Making of Three Russian Revolutionaries: Voices from the Menshevik Past* (New York: Cambridge University Press, 1987), 484; Jonathan Edwards Sanders, "The Union of Unions: Political, Economic, Civil, and Human Rights Organizations in the 1905 Russian Revolution" (PhD diss., Columbia University, 1985); Zbyněk Anthony Bohuslav Zeman and Winifred B. Scharlau, *The Merchant of Revolution: The Life of Alexander Israel Helphand (Parvus), 1867–1924* (New York: Oxford University Press, 1965), 81–82.

72. Zeman and Scharlau, *Merchant of Revolution*, 79–83.

73. Theodore Weeks, "Managing Empire: Tsarist National Policies," in *The Cambridge History of Russia*, vol. 2: *Imperial Russia, 1689–1917*, ed. Dominic Lieven (Cambridge: Cambridge University Press, 2006), 2:42.

74. Bushnell, "Specter of Mutinous Reserves," 345.

75. George Garvy, "The Financial Manifesto of the St. Petersburg Soviet, 1905," *International Review of Social History* 20, no. 1 (1975): 16–32.

76. Leo Deutsch, *Viermal Entflohen* (Stuttgart: Dietz, 1907), 170–198; *Hamburger Anzeiger*, October 17, 1906. On Parvus in the 1905 Revolution generally, see Anne Dorazio Morgan, "The St. Petersburg Soviet of Workers' Deputies: A Study of Labor Organization in the 1905 Russian Revolution" (PhD diss., Indiana University, 1979).

CHAPTER 12: ORIENT EXPRESS, ARMY OF ACTION

1. On Parvus's sense of the instability of the Russian Empire, see Parvus, "Eine Neue Äera [sic] in Rußland," *Sächsische Arbeiter-Zeitung*, July 9, 1896.

2. Zbyněk Anthony Bohuslav Zeman and Winifred B. Scharlau, *The Merchant of Revolution: The Life of Alexander Israel Helphand (Parvus), 1867–1924* (New York: Oxford University Press, 1965).

3. Nikolai Yakovlevich Danilevsky, *Rossiya y Evropa* (St. Petersburg: brat. Panteleevykh,1895); Cyrus Hamlin, "The Dream of Russia," *The*

Atlantic 58 (December 1886); Mose L. Harvey, "The Development of Russian Commerce on the Black Sea and Its Significance" (PhD diss., University of California, Berkeley, 1938).

4. Alliance with Germany was complicated by the kaiser's previous support of Abdul Hamid II and the kaiser's ambivalence about supporting Turkey against Germany's ally Austria-Hungary, which sought to carve Turkey up. M. Şükrü Hanioğlu, *A Brief History of Late Ottoman Empire* (Princeton, NJ: Princeton University Press, 2008), chap. 6.

5. On the *carbonari*-style organization of the 1820s, see Eric Hobsbawm, *The Age of Revolution* (New York: Vintage Books, 1962), 114–116. A lot of nonsense has been written about Jewish and Masonic infiltration of the ranks of the Unionists. The Unionists, like all *carbonari*, understood that exposure meant assassination and so sought to prevent this by adopting rituals that were turned in nationalist directions.

6. Mehmed Naim Turfan, *Rise of the Young Turks: Politics, the Military and Ottoman Collapse* (London: I. B. Tauris, 1999), chap. 3; Ayşe Hür, "31 Mart 'ihtilal-i askeriyesi'," *Taraf*, April 6, 2008, https://web .archive.org/web/20160214154016/http://arsiv.taraf.com.tr/yazilar/ayse -hur/31-mart-ihtilal-i-askeriyesi/375 (accessed June 29, 2020).

7. Erol A. F. Baykal, *The Ottoman Press (1908–1923)* (Leiden: Brill, 2019), chap. 6.

8. Y. Doğan Çetinkaya, *The Young Turks and the Boycott Movement: Nationalism, Protest and the Working Classes in the Formation of Modern Turkey* (London: I. B. Tauris, 2014); Yunus Yiğit, "Aleksander Israel Helphand (Parvus)'in Osmanli Malî Ve Sosyal Hayatina Daİr Değerlendİrmelerİ" (unpublished master's thesis, Istanbul University, 2010), 5.

9. Hanioğlu, *A Brief History of Late Ottoman Empire*.

10. Parvus, "Die Integrität der Turkei," *Sächsische Arbeiter-Zeitung*, March 11, 1897.

11. Christopher M. Clark, *The Sleepwalkers: How Europe Went to War in 1914* (New York: Harper, 2013), chap. 1.

12. "Sanayi ülkeleri için yararlı olan bu düşüş, tarım ülkelerine çok büyük zarar vermektedir." Parvus, *Türkiye'nin malî tutsaklığı*, trans. Muammer Sencer (İstanbul: May Yayınları, 1977).

13. Parvus, *Türkiye'nin malî tutsaklığı*.

14. Justin Yifu Lin, *Demystifying the Chinese Economy* (Cambridge: Cambridge University Press, 2012), describes how China overtook Russia in the 1990s by using a slow, infrastructure-based development strategy that emphasized private property in agriculture and a mix of state-owned enterprises and some private firms. Parvus initially laid out this strategy in his 1895 rebuttal to Eduard Bernstein's arguments

about a Marxist agrarian program in "Zur Diskussion über den Agrar-programmentwurf," *Leipziger Volkszeitung* (summer 1895). This is use-fully transcribed on Wolfram Klein's *Sozialistische Klassiker 2.0* website at https://sites.google.com/site/sozialistischeklassiker2punkt0/parvus /parvus-zur-diskussion-ueber-den-agrarprogrammentwurf (accessed June 26, 2020).

15. Ayfer Karakaya-Stump, personal conversation, September 2016; Feroz Ahmad, "Vanguard of a Nascent Bourgeoisie: The Social and Eco-nomic Policy of the Young Turks, 1908–1918," in *From Empire to Re-public: Essays on the Late Ottoman Empire and Modern Turkey* (Istanbul: Istanbul Bilgi University Press, 2008), 40.

16. Parvus, *Türkiye'nin mali tutsaklığı*.

17. Parvus, *Türkiye'nin mali tutsaklığı*.

18. It is possible that these were Maxim guns rather than artillery. One ship manifest refers to 439 crates of "seri ateşli top," or "fast fire-balls," delivered from Hamburg. Footnote in Yiğit, "Aleksander Israel Helphand (Parvus)," 8.

19. On the Ziraat Bankesi, see Donald Quataert, "Ottoman Reform and Agriculture in Anatolia, 1876–1908" (PhD diss., University of Cal-ifornia, Los Angeles, 1973).

20. Ioanna Pepelasis Minoglou and Helen Louri, "Diaspora Entre-preneurial Networks in the Black Sea and Greece, 1870–1917," *Journal of European Economic History* 26, no. 1 (1997): 69–104.

21. On Parvus as provisioner, see Parvus, "Meine Entfernung aus der Schweiz," *Die Glocke*, February 21, 1920, 1482–1489. See also Mine-glou and Louri, "Diaspora International Networks in the Black Sea and Greece," 84.

22. Elisabeth Heresch, *Geheimakte Parvus: die gekaufte Revolution* (München: Herbig, 2013), chap. 1.

CHAPTER 13: A WORLD WAR OVER BREAD

1. This is the argument Fritz Fischer made most strongly in *Griff nach der Weltmacht: Die Kriegszielpolitik des kaiserlichen Deutschland 1914/18*, 3 vols. (Düsseldorf: Droste Verlag, 1964), published in En-glish as *Germany's Aims in the First World War* (New York: W. W. Nor-ton, 1967).

2. Sean McMeekin, *The Russian Origins of the First World War* (Cam-bridge, MA: Harvard University Press, 2011), 37.

3. McMeekin, *The Russian Origins of the First World War*.

4. Elisabeth Heresch, *Geheimakte Parvus: die gekaufte Revolution* (München: Herbig, 2013); M. Asim Karaömerlioglu, "Helphand-Parvus

and His Impact on Turkish Intellectual Life," *Middle Eastern Studies* 40, no. 6 (2004): 158.

5. Sean McMeekin, *The Berlin-Baghdad Express: The Ottoman Empire and Germany's Bid for World Power* (Cambridge, MA: Harvard University Press, 2010).

6. Avner Offer, *The First World War: An Agrarian Interpretation* (New York: Oxford University Press, 1989).

7. Zbyněk Anthony Bohuslav Zeman, ed., *Germany and the Revolution in Russia, 1915–1918: Documents from the Archives of the German Foreign Ministry* (Oxford: Oxford University Press, 1958), 140–149.

8. Friedrich Engels, *Die Preußische Militärfrage und die deutsche Arbeiterpartei* (Hamburg: O. Meissner, 1865). It is possible Parvus thought that cutting off France and England from Russian grain would end the war quickly because of its effect on those two consumers, just as the Crimean War had demonstrated how completely France and Britain depended on that grain in 1853.

9. Boris Chavkin, "Alexander Parvus: Financier der Weltrevolution," *Forum für Osteuropäische Ideen-und Zeitgeschichte* 11, no. 2 (2007): 31–58.

10. McMeekin, *The Russian Origins of the First World War.*

11. Offer, *The First World War.*

12. Nikolai D. Kondratieff, *Rynok khlebov i ego regulirovanie vo vremia voiny i revoliutsii* (1922; repr. Moscow: Nauka, 1991).

13. McMeekin, *The Berlin-Baghdad Express.*

14. Zeman, *Germany and the Revolution in Russia,* 1–2.

15. Zeman, *Germany and the Revolution in Russia.*

CHAPTER 14: GRAIN AS AUTHORITY

1. Lars T. Lih, *Bread and Authority in Russia, 1914–1921* (Berkeley: University of California Press, 1990); Arup Banerji, *Merchants and Markets in Revolutionary Russia, 1917–30* (New York: Springer, 1997), 9.

2. Thomas Fallows, "Politics and the War Effort in Russia: The Union of Zemstvos and the Organization of the Food Supply, 1914–1916," *Slavic Review* 37, no. 1 (1978): 70–90; Thomas Porter and William Gleason, "The Zemstvo and Public Initiative in Late Imperial Russia," *Russian History* 21, nos. 1–4 (1994): 419–437.

3. Lih, *Bread and Authority in Russia.*

4. Nikolai D. Kondratieff, *Rynok khlebov i ego regulirovanie vo vremia voiny i revoliutsii* (1922; repr. Moscow: Nauka, 1991); Lih, *Bread and Authority in Russia*; Banerji, *Merchants and Markets,* chap. 1; Peter Holquist, *Making War, Forging Revolution: Russia's Continuum of Crisis, 1914–1921* (Cambridge, MA: Harvard University Press, 2002).

5. Zbyněk Anthony Bohuslav Zeman, ed., *Germany and the Revolution in Russia, 1915–1918: Documents from the Archives of the German Foreign Ministry* (Oxford: Oxford University Press, 1958), 24–35.

6. Catherine Merridale, *Lenin on the Train* (New York: Metropolitan Books, 2017), 62–68.

7. Parvus, "Die Plan für die russische Revolution," appendix to Elisabeth Heresch, *Geheimakte Parvus: die gekaufte Revolution* (München: Herbig, 2013).

8. Merridale, *Lenin*, 62–68, 251–261; Heresch, *Geheimakte Parvus*, 153ff; Michael Futrell, *Northern Underground: Episodes of Russian Revolutionary Transport and Communications Through Scandinavia and Finland, 1863–1917* (New York: Faber & Faber, 1963), chap. 7.

9. William Henry Chamberlain, *The Russian Revolution, 1917–1921* (New York: Macmillan, 1935), vol. 1, chap. 8.

10. State Secretary Zimmerman to the Minister in Bern, June 3, 1917, in Zeman, *Germany and the Revolution in Russia*, 61.

11. Zeman, *Germany and the Revolution in Russia*, 68.

12. State Secretary Kühlmann to the Foreign Ministry Liaison Officer at General Headquarters, September 29, 1917, in Zeman, *Germany and the Revolution in Russia*, 70.

13. Lih, *Bread and Authority in Russia*, 76–77.

14. The following three paragraphs rely almost exclusively on William G. Rosenberg, "The Democratization of Russia's Railroads in 1917," *American Historical Review* 86, no. 5 (December 1981): 983–1008.

15. Rosenberg, "The Democratization of Russia's Railroads."

16. Vladimir P. Timoshenko argues, in *Agricultural Russia and the Wheat Problem* (Stanford, CA: Food Research Institute, 1932), 44–46, that in 1917, 21 to 30 percent of agricultural land was fallow in Ukraine. David Moon argues, in *The Plough That Broke the Steppes: Agriculture and Environment on Russia's Grasslands, 1700–1914* (New York: Oxford University Press, 2013), that Ukraine used three- and four-field rotation rather than shifting cultivation, but this still apparently left a great deal of fallow land.

17. Daniel Thorner et al., eds., *A. V. Chayanov on the Theory of Peasant Economy* (Homewood, IL: American Economic Association, 1966).

18. Robert Louis Koehl, "A Prelude to Hitler's Greater Germany," *American Historical Review* 59, no. 1 (October 1953): 59; Holger Herwig, "Tunes of Glory at the Twilight Stage: The Bad Homburg Crown Council and the Evolution of German Statecraft, 1917/1918," *German Studies Review* 6, no. 3 (October 1983): 475–494; Judah Leon Magnes, *Russia and Germany at Brest-Litovsk: A Documentary History of the Peace Negotiations* (New York: Rand School of Social Science, 1919), 181.

19. Lih, *Bread and Authority in Russia*, 131.

20. Robert Conquest, *The Harvest of Sorrow: Soviet Collectivization and the Terror-Famine* (New York: Oxford University Press, 1986), 46.

21. Mark Von Hagen, *School of the Revolution: Bolsheviks and Peasants in the Red Army, 1918–1928*, vols. 1 and 2 (PhD diss., Stanford University, 1984).

22. Stephen Anthony Smith, *Russia in Revolution: An Empire in Crisis, 1890 to 1928* (New York: Oxford University Press, 2016), chap. 4.

23. G. V. Melikhov, *Man'chzhuriya, dalekaya i blizkaya* (Moscow: Nauka, 1991).

24. Frederick C. Corney, *Telling October: Memory and the Making of the Bolshevik Revolution* (Ithaca, NY: Cornell University Press, 2004).

25. Dmitri Volkogonov, *Lenin: A New Biography* (New York: The Free Press, 1994), chap. 3.

26. Frederick C. Corney, *Trotsky's Challenge: The "Literary Discussion" of 1924 and the Fight for the Bolshevik Revolution* (Boston: Brill, 2015).

CONCLUSION

1. Though his mother was named Tatyana Berman, Yevgeny assumed the last name of Gnedin. Paul Raymond, in "Witness and Chronicler of Nazi-Soviet Relations: The Testimony of Evgeny Gnedin (Parvus)," *Russian Review* 44, no. 4 (1985): 379–395, says that he took this last name in 1920.

2. Central Intelligence Agency, Electronic Reading Room, "OSS—Soviet Defector L. Borisovitch Gelfand/Comments on Stalin and the Course of the War, Aug. 12, 1942," file citation CIA-RDP13X00001R000100210002-9; Central Intelligence Agency, Electronic Reading Room, Breve Biographie De Leon Moore (Precedement Leon Helfand), file citation DOC_0001165778; US House of Representatives, 81st Cong., 1st Sess., Report No. 1283, "Report on the Bill to accompany S. 627 for the Relief of Leon Moore"; Office of Strategic Services, "Leon Borisovitch HELFAND: American. A Soviet Diplomat in the 1920s and 1930s," catalogue reference KV 2/2681, National Archives, Kew, Richmond, Surrey, United Kingdom.

3. *Dun & Bradstreet Middle Market Directory*, 1971, 608; "Sonia Moore, 92, Stanislavsky Expert," *New York Times*, May 24, 1995.

4. Raymond, "Witness and Chronicler of Nazi-Soviet Relations," 379–395; Pryanikov Pavel, "Put' marksista Yevgeniy Gnedin glazami docheri," *Russkaya Zhizn'*, September 28, 2007.

5. Tatyana Gnedina, *Posledniy den' Tugotronov: povesti-skazki* (Moscow: Molodaya Gvardiya, 1964).

INDEX

Scott Reynolds Nelson is the UGA Athletics Association Professor of the Humanities at the University of Georgia. He is a Guggenheim fellow and the author of five books, including *Steel Drivin' Man*, which received the Merle Curti Prize for American Social History and the National Award for Arts Writing. Nelson lives in Athens, Georgia.